LIKE WILDFIRE

Studies in Rhetoric/Communication

Thomas W. Benson, series editor

LIKE WILDFIRE

The Rhetoric of the Civil Rights Sit-Ins

Edited by
Sean Patrick O'Rourke &
Lesli K. Pace

THE UNIVERSITY OF
SOUTH CAROLINA PRESS

© 2020 University of South Carolina

Published by the University of South Carolina Press
Columbia, South Carolina 29208

www.uscpress.com

Manufactured in the United States of America

29 28 27 26 25 24 23 22 21 20
10 9 8 7 6 5 4 3 2 1

Library of Congress Cataloging-in-Publication Data
can be found at http://catalog.loc.gov/.

ISBN 978-1-64336-066-9 (hardback)
ISBN 978-1-64336-083-6 (ebook)

This book was printed on recycled paper with
30 percent postconsumer waste content.

To our parents:

John W. O'Rourke, Jr., and Lois O'Rourke
Bob Pace and Jeanette Pace

Contents

Series Editor's Preface

In *Like Wildfire: The Rhetoric of the Civil Rights Sit-Ins*, editors Sean Patrick O'Rourke and Lesli K. Pace bring together a group of scholars to investigate the rhetorical structure, antecedents, and descendants of the Southern student lunch counter sit-ins of 1960. The resulting account of sit-ins and their variations through American history and across the American landscape, especially in the Jim Crow South, celebrates the courage, decency, and rhetorical acuity of the movement leaders and participants, against the backdrop of stubborn hatreds and habits of exclusion and exploitation, the recurring sin of American racism. O'Rourke, to take one small example, finds in the 1958 Code of Greenville, South Carolina, a requirement that public eating establishments maintain separate sets of dishes and utensils for black and white customers and that "a separate facility shall be maintained and used for the cleaning of eating utensils and dishes furnished the two races." The hateful delicacy and rotten purity of such practices were made visible and untenable when well-dressed, young black customers, with modest courtesy and loving courage, simply sat at white lunch counters and ordered a Coke. The actions of the college students who participated in those sit-ins were hardly protests at all but simply the enactment of ordinary, everyday shopping; they were protests only in context of the opposition with which they were met and not in the form that they presented in their enactment, and yet they are central to the history of American social protest and nonviolent direct action. The essays in this book help to illuminate the design, context, and development of the sit-ins as a rhetorical practice and open the way to ongoing work.

Thomas W. Benson
Series Editor

Acknowledgments

Completion of this book has been long and arduous. We want to take a moment to thank the wonderful staff of the USC Press, who could not have helped more. We also want to acknowledge here our sincere appreciation and respect for one another, as well as note the value we place on our friendship even in the face of the most challenging aspects of this scholarly endeavor. Deep thanks also to Mike McDonald, Lili and Ian Pace McDonald, Tierney O'Rourke, Jamie Capuzza, and our wonderful contributors for their support, patience, flexibility, and encouragement. Sean would also like to thank his Sewanee colleagues Melody Lehn and Terry Papillon, and Lesli would like to thank her ULM colleague C. Turner Steckline Wilson, for their good cheer, unflagging support, continued friendship, and unwavering encouragement. We would also like to thank the University of Louisiana, Monroe's College of Arts, Education, and Sciences Research Hub for awarding a mini-grant that allowed us to hire Teresa Abney to support the development of a master list of citations and Sewanee: The University of the South's Faculty Research Grants Committee for funding Camille Stallings's work on the book's index. Finally, we wish to thank Adam Hawkins for his considerable help with the manuscript.

INTRODUCTION

Civil Rights Sit-Ins and the Rhetoric of Protest

Sean Patrick O'Rourke & Lesli K. Pace

The sit-ins of the civil rights movement were some of the most extraordinary acts of protest in an age defined by protest. By sitting in at "whites only" lunch counters, libraries, beaches, swimming pools, skating rinks, and churches, young men and women put their bodies on the line, fully aware that their actions would almost inevitably incite savage, violent responses from entrenched and increasingly desperate white segregationists. And yet they did so in enormous numbers: estimates suggest that in 1960 alone more than seventy thousand people participated in sit-ins across the American South, and more than three thousand were arrested.[1] The simplicity and purity of the act of sitting in, coupled with the dignity and grace with which most participants acted, lent to the sit-in movement a kind of sanctity difficult to find in other protest demonstrations.

Nearly everyone recognizes the importance and galvanizing influence of the sit-ins, both on the civil rights movement generally and on student activism more particularly. The sit-ins had, as Howard Zinn puts it, "an electrical effect" that "marked a turning point" for black Americans.[2] Clayborne Carson focuses Zinn's broad point by arguing that the sit-ins were "the beginning of a new stage of black political development," because they spawned the notion that the guiding ideas of the movement "should not come from the pre-existing ideologies but from the intellectual awakening that had begun on black campuses."[3] Others describe the sit-ins as a "bolt out of the blue," "the spark that ignited a raging prairie fire," and an accelerant that spread "like wildfire throughout the South."[4] Most commentators agree that the sit-ins rejuvenated a flagging civil rights movement and challenged not only segregation but also the older generation of African American civil rights leaders.[5]

The standard story of the civil rights sit-ins is well known. According to that narrative, the sit-ins began in Greensboro, North Carolina, on February 1, 1960, expanded to Nashville, Tennessee, and other cities in Virginia and the Carolinas later that month, and swept across the South that spring and summer. They gave rise to the Student Nonviolent Coordinating Committee (SNCC), provided black students a powerful and effective forum for protest, transformed the social and economic culture of the segregated South, and opened a new front in the battle to desegregate.[6]

And yet that narrative is partial at best and misleading at worst. It endures in part because of a disturbing lack of scholarship on the sit-ins. For decades the sole single-authored, book-length study of the movement was Martin Oppenheimer's *The Sit-In Movement of 1960*, written in 1963 as the author's Ph.D. dissertation and published, without changes, in 1989.[7] As David Garrow notes in the introduction to the 1989 publication and Adam Fairclough echoes in his review of it, Oppenheimer's work was the best single source on the sit-ins to date, an invaluable resource for the spread of the movement and the many shapes it assumed across the South.[8] However, Oppenheimer himself acknowledges in his preface to the 1989 edition that the work is a bit heavy on early-1960s sociological constructs, his focus is on the year 1960 alone, and important follow-up studies "remain to be done."[9] Two other book-length treatments have appeared more recently. The first, the 2012 collection of essays edited by Iwan Morgan and Philip Davies, is a much-needed treatment drawn from papers presented at the 2010 conference held by the British Library's Eccles Centre for American Studies and the Institute for the Study of the Americas at the University of London to mark the fiftieth anniversary of the sit-ins. The collection makes important advances in our understanding of white segregationists' responses to the movement, the impact of the sit-ins on U.S. constitutional law, and the formation of the Student Nonviolent Coordinating Committee.[10] The second, Christopher W. Schmidt's *The Sit-Ins: Protest and Legal Change in the Civil Rights Era,* considers the sit-ins and the legal cases that grew out of them as important moments of legal and especially constitutional struggle. Schmidt shows how the sit-ins raised important questions about equal protection, state action, private property/public accommodation, and judicial versus legislative action in U.S. controversies over social change.[11]

There are, of course, a few studies of sit-ins in individual cities, but a good portion of these are short essays, some aimed at more popular audiences, and the group as a whole represents a mere fraction of what can and needs to be done.[12] The truth is that despite considerable scholarship on the movement's most visible high points (e.g., Greensboro and Nashville), local and regional historians have only recently begun the long and difficult effort of recovering the lost and all too often forgotten chapters of the sit-in movement. As a result we lack even shallow histories of the hundreds of other sit-ins against segregation during the 1960s and have very little at all on the important sit-ins before Greensboro. Perhaps even worse, the rhetorical aspects of the sit-ins remain *terra incognita,* for only a handful of studies touch even indirectly on the persuasive strategies and tactics the sit-ins employed.

By "rhetorical" we mean that the sit-ins were essentially persuasive activities. They were planned, strategic, carefully executed attempts to alter existing attitudes, values, beliefs, and actions. They functioned, to use James Boyd White's language, as "ways in which character and community—and motive, value, reason, social structure, everything, in short, that makes a culture—[were] defined and made real" in meticulously conceived real-world performances.[13] They were serious efforts to adapt ideas to people and people to ideas, attempts to begin to transform the discriminatory realities of segregated living into at least the beginnings of desegregated communities.[14] And like most episodes in larger mass movements, they were joined by common concerns and commitments but also radically situated in time, place, and culture.[15] Our working assumption is that in many ways sit-ins were similar—black bodies occupying and, in so doing, contesting white spaces—but that the sit-ins varied not only in time and place (historically and geographically) but also in how protesters sat-in, why they did so, the timing of their efforts, and the strategic targeting of different types of places (public forums versus private businesses, restaurants or libraries or swimming pools or beaches)[16] and also in the responses to those demonstrations, not only by counterdemonstrators but also by the media, the police, and the government.

This dearth of rhetorical scholarship is all the more disturbing when we remember that the sit-ins were transformative rhetorical activities where rhetorical voice (being *heard*) was transfigured into bodily protest (being *seen*). Indeed seeing and being seen were precisely the goals of the sit-ins. As John Lewis explains in his memoir, *Walking with the Wind:* "We *wanted them to see us.* . . . We wanted white people, everyday citizens, everyday customers to be exposed to us, *to see us as we were,* not as something in their minds, in their imaginations. We wanted them *to watch how we responded* to the people who refused to serve us. And we wanted them *to watch those people as well.*"[17] To be sure, rhetorical scholars recognized early on that the protests of the 1960s represented new persuasive practices, and they struggled to adapt rhetorical theories derived from primarily discursive, polite forms of persuasion to the new struggles. As Robert Scott and Donald Smith acknowledged in their "Rhetoric of Confrontation," "A rhetorical theory suitable to our age must take into account the charge that civility and decorum serve as masks for the preservation of injustice, that they condemn the dispossessed to non-being, and that as transmitted in a technological society they become instrumentalities of power for those who 'have.'"[18] True enough, but as Marilyn DeLaure points out in her essay in this book, rhetorical critics scrambled, often unsuccessfully, to escape the norms of more traditional rhetorical theories. Franklyn Haiman, in his "Rhetoric of the Streets," explained that "many objective observers of the contemporary 'rhetoric' of the streets . . . have misgivings about its propriety and even its legality,"[19] and Gladys Ritchie, in her essay "The Sit-In: A Rhetoric of Human Action," admitted that the sit-ins were rhetorically effective but nonetheless understood that some could consider them a "despicable" display of "bad manners."[20]

Rhetorical critics no longer have to struggle in these ways. Over the past forty years, theorists and critics have developed an extraordinary array of insights that allows the sit-ins to be reconsidered from at least four perspectives. Somatic rhetoric—the rhetoric of the body—considers movement, gesture, and the very presence of the body to be central sites not only of rhetorical activity but also of invention and, potentially, moral judgment. From this perspective rhetorical appeals are material, at times resistant to discursive constraints and at other times functioning to elaborate, extend, and amplify verbal appeals.[21] Similarly visual rhetoric/visual argument studies concentrates on the persuasive appeal of images—not just bodies—and consider the aesthetic, rational, and affective dimensions of iconic photographs, museum exhibits, and even sculpture as rhetorical forms of proof.[22] Performance studies, a third perspective related to somatic and visual rhetoric, seeks to comprehend and explain the persuasive meanings of human performance writ large. As such it offers students of the sit-ins a rich vocabulary drawn from the intersection of multiple disciplines and practitioners.[23] Finally public memory studies, concerned with the ways in which we cultivate, contest, and communicate our shared past, suggests ways to consider and reconsider the sit-ins in dialectical tension with more traditional historical studies.[24]

Each of these perspectives enlivens the possibilities for social movement studies in rhetoric. The essays here contribute to this reinvigoration by narrating and analyzing the rhetorical history of the sit-ins. The authors of the essays in this book not only find value in but also feel a sense of obligation to highlight those underrepresented moments. Their analyses and explications of the rhetorical strategies of lesser-known events in the civil rights movement not only contribute to the production of knowledge but also memorialize and provide depth of understanding that can translate well for future generations.

With these thoughts in mind, then, our edited collection presents the sit-ins as the rhetorical protests articulated by Lewis and argues that the sit-ins are best understood as rhetorical events connected to one another but nonetheless radically situated in their local contexts. As such, we argue, the sit-ins were critical persuasive episodes that, taken as a whole, unleashed a powerful and needed accelerant to the civil rights movement and continue to exert a potent, although contested, influence on our civic life. Our book brings together scholars who have studied civil rights, protest, visual argument, and rhetorical history and criticism and applies our individual expertise and collective energies to understanding the complexity and power of the sit-ins. Thus our goal for this text is threefold: (1) to articulate the rhetorical facets of sit-ins; (2) to emphasize the strategic rhetorical interplay between the goals and methods of the national movement and the inventiveness of radically situated protest in local communities; and (3) to suggest, at least in outline form, the long and complex trajectory of the sit-in movement. Toward that end each essay establishes and maintains a distinctive, critical rhetorical approach that grows out of, and helps illuminate, the unique elements of the local sit-in protests. All essays evidence an understanding that media reports of the day were always already biased and accordingly cast a wide net for artifacts and resources that challenge those biases and provide new understandings of the demonstrations. The essays are therefore supported by archival materials, original interviews with surviving participants, reports from the black media, unpublished correspondence, police reports, FBI files, oral histories, and often suppressed photographic and filmic evidence.

The book is united into a coherent whole in three ways. First, every essay challenges our received wisdom, whether by extending our understanding of the movement to the pre-Greensboro episodes, offering fresh perspectives on well-known sit-ins such as Nashville and Greensboro, or providing analyses of important protests for the very first time. Second, in addition to the main introductory essay, the volume editors provide short "part introductions" that guide readers from one section to the next, fill in some of the historical gaps, and build the book's main argument. Third, in addition to organizing the book chronologically, three themes unite the essays into a cohesive whole: somatic rhetoric, visual argument, and public safety/personal risk. In each essay we see evidence of the significance of somatic rhetoric. The bodies on the line for civil rights make cogent the risk involved for protestors who chose to sit, swim, or wade in. These analyses bring to light the material implications of rhetorical force. In addition across these essays is evidence of the power of visual argument. The backlash against black bodies occupying "white spaces" is emphasized in images of people being beaten, cuffed, forcibly removed from buildings, covered in food, or attacked when wearing, in some cases, no more than a swimming suit. The rhetorical analysis of these images makes clear the significance and power of these protests. Finally the theme of public safety and personal risk moves this collection beyond Gene Roberts and Hank Klibanoff's 2007 study of reporting in *The Race Beat* to consider, inter alia, the rhetorical constructions of victimhood, crime, trespass, and the like.[25] Through exploration of the rhetorical aspects of safety and risk, we gain further insight into how and why sit-ins changed communities.

Our book is not a comprehensive history of the sit-in movement. It is, however, a new story of the sit-ins, one that emphasizes the long and fragmentary nature of the movement's evolution without losing sight of the important place of the protests in Greensboro and Nashville. It also stresses the decidedly local and dangerous nature of each sit-in without losing touch with the regional and national influences one demonstration had on the others. Finally the story told in this book underscores the rhetorical creativity and inventiveness at the heart of the sit-in movement and explores the ways in which local citizens harnessed and directed the resources of persuasion available to them. The book consists of three main sections, preceded by an introductory essay and followed by a concluding essay and bibliography.

Part 1: Sparks: The Origins of the Sit-Ins before Greensboro

Each essay in this section explores key demonstrations that preceded and sparked the February 1, 1960, Greensboro protest, the event most widely associated with the "beginning" of the civil rights movement's sit-ins. This section makes clear that the sit-ins did not, as some histories now suggest, erupt spontaneously on February 1, 1960, but rather emerged from a long history of sporadic, localized efforts that, gathered together as learning experiences, formed a kind of tinderbox for what was to follow. The short part introduction charts this evolution, stressing the centrality of the philosophy of nonviolence and decorum to the movement, while the essays themselves explore where and how sit-ins emerged as rhetorical events in places that have gone largely unnoticed in the scholarly literature. Organized by date of occurrence, the essays span the twenty-two years leading up to the moment the sit-ins flared up across the South, contain analyses of these early sit-ins, and provide readers with a broader and deeper history of the sit-in movement than has been available to date. More specifically the essays examine different forms of sitting in and the evolution of the rhetorical dynamics of sit-in protests, detailing the organizational strategies they employed and connecting them to later protests. Melody Lehn demonstrates the early symbolic importance of white elites bridging the racial divide by "sitting between," a liminal act, she argues, that had far-reaching rhetorical implications for blacks and whites, south and north. David Miguel Molina and Joshua Daniel Phillips examine two important early sit-ins in Washington, D.C. (1942–44), and St. Louis (1948), respectively, showing how both events, now nearly forgotten, tested the rhetorical resources available to protesters combating segregated public and private facilities. Victoria J. Gallagher, Kenneth S. Zagacki, and Jeffrey C. Swift connect the sit-ins to the larger civil rights movement in their tracing of the 1957 Durham, North Carolina, Royal Ice Cream Parlor sit-ins to Martin Luther King's speech endorsing the sit-in movement, delivered in Durham after the Greensboro sit-ins in February 1960. Judith Hoover's essay concludes the section by examining the "test sit-ins" that led up to the Nashville protests, some of the most well-known sit-in demonstrations, and sheds new light on the rhetorical strategy sessions these tests provided. Nonviolent training, Hoover argues, functioned as a kind of rhetorical pedagogy in which students learned to invent forms of resistance and improvise responses to violent and abusive behavior. In this section readers are given a glimpse into the long history of the sit-in movement, as well as the breadth of strategies protestors incorporated into it. The rhetorical approaches taken in this section allow the reader to see the implications of location, social and legal situations, and participants/personalities, thus highlighting ways each sit-in is distinctive but still identifiable as a part of a larger national movement.

Part 2: Conflagration: The Spread of the Sit-Ins across the South

The essays in the "Conflagration" section analyze sit-in protests as they spread across the South, focusing for the most part on events unknown outside their respective localities or on unfamiliar features of well-known demonstrations. This section extends the analyses of the first section and argues that the sit-ins spread "like wildfire" because they were unified by common features (philosophy of nonviolence, sacrifice by youth, assertion of rights by disarmingly simple acts) and yet freely and imaginatively adapted to the changing demands of local conditions and circumstances. The short part introduction provides a wide overview of the sit-in movement as it spread across the South after Greensboro, charts the vast scope and duration of the protests, and sketches a profile of the movement's participants—mostly young students—and the grave risks they faced. Moving again in chronological order, the essays in this section offer case studies of six protests. Sean Patrick O'Rourke begins the section by directing attention to the little-known Greenville, South Carolina, sit-ins of 1960. His study reveals the importance of rhetorical somatics and visual imagery to the movement while deepening our understanding of the ways in which specifically local conditions brought forth unique responses rhetorically adapted to those conditions. Stephen Schneider considers the "bodily rhetoric" of Louisville, Kentucky's "Nothing New for Easter" campaign of 1961 to illustrate how such protest created collective action frames of justice, identity, and agency. Roseann M. Mandziuk, William H. Lawson, and Lindsay Harroff study three important sit-ins of 1963 (the Birmingham, Alabama, youth demonstrations, the Jackson, Mississippi, Woolworth protest, and the Cambridge, Maryland, "Treaty of Cambridge" controversy) to explore the power of symbols. Mandziuk and Lawson look at the rhetorical force of the visual arguments that emerged from Birmingham and Jackson, respectively, while Harroff traces the continuity of the movement's trajectory from *sitting in,* during the phase of public protests, to *sitting out* the referendum vote in Cambridge. In somewhat different ways, each of these essays demonstrates that, rhetorically speaking, sit-ins as physical acts are largely inseparable from sit-ins as symbolic acts. Rebecca Bridges Watts brings the section to a close with her provocative rhetorical history of the move from sit-ins to "swim-ins" in St. Augustine, Florida, in the summer of 1964. Combining many of the approaches of the other essays in this section, Watts shows how, by 1964, striking visual rhetoric from "new" settings propelled the movement forward.

Part 3: Embers: The Legacies of the Sit-Ins

In this final section, we consider the legacies of the civil rights sit-ins and the ways in which they continue to exert an enduring force in our civic life. We maintain that the legacies of the civil rights sit-ins are many, complicated, and difficult to discern. One way to grasp this legacy is to focus on public remembering and forgetting, which draws attention to the ways in which documenting and memorializing the sit-ins are in and of themselves rhetorical acts. Though documentaries and memorials are meant to help us remember and pay homage to that which has come before, they are also rhetorical constructions that include some aspects of an event and exclude and forget other aspects. Three of our essays take this approach. Marilyn DeLaure looks at *NBC White Paper*'s hour-long episode on the sit-ins that aired in late 1960 to show how the discursive aspects of the report suggested a detached, evenhanded view of the sit-ins while the nondiscursive, visual rhetoric portrayed the demonstrators and the cause of desegregation in a much more positive light than their opponents. Casey Malone Maugh Funderburk and Wendy Atkins-Sayre contrast the "wade-in" narratives and images documenting the Biloxi, Mississippi, protests in 1960 with those used to commemorate the events fifty years later, revealing that the earlier depictions gave the protesters voice while the later versions served to mute those same voices. Diana I. Bowen studies the historical lunch counter at the Smithsonian National Museum of American History and corresponding barstools at the Greensboro Historical Museum from the perspective of visual rhetoric and memoryscapes and argues that the installations serve to perform the act of "sitting" as a haunting cultural icon of nonviolence.

Two other essays take a quite different approach. Fully aware of the dangers of attributing historical "influence," these essays nonetheless explore the connections between the civil rights sit-ins and later developments. Jason Del Gandio explores parallels and differences between the civil rights sit-ins and 2011's Occupy Wall Street movement, and David Worthington draws our attention to the "presence," outside the National Civil Rights Museum in Memphis, Tennessee, of a lone protester who has been "sitting in" since she was thrown out of the Lorraine Motel in 1988—ironically so that the museum could be opened. Both of these essays warn us against claims of "influence" that are too facile and yet expand, with a provocative insistence, the different ways in which the civil rights sit-ins may have continued to exert a presence in our civic life long after the lunch counters and libraries were desegregated.

In the book's afterword, Keith D. Miller explores the "larger picture" of the sit-ins, their place in the civil rights movement, and the implications the studies in this book have for future scholarship.

Notes

1. For the statistics noted here, see Farber and Bailey, *Columbia Guide*, 16. The International Civil Rights Center and Museum reports that "by the end of March 1960, the sit-in movement had spread to more than 55 cities in 13 states." See "Celebrating Civil Rights in Greensboro."

2. Zinn, *SNCC*, 17–26. We recognize that some readers may see the late Howard Zinn as more advocate than historian, or perhaps more accurately, more representative of an older historiography of the civil rights movement than of newer approaches. On this distinction see Lawson, "Freedom Then, Freedom Now." We hope that our book answers Lawson's call for a deeper examination of the factors that influenced the movement's development and growth and his desire to see studies that "add a critical edge and great complexity" (471) to movement studies.

3. Carson, *In Struggle*, 17–18.

4. Farber and Bailey, *Columbia Guide*, 16. See also the website of the International Civil Rights Center and Museum at https://www.sitinmovement.org/history/sit-in-move ment.asp, where the active "spread like wildfire" image is also deployed. The conflagration metaphor is especially prominent among those involved in the sit-ins. See, e.g., "The Sit-Ins of 1960," at http://www.crmvet.org/info/sitins.pdf.

5. See, e.g., Morgan, "New Movement," 2.

6. This narrative is evident in Fayer, "Ain't Scared of Your Jails," episode 3 of *Eyes on the Prize,* which starts with the Greensboro sit-ins and then focuses on the Nashville struggle. More recently websites devoted to the sit-ins perpetuate this account. See, e.g., https://www .ncpedia.org/civil-rights-sit-ins and https://www.cnn.com/2017/02/08/us/gallery/tbt-civil -rights-sit-ins/index.html (where Greensboro is described as the "Launch of a Civil Rights Movement" and where visitors are told that "the Story begins here") and https://www.sitin movement.org/history/america-civil-rights-timeline.asp (the Greensboro sit-ins "triggered similar nonviolent protests throughout the South"). The documentary film *February One: The Story of the Greensboro Four* (Video Dialogue, 2003) offers a similar storyline.

7. Oppenheimer, *Sit-In Movement of 1960.*

8. Garrow, introduction to Oppenheimer, *Sit-In Movement of 1960,* xi–xii; Fairclough, review of *The Sit-In Movement of 1960,* 769.

9. Oppenheimer, *Sit-In Movement,* xvi.

10. Morgan and Davies, eds., *From Sit-Ins to SNCC.*

11. Schmidt, *Sit-Ins.*

12. See, e.g., Bayor, "Atlanta, Georgia, 1960–1961" (briefly sketching the events and timeline of the Atlanta movement); Eick, *Dissent in Wichita* (exploring the Dockum Drug Store sit-ins of 1958 as part of her larger history of the civil rights movement in Wichita); Fleming, "White Lunch Counters" (connecting the Knoxville sit-ins to the emerging conceptions of black consciousness); Garrow, *Atlanta, Georgia, 1960–1961* (setting Atlanta's sit-ins in that city's larger student movement); Graves, "The Right to Be Served" (describing Oklahoma City's tumultuous sit-ins); Hurst, *It Was Never about a Hot Dog and a Coke!* (a memoir of the author's civil rights activities); Lawrence, "'Since It Is My Right, I Would Like to Have It'" (providing perspective on the important Katz Drug Store sit-in); Mohl, "'South of the South'" and "Interracial Activism" (considering the Miami sit-ins of 1959 as part of the city's larger intercultural civil rights movement); O'Brien, *We Shall Not Be Moved* (contextualizing the Jackson, Mississippi, sit-ins within the larger Mississippi struggle); Proudfoot, *Diary of a Sit-In* (providing firsthand impressions of the Greensboro sit-ins); and Seals, "Wiley-Bishop Student Movement" (detailing the March 1960 sit-ins in Marshall, Texas).

13. White, *When Words Lose Their Meaning,* xi.

14. In these ways sit-in demonstrators enacted conceptions of rhetorical action envisioned by theorists as different as Donald C. Bryant, *Rhetorical Dimensions in Criticism,* and Judith Butler (see, e.g., *Excitable Speech, Bodies That Matter,* and *Gender Trouble*). See also Butler's talk "Public Assembly and Plural Action."

15. On rhetoric as radically situated, see Leff, "Habitation of Rhetoric."

16. The choice between a public forum and a private business engaged issues of ownership, First Amendment protection, and Fourteenth Amendment "state action" requirements and raised important questions about the reach of constitutional protections. The thoughtful selection and targeting of restaurants, movie theaters, libraries, skating rinks, and a wide variety of other contested places involved consideration of the multitudinous activities of citizenship and presented questions not only about the reach of "integration" but also, and ultimately, about levels of "equality" in an integrated community.

17. Lewis, *Walking with the Wind,* 105 (emphasis added).

18. Scott and Smith, "Rhetoric of Confrontation," 8. For other efforts to come to grips with the new rhetoric of protest, see, e.g., Andrews, "Confrontation at Columbia," and Bowen, "Does Non-violence Persuade?"

19. Haiman, "Rhetoric of the Streets," 99.

20. Ritchie, "Sit-In," 22–25.

21. On somatic rhetoric, see, e.g., Hawhee, *Moving Bodies;* Hawhee, "Somatography."

22. For a sense of the growing field of visual rhetoric, see, e.g., Olson, Finnegan, and Hope, *Visual Rhetoric,* and Hill and Helmers, *Defining Visual Rhetorics.*

23. Performance studies has already contributed to our understanding of the sit-ins. See Foster, "Choreographies of Protest"; Kowal, "Staging the Greensboro Sit-Ins"; and De-Laure, "Remembering the Sit-Ins."

24. Public memory studies are now too numerous even to summarize. For a helpful entrée to the field, see Phillips, *Framing Public Memory.* For a sense of the connections between public memory studies and visual rhetoric, consider Demo and Vivian, *Rhetoric, Remembrance, and Visual Form.*

25. Roberts and Klibanoff, *Race Beat.*

1

SPARKS

*The Origins of the Sit-Ins
before Greensboro*

While what we now call the "Sit-In Movement" may have emerged in 1960 out of the larger civil rights movement, its origins are much older. Even those who mention the sit-ins before February 1, 1960, tend to underestimate the duration and frequency of early sit-in protests. In all probability these estimates are low, because it is difficult to determine what is counted as a "sit-in" and by whom, and does not include sit-in protests outside the South. It also does not account for the rich, diverse, and often unorganized efforts of individual protesters.

A cursory look at the preceding century reveals that, even before the Civil War, African American citizens protested their exclusion from, and segregation in, many public and semiprivate facilities, accommodations, and services. These early protests tended to be localized, deployed a wide array of tactics and strategies (not all of which were successful), and slowly created, however knowingly, a tinderbox of sorts for future accommodation protests.

As Blair Kelley has shown, the deepest sit-in roots extend back to the antebellum period, when African Americans resisted segregated trains, streetcars, and ferries in Massachusetts and New York. There Frederick Douglass, Sarah Adams, Elizabeth Jennings and her father, Thomas L. Jennings, the Reverend James W. C. Pennington, and the Legal Rights Association chose to protest segregated streetcars not by boycotting but by riding—by sitting in segregated cars until they were pulled out of their seats and, sometimes, thrown forcefully from the train. The sit-ins had mixed results: New England rail cars were eventually desegregated, and in New York, Elizabeth Jennings sued for damages after being dragged from a car in 1854 and won. The protesters lost other cases.[1] But they established, over the course of their protests, both an effective method—sitting in—and a precedent of resistance.

Sit-ins were also prevalent in the postbellum period, especially during Reconstruction. Once again the targets were streetcars and similar forms of public transportation. In March 1867 African Americans in Charleston, South Carolina, began sitting in the city's new streetcars and by May had won legal access to them. In June the military commander of the town extended those rights to railroads and steamboats.[2] That same May newly freed Anglicized African Americans and mixed-race Francophone Afro-Creoles joined forces to overthrow New Orleans, Louisiana's "star-car" system, in which black riders were forced to ride in separate cars set aside for them.[3] Similar streetcar sit-ins took place in Richmond, Virginia (1867),[4] and Louisville, Kentucky (1870–71).[5] In many of these protests, especially those that lasted for weeks and months, protesters used a combination of tactics, adding boycotts, legal actions, speeches, and demonstrations to their sit-in campaigns.

The Jim Crow era, especially the period after the Supreme Court's "separate but equal" interpretation of the Fourteenth Amendment in *Plessy v. Ferguson*,[6] presented African Americans with new and virulent rules and rituals of segregation. In this period, as Kelley and, before her, August Meier and Elliott Rudwick[7] have shown, resistance more often took the form of boycotts rather than sit-ins, again with mixed results. This period also saw the rise of new organizations—the Niagara Movement in 1905, reformed, of course, as the National Association for the Advancement of Colored People (NAACP) in 1909, and the Congress of Racial Equality (CORE) in 1942—as well as the changed conditions of the Great Depression sandwiched between two world wars, all wrapped in the Great Migration of six million African Americans from the South to the Northeast, Midwest, and West.[8] These changed conditions shaped the resistance and response of the time, providing new demands (and opportunities) for sit-in protests.

The essays in this section consider five early sit-ins, each important in its own right but also crucial in the arc of the sit-in movement from the Great Depression to Greensboro. That arc runs from Eleanor Roosevelt's "sit-between" in 1938 Birmingham to the 1948 Stix, Baer, and Fuller department store sit-in in St. Louis, then on to the 1957 Royal Ice Cream Parlor sit-in in Durham, North Carolina, and the Nashville sit-ins with its long-running rhetorical training sessions. In between, however, were many other sit-ins we were unable to include in this volume: the 1939 sit-ins at Alexandria, Virginia's public library[9] and New York's Shack Sandwich Shops,[10] the Little Palace sit-in by Howard University students between 1942 and 1944,[11] CORE's sit-in at Jack Spratt's in Chicago in 1943,[12] the CIO sit-in in Columbus, Ohio, in 1947,[13] and Des Moines, Iowa's Katz Drugs sit-in of 1948.[14] After Stix, Baer, and Fuller, protesters staged sit-ins in Washington, D.C., at Thompson's Restaurant from 1950 to 1953;[15] in Baltimore, Maryland, at Read's Drugs (1955);[16] in Wichita, Kansas, at Dockum Drugs (1958);[17] in Oklahoma City at Katz Drugs (1958);[18] and in Miami, Florida (1959),[19] just months before the Greensboro sit-ins of February 1, 1960. There are no doubt others, some we have heard of but for which we have no reliable sources, others that, given the nature of a sit-in, have almost certainly been lost to us, buried in a police report or never reported at all.

The essays in this section provide glimpses into protest moments between 1938 and 1959, moments that sparked the fires of the early 1960s.

Notes

1. Kelley, *Right to Ride*, 15–32.

2. Hine, "1867 Charleston Streetcar Sit-Ins."

3. Fischer, "Pioneer Protest."

4. For the beginnings of the Richmond protest, see Regnault, "Indictment of Christopher Jones."

5. Norris, "An Early Instance of Non-violence."

6. *Plessy v. Ferguson*, 163 U.S. 537 (1896).

7. See, e.g., Meier and Rudwick, "Negro Boycotts of Segregated Streetcars." See, more generally, Meier, *Negro Thought in America*.

8. On the importance of these changes, see especially Wilkerson, *The Warmth of Other Sons*.

9. See, e.g., Sullivan, "Lawyer Samuel Tucker."

10. "Divine's Followers Give Aid to Strikers."

11. Bynum, *NAACP Youth*, 39–40.

12. Grossman, "Birth of the Sit-In."

13. "CIO Delegates 'Sit In'"; "CIO Group Stages Coffee Shop 'Sit-In.'"

14. Lawrence, "'Since It Is My Right, I Would Like to Have It.'"

15. Quigley, "How D.C. Ended Segregation."

16. Cassie, "And Service for All."

17. Eick, *Dissent in Wichita*.

18. Walker, "50 Years Ago."

19. "Close Counter Rather Than Serve Negroes."

LIMINAL PROTEST

Eleanor Roosevelt's "Sit-Between" at the 1938
Southern Conference for Human Welfare

Melody Lehn

In November 1938 the first meeting of the Southern Conference for Human
Welfare (SCHW) convened in Birmingham, Alabama. Although the conference
began as an integrated event, the commissioner of public safety, Theophilus
Eugene "Bull" Connor, arrived with local police on the second day. Connor's
purpose was to enforce a city ordinance mandating that the audience be divided
along racial lines. Following a heated debate, conference participants reluctantly
submitted to the ordinance, with one notable exception. Refusing to be segregated, first lady Eleanor Roosevelt moved her chair to sit in the aisle, effectively
"sitting between" the two races in a visual rhetorical event that protested the
segregation law and its enforcement by police. Wise enough not to arrest the
wife of the president, Connor and his men were powerless to challenge a display
of dissent that was both irenic and confrontational.

This essay begins with an account of the SCHW's origins, the fear and
frustration inspired by Bull Connor's appearance at its inaugural meeting, and
Eleanor Roosevelt's public eschewal of segregation. Despite some threads of
agreement about its significance, historical treatments of Roosevelt's participation at the meeting are inconsistent and inadequate. Widening the view, I argue
for a rhetorical reading of Roosevelt's aisle-sitting as a deliberate, polysemic
rhetorical strategy of "sitting between." This strategy exemplifies what I call
"liminal protest": a rhetorical act that invents and temporarily occupies an un-
defined or contested space in protest, all the while transforming that space into
an interpretative place of meaning, argument, and dissent. The "in between"
protester—neither here nor there—momentarily traverses, defies, and subverts

boundaries and binaries to offer a fresh, though necessarily contingent and impermanent, revision to the status quo.

Drawing on cultural anthropologist Victor Turner's work on ritual processes, I then examine the liminal aspects of Roosevelt's sit-between. Following a brief description of Turner's three stages of ritual, I read Roosevelt's sit-between within and against the order and vocabulary of these stages. This analysis shows that Roosevelt strategically harnessed liminality as a protest strategy to confound and critique the ritual performance of southern segregation. To complicate the law and animate her protest, Roosevelt drew from several intersecting and distinctive privileges to enable and bolster her protest. After considering the rhetorical opportunities and limitations of enacting these privileges, I discuss the legacy of Roosevelt's liminal protest as a provisional yet potent precursor to what later emerged as an indispensable strategy throughout the civil rights movement.

Connor Arrives and Roosevelt Sits at the 1938 SCHW

The idea for the SCHW can be traced to Joseph Gelders. A former professor of physics at the University of Alabama, Gelders was an outspoken advocate and member of the National Committee for the Defense of Political Prisoners. In September 1936 four Birmingham men kidnapped, robbed, stripped, and brutally beat Gelders with a leather strap. Though Gelders positively identified two of the men, the case never reached trial and the assailants escaped punishment.[1] The attack and its aftermath prompted Gelders to envision "a regional conference on civil liberties to publicize police and vigilante brutality, to elicit suggested solutions to the violation of the Constitution incident to the class war in Birmingham, and to establish a permanent organization devoted to the protection of Constitutional rights in the South."[2]

Aware of his proposal and convinced of its potential, labor activist Lucy Randolph Mason arranged a meeting between Gelders and her friend Eleanor Roosevelt. In June 1938 Gelders visited the Roosevelts at Hyde Park to discuss what would become the Southern Conference for Human Welfare.[3] Eager to lend her support, the first lady promised to deliver a keynote address at the meeting. Notably she reasoned that if the conference was to do any good, it ought to be inclusive. Women, blacks, tenant farmers, and union members must not only be invited, she insisted, but should also serve as conference delegates.[4]

The first SCHW convened in Birmingham, Alabama, November 20–23, 1938, in the city's Municipal Auditorium, the First Methodist Church, and the Tutwiler Hotel. Delegates and attendees exemplified the diversity Roosevelt had envisioned. Activists, union leaders, educators, politicians, journalists, and others gathered together for the common purpose of improving southern welfare.

Of the 1,200 registered delegates hailing from thirteen southern states, nearly twenty-five percent were black.[5] Governor Bibb Graves and his wife, Dixie, attended, as did both Alabama senators. Supreme Court Justice Hugo Black, an Alabamian, was on hand to speak and accept the Thomas Jefferson Medal honoring "the Southerner who has done most to promote human welfare."[6] Panel topics were as varied as the attendees. Sessions facilitated conversation about constitutional rights, the poll tax, credit, housing, labor relations, farm tenancy, suffrage, youth problems, prison reform, and race relations. "The strategy of the conference was sound," Charles S. Johnson remarked in the *Crisis* two months later: "It aimed at being neither a labor meeting, nor a social work body, nor a race relations assembly. It sought to present the total regional configuration, with special elements and problems in their functional setting."[7] All told, there had never been a gathering—or even an attempt at a gathering—such as this in the South.[8]

Even as hotel accommodations and dining strictly adhered to segregation standards of the time and place, participants sat unsegregated at the opening meeting on Sunday evening. The desegregation mostly had to do with logistics. With more than 5,500 seats arranged to accommodate the thousands set to attend, people claimed chairs wherever they could find them. The "subtle relaxation of the old rules" of segregated seating, coupled with fiery and inspirational words from the speakers, made for a memorable first day.[9] "We had a feeling of exhilaration, like we had crossed the river together and entered the Promised Land," conference organizer Virginia Durr later remembered.[10]

But that feeling of exhilaration would not—indeed, could not—last. When Bull Connor arrived with officers the next morning, he loudly announced, "We're not going to have white folks and nigras segregating [*sic*] together in this man's town," before threatening to arrest anyone who did not comply with the order.[11] Hereafter the central aisle constituted the barrier separating the two races, sharply emphasized by the fact that police "drove a peg into the lawn, tied a cord to it, and then teased it through the auditorium doors, down the central corridor, and onto the stage."[12] Each race now had an assigned side: whites on one side, blacks on the other.[13] Officers strictly monitored the remaining sessions to ensure that whites and blacks stayed separate and used their designated race-specific entrances.[14] Anyone who disobeyed the order risked arrest or worse.

The new arrangements detrimentally affected the proceedings. While the audience physically split down the middle easily enough, speakers and members of the conference leadership struggled to implement the ordinance onstage. Several hours of debate ensued about whether or not whites and blacks could congregate together on the platform or even pass by each other when transitioning between speakers.[15] Most reluctantly agreed to abide by the law so that the conference could continue. Nevertheless some took great offense at the prospect of segregating. An administrator from a historically black university, after agreeing to sit on the designated black side, vehemently protested the order to use a "blacks only" entrance.[16] Several delegates threatened to cause embarrassment by boycotting Roosevelt's address if segregated seating took effect.[17] Once segregated, a few made good on the threat to walk out in protest. The president of Fisk University left and swore he would attend no future meetings of the SCHW.[18]

Some, however, opposed the anti-segregation turn the conversation had taken. An unnamed "dean of women in a certain educational institution," the *Chicago Defender* reported, announced that she found segregated seating "desirable for the interest of the two races."[19] One conference planner, Birmingham postmaster Cooper Green, denied having ever been a delegate and declared his support for segregation. Several of the SCHW's sponsors later withdrew support and "pleaded ignorance" of the anti-segregation stances taken after Connor's appearance.[20] The most prominent censure came from Governor Graves, who left the conference so swiftly that he "nearly tripped" on the way out.[21] After departing, Graves told the press he was "shocked and surprised . . . that a group of people who call themselves Southern should come out with such open and contemptuous opposition to the ancient Southern principle of the segregation of the races."[22] Graves gave voice to a wider concern with the SCHW's agenda, which many had already perceived as a threat to southern segregation. Now, seemingly, they had all the proof needed to condemn the proceedings. Editors at the *Tuscaloosa News* lamented that the organizers and delegates apparently sought to "destroy the harmony which has taken us so many years to achieve."[23] In any case the once-harmonious meeting—a gathering meant to unify— proceeded diminished and divided, yet hopeful.

Amid the controversy and confusion that had taken hold of the meeting, Eleanor Roosevelt arrived in Birmingham early Tuesday morning with Aubrey Williams, head of the National Youth Administration. After touring a local community center and holding a joint press conference with Dixie Bibb Graves, Roosevelt rushed to the conference site, entered during a session, walked to the front, and sat down on the designated black side. Almost immediately an officer approached and told her that she was sitting on the "colored side."[24] In response Roosevelt took her chair, moved it to the center aisle, and remained there.[25] Meanwhile Connor's officers shook their heads in helpless frustration at the maneuver.[26]

As the conference's most distinguished guest, Roosevelt made the most of her time in Birmingham. In addition to her tour and press conference, she gave an unscheduled talk following an afternoon panel on youth problems.[27] At one point in the day, she "rose," "extended her hand," and engaged in a "hearty handshake" with her good friend, educator and civil rights activist Mary Bethune. As white and black hands touched, many interpreted the exchange as yet another unmistakable effort to push back against the segregation ordinance. The *Chicago Defender* reported on the significance of the exchange, wryly observing that no major news outlets mentioned it when covering the proceedings.[28] During a discussion about the recent lynching of a black youth in Mississippi, the audience applauded when Roosevelt questioned Representative Luther Patrick (D-AL) about his lack of support for a federal anti-lynching law. The tense exchange between the two constituted Roosevelt's most strongly voiced challenge to racism while in Birmingham.[29] In her rousing plenary address, "Democracy in Education," on Tuesday evening, the first lady told the segregated audience in the overflowing Municipal Auditorium that "every one of our citizens . . . regardless of nationality, or race, every one contributes to the welfare and culture of the nation."[30] For more than an hour afterward, she answered audience questions before yielding the floor. After only eighteen hours in Birmingham, Roosevelt boarded a train to Warm Springs, Georgia, to join her family for Thanksgiving.[31]

Sitting-Between: A Liminal Protest Strategy

An early and unusual variation of the sit-in, Eleanor Roosevelt's demonstration in Birmingham is an uncharted example of protest. Upending social norms and impugning legal mandates, Roosevelt's sit-between employed a strategy of "liminal protest." Liminality, rooted in the Latin *limen* (threshold), conveys a sense of "in-betweenness" ripe with potential.[32] Inspired by Arnold van Gennep's work on rites of passage, Victor Turner theorizes liminality as the second part of a three-stage ritual process in which a subject departs from existing norms and structures, temporarily exists in a transitional state, and rejoins society transformed. The first (separation) and last (reincorporation)[33] of these stages, Turner suggests, "speak for themselves" as moments that "detach ritual subjects from their old places in society and return them, inwardly transformed and outwardly changed, to new places."[34] Taken together, separation and reincorporation signify an exit from and reentry back into social structures, which for Turner means "a more or less distinctive arrangement of specialized mutually dependent institutions and the instructional organization of positions and/or of actors which they imply."[35]

Turner finds the middle stage of liminality, the "betwixt and between," to be the most complex and promising in understanding human behavior within the context of sociocultural performances of ritual. The period of liminality separates a subject from that which is known: that is, the liminal subject withdraws from "the familiar space, the routine temporal order, or the structures of moral obligations and social ties."[36] Between separation from and reincorporation into these structures through ritual, liminality constitutes a period of "anti-structure" where the subject engages in "a transformative performance, revealing major classifications, categories and contradictions of cultural processes."[37] Given its potentialities for locating, disclosing, and destabilizing taxonomies and their incongruities, liminality can stimulate individual, as well as group and societal, liberation from constraining social structures, rules, and customs.[38]

Central to its prospects for rhetorical analysis, liminality can spark *communitas*. The Latin *communitas* originally conveyed a sense of community and publicness.[39] For Turner communitas is "social antistructure, meaning by it a relation quality of full, unmediated communication, even communion, between definite and determinate identities, which arises spontaneously in all kinds of groups, situations, and circumstances."[40] Though unstructured and spontaneous, communitas manifests, often quite profoundly, "between concrete, historical, idiosyncratic individuals."[41] Communitas is distinguishable in at least three different forms. First, *existential* or *spontaneous* communitas is a short-lived yet intense and intoxicating "happening" of mutuality enjoyed in the liminal period. More far-reaching and enduring is *normative* communitas, which fosters group unity around shared goals and motivates collective action toward these goals. Normative communitas reflects the possibilities for existential/spontaneous communitas to produce something more permanent that then assimilates back into existing social structures. Finally *ideological* communitas is "utopian" in nature: it reflects, at its very best, "the optimal social conditions under which social experiences might be expected to flourish and multiply."[42]

Liminality has proven useful as an analytic framework and conceptual vocabulary for those seeking to understand when and how people strategically assume a liminal status and/or rhetorically enact liminality. Rhetorical critics have identified liminality's prospects for exercising agency, negotiating identity, rejecting binaries, and reshaping contexts.[43] Reading Roosevelt's sit-between within and against the order and terminology of Turner's stages of ritual, this analysis echoes liminality's potential to shed light on acts that elide the either/or and instead embrace the betwixt and between.

Variations on Separation: Disrupting the Ritual Performance of Racial Segregation

Upon arrival, Roosevelt's initial choice to sit with black attendees immediately located her outside of the ritualized "racial routine" of southern whites and blacks performing segregation.[44] She did not, as Turner's framework suggests, deviate from a place within "an earlier fixed point in the social structure."[45] She missed the exhilaration of the integrated opening session, as well as Connor's arrival to enforce segregation the next morning. Rather she arrived already an outsider, suspended the ritual, and impeded its completion. As a variation on Turner's separation, her departure from segregation necessarily came not from within the ritual but from without.

The police officer amplified Roosevelt's violation when he told her to move, further dramatizing the fact that she had behaved improperly and, in fact, illegally by sitting on the black side. According to the Birmingham city code's section on "separation of races,"

> It shall be unlawful for any member of one race to use or occupy any entrance, exit or seating or standing section set aside for and assigned to use of members of the other race. It shall be unlawful for any person to conduct, participate in or engage in any theatrical performance, picture exhibition, speech, or educational or entertainment program of any kind whatsoever, in any room, hall, theatre, picture house, auditorium, yard, court, ball park, public park, or other indoor or outdoor place, knowing that any of the two preceding subdivisions has not been complied with. The chief of police and members of the Police Department shall have the right, and it shall be their duty, to disperse any gathering or assemblage in violation of this section, and to arrest any person guilty of violating the same.[46]

Since the ordinance made participation in unsegregated meetings unlawful for *any* person in the city of Birmingham, Roosevelt clearly violated the law and, momentarily at least, rendered the audience a body of coconspirators in her crime.

When accounting for her arrival, historians have cautioned against "reading too much" into Roosevelt initially sitting on the black side. Several, though not all, strongly maintain that she did not seek to fulfill a dissenting impulse. For example, William E. Leuchtenburg suggests that no seats remained,[47] while Allida M. Black, Patricia Bell-Scott, and others reasonably claim that Roosevelt merely wanted to sit with her good friend Mary Bethune.[48] John Egerton has advanced the reading that, somehow, Roosevelt moved to the front and sat down unaware that the audience around her was segregated.[49]

No conclusive evidence exists to suggest that Roosevelt did, or for that matter did not, sit on the black side as a deliberate act of civil disobedience.[50] In fact Roosevelt chose to leave the historical record ambiguous on this subject. In her 1948 memoir *This I Remember,* she offered no explanation for why she originally "sat down on the colored side." She did say that "at once the police appeared to remind us of the rules and regulations on segregation," and an officer told her that she "could not sit on the colored side."[51] Still Roosevelt did not raise or preclude the possibility, here or anywhere else, that she acted willfully to confront segregation at this point in the meeting.

"Rather Than Give In": Sitting Between as Liminal Protest

Once engaged by Birmingham police, Roosevelt had a choice to make. The easiest option was for her to obey the order and remain silent about the subject of segregation. Conversely she might join her white peers and challenge the point later in her plenary address or another forum. Or she could be direct and confrontational. Question the officer then and there? Refuse to move and see what happened? Leave in protest, as others had? All were potential options for dissent that might, then again, derail the proceedings altogether. Either way Roosevelt was determined not to "give in."

Instead she moved to the aisle. At this point her choice of seating could no longer be, if it ever had been, seen as a blunder, a matter of practical convenience, or an unthinking deed. Nor could it, as one Roosevelt biographer has suggested, be perceived as merely a "simple gesture of solidarity."[52] Segregationists and anti-segregationists alike widely regarded the maneuver of "sitting between" as a deliberate act of rhetorical protest: a rich, multifaceted "demonstration of defiance and courage" that publicly resisted southern segregation.[53] Testimony shows that those there viewed her sit-between as a "refusal" to be segregated.[54] Neither fully obeying nor disobeying the ordinance but nonetheless disrupting it, Roosevelt conspicuously entered into a self-induced state between order and disorder, between lawfulness and lawlessness, and between silence and speech.

Unlike her evasive description of arriving, sitting, and encountering local police, Roosevelt later characterized the move to the aisle as one of thoughtful resistance, even as she refrained from saying more. "Rather than give in," she explained of the decision-making moments following the police intervention, "I asked that chairs be placed for us with the speakers facing the whole group." Making no mention of her sit-between, Roosevelt went on to say that everyone knew violating "one of Birmingham's strongest laws against mixed audiences" meant arrest and jail. Nevertheless, she concluded, "nothing happened and the meetings for the rest of the day went off well."[55]

Sitting between, Roosevelt's body displayed and deployed her protest. Liminal bodies are those that exist in "the stage of being between categories and the power inherent in that process."[56] These bodies, Andrew Clark explains, "do not neatly fall into a single category, but rather have the ability to slip in and out of categorical spaces."[57] In turn liminal bodies are well poised "to use the current system to their advantage while simultaneously exposing the cracks in the system through their occupation of liminal political and cultural space."[58] To expose the flaws inherent in segregation, Roosevelt's protest drew on intertwined privileged aspects of her body, identity, and status to serve as symbiotic appeals for the argument that integration was practical, necessary, and possible.

Because segregation was defined by race, the most immediately distinguishable feature of Roosevelt's body in protest was its signification of whiteness. As Carrie Crenshaw argues, whiteness "functions ideologically when people employ it, consciously or unconsciously, as a framework to categorize people and understand their social locations."[59] In this case the social location was a segregated conference where whiteness served as the ideological category for the racially privileged. Together but in disunity, police and white conference participants upheld segregation between the time of Connor's appearance and Roosevelt's arrival.

Sitting between, Roosevelt's whiteness functioned as a "strategic rhetoric"[60] that harnessed its concomitant privilege as a resource for protest. Her whiteness contrasted with that of the oppressor, along with that of whites who, despite strenuously condemning segregation, still obeyed the order and submitted to segregation. By sitting between, Roosevelt performed whiteness to disclose further and then mediate the relationship between the oppressor and the oppressed, upsetting white privilege by drawing it from its "proper" place to make even more tangible the injustice at hand. In protest her whiteness took on a liminal status as she paradoxically embodied and rebuked white political authority.

In concert with whiteness, the display of Roosevelt's womanhood contradicted and undermined the symbolic way white women were regularly cast in the South. The images and spectacles created by Bull Connor throughout the later civil rights movement embodied masculinity, aggression, and violence, as did the image he created early in his career at the Birmingham SCHW. Connor, commonly known for his impulsiveness and brutality, would go on to rely routinely upon the manpower and assets of his office to enforce segregation as he saw fit. Such a characterization supports Craig Thomas Friend's portrayal of certain postbellum southern men who "viewed themselves in opposition to what they described as urban, industrial, liberal, corrupt, effeminate men of the North."[61] A refined white woman sitting peacefully in the center aisle offered a steely yet serene counterpoint to the masculinized spectacle of Birmingham's law enforcement surveilling what had otherwise been a collegial gathering.

Importantly Roosevelt's white womanhood did more than present a contrasting feminine image to Connor's brute aggression. As one southern historian explains of this period, "white male patriarchy required that white women possess feminine virtue and maintain the communal hierarchy of being subordinate to and dependent on white males" in a gendered relationship constituted through a "rhetoric [that] represented [and perpetuated] an idealized conception of womanhood."[62] But it was the idealized white southern lady, not the visiting northern woman, who functioned as a "construct that depended on passivity, male protection, and life on a pedestal."[63] Cultural perceptions of women possessing virtuous character that needed rigorous protection by male authority figures further legitimized the conduct of Connor and others, who in part relied upon the perceived dependency of vulnerable white women to explain and justify their segregationist policies, practices, and politics.

Roosevelt, however, was neither vulnerable nor southern, a fact her critics frequently cited when calling for her to be silent about southern problems and race relations.[64] Therefore she was not subject to the same social guidelines governing white womanhood in Birmingham. By not sitting on the "safe" white side, she drew on distinct privileges embedded in her whiteness and her (northern) womanhood to reject the view that she was reliant on white southern men for protection or guidance. Between white and black bodies, sitting undisturbed and unharmed, Roosevelt belied the patriarchal stereotypes and racial prejudices guiding Connor's so-called authority. The purpose of white male law enforcement was not to guard or to protect white females from any real threats against their bodies or virtue. Rather Connor enforced the ordinance simply to avoid having people of different races mingle together publicly in "this man's town." Punitive action was Connor's chief objective, a fact that Roosevelt's sit-between further accentuated.

As a strategic rhetorical performance of white womanhood, Roosevelt's sit-between cannot be detached from its relationship to her position as U.S. first lady, which arguably lent her the most salient authority to challenge Connor and the segregation ordinance. By its very (lack of) definition, the role of first lady exists in a perpetual state of liminality. She enjoys an intimate connection to the executive branch and, depending on the nature of her marriage and the various contextual factors enabling and constraining her performance, she may hold unrivaled influence over presidential decision-making. Even so, a first lady is unelected, uncompensated, and formally unrecognized in the nation's founding documents. She occupies a distinct yet otherworldly place in American political culture, somewhere between an elected official and an ordinary citizen.

Because it has historically been a prominent "symbol of traditional white middle-to-upper-class femininity in America," the first lady position is the archetypal convergence of whiteness and womanhood in an elite, universally recognizable body.[65] The position has historically assumed whiteness in its occupant, at least until Michelle Obama's tenure "disrupted, revised, and refigured the historical battle over ladyhood" in and beyond the White House.[66] Since the nation's founding, white first ladies have rhetorically navigated the tensions inherent in what Rebecca Traister calls "a kind of proximal political power . . . via their relation to powerful white men."[67] Quite often first ladies use their proximal power for civic engagement and advocacy that, concurrently, works to "'open up' opportunities for stretching or extending gendered roles."[68] In its most flattering light, proximal power is construed as beneficial to the extent that some first ladies have used their proximity to influence presidential decision-making directly, affect policy and legislation, and advance political agendas.[69] And yet, as some rhetorical scholars have countered, a first lady's proximal power upholds and depends on patriarchal configurations to do so—even when critiquing those very configurations.[70]

Mutually enabling and problematic in its association with presidential privilege, Roosevelt's protest relied heavily on the proximal power and protection gained through her marriage. Everyone there recognized that while she unofficially represented the Roosevelt administration, her presence was not merely symbolic. "We knew Eleanor just had to pick up the telephone and call Franklin. We had the feeling of having the power of the government on our side," Virginia Durr explained.[71] Hence Roosevelt's protest also exploited the patriarchal aspects of both her marriage and the presidency itself. Challenging Connor on these grounds did require that Roosevelt "acquiesce to male authority in order to gain some protections from male violence."[72] Nonetheless her protest rhetorically worked to "leverage that proximal power enjoyed by white women—who can draw media attention, who have more access to political power . . . and [who] can use that power as a cudgel against the minority of white men who have had everyone in their grip."[73] Connor simply could not risk arresting the president's wife, even though she failed to follow the laws and customs of the region. Strategically leveraging her proximal power, Roosevelt's protest ultimately diluted the threat by subjecting it to her husband's presidential authority, government oversight, and national scrutiny should Connor or his officers attempt to follow through.

Beyond her sit-between, Roosevelt did not speak out about or challenge the ordinance, Bull Connor, or southern segregation during or immediately after the conference. Her inclination in these early years was not to be overtly confrontational in either substance or style, especially when it came to race relations.[74] When given the chance to condemn segregation at the meeting, Roosevelt elected to let her protest speak for itself. After her plenary address, she took an audience question about her views on segregated seating and replied in a way that placed the burden to change both law and practice on the people themselves: "What do I think of the segregation of white and Negro here tonight? Well, I could no more tell people in another state what they should do than the United States can tell another country what to do. I think that one must follow the customs of the district. The answer to that question is not up to me but up to the people of Alabama."[75]

She maintained a measured approach when writing about the SCHW in her "My Day" newspaper column. Only subtly critiquing segregation on the vague grounds of needlessness, Roosevelt made no mention of her sit-between but did praise the cool heads of those who obeyed the law so that the meeting could carry on: "A city ordinance was enforced at this meeting, which to some of us seemed somewhat unnecessary, but the young people showed wisdom and respect for law and order. They complied without question to this ordinance and reserved the right to protest after discussion, as certain other groups have done. I do not know, but I feel that many present objected to the ordinance, but they showed their good sense and self-restraint in not making a real issue on the spot—which might have spoiled the value of the entire meeting."[76]

Even as her public speaking and writing remained purposefully ambiguous, Roosevelt privately expressed frustration that she should not say or do more, lending some insight into her feelings about segregation at the conference. In a letter to confidante Lorena Hickok the day after her sit-between, Roosevelt wrote that she "felt uncomfortable and longed to answer [the questions] not as a visitor should."[77] The contradictions between her public words and private feelings underscore the ways that liminal protest is fraught with contingencies and constraints even as it opens up rhetorical possibilities.

After Sitting Between: The Prospects for Communitas

Once the conference ended, Eleanor Roosevelt left Birmingham and business as usual resumed. Since she challenged, rather than completed, the ritual of southern segregation, Roosevelt did not depart as a transformed subject in the sense of what Turner's third stage of ritual necessitates. Likewise her protest did not culminate in the broad, long-term effects that liminality sometimes makes possible, for she alone could not dismantle the norms, customs, and laws of segregation.[78] Over time Bull Connor's power grew and his reach spread, as did his willingness to use any means necessary to uphold segregation. In the meantime the tactic of sitting in—purposefully entering and fully occupying a public space designated for a race different from that of the protestor—did not become a concerted, organized protest strategy until the 1960 Greensboro, North Carolina, sit-ins. No evidence suggests that Eleanor Roosevelt's "sit-in of sorts" directly informed or inspired any later civil rights sit-ins.[79]

Roosevelt's protest also did not spark the permanence required to achieve normative or ideological communitas. Conference attendees did not rally around her protest, as normative communitas might inspire. Nor did they ever return to the utopian "love feast," as Virginia Durr described the evening before Bull Connor arrived.[80] Most telling on this score is the fate of the SCHW itself. Though it made concrete and positive gains in the decade after its inaugural meeting, the SCHW eventually fractured and, as one historian ruefully explains, "died in obscurity, poor and neglected, forgotten by both its friends and enemies."[81] Eleanor Roosevelt, once its most prominent friend, had already distanced herself from the SCHW by the time it disbanded in 1948 with many of its goals unreached and recommendations unanswered.

Still Roosevelt's act quite clearly generated existential/spontaneous communitas at the conference and in its immediate aftermath. Her sit-between, as evidence shows, almost instantly "warmed the hearts of conferees, angered segregationists, and thrilled the black press."[82] The Washington, D.C.–area weekly *Afro-American* aptly summarized a feeling many black Americans shared at the time: "If the people of the South do not grasp this gesture, we must. Sometimes actions speak louder than words."[83] The actions of Bull Connor and the Birmingham police also stirred the hearts and minds of white liberal southerners, many of whom consequently became more involved in the fight against racial inequality after the conference.[84] Roosevelt's demonstration at that meeting helped to strengthen, legitimize, and advance this determination. As SCHW leader James Dombrowski later indicated, "support for any kind of interracial activity was very scarce. . . . Roosevelt's stand strengthened the backbone of Southerners who wanted to take a decent stand. Her moral stature was very meaningful."[85]

As well Roosevelt's protest created opportunities to forge new relationships with black activists, some of whom had previously been skeptical of her capacity to support racial equality boldly or meaningfully. Less than two weeks after the SCHW meeting, a budding activist named Pauli Murray wrote to Roosevelt tentatively, but as a potential ally, to discuss the status of southern blacks. That she wrote to Roosevelt at all was remarkable given Murray's prior criticism of what she perceived as FDR's inadequate "armchair liberalism" and troubling "coziness with white supremacy in the South."[86] The ensuing exchange of letters between the two women initiated a long, candid, and occasionally tumultuous relationship. Against all odds and the deep inequalities between them, they formed the unlikeliest of friendships.[87] Near the end of her life, Murray said of Roosevelt's evolution as a champion of civil rights, "I learned by watching her in action over a period of three decades that each of us is culture-bound by the era in which we live, and the greatest challenge to the individual is to try to move to the very boundaries of our historical limitations and to project ourselves toward future centuries."[88]

Eleanor Roosevelt did just that when she moved to, dissented upon, and imagined beyond the boundaries of southern segregation in Birmingham. The polysemic, liminal quality of her protest allowed Roosevelt to create, claim, and complicate the interpretative space surrounding the law, the power of law enforcement, and the ritual practice of segregation. Whereas initially sitting on the "wrong" side halted the ritual, dwelling in the aisle exposed the ordinance's ambiguity, paralyzed its enforcer, and confounded the logics of segregation. Accordingly Roosevelt's sit-between could be read in at least one of two ways: as a violation of an ordinance that made any public event "unlawful" if segregation "has not been complied with" *and/or* a non-violation of the law because she did not "use" or "occupy" an entrance, exit, seat, or standing section reserved for a single race.[89] Her deliberate act exposed the ambiguity of the law and prohibited police from exercising their right and duty "to disperse any gathering or assemblage in violation of [segregation], and to arrest any person guilty of violating the same."[90] A mandate that had once seemed clear and binding now appeared murky, vulnerable, and baseless in her act of violating, but not violating, the ordinance without police retribution. Although Roosevelt voiced no opinion either way, her sit-between made the problems with segregation apparent enough for all to see.

Conclusion

In at least three ways, Eleanor Roosevelt's participation at the 1938 SCHW contributes to our understanding of protest. First Roosevelt's sit-between unequivocally *was* a protest. By advancing this argument, my analysis addresses the problems within historical readings that mischaracterize her sit-between as an "imaginative bit of political theater."[91] Rightly some historians have warned that Roosevelt's sit-between should not take on "mythic proportions" in its telling and retellings.[92] A rhetorical reading, however, reveals ways of seeing and addressing both the significance and limitations of her protest. Implicitly this study also signals the likelihood that other inventive instances of protest remain elusive, forgotten, or misunderstood within the annals of American history. Rhetorical critics are ideally suited for the work of locating, excavating, and analyzing these protests.

This study also demonstrates the potential for reading protests and demonstrations within and against Victor Turner's stages of ritual, particularly his conceptualization of the liminal stage. As a critical lens, liminality can offer fruitful ways to account for protests that defy binary definitions, categorizations, and occupations. Unlike later sit-ins, Roosevelt's sit-between straddled and transformed the boundary itself into a conspicuous field of rhetorical action.[93] Liminal protest is, accordingly, a rhetorical strategy that is at once confrontational, concessional, and conditional. While committal in its refusal to choose between an either/or, liminality is also noncommittal in requiring the protestor definitively to claim a side. It both permits and insists the protester dwell in the gray realm of "both/and" rhetorical action and interpretation. The recovery and study of other cases will no doubt yield further insight into the creative, multifaceted nature of liminal protest, as well its potential to stimulate different kinds of communitas. Although it did not generate normative or ideological communitas, Roosevelt's sit-between did produce existential/spontaneous communitas that in many ways positively shaped her social location and encouraged her relationships with emerging civil rights activists, white and black alike. Further investigation might extend the findings of this case and offer examples where liminal protest sparks a more enduring effect.

Finally this study takes seriously the need to account more fully for how privilege can rhetorically animate and problematize the alliances between the powerful and the powerless. Unmistakably Roosevelt enacted whiteness as a rhetorical strategy to enable her protest. Yet privilege is rarely, if ever, one-dimensional. Roosevelt drew authority and meaning from other intersecting aspects of her body, identity, and status. Her gender, class, northernness, role in the proceedings as a keynote speaker, marriage to the president, and status as an unofficial representative of the Roosevelt administration all informed and were informed by her whiteness. Perhaps no one has articulated the multidimensional aspects of Roosevelt's privilege more eloquently than Alabama's own first lady did the year before the Birmingham SCHW. Dixie Graves, familiarly known as "Miss Dixie" to her fellow Alabamians, introduced Roosevelt at an event in the warmest, most discerning of terms: "This woman, born to leisure, busily seeks the truth; highly placed, finds friendship with the lowly; clothed with privileges, strives passionately for social justice; sustained in character, understands commiseratingly human frailty."[94] These words capture the dynamic and thorny interplay between Roosevelt's advantages and the powerlessness of others to do anything other than obey or leave. Taken together, the interweaving aspects of her privilege served as rhetorical clout for a protest that both relieved and troubled pressures between the enfranchised and the disenfranchised. Neither dismissing outright nor fully embracing the hegemonic configurations that allowed Eleanor Roosevelt to sit between, this analysis—like liminality itself—occupies the critical space betwixt and between.

Notes

1. Krueger, *And Promises to Keep*, 3–11; Ingalls, "Flogging of Joseph Gelders," 576–78.

2. Krueger, *And Promises to Keep*, 10–11.

3. Ibid., 13–17. See also Dunbar, *Against the Grain*, 188.

4. "First Southern Conference for Human Welfare," oral history interview with Virginia Foster Durr, 16 October 1975; Egerton, *Speak Now*, 181.

5. Egerton, *Speak Now*, 186–89.

6. Kilpatrick, "Bungled Opportunity."

7. Johnson, "More Southerners Discover the South," 14–15.

8. Egerton, *Speak Now*, 186–87.

9. Ibid., 187–88.

10. Ibid., 188–89.

11. Quotation from Stanton, *Journey toward Justice*, 58; see also Sullivan, *Days of Hope*, 16, 100.

12. McWhorter, *Carry Me Home*, 32.

13. Egerton, *Speak Now*, 192.

14. Johnson, "More Southerners Discover the South," 14.

15. "First Southern Conference for Human Welfare."

16. Thomas, "Conflicts in Intra-racial Culture."

17. Kilpatrick, "Bungled Opportunity."

18. "Southern Whites Flay Jim Crow Laws."

19. Thomas, "Conflicts in Intra-racial Culture."

20. Egerton, *Speak Now,* 292.

21. Stanton, *Journey toward Justice,* 58.

22. "Shocking And Surprising."

23. Ibid.

24. Roosevelt refers to it as the "colored side" in her memoir. See Roosevelt, *This I Remember,* 173.

25. Sullivan, *Freedom Writer,* 11–12; Cook, *Eleanor Roosevelt,* vol. 2, *1933–1938,* 565.

26. Fleming, *In the Shadow of Selma,* 100.

27. Mallon, "Sweeping Moves Urged to Aid South."

28. "Mrs. Eleanor Roosevelt Greets Mrs. Mary Bethune."

29. Allida M. Black notes the irony of how Roosevelt's "outspoken attack on Birmingham politics received little coverage" in the press. See Black, *Casting Her Own Shadow,* 41. Though with limited effects, Roosevelt was already deeply involved in anti-lynching advocacy by this point. See also Cooper, "Reframing Eleanor Roosevelt's Influence."

30. Excerpts of Roosevelt's address can be found in Black, *Courage in a Dangerous World,* 40–41.

31. Egerton, *Speak Now,* 194.

32. Turner, *Ritual Process,* 94–95. See also Turner, "Variations on a Theme of Liminality," 37.

33. Turner, *Ritual Process,* 94. Across his writings Turner's naming of the third stage alternates between "aggregation," "reaggregation," and "reincorporation." The language of "aggregation" is van Gennep's, while "reincorporation" is Turner's usage. For clarity and consistency, I use the term "reincorporation" throughout this analysis.

34. Turner, "Variations," 36.

35. Turner, *Ritual Process,* 166–67.

36. Yang, "Liminal Effects of Social Movements," 383.

37. Turner, "Process, System, and Symbol," 77. See also Coman, "Liminality in Media Studies," 94–95.

38. Yang, "Liminal Effects," 383; Turner, *Process, Performance and Pilgrimage,* 41.

39. Turner, *Ritual Process,* 96.

40. Turner, "Variations," 46.

41. Turner, *Ritual Process,* 131.

42. Ibid., 96–97, 131–33.

43. See, for example, Morris, "Contextual Twilight/Critical Liminality"; Roberts, "Liminality, Authority, and Value"; Whalen, "Introduction: Rhetoric as Liminal Practice"; Gardner, "'Created This Way.'"

44. Berrey, *The Jim Crow Routine,* 2.

45. Turner, *Ritual Process,* 94.

46. The General Code of City of Birmingham Alabama of 1930 (includes all ordinances of a general and permanent nature except as specified in Sec. 6113), Sec. 5516: "Separation of races" (Birmingham: Birmingham Printing Company, 1930), 242–43.

47. Leuchtenburg, *White House Looks South,* 114.

48. Black, "Civil Rights," 91; Black, *Casting Her Own Shadow*, 41; Bell-Scott, *Firebrand and the First Lady*, 25; "Eleanor Roosevelt and Civil Rights," The Eleanor Roosevelt Papers Project, https://www2.gwu.edu/~erpapers/teachinger/lesson-plans/notes-er-and-civil-rights.cfm (accessed 10 October, 2019).

49. Egerton, *Speak Now,* 193.

50. A lone exception worth mentioning here is uncorroborated testimony from NAACP leader and civil rights activist Modjeska Simkins. In a 1990 oral history with John Egerton, Simkins revealed that her friend Seymour Carroll, who attended the Birmingham SCHW, confided in her that Roosevelt was informed of segregated seating before entering the church, implying that she was purposeful and strategic (rather than unthinking or impulsive) from the start. See "Eleanor Roosevelt Reacts to Segregation," oral history interview with Modjeska Simkins, 11 May 1990.

51. Roosevelt, *This I Remember*, 173.

52. Black, *Casting Her Own Shadow,* 41.

53. Cook, *Eleanor Roosevelt,* 568.

54. See Foreman, "Decade of Hope," 141; Durr, *Outside the Magic Circle*, 121; Frantz and Shaylor, "American Radical Traditions," 176–79.

55. Roosevelt, *This I Remember*, 173–74.

56. Smith-Rosenberg, *Disorderly Conduct*, 98.

57. Clark, "Falling through the Cracks," 26.

58. Ibid.

59. Crenshaw, "Resisting Whiteness' Rhetorical Silence," 255.

60. See Nakayama and Krizek, "Whiteness: A Strategic Rhetoric."

61. Friend, "From Southern Manhood to Southern Masculinities," x.

62. DuRocher, "Violent Masculinity," 55.

63. Hoelscher, "Making Place," 666.

64. In a much-circulated 1950 pamphlet, radio commentator W. E. Debnam criticized the hypocrisy of Roosevelt, a "Southern visitor," for observing problems in the South while neglecting to mention where the North fell short in the very same areas. See Debnam, *Weep No More, My Lady*, 52; Lehn, "In Defense of Crap Archives."

65. Anderson, "First Lady," 18.

66. Cooper, "A'n't I a Lady?" 47.

67. Traister, *Good and Mad*, 118.

68. Blair, "'I Want You To Write Me,'" 416. See also Parry-Giles and Blair, "Rise of the Rhetorical First Lady."

69. See, for example, Campbell and McCluskie, "Policy Experts."

70. See, for example, Erickson and Thomson, "First Lady International Diplomacy."

71. Durr, *Outside the Magic Circle,* 127.

72. Dworkin, *Right-Wing Women*, 14.

73. Traister, *Good and Mad*, 131.

74. See Black, "Reluctant but Persistent Warrior."

75. Egerton, *Speak Now,* 194.

76. Roosevelt, "My Day."

77. Qtd. in Black, *Casting Her Own Shadow,* 41.

78. See also Yang, "Liminal Effects."

79. Reed, *Simple Decency and Common Sense*, 180. Reed reaches this conclusion based on a personal interview with Anne Braden, a longtime civil rights activist, ally to the

Student Nonviolent Coordinating Committee, and organizer of the Southern Conference Educational Fund, an outgrowth of the SCHW.

80. Durr, *Outside the Magic Circle*, 120.

81. Krueger, *And Promises to Keep*, 192.

82. Bell-Scott, *Firebrand and the First Lady*, 25.

83. Reprinted in Cook, *Eleanor Roosevelt*, 565.

84. Reed, *Simple Decency*, 17.

85. Reprinted in Sullivan, "Virginia Foster Durr," 150–51.

86. Bell-Scott, *Firebrand and the First Lady*, 21–28.

87. See ibid.

88. Ibid., 354.

89. General Code, "Separation of races," 242.

90. Ibid., 243.

91. Leuchtenburg, *White House Looks South*, 114.

92. Black, *Casting Her Own Shadow*, 41. See also Egerton, *Speak Now*, 193–94.

93. Leff, "Things Made by Words," 226.

94. Dixie Graves, "Welcome to the First Lady of the Land from the First Lady of Alabama," official program for the visit of Mrs. Franklin Delano Roosevelt, March 1937, Birmingham Public Library Digital Collections. For her part Graves possessed a troubling and inconsistent record when it came to race relations. See also Burge, "Senator Graves's Speech."

"OUR BOYS, OUR BONDS, OUR BROTHERS"

Pauli Murray and the Washington, D.C.,
Sit-Ins, 1943–1944

David Miguel Molina

On Saturday, April 17, 1943, a group of three Howard University students entered the Little Palace Café, located at the corner of Fourteenth and U in Washington D.C., and requested to be served. A fourth student positioned herself outside, observing. As the café—situated in "the heart of a Negro business neighborhood" and about a half mile from the Howard campus—maintained a "white trade only" policy in its dining room, her classmates were denied service.[1] They had prepared for this; the students inside each took an empty cafeteria tray, sat at an empty table, and took out something to read. Soon after a second group arrived: three more empty trays, three more empty tables, three more things to read, and a witness outside. Then a third group, and a fourth, until the cafeteria "was more than half-filled with staring students on the inside, and a staring public grouped in the street."[2]

As the students inside maintained their attitude of concentrated study, those positioned outside began to form a picket line, holding up posters prepared by the Office of War Information and displaying signs with slogans such as "Our boys, Our bonds, Our brothers are fighting for YOU, Why Can't We Eat Here?" and "There's No Segregation Law in DC. What's your story Little Palace?" After repeated threats by the café's owner to call the police, a group of about a half dozen officers arrived, though they concluded that the students were not violating any laws. And so, after about an hour of waiting and witnessing, the Little Palace Café closed for the day. Interviewed by the *Chicago Defender* afterward, the owner remarked: "I'll lose money, but I'd rather close up than practice democracy this way. The time is not yet ripe."[3] Perhaps time was a little riper, then, on April 19; on Monday the students returned, and after another forty-eight hours of empty trays, open books, and staring publics, the Little Palace agreed to serve black customers.[4]

Though cursorily dismissive of the student's actions in his remarks to the *Defender*, the owner's comments reveal as much as they refuse: First, what had taken place at the Little Palace Café was recognizably a democratic practice (albeit one he rejected). That is, these performances of waiting and witnessing —these enactments of seeing and being seen—evoke a particular "way" in which democracy might be practiced. Second, this mode of contestation has a particular relation to time or, more precisely, timeliness. By discussing time's "ripeness" with respect to the protestors' democratic envisioning, the café owner acknowledged that these practices work both in and upon a time. Alternatively, to draw on rhetorical theory, one might argue that in their unfolding across the quantitative time (*chronos*) of that first hour at Little Palace Café, these performances of waiting and witnessing staged a crisis in the qualitative time (*kairos*) of embodied democratic practice.[5] As Pauli Murray, one of the key organizers of the protest, reflected in a November 1944 article in the *Crisis,* these students "led the way toward a new, and perhaps successful technique to achieve first class citizenship in one area of life in these United States."[6]

Taking a cue from the title of Murray's *Crisis* article "A Blueprint for First Class Citizenship," this essay examines the inventional process for developing this blueprint for democratic practice. As I will argue, the "new, and perhaps successful" mode of protest enacted at Little Palace Café developed within a particular fusion of discursive and performative genealogies available to the Howard University students at the time. By drawing on emergent discourses on race, gender, and wartime citizenship in the nation's capital and mobilizing experimental modes of mass protest and collective action, the protestors at Little Palace Café and in a second campaign conducted at Thompson's Café in the spring of 1944 developed a novel strategy for politicizing the legibility of embodied space.[7] The effects of this development would be widespread, as the Little Palace and Thompson's protests contributed significantly to the development of what is now recognizable as a sit-in. However, in its moment this important blueprint for action was, as Murray reflects, still decidedly *new*. This essay, then, is an investigation into the conditions of this newness.

Drawing on Pauli Murray's publications, notes, and reflections during the buildup, implementation, and aftermath of the Little Palace Café and Thompson's protests, this essay constitutes an attempt to tease out the constituent elements of their emergence. The basic components were a convergence of civil rights, labor, and pacifist discourses during the buildup, struggle, and aftermath of the Second World War. The sections that follow explore how and why these discourses came to overlap in the Little Palace Café: how Murray's involvement in an ensemble of wartime projects facilitated this accumulation, how planning and enacting the Howard University protests drew upon these available repertoires, and how this process contributed to the emergence of a blueprint for rhetorical performance that would, in the long accumulation of iterations, come to be called a sit-in.

Before proceeding, however, I want to make some preliminary remarks about two aspects of the Little Palace and Thompson's protests that frame my project's investment in them. The first is the central involvement of Pauli Murray in their organizing and enactment. At the time Murray was studying law at Howard University and initiating a project of legal research that culminated in an early theorization of what became the NAACP's legal strategy in *Brown v. Board of Education:* a "frontal assault on the constitutionality of segregation per se" that drew upon psychological and sociological data to argue that segregation did "violence to the personality of the individual affected, whether he is white or black."[8] Existing scholarship on Murray generally attends to her crucial (though crucially unrecognized) role in the intellectual and organizational vanguard of this and various other civil rights, feminist, and human rights struggles across the latter half of the twentieth century: her arguments for the inclusion of "sex" in Title VII of the 1964 Civil Rights Act, her participation in the founding of the National Organization for Women, her time teaching constitutional law in post-independence Ghana, her theorizations of black feminist theology as an Episcopal priest, her discursive and performative negotiations of the categorical interplay of race, gender, and sexuality, and so forth.[9] Moreover, while Murray's role in the Washington, D.C., protests is often mentioned in biographic overviews and amidst contextual framings along the way to a more sustained analysis of her later work, the protests themselves have rarely received sustained scholarly focus.[10] Much of what we know about Little Palace and Thompson's comes from Murray's writings—via publications like the article in the *Crisis,* reflections in her autobiography, and archival notes, correspondence, and materials. Furthermore two of Murray's central interventions in critical discourses of race and gender—the constitutional research on segregation mentioned above and Murray's theorization of "Jane Crow" as an analytic for the position of the "Negro woman . . . within the framework of 'male supremacy' as well as 'white supremacy'"—were developed during her involvement in the planning and implementation of the Howard University protests.[11] So inasmuch as this essay looks to understand better the particularity of these emergent protests as embodied democratic practices, it will do so with an emphasis on Murray's theoretical and organizational role in the rhetorical production of staring students and staring publics, as well as the effects of this process on Murray's thought.

The second aspect of the Little Palace and Thompson's protests that is central to this essay is the notion of the sit-in protest. As Theodore Carter Delaney notes in his article "The Sit-In Demonstration in Historic Perspective," "When North Carolina A&T students Joseph McNeil, Izell Blair, Franklin McCain, and David Richmond took their places at the Woolworth lunch counter in Greensboro, North Carolina, on February 1, 1960, they were not the first black activists to use this form of protest."[12] The scene at the Little Palace Café described above resonates with our understanding of sit-ins via Greensboro, or Nashville, or Jackson: students occupying seats in a "whites only" dining space, picket lines outside, angry threats, police involvement. Staring students on the inside, and a staring public grouped in the street. Admittedly, though, in these later sit-ins, the public did much more than stare—they often intervened violently—and the police did not always conclude that no law had been violated. Nevertheless it seems clear that there is some performative homology between these protest actions. They are all easily legible as sit-ins, despite more than fifteen years of separation between their enactments.

Moreover I want to suggest that simply calling all of these protests sit-ins and moving on risks anachronism or—more important—misses the productive possibilities of a near-anachronism, a moment in which the concept of the sit-in is approaching, but not yet at, its accumulation and condensation as a legible form. In fact the term *sit-in* does not appear in any of the writings or archival material produced in and around the time of the Little Palace and Thompson's Café protests—though Murray uses the phrase in her autobiography to refer to the events. Instead many near neologisms abound in contemporaneous writing about the protest actions, including *sit down, stool sitting, sitting,* and *sitting in.* This is to say not that the D.C. protests were not sit-ins but that this terminological disjuncture suggests that the Little Palace and Thompson's protests offer an opportunity to think through a moment in which the sit-in was a decidedly emergent practice.

Importantly, the D.C. protestors themselves are by no means the first to experiment with these strategies of protest. As recently as May 1942, CORE had sponsored similar actions in Chicago—organized in part by James Famer, who had close ties with Murray as a member of the Fellowship of Reconciliation (FOR) and later, along with Bayard Rustin, as resident at the Harlem Ashram.[13] Even so one might claim that the performative availability of similarly articulated strategies can be seen in the spread of the sit-down strike in 1936–37 as a popular strategy for labor action.[14] However I am more interested in investigating the shared conditions of possibility for the sit-in as a protest than in delineating some authorial through line of development. So in the interest of heeding Delaney's call for a more robust understanding of "how the activists of the 1940s and 1950s fit into the story of the later civil rights era," what is important here is the possibility that the 1937 sit-downs, the Washington, D.C., and Chicago sit-ins, and any number of similar and contemporary protest actions emerged within a shared rhetorical milieu and engaged similar conditions of possibility.[15]

From "Double V" to "This Means Me": Addressing Jim Crow Publics

"In January 1943 three women students were arrested in downtown Washington for the simple act of refusing to pay an overcharge for three hot chocolates in a United Cigar store on Pennsylvania Avenue."[16]

By Murray's account this simple act of refusing initiated the organizing build-up that culminated in the Little Palace Café and Thompson's Café protests. In a "Blueprint for First Class Citizenship," Murray states that after the incident at the United Cigar store a "flood of resentment against the whole system of segregation broke loose."[17] Finding little support from the Howard University administration, the women turned to the Howard chapter of the NAACP, which formed a "Civil Rights Committee" charged with undertaking a lobbying and direct action campaign to "bring equal accommodations to the District of Columbia."[18] Soon after Murray herself was asked to advise the mostly undergraduate—and predominantly female—group, working to "make sure that [their] proposed actions were within the framework of legality so not as to arouse the official disapproval of the university administration."[19]

In its initial meetings in the aftermath of the United Cigar store arrests, the Civil Rights Committee got right to work on translating a flood of resentment into political action. Taking the situatedness of their classmates' act of refusal as a performative entry point into a whole repertoire of resistance—the act's very "simplicity" marking it as just one of the innumerable instances of African Americans' refusal to comply with prejudicial treatment during the Jim Crow era in the United States—the committee worked to identify preexisting practices that could be articulated together as an organized, and organizable, mode of contestation. In Murray's accounts of the students' organizing efforts, the group's proposed actions were intended to be a merging of two recognizable protest forms occasionally deployed by Howard University students as strategies of everyday resistance to the habitus of Jim Crow. The first was a method suggested by William Raines, a law school classmate of Murray's, as the "stool-sitting technique." Of Raines's "disruptive" strategy, Murray states: "His reasoning was that if white people wanted to deny us service, they should be made to pay for it. Since no lunchroom open to the public could keep us out, Raines argued, 'Let's go downtown some lunch hour when they're crowded, and if they don't serve us, we'll just sit there and read our books. They'll lose trade while that seat is out of circulation.'"[20] The other method, identified by Murray as a "one-person campaign along the very lines Bill Raines was proposing," was a string of "sittings" enacted individually by Ruth Powell, one of the three women who were arrested at the United Cigar store and, by Murray's account, "the essence of respectability." Where Raines's method was theorized as an economic intervention, Powell's one-woman campaign was understood as one of "self-respect": "Ruth would go in, ask politely for service, and when she was refused, would sit quietly, sometimes for hours at a time. During those 'sittings' she would pick out a waiter and just stare at him with a perfectly blank expression on her face. Waiters found it very confusing and nerve-racking to be singled out and simply stared at for an hour or more."[21] And so, as Murray notes in "Blueprint," in the deliberations of the direct action subcommittee of the Howard Chapter NAACP's Civil Rights Committee, "the 'stool sitting' idea combined with the 'sit-it-out-in-your-most-dignified-bib-and-tucker' idea to make a fundamental thrust at the heart of jim crow [sic]."[22]

Though at first glance Murray's account of the protests' immediate genealogy suggests a rather accelerated transition from "simple act" to "fundamental thrust," it also opens up a host of critical questions. How, for instance, did this suturing happen? That is, what enabled the various articulations implied in the combination above—between the performative availability of Raines's stool sitting and Powell's sittings; between their economic (to be made to "pay for it") and ideological contestations (to be "simply stared at"); between their denied ("service") and fugitive consumption ("just stare at him"/"read our books"); between their confrontation ("disruptive") and respectability politics ("bib-and-tucker")? In many ways these varied antagonisms were already present before the United Cigar arrests—otherwise the "simple act of refusal" itself might not have been so salient. So, crucially, why come together then? What about the historical moment served as the conditions of possibility for the arrest of those three women to allow for "the flood of resentment against the whole system of segregation [to break] loose"?

As Ruth Powell put it in her reflections on the initiation of her practice of sittings, the composite protest form that emerged out of the committee's deliberations might be primarily understood as a site through which the participants negotiated a shared conjunctural inflection point, the felt sense that "then came the war."[23] Indeed in planning and implementing the Little Palace and Thompson's protests in 1943 and 1944, the Howard University students were working within and upon a shifting rhetorical terrain marked by wartime challenges to the articulation and maintenance of democratic practice. Moreover, in imagining their composite protest as staging a *kairotic* crisis in the available ways of practicing democracy, perhaps no shift was more timely for the Howard women than the recent entry of "Double V" discourse into the black public culture.

In her essay on the D.C. protests, Flora Bryant Brown argues that "American entry into World War II heightened [these students'] awareness of political issues," most recognizably through their strategic appropriation of the "Double V" slogan—"victory against fascism abroad and victory over discrimination at home"—coined by the *Pittsburgh Courier* in February 1942 and quickly taken up in African American newspapers throughout the country.[24] In fact, as Murray states in her autobiography, Howard's situatedness in the nation's capital seems to have made a specific Double V framing particularly attractive to the organizers —as "Washington was seen by many as the symbolic capital of the nations allied against the Axis, and its advocacy of war aims such as the Four Freedoms made it the logical place for Negro activists to press their claims for equality."[25]

Moreover, Brown argues, the students' heightened political awareness at the time was articulated through the particularly gendered implications of Double V in light of the draft—that is, the students' shared feeling of a "duty to continue the struggle for equality at home while the young men who had been their classmates were fighting overseas."[26] As nearly all of the Howard University students involved in the protest were women, the ability of Double V arguments to be amplified by legibly gendered citizenship claims did not go unheeded. For example a placard frequently remarked upon in reportage and reflections on the event—"Our boys, Our bonds, our brothers are fighting for YOU. Why can't we eat here?"—alliteratively positions the protest at the intersection of Double V rhetoric and a strategic gendering of the war's effect on everyday life. In doing so the Howard University students were able simultaneously to fix and displace the addressivity of their protest—compounding the situatedness of staring students and staring publics. On the one hand, the appeal's conflation of familial, capital, and fraternal stakes in the war effort indexes the protestors' *our/we* as having not only a raced but also a gendered relationship to struggles at home and abroad. This works to fix the *here* of the protest within what Murray later described as her and her fellow students' frustration with the contradictions of their "protected position" during wartime—a position nonetheless constrained within the daily indignities of race and gender discrimination.[27] On the other hand, the protest's (and Howard University's) marked situatedness in the nation's capital extended the possible legibility of the *YOU* in the "Our boys" placard to interpolate a whole range of audiences. In this way the addressivity of the protests hailed not only the multiple staring publics of Jim Crow Washington, D.C., but also (by way of apostrophe) the federal government whose institutional enactment establishes the district's political geography and (by way of synecdoche) the broader *demos* by which this government is representatively constituted.

This is not to say, however, that the availability of Double V discourse to the protestors and their audiences was somehow automatic, or its articulation to their demands at the Little Palace Café was simply transparent. Nor were the mechanics of Double V somehow necessarily embedded in the performative articulation between "sitting," "stool sitting," and the "Our boys" placard. Importantly, further consideration of Murray's writing at the time sheds light on some of the available discursive and performative mechanisms for not just invoking Double V but also enacting it. Murray's written engagement in Double V arguments spans across her participation in the D.C. protests in 1943 and 1944, and many of her publications at the time explore the multiple staring publics made available by the "Our Boys" placard. A closer look at one of these texts, Murray's August 1943 article in *Common Sense*, "Negroes Are Fed Up," is useful for considering the specific range of rhetorical possibility through which a "strategy of using wartime aims to attack Jim Crow" could be mobilized within the addressivity of the D.C. protest actions.[28]

Published in the time between the Little Palace Café protest in April 1943 and the second protest at Thompson's Café in April 1944, "Negroes Are Fed Up" takes up the repertoire of Double V in the interest of understanding the underlying causes and official response to the June 1943 riots in Detroit.[29] As the article progresses, Murray looks to understand the riots not as a deviation from the Double V strategy, nor as the machinations of rumored "fifth columnists," but precisely as a violent articulation of one of the central interventions of Double V itself—the fact that "the Negro is adopting the war slogans as his own."[30] Turning her attention to the concluding remarks in a June 7 radio address by President Roosevelt in which he offered yet another reflection on the "Four Freedoms" thematic, Murray states: "At these words, the most humble Negro lifts his head, points to his war stamps, or to the picture of his son in uniform, and says, 'This means me.'"[31]

For Murray, then, the conflict in the Detroit riot represented a possible expression of "this means me"—a confirmation not only that "Negros in America are determined to obtain justice and nothing will stop them," but also that "rebellion against the denial of these rights is speeded by war." To reinforce this claim, Murray turned to the particular situatedness of the nation's capital in the interest of providing a representative list of "individual acts" that contributed to "[creating] of tension from which the victims must find relief": "A white sailor dashes the tray of a Negro girl war worker in Washington to the floor in a crowded government cafeteria. . . . Two Negro war workers are arrested and fined for riding in their accustomed seats to the Pentagon building. . . . Three Howard University girls are jailed because they refuse to pay an overcharge in a Washington restaurant."[32]

Crucially the last example is precisely the "simple act of refusing" that functions in "Blueprint for First Class Citizenship" as the ruptural moment through which a "flood of resentment against the whole system of segregation broke loose" for the Howard University students involved in the Little Palace Café and Thompson's Café protests.[33] Moreover, while Murray does not address the Little Palace protest directly in "Negroes Are Fed Up," she gestures toward the organizing efforts in her concluding comments, remarking that "those of us who will not yield to despair will continue to fight for a solution through long-range and immediate programs of group action."[34] In this light the Little Palace and Thompson's protests might be thought through as attempts to articulate "this means me" differently, to enact an alternate contestatory outlet for the Howard University women to "[adopt] the war slogans as [their] own," and to do so in a way that both enacted Double V and avoided reproducing of the particular mode of violence deployed in the 1943 Detroit uprising.

And yet, as Murray's concludes in "Negroes Are Fed Up," it became clear that the availability of Double V alone—while a productive initial framework for thinking through the multiplicity of address and the fixity of place in the Little Palace and Thompson's protests—failed to account for the full range of discursive suturing present in their planning and implantation, let alone their articulation to the experiences of black women during wartime. She continues: "But I think the situation also demands a revolution in our individual thinking. It requires a moral ethic which reaffirms a fundamental kinship in all mankind."[35] To understand properly Murray's call here for a "revolution in our individual thinking" and "a moral ethic," and to bring the notion of "kinship in all mankind" in conversation with the strategic production of staring students and staring publics in the D.C. protests, we must also consider the ways in which the Little Palace and Thompson's protests should also be seen as early experiments in particular understandings of "nonviolent civil disobedience" and legal activism that were just taking shape as an ensemble of pacifist, leftist, labor, and civil rights organizations worked to rethink the political possibilities of direct action.

"Satyagraha on the Spot": Experiments with Nonviolence

In her autobiography Murray remarks that though still quite controversial—and recently denounced by the Double V–coining *Pittsburgh Courier* as "dangerous demagoguery"—"ideas about nonviolent resistance to racial injustice, modeled on Gandhi's movement in India, were in the air" during the buildup to the Little Palace and Thompson's Café protests in 1943.[36] For Murray, at least, such ideas had been in the air since early 1940. As a member of the Fellowship of Reconciliation and one of the few black members of the recently established Harlem Ashram, Murray was engaged at the time in what Ashram founder J. Holmes Smith offered as the "special study of, and experimentation with, methods of nonviolent direct action as an effective substitute for international or class war."[37] The added emphasis on "experimentation" in Smith's announcement here is key. Smith, a FOR member and former missionary to India, initiated the Ashram's program of voluntary poverty and communal living on Fifth Avenue and 125th Street amid a larger debate within the FOR about the capacity of pacifism to enact social change—and the controversial, experimental role of nonviolent resistance therein.

As Leilah Danielson notes, just as Gandhian nonviolence "only took root in the African American community after a process of adaptation and modification," likewise "a complex historical and cultural process occurred in the translation of Gandhian nonviolence to the pacifist community in the United States."[38] Alternatively, as Aldon Morris puts it, "it took time to create the nonviolent protester."[39] Through her involvement with FOR and the Harlem Ashram project, Murray found herself doubly embedded in these then-uncertain processes of adaptation. Situated at the interstices of a complex, transnational exchange between theories of Gandhian nonviolence, Christian pacifism, and civil rights activism, the Harlem Ashram positioned Murray in unique, conjunctural space for theorizing the possibility of "applying the technique [of satyagraha] to the racial struggle in the United States."[40] Again, a closer look at Murray's writings at the time helps illuminate the process of imagining how a Double V–inflected reconsideration of nonviolent resistance could provide the groundwork for the mode of group action heralded in "Negroes Are Fed Up" and enacted at Little Palace Café.

In a series of notes on nonviolence taken in March 1940, Murray offered an early illustration of her engagement in this process. Set on a single sheet of paper, Murray's notes are roughly divided into two sections: a numbered group of summary data regarding the labor, legal, and political situation in India and a two-columned table setting "India" and "Am. Negro" in comparative analysis.[41] A double-underlined phrase, "War without Violence," is set off to the side of the page—functioning as both a visual separator and discursive connector between the sections. It is also the title of a book: Krishnalal Shridharani's *War without Violence: A Study of Gandhi's Method and Its Accomplishments,* published by the Fellowship of Reconciliation the previous year. One of the central texts of FOR's reengagement in theories of nonviolent direct action, *War without Violence* provides an account of satyagraha's role in "Gandhi's war with the [British colonial] government."[42] Distinguishing nonviolent direct action from, on the one hand, coercion (with its violent implications of "revenge and punishment") and, on the other hand, Western pacifism (which he likened to "[taking] the invasion supinely"), Shridharani's work carved out a space for thinking through satyagraha as a practice of "compulsion" through "psychological suggestion."[43]

In the structuring of her notes as a series of analytic links between the situation in India and the "Am. Negro," Murray's initial attempts to theorize the mobilization of nonviolent compulsion in a Western context begin to emerge.

Notably much of the comparison points to the relative incongruence of conditions of possibility in the American situation for the development of the sort of direct action campaigns deployed in India. Characterized by Murray's notes as a relatively "peaceful" minority population trapped between the "lack of a well-disciplined movement," the rigidly legalistic "court test" strategies of the NAACP, and segregated "Jim Crow unions," the black community in the United States appeared to lack many of the constitutive factors for mass civil disobedience ascribed to Indian anticolonial struggle. In contrast the Gandhian effort is portrayed as a "well-disciplined movement" emergent within a majority population with a tradition of nonviolent practices and "unified labor," resulting in a widespread "willingness to sacrifice for your ideal—to change the heart of the enemy."[44]

While these notes suggest a somewhat reductive, pessimistic view of the likelihood of adapting satyagraha to civil rights struggles in the United States, they nevertheless mark an important turning point in the very possibility of considering such an adaptation at all. The Fellowship of Reconciliation had not yet formally endorsed nonviolent resistance as a part of its program—it would do so in 1941 under the leadership of A. J. Muste—and Shridharani's *War without Violence* had only just been published. In fact it was the unexpected and popular success of the 1936–37 sit-down strikes in Flint, Michigan, that offered a breakthrough for Muste, Shridharani, and others to urge FOR members to reconsider Gandhian nonviolence. The technique presented such a compelling case for the adoption of nonviolent resistance techniques that FOR's Fellowship Council eventually responded with a statement admitting that, while the strategy remained "far from fully exemplifying the spirit of nonviolence," it was born of a valid interest by workers to "organize and bargain collectively."[45] Murray's notes taken at the Harlam Ashram are written toward the culmination of this contentious reassessment of Gandhian nonviolence across the arc of the 1930s, during which organization leadership had transitioned from deploring an approach that placed "pressure and punishment on innocent and guilty alike with no regard to individual personality" to admiring nonviolence's capacity for "moral jiu-jitsu"—a compelling willingness to suffer that showed conviction-challenging "respect for the personality and moral integrity of the assailant."[46]

In the years between March 1940's notes on nonviolence" and April 1943's protest at the Little Palace Café, Murray encountered multiple opportunities to experiment actively with the potential application of Gandhian nonviolence techniques to civil rights concerns. In fact the first such instance occurred just a few weeks after these notes were taken—when Murray and a travel companion were arrested on Easter weekend of 1940 for refusing to give up their seats to accommodate Jim Crow policies on a Greyhound bus entering Virginia from Washington, D.C. And though at the time Murray had just "read Krishnalal

Shridrami's [sic] *War without Violence* . . . and had pondered the possibility of applying the technique to the racial struggle in the Unites States," the bus confrontation was not a planned action.[47] In a letter describing the episode to a friend, Murray reflected: "We did not plan our arrest intentionally. The situation developed and, having developed, we applied what we knew of *Satyagraha* on the spot."[48]

Less than a year later, another situation developed—and on a much larger, much more intentional scale. In January 1941 A. Philip Randolph announced that ten thousand African Americans would march in the nation's capital on July of that year to demand the end of racial segregation in defense industries and the military. This March on Washington Movement (MOWM) grew quickly into a national organization with thirty-six chapters and significant support throughout the black community in the United States—so much so that after a meeting in July with MOWM organizers, President Roosevelt issued Executive Order 8802 creating a temporary Fair Employment Practices Committee.[49] Though this resulted in the cancellation of the march, it did not mark the end of the MOWM's push for a mass protest strategy to combat segregation—and Murray, seeing the MOWM as "the only available vehicle for mass protest," devoted much of her early years at Howard University to the organization's initiatives.[50]

In just a short time, then, the conditions of possibility for the sort of satyagraha campaign against Jim Crow sketched out in the notes on nonviolence were becoming much less conducive to pessimism. At a MOWM planning conference, Murray's committee was able to propose the development of a "carefully planned non-violent technique of refusal" for "breaking down discrimination in Restaurants [sic], hotels, buses, movies, etc."[51] And during his address to the MOWM in September 1942, it became clear that in the interim Randolph himself was increasingly drawing upon newly available accounts of Gandhian nonviolence to envision future action. Despite persistent resistance to such techniques in the black community, he challenged members to "witness the strategy and maneuver of the people of India," particularly their examples of "mass civil disobedience and noncooperation and marches to the sea."[52] By 1943 MOWM was explicitly calling for a nonviolent movement against racism, a transition that coincided with experiments by Murray, Bayard Rustin, and other FOR members with the adaptation and modification of Gandhian nonviolence techniques to the struggle against segregation and their taking on leadership and pedagogical roles in the organization.[53]

Thus three years after Murray's notes on nonviolence, the Civil Rights Committee of the Howard NAACP Chapter presented Murray with a new, concrete opportunity to continue these experiments in deploying satyagraha in the struggle against Jim Crow laws. In the interim it had become increasingly clear to Murray that whatever form they took, the nonviolent techniques developed for the Howard University students' actions would need to work within and upon distinctly African American claims for citizenship. That is, if demand for action could be routed through the particular—and particularly American—disjuncture of Double V's "this means me," then the practice of civil disobedience itself could draw upon the situatedness of black Americans' everyday life. The resultant challenge, as she remarks in her autobiography, was that "the most effective way to use nonviolence in our racial struggle was to combine it with American techniques of showmanship."[54]

As Murray and the Howard University students worked to catalyze a "simple act of refusal" into a blueprint for democratic practice at Little Palace Café and Thompson's Café, the performative contours of this insurgent, nonviolent showmanship eventually gained shape. Along the way all the conjunctural vectors of combination summarized in Murray's comment were in play: the challenge to combine Gandhian nonviolence techniques of direct action with "American techniques of showmanship" now compounding the simultaneous challenge to merge the preexisting practices of "stool-sitting" and "sit-it-out-in-your-most-dignified-bib-and-tucker"; to situate the "this means me" of Double V discourse within the alternative weapons of nonviolence; to transform a single, everyday refusal into a fundamental thrust at the heart of Jim Crow. As we return to analyze more closely the composite mode of protest that emerged from the Howard University students' efforts in 1943 and 1944, the questions become: How does this strategy work to break down Jim Crow—and do so in such a way that is recognizable as both showmanship and satyagraha? And which aspects of this whole performative fusion of "contradictions and problems and antagonisms" constitute challenges to the existing social order? Which contribute to its reproduction?

"To Occupy Space": The Sit-In as a Genre of Protest

"The purpose of 'Sitting' is to occupy space, to defeat the argument that the presence of Negroes will cause the management to lose trade, and to custom the white public to the presence of Negroes in a place of public accommodation."[55] This quote comes from a flyer distributed on the Howard University campus by the Civil Rights Committee of the Howard Chapter NAACP. Likely circulated in the spring of 1943 as the group gathered support and participants for their forthcoming action at Little Palace Café, this text functions as a concise statement of purpose for the composite protest form developed by Murray and her fellow students. Just one of many discursive tools developed by the Howard group as they drew on available discourses and homegrown innovations to articulate their new technique, the flyer named the intended mode of action most directly.[56] It was an occupation: a dramatization of space, an argument of presence.

At Little Palace Café and Thompson's Café, the Howard University student protesters staged an intervention in the very spatiality of Jim Crow publics—effectively dramatizing these publics' core racialized logics of embodied, situated visuality by holding the practices of seeing and being seen in *kairotic* suspension. To put it another way, the students occupied space in a way that exposed space's social functioning. As discussed, the accumulation of civil rights, labor, and pacifist discourses and practices marked the conditions of possibility for sitting-as-protest through a rather complex process contingent on historical situatedness, individual experience, and collective invention. Finally this analysis allows a look into a noticeably emergent protest genre, the sit-in, at a time in which the "internal dynamic" binding together its "constellation of recognizable forms" was still in flux.[57] Following Karlyn Kohrs Campell and Kathleen Hall Jamieson (1978), offering a "generic claim" about the Little Palace and Thompson's protests allows us to consider not only the work that these rhetorical performances were doing in their enactment but also the tensions that were left embedded in their contribution to the developing "synthetic core" of the sit-in genre.

Starting with the nascent, individual practices of Bill Raines's stool-sitting and Ruth Powell's sittings, the Howard University students reached out to the full repertoire of forms made available by "then came the war" and reinforced by Murray's experience and credibility as a theorist and activist. As a result the production of staring students was able to effect a sit-down strike–cum–"compulsion to witness" inside the Little Palace Café and Thompson's Café. In doing so the protestors brought identifiably Gandhian nonviolence techniques closer to the center stage of American showmanship—the arena of consumer culture and middle-class leisure. This allowed for an attitude of nonviolent "compulsion" projected toward their non-protesting audiences; other patrons were not *coerced* into performatively withholding being served themselves but rather *compelled* into considering the conditions of their ability to "eat here." The spatial mechanics in the newly politicized practice of sitting effected a mode of uncanny availability to the forestalled action at hand. "Occupying" in this sense is a performance of being present to act in all ways but one, a sole felicity condition withheld now amplified in sharp relief by the fact of its withholding.[58] For the sitting students, this was a condition of their situatedness as black female consumers within a Jim Crow habitus persisting amid a global war for liberal democratic freedoms: "Our boys, Our bonds, our brothers are fighting for YOU. Why can't we eat here?"

Consequently as these staring students on the inside performed their inability to eat under Jim Crow conditions, a staring public grouped on the street found itself hailed to witness by a picket line captioning this uncanny, nonviolent suspension of everyday life with a barrage of Double V–inflected address. It was as if this composite performance functioned to render visible the seams of daily relations of power and simultaneously to give its publics a reading strategy for reflexive interrogation into their complicity in its reproduction. As another sign pronounced, "We die together—why can't we eat together?" In the interplay between the multiplicity of address and the fixity of place that Double V citations provided the protestors—the placard's multiple *wes* converging on the rigid facts of the students' situatedness to wartime death and domestic life—we have once again the sort of insurgent invocation that the students' choral performance of "this means me" facilitates. By holding the everyday in occupied suspension, by articulating that suspension as a withholding of their own availability to the everyday, and by compelling their audience to reflect on their complicity in that withholding, the students transformed a simple act of refusal into a strategy for staging a coproduction of staring students and staring publics that punctured the *kairos* of civic life.

These generic tensions—between alienation and absorption and between suspended and shared conditions of availability—came to inhabit the synthetic core of the sit-in, bound up in its recognizable production of a *kairotic* crisis of embodied democratic practice. The Howard University student protesters' role in the development of this fusion, however, ended after the second protest at Thompson's Café. The university administration, under threat of revoked federal funding from segregationist and chair of the District of Columbia Committee Sen. Theodore Bilbo of Mississippi, issued a directive requesting that students "cease all activities designed to accomplish social reform affecting institutions other than Howard University itself."[59] Murray, for her part, soon turned her attention to two projects for which she would become much more well-known: the initial research for *States' Laws on Race and Color,* a compendium of each U.S. state's statutes on racial segregation that Thurgood Marshall dubbed the "bible" of the NAACP's preparation for *Brown v. Board of Education;* and critical reflection on the situatedness of black women in the freedom struggle, which culminated in Murray's theorization of what she would coin "Jane Crow."[60]

The proximity between the truncated development of this "new, and perhaps successful technique to achieve first-class citizenship" and Murray's deepening engagement in a multiply situated critique of the interplay of race, gender, class, and sexuality in the reproduction and maintenance of power—that is, a mode of recognizably black feminist analysis of what was termed "intersectionality" —warrants additional scrutiny. Though outside the scope of the current project, such an inquiry might initiate in considerations of the rhetorical linkages between the Howard University students' protests, Murray's articulation of "Jane Crow," and what Evelyn Brooks Higgenbotham calls the "politics of respectability"—a repertoire of resistance that leverages discourses of personal uplift, fine manners, and proper morals to facilitate oppositional practices and networks for confronting systems of oppression. Developed in the women's movement of the black Baptist church and social clubs in the late nineteenth and early twentieth centuries, these politics had a strategically ambivalent relation to power—"reflect[ing] and reinforc[ing] the hegemonic values of white America," while "simultaneously subvert[ing] and transform[ing] the logic of race and gender subordination."[61]

Similarly, in working to "custom the white public" to the presence of black bodies, the composite protest form developed by the Howard University students hinged much of its disruptive force on specific notions of gender embedded in the performance of "respectability." That is, in their efforts to make legible a suspended availability to public life, the protestors leveraged those conditions of availability that were otherwise shared with the various publics of their performance. First and foremost was the legibility of potentially shared class status, given the fact of the students' enrollment at Howard University, the "Capstone of Negro Education."[62] To effect the uncanny forestallment of availability to eat at Little Palace Café and Thompson's Café, the student protestors took efforts to leverage the productive force of the "dignified-bib-and-tucker." In this way, the "first-class citizenship" sought by the student protestors in part functioned metonymically for a specifically middle-class citizenship. However, in line with Higgenbotham's theorization of respectability politics, this class- and gender-specific uptake was not entirely uncritical. Though participants pledged "to look their best" and "use dignity and restraint at all times" during the protest actions, in her autobiography Murray describes these considerations as wholly strategic: since the risk of breaking the student's entrenched code of "middle-class standards of respectability" was itself "as formidable a psychological barrier to action as the prospect of police brutality," what made Ruth Powell's one-woman campaign of sittings so compelling as a model for the students was precisely the force of its articulation within "the essence of respectability."[63] Nevertheless by embedding their "fundamental thrust at the heart of jim crow" with a distinctly middle-class articulation of black womanhood, the students risked delimiting the availability of the first-class citizenship they sought within the respectability of politics upon which the protests' intervention hinged. Again, future study is necessary to understand the stakes and consequences of this rhetorical choice on the enactment, reception, and legacy of the Little Palace and Thompson's protests.

However by 1944 the initial work of constellating an array of discourses and practices had been set in motion—and continued to inform Murray and her contemporaries' struggle for years to come. The Howard University students were not the first activists to use this form of protest, nor would they be the last. Over time the various parts sutured together in the conjunctural space of "then came the war" became smoothed out, naturalized into a generic whole now called the sit-in. And yet this way of practicing democracy—with all its possibilities and limitations—did not spring forth fully formed in this or any of the constitutive moments of its long accumulation. Though it was often offered as a "new, and perhaps successful" blueprint for collective action, the sit-in was always an obscured bricolage of recognizable and emergent modes of performative occupation—with each iteration equal parts revision and repetition. Embedded in this generic *dureé,* then, are some echoes of the Howard University students' constitutive attempts to negotiate the particular "flood of resentment" opened up when a simple act of refusal became articulated to a whole ensemble of discourses and practices. That is, the students' felt sense of the "purpose of sitting" is in some ways always available to future practices of sitting in—always part of the iterability of its blueprint and always part of its openness to further accumulation. In this way what becomes recognizable as a sit-in is always in some ways a return to Little Palace Café: an occupation that enacts "this means me," a dramatization that implements satyagraha on the spot, an argument that affixes a ripeness of time to the forestalled practice of everyday life. These attempts to transform floods of resentment into frameworks for collective action inhabit the dynamic core of this resilient blueprint for building up a new society within the declining old.

Notes

1. McAlpin, "Howard Students Picket Jim Crow Restaurant."
2. Murray, "Blueprint for First Class Citizenship," 359.
3. McAlpin, "Howard Students Picket Jim Crow Restaurant."
4. Murray, *Song in a Weary Throat,* 207–8; Murray, "Blueprint for First Class Citizenship," 359.
5. Kinneavy, "*Kairos* in Aristotle's *Rhetoric,*" 433.
6. Murray, "Blueprint for First Class Citizenship," 359.
7. The second campaign sought to challenge a similar "white trade only" policy at Thompson's at Fourteenth and Pennsylvania—i.e., situated in the "shadow of the White House" instead of the shadow of the University. Ibid.
8. This project was later published as *States' Laws on Race and Color*—a compendium of each state's statutes on racial segregation that grew out of this research at Howard. Azaransky, *Dream Is Freedom,* 38; Murray, *Song in a Weary Throat,* 221, 254, 284–85.
9. See Rosenberg, "Conjunction of Race and Gender"; Gilmore, "From Jim Crow to Jane Crow"; Azaranzy, "Jane Crow."
10. The notable exception being Glenda Elizabeth Gilmore's *Defying Dixie*, which plays a significant role in the research for this essay.
11. Azaransky, "Jane Crow," 38; Murray, "Why Negro Women Stay Single."

12. Theodore Carter Delaney, "Sit-In Demonstration in Historic Perspective," 432.

13. The date of the original CORE sit-ins is unclear. In his autobiography Farmer identifies the first sit-ins in Chicago as starting at the segregated Jack Spratt coffee shop in May 1942. But the only available reportage for activity at Jack Spratt is in May 1943—three weeks after Little Palace—which is the date Meier and Elliot use in *CORE*. The reality is likely a combination of both—a series of individual or spontaneous actions starting in 1942 and building toward organized, publicized direct action. This only reinforces the fact of the protest's emergent status and the general futility of attempts to designate authorship in any strict sense. However Murray's absence from Farmer's reflections on FOR, CORE, and the Harlem Ashram is conspicuous. Farmer, *Lay Bare the Heart*, 106; Meier and Elliot, *CORE*; Gilmore, *Defying Dixie*, 386.

14. As Robert Shogan states ("Labor Strikes Back," 40): "The UAW's triumph [at Flint] inspired an epidemic of sit-down strikes the like of which neither the United States, nor any country, had ever seen." However Torigan notes that in the wake of the successful passage of the 1937 Wagner Act, which "protected unions from employer interference and enabled the National Labor Board to conduct certifying elections," sit-downs decreased as unions opted to pursue their goals "through procedural means." Then in 1939 a Supreme Court ruling that designated sit-downs as "illegal seizures" all but ended the practice's availability to the labor movement. Torigian, "Occupation of the Factories," 324, 346–47.

15. Delaney, "Sit-In Demonstration in Historic Perspective," 438.

16. Murray, "Blueprint for First Class Citizenship," 358.

17. Ibid.

18. Ibid.

19. Murray, *Song in a Weary Throat*, 205. In fact, as Murray and the student organizers would soon discover, segregation had technically been illegal in Washington, D.C., since 1872—via an unrepealed statute that made it a misdemeanor to refuse to serve "any respectable, well-behaved person without regard to race, color or previous condition of servitude . . . in the same room, and at the same prices as other well-behaved and respectable persons are served." Ibid., 230.

20. Ibid., 203.

21. Ibid.

22. Murray, "Blueprint for First Class Citizenship," 359.

23. Drawing on the work of Stuart Hall, this essay understands "conjuncture" as "a period in which the contradictions and problems and antagonisms, which are always present in different domains in a society, begin to come together. They begin to accumulate, to fuse, to overlap with one another. . . . The aftermath of the fusion, how that fusion develops, its challenges to the existing historical project or social order, the efforts [to contain it], or the success of change and transformation—*all* of that constitutes conjuncture." Hay, Hall, and Grossberg, "Interview with Stuart Hall," 16; Murray, *Song in a Weary Throat*, 204.

24. The "Double V" slogan was originally unveiled via an emblem printed prominently on the front page of the 7 February edition of the *Courier*. The image featured an eagle with spread wings perched on top of a ribbon displaying the text "Double Victory." Two large Vs overlay the eagle image and straddle the ribbon. The word "Democracy" is printed at the top of the emblem, and the text "At Home-Abroad" is at bottom. Looking to "test the response and popularity of such a slogan," the *Courier* published this unveiling without any explanatory text or acknowledgement. An article in the 14 February issue explained the logic of publishing the new slogan "without public announcement or fanfare" and—in light of an "overwhelming" amount of letters and telegrams received in support of the slogan—unpacked the image's intended meaning: "the Double 'V' war cry—victory over

our enemies at home and victory over our enemies on the battlefields abroad." Flora Bryant Brown, "NAACP Sponsored Sit-Ins," 276; untitled article, *Pittsburgh Courier*, 7 February 1942; *"Courier's* Double 'V.'"

25. Murray, *Song in a Weary Throat*, 200.

26. Brown, "NAACP Sponsored Sit-Ins," 276.

27. McNeil, interview with Pauli Murray, 67.

28. Penny M. Von Eschen, *Race Against Empire: Black Americans and Anticolonialism, 1937–1957* (Ithaca: Cornell UP, 1997), 33–34.

29. Sparked by a confluence of "black and white Detroiters clashing regularly and everywhere for their stakes in the rapidly changing [city]" and fast-spreading dual rumors that "whites had thrown a black mother and her child into the Detroit River" and that black men "[had] accosted white women" throughout the city, the Detroit riots lasted three days, from 20 to 23 June 1943. Throughout the turmoil thirty-four people were killed, twenty-seven of whom were black (and seventeen of these deaths were at the hands of the police). In her autobiography Murray notes that "few Negroes were surprised when the Detroit riot broke out . . . for the racial tensions that produced it had been building steadily throughout the war." Detroit's black population was increasing rapidly as southern migrants sought defense-contract work—however the persistence of segregated neighborhoods and increasingly fraught competition with white laborers for industrial work produced tenuous living conditions for many black Detroiters. Capeci and Wilkerson, "Detroit Rioters of 1943," 52–53; Murray, *Song in a Weary Throat*, 211.

30. Murray, "Negroes Are Fed Up," 274.

31. Ibid. The Four Freedoms are freedom of speech, freedom of worship, freedom from want, and freedom from fear.

32. Ibid.

33. In "Negroes Are Fed Up," the event is described as "three Howard University girls are jailed because they refuse to pay an overcharge in a Washington restaurant." Ibid.

34. Ibid.

35. Ibid.

36. Murray, *Song in a Weary Throat*, 201.

37. Smith, "Our New York Ashram," 2. In January 1941 Smith boasted that the "present group of eleven members includes three negroes and a Hindu" and promoted the ashram as a way to "get away from New York while living in the midst of it" (ibid.). Notably the ashram's predominantly white membership and orientation of worldly detachment—coupled with the widespread skepticism about nonviolent tactics among civil rights leaders and activists—prompted CORE founder and occasional ashram member James Farmer to remark later that though it "was not all idiocy," it "was as incongruous in Harlem as the Bucket of Blood Bar, which faced it, would have been in a street in Bombay." Farmer, *Lay Bare the Heart*, 149, 152.

38. Danielson, "'In My Extremity I Turned to Gandhi,'" 362.

39. Morris, *Origins of the Civil Rights Movement*, 161.

40. Ibid., 361; Murray, *Song in a Weary Throat*, 138.

41. Murray, "Notes taken by P.M. on Non-violence."

42. Shridharani, *Selections from "War without Violence,"* 8. Shridharani completed the text as his doctoral thesis while studying sociology at Columbia University—during which he "became a mentor to American pacifists interested in Gandhian nonviolence" and contributed to the establishment of the Harlem Ashram. Danielson, "'In My Extremity I Turned to Gandhi,'" 385.

43. Shridharani, *Selections from "War without Violence,"* 45, 53.

44. Murray, "Notes Taken by P.M. on Non-violence."

45. In a 1937 article, "Sit Downs and Lie Downs," Muste draws a tentative connection between the admittedly "coercion"-dependent Flint sit-downs and "actual experiments in non-violent resistance" attempted by FOR members of the Hosiery Workers Union in initiating a "lie-down picketing" strategy in Reading, Pennsylvania, in December 1936. And in *War without Violence,* Shridharani points to a transnational resonance between the Indian practice of *dhurna*—which he dubs "the father of all sit-down strikes"—and modern examples of successful deployment of the technique in the Punjab, Bengal, and "especially the United States." "Sit-Down Technique," 6; Muste, "Sit Downs and Lie Downs," 5; and Shridharani, *Selections from "War without Violence,"* 18.

46. Qtd. in Fox, "Passage from India," 25; Danielson, "'In My Extremity I Turned to Gandhi,'" 368, 373, 375.

47. Murray, *Song in a Weary Throat,* 138.

48. Ibid., 144.

49. Gilmore, "From Jim Crow to Jane Crow," 359–60.

50. Ibid., 364–65. Murray even led the only actual march that occurred under the MOWM's auspices in the 1940s: a "Silent Parade" carried out by the New York Division of the March on Washington Movement in collaboration with the Workers Defense League in July 1942. Murray, *Song in a Weary Throat,* 175.

51. Qtd. in Gilmore, "From Jim Crow to Jane Crow," 385.

52. Fox, "Passage from India," 25; "Citizen's Repudiate Non-violence Program."

53. Gilmore, "From Jim Crow to Jane Crow," 365; Prashad, "Black Gandhi," 12.

54. Murray, *Song in a Weary Throat,* 201.

55. Flyer, Civil Rights Campaign, Howard University Chapter NAACP, quoted in Brown, "NAACP Sponsored Sit-Ins," 277.

56. Murray, *Song in a Weary Throat,* 223.

57. Campbell and Jamieson, "Form and Genre in Rhetorical Criticism," 17.

58. Cf. Austin, *How to Do Things with Words.*

59. Murray, "Blueprint for First Class Citizenship," 359.

60. Azaransky, *Dream Is Freedom,* 38; Murray, "Why Negro Women Stay Single," 4.

61. Higgenbotham, *Righteous Discontent.*

62. Brown, "NAACP Sponsored Sit-ins," 275.

63. Murray, *Song in a Weary Throat,* 204.

LUNCH COUNTERS AND THE PUBLIC SPHERE

The St. Louis Sit-In as an
Emerging Counterpublic

Joshua D. Phillips

In the 1940s St. Louis was a city divided by W. E. B. Du Bois's infamous color line.[1] While geographically north of the Mason-Dixon Line, St. Louis faced the predicament of being a northern city in a former slaveholding state. Throughout Reconstruction and through the first half of the twentieth century, St. Louis remained rife with racism, as the legacy of slavery turned into de facto segregation. While St. Louis's African American population was proportionally small and did not present a political threat to the social and economic policies of the day, Jim Crow attitudes "permeated St. Louis's institutional life [and] Missouri state law protected segregated public education and prohibited interracial marriage."[2] Most of these segregating social ordinances were enforced quietly, for racist white leaders recognized the need to save face and appear hospitable in the more racially tolerant north. As such St. Louis's white leaders "fostered a public perception of interracial cooperation, and used discourses of racial 'civility' to maintain black subordination, with outright brutality as an unspoken corollary."[3]

However, these racist attitudes were socially and legally challenged as integrationists acquired more political standing in St. Louis. For instance in December 1943 "several black organizations started a letter-writing campaign, urging downtown [St. Louis] department stores to end discrimination at their lunch counters."[4] No business replied to these letters, and eventually the organizations took their concerns to the St. Louis Board of Aldermen. Because department stores were private businesses, there was constitutional uncertainty about whether or not the city had any legal authority to prohibit this type of discrimination. However the city did have a say over city-owned buildings, and in April 1944 Rev. Jasper C. Caston led the passage of a law that integrated the cafeterias of public buildings.[5] Integrating public cafeterias was a widely broadcast victory, and organizations such as the Citizens Civil Rights Committee (CCRC) and the National Association for the Advancement of Colored People (NAACP) viewed this victory as an opportunity to leverage privately owned department stores to reconsider their policies of segregated lunch counters.

In the coming months, the closed-door negotiations among the CCRC, the NAACP, and the department stores reached another standstill. Void of any progress, some citizens began to feel that protesters could no longer afford closed-door meetings. Instead protesters needed to be visible. Essentially they believed that visible and direct action was the only way to get the attention of the department stores and persuade them to change their segregationist policies. In the summer of 1944, Pearl Maddox, a middle-class black woman, decided to act and led the first known sit-in at the Stix, Baer and Fuller department store.[6] Using World War II as leverage, these early protesters carried signs asking "Fox holes are democratic, are you?"[7]

While these tactics did not integrate lunch counters at Stix in 1944, they did open dialogue with store employees. Reportedly the manager at Stix was not ready to lead on lunch counter integration in 1944 but did say that "if other stores opened their lunch counters to blacks, Stix would follow suit."[8] Knowing that Stix was open to integration was just the leverage the sit-in movement needed to recruit more participants and organize a full-scale advance. After lengthy deliberations among activists, protestors agreed upon a strategy, and four years after Pearl Maddox was refused service at Stix, the well-organized and numerically strong Congress of Racial Equality (CORE) returned to Stix in July 1948 to try its luck at finally ending lunch counter segregation.

The Public Sphere and Emerging Counterpublics

Before discussing the specific strategies CORE used in its sit-in campaign, it is important to have a foundational understanding of the "public sphere" and how it intersects with the notions of democratic inclusion and leveraging social capital. Like other social movements, the civil rights movement was constantly shifting, evolving, and transforming its strategies based on the temperament of the day. By understanding how the public sphere has expanded and evolved over the centuries, we can better understand how the Stix sit-in fits within America's narrative as an expanding democratic institution.

In *The Structural Transformation of the Public Sphere,* Jürgen Habermas traces contemporary understanding of the public sphere back to eighteenth-century Europe. Habermas's widely cited argument suggests that the modern roots of democracy were formed during the eighteenth century and that these roots made a more active and politically engaged citizenry possible. Before this period European citizens were quelled under oppressive feudalism. However the rise of capitalism and the mercantile class in the eighteenth century expanded individual property rights and provided some commoners enough social capital to unite in challenging the prevailing political beliefs and practices of the monarchies.[9] In working toward a political voice, politically engaged citizens convened in coffee shops and salons, hoping that a civically literate public could transform oppressive state policies from the bottom up. In theory the public sphere ought to provide equal access to all citizens and should be open to diverse viewpoints. In practice these early public gatherings had their limitations, and only property-owning males were allowed to participate. While this early European model was exclusive, its model of public gatherings and public debate was quite similar to the framework used by the civil rights movement that challenged America's racist and segregationist institutions of power.

Before the civil rights movement, America had already witnessed the evolution of the public sphere through demonstrations that challenged the ways government and institutions recognized citizenship and the democratic process. For example, the early American aristocracy—mostly comprising white, educated men—had absolute reign over public authority and de jure control over the U.S. populace in their personal, political, and economic lives. However, as African Americans, women, Native Americans, poor whites, and other disenfranchised groups publicly vocalized their grievances as well as acquired modest amounts of capital, the once-exclusive public sphere was forced to expand and listen to the political opinions of marginalized peoples. While progress was slow (and is still ongoing), the inclusion of more voices in the public sphere ultimately led to more people being represented in the democratic process.[10]

One way scholars have begun to understand the expansion of the public sphere is by theorizing the emergence of counterpublics. The concept of "counterpublics" challenges the foundational aspects of the public sphere that have often excluded people based on race, class, and gender.[11] Therefore counterpublics aim to encourage more inclusive public dialogues and actively highlight the viewpoints of those individuals who have traditionally been left out of the public sphere's debates. Notably the public sphere does not need to be pitted against the emergence of counterpublics.[12] Instead each of these concepts provides value that betters people's understandings about the transformation of political inclusion. At its core the public sphere can be viewed as a theoretical framework for critiquing, analyzing, and mobilizing public opposition to the state. Correspondingly counterpublics remind people always to be mindful of how power, privilege, and marginalization operate within democracies. An analysis of the Stix, Baer and Fuller department store sit-in as a rhetorical act shows how conceptualizing both the public sphere and counterpublics helps us understand better why specific strategies were utilized and, ultimately, successful.

1948 St. Louis: Ripe for Change

While the sit-ins lay dormant in 1944–48, St. Louis debated other civil rights issues and attempted to mold a new racial climate. Most notably, during the first half of 1948, the U.S. Supreme Court case of *Shelley v. Kraemer* placed the city in the national spotlight. Essentially the *Shelley* case debated the merits of racially restrictive neighborhood covenants that forbade African Americans from purchasing homes in white neighborhoods. In May 1948 the Supreme Court ruled that the Fourteenth Amendment prohibits the government from enforcing "race restrictive ordinances."[13] White property owners could, the court declared, refuse to sell their private property to African Americans, but those owners could not legally require that their white neighbors do the same, because state courts could not enforce such racially restrictive covenants. While the timing of *Shelley v. Kraemer* and the onset of the Stix sit-in in July 1948 may have been coincidental, *Shelley*'s proximity and national prominence seemed to influence the racial atmosphere of St. Louis in the summer of 1948. At the very least, the *Shelley v. Kraemer* decision was indicative of changing race relations in St. Louis and helped pave the way for a following wave of sit-ins.

In acknowledging the timing of the *Shelley* decision, we can better understand St. Louis as a site already ripe with an emerging counterpublic. This type of challenge to the city's status quo directly influenced people's perceptions on expanding citizenry and democratic participation and also influenced strategies for confronting lunch counter segregation at the Stix, Baer and Fuller department store. Therefore this analysis is primarily concerned with the following questions: (1) How did the Stix, Baer and Fuller sit-in work to abolish the status quo of lunch counter discrimination? (2) How did participants of the Stix, Baer and Fuller sit-in articulate their ideological motivations and experience? By analyzing the sit-in through interviews, historical accounts, and news reports, we find that several rhetorical strategies were used throughout the six-year duration of the sit-in. Additionally we discover how ordinary citizens used the leverage of an emerging counterpublic in the aftermath of *Shelley v. Kraemer* to expand political engagement and transform the public sphere.

Strategies of the Stix, Baer and Fuller Department Store Sit-In

In July 1948, only two months after the *Shelley v. Kraemer* decision, the St. Louis sit-ins began as a political protest against the maltreatment of African Americans in St. Louis's public eateries. However, small interracial groups of activists had been planting roots for several years before July 1948 as activists met in living rooms and church basements across the city to strategize the sit-in efforts. Now that the U.S. Supreme Court had ruled against enforcing segregated housing in St. Louis (and therefore across the country), these organizing activists had an opportunity to strike with momentum on their side. In their sights were "three large department stores: Famous-Barr; Scruggs, Vandervoort, Barney; and Stix, Baer & Fuller."[14] Not only were these stores well known in downtown St. Louis, but they were also large, several floors high, and "their window displays attracted shoppers during the day and window shoppers after hours."[15] These highly visible and frequently visited businesses created the perfect opportunity to draw public awareness to segregationist policies. Additionally some citizen activists felt that because Stix's "owners had reputations as humanitarian civic leaders,"[16] protesters could use these sentiments to their advantage.

The group that garnered the most participation among citizen activists was the Congress of Racial Equality (CORE). While CORE's numbers fluctuated between only ten and a few dozen members throughout the 1948–54 Stix sit-in,[17] CORE found its strength as a leading activist group in its eclectic membership of everyday citizens, including teachers, students, custodians, mechanics, seamstresses, factory workers, and stay-at-home moms. Whereas the NAACP and other civil rights groups used lawyers to negotiate legal policy with city leaders behind closed doors, CORE's demonstrations took place in the open and allowed average citizens to debate public policy in the public sphere openly. Paralleling Habermas's idealized public sphere, publications from CORE stated that "legal action is necessarily limited to lawyers. CORE's techniques enable large numbers of ordinary people to participate in campaigns to end discrimination."[18] By formulating consensus with everyday citizen activists, CORE obtained a level of public support and public participation that was out of reach for more legalistic groups.

Strategies of Interracial Solidarity and Stressed Similarities

One of the early members of CORE was a local African American schoolteacher named Marian O'Fallon Oldham.[19] Like many of her colleagues, Oldham held no official political title but yearned to be involved in shaping public policy. Of her commitment to CORE's mission, Oldham states, "We were very dedicated and very sincere and very non-violent. We studied Gandhi. We knew the techniques that he had used. And we were committed to what we were doing."[20] Another member who held no official title was a white college student named Judith Stix (no relation to the department store). Like Oldham, Stix was dedicated to Gandhi's philosophy of nonviolence, and she later wrote that CORE's objective was "to avoid friction and to win hearts."[21] The ideological goals of nonviolence and persuasion were paramount in CORE's early years (the 1940s) and remained a central concern of CORE's when it later articulated its mission to a national audience in formal newsletters. For instance a 1963 publication, "All About CORE," reads: "CORE seeks understanding, not physical victory. It seeks to win the friendship, respect, and even support of those whose racial policies it opposes. People cannot be bludgeoned into a feeling of equality. Integration, if it is not to be tense and artificial, must, in CORE's view, be more than an armed truce. Real racial equality can be attained only through cooperation; not the grudging cooperation one exacts from a beaten opponent, but the voluntary interaction of two parties working toward a solution of a mutual problem."[22]

In addition to nonviolence and persuasion, CORE upheld a strong ethos of interracial solidarity. For many, winning the hearts of segregationists through interracial solidarity and nonviolence was an overwhelming and sometimes dangerous task. The difficulty of this task was not lost on CORE's members, and they held very thorough strategy sessions that provided detailed explanations of what the community expected of its members. While celebrated acts of interracial solidarity may seem commonplace in the collective narratives of the civil rights movement, solidarity with whites was not a preferred strategy among all black freedom organizations. More specifically 1948 rested in the shadow of Marcus Garvey's Pan-Africanism movement and also witnessed the rise of the Nation of Islam, which advocated black separatism. In contrast CORE had deep interracial ties among members; as Oldham noted at the time, "My husband is white. He was with a law firm that gave him an ultimatum. Either you stay with the law firm and you stop the CORE activities. . . . And he chose to stay with the group and leave the law firm. . . . and we always went in interracial groups."[23] Stressing this type of interracial solidarity in 1948 was highly political and caused disdain among some white and black people. Not only was interracial solidarity a political position within CORE's membership, but interracial solidarity was also used as a sit-in strategy. In fact one of the earliest, and most widely reported, lunch counter conflicts happened because of interracial unity. In May 1949 Billie Ames, a white woman, tried to eat at the Stix lunch counter with her friend Connie Williams, a black woman. The server welcomed Ames to receive service on her own, but Ames was insistent on ordering and eating lunch with Williams. Ultimately management refused service to both Ames and Williams, citing policies against interracial amalgamation.[24]

Beyond interracial solidarity, CORE was also concerned with being viewed as a respectable organization and demanded that "men should wear shirts and ties [and c]orrect posture should be remembered."[25] While clothing seems trivial given the larger issues of 1948, it provides significant insight about the ideological position of the group. In short it helped CORE demonstrate to the public that sharply dressed African Americans were just as civil as their white counterparts. Through shared attire, black and white members of CORE underscored their solidarity as well as demonstrated that the difference between the races was not based on social behaviors as many segregationists assumed. Instead the difference between races was superficial skin color.

To amplify the similarities between the races, "the smartly dressed demonstrators often sat quietly the length of the day, occupying the silences with knitting, academic studies, or the Bible."[26] By studying the Bible, protesters communicated shared values across racial differences as well as demonstrated that people are all "children of God" and, therefore, are each entitled to the same basic rights. While this type of ideological doctrine was not unique to CORE, the Bible's physical usefulness was unique on one important occasion. As recalled by CORE member Walter Hayes, "one of our tactics was to occupy seats so that no one else could sit there to eat and spend money."[27] However, the weekly sit-ins averaged only twenty to thirty participants, which was relatively small compared to a cafeteria that sat ninety-seven people.[28] Therefore a small group of people had a difficult time making an economic, or even a visual, impact by demonstrating only once a week in "a huge place with many, many seats."[29] Furthermore, unlike the violent conflicts of the South, which included police beatings and pouring hot coffee onto protesters' heads, white segregationists of St. Louis simply ignored the protesters or engaged them in polite conversations that took a "that's just the way it is" position on lunch counter segregation. By not creating an economic or emotional stir among the management, the customers, or the police, the CORE protesters had little chance of changing the policy. In short the protest had to make the status quo economically and emotionally uncomfortable enough to make a change toward integration.

This would be the case when one unplanned accident changed the economic and visual impact of the sit-in situation and forced the segregationist customers and staff to react. As Hayes told the story: "One day a CORE member got up from his seat for a few minutes and left his Bible, which I was reading, open on the counter. When customers came in to eat, amazingly, none of them would sit within five or six seats of that open Bible. The next day, we all brought Bibles and spread them throughout the cafeteria. With only a few people and several Bibles we almost shut the place down."[30]

Apparently the ideological power of the Bible was understood by the integrationists, the segregationists, and the indifferent patrons. By highlighting this power, CORE members were able to take advantage of the common ground shared across differing political policy: belief in a powerful God. Furthermore Hayes's testimony suggests that the segregationists, as well as indifferent whites, avoided the Bibles in the cafeteria because of the Bible's inherent power to create emotional appeals and change behavior. Presumably Hayes's context implies that these groups avoided the Bibles out of guilt, shame, or fear of God's judgment. If this is the case, then perhaps the segregationists felt guilty in the eyes of God for denying African Americans' humanity, and the indifferent whites felt guilty for not speaking against an injustice. Whatever the reason, the presence of Bibles successfully worked as a rhetorical strategy because the Bible made the segregationists and indifferent whites uncomfortable enough to change behaviors.

Beyond the formal clothing and Bibles, protesters also relied on persistence and consistency. As some protesters recalled, members of CORE stuck to a strict schedule and would sit-in at Stix every Saturday with signs stating, "I am waiting for service."[31] Some even wore signs around their necks that read "We have been waiting for service ___ hours and ___ minutes" and updated the blanks throughout the day.[32] These types of grandiose displays created many opportunities for conversations and debates with management and customers. One of CORE's more common talking points was that Stix allowed blacks to shop in the department store section but not to eat in the cafeteria. This partial segregation may have been rooted in Stix's misconceptions about whether or not white customers felt comfortable eating next to black customers. Essentially shopping required little contact or social interaction with other customers. However eating at a lunch counter was more intimate and required close contact with other patrons. In the South these assumptions may have been correct, and integration may have driven away southern whites who felt that eating with African Americans was an unsanitary and deplorable act. Yet CORE found it laughable that northern whites would be driven away by integration, because northern whites already routinely interacted with African Americans on a daily basis. Furthermore Stix's white customers continued to eat next to and converse civilly with black protesters throughout the sit-in.[33] Therefore protesters simply highlighted how racially accepting St. Louis already was by pointing to the examples of widespread interracial interaction. In the end CORE was confident that there was only the matter of time before private businesses would cave to the public's acceptance of integration.

Strategies of Leadership and Evolving Tactics

However time moved slowly with regard to race in the late 1940s, and after eighteen months of protests and negotiations with management, the Stix, Baer and Fuller department store sit-in had not yielded any results. Finally in December 1949 CORE's efforts collapsed. To hear some historians tell it, the protesters left as part of a bargaining strategy to give Stix "an opportunity to voluntarily open the lunch counter while saving face."[34] The facts seem to indicate that abandoning the sit-in was an admission of defeat as opposed to some clever strategy. As CORE member Billie Ames remembered the solemn exit in December 1949,

"We then swallowed our pride, retreated and went to work on lesser stores."[35] This account seems like a far more plausible scenario given the fact that without the visual presence of the protesters, Stix would have no incentive to change its policy. If Stix was not going to integrate when African Americans were at the lunch counter, why would they have a change of heart in their absence? While retreating from Stix in December of 1949 was not a direct strategy to coax Stix into changing its policies, Ames's mention of going to work on "lesser stores" brings to mind managements' earlier statement to Pearl Maddox in 1944 "that if other stores opened their lunch counters to blacks, Stix would follow suit." Stix did not have to be the first lunch counter to integrate. Rather the store had to continue to feel public pressure regarding integration. If Stix was not feeling that pressure from protesters within its store, then perhaps it would feel pressure from the outside once other lunch counters began to integrate.

CORE's movement from one location to another did not signify surrender. Instead the group spent the next two years (1950–51) adapting to the community's racial climate and figuring out how to stay visible as a counterpublic. By and large adaptation is essential for counterpublics to survive political resistance within the public sphere because the public sphere is not a static concept.[36] Instead the public sphere is malleable, shifting, and dynamic. Additionally when the public sphere ignores the counterpublic narrative, the counterpublic must change its strategy to gain entrance into the public sphere. If a counterpublic fails to shift with the public sphere, then it risks becoming irrelevant. However once a counterpublic has a footing on the public stage, the dynamic aspects of the public sphere shift, and the counterpublic narrative becomes integrated into the public sphere.

Leaving Stix in December 1949 highlighted the evolving and complicated transformation process of a counterpublic trying to stay relevant in the public sphere as the public sphere shifted and evolved. In short Stix had been hearing CORE's arguments for eighteen months and was unmoved. CORE's protest had become stagnant in late 1949, and Stix was no longer shocked by CORE's campaign or its message. In some ways Stix had become comfortable with CORE's predictable tactics and simply operated business accordingly, hoping that the protesters would soon grow tired. CORE had to discover new ways to convey its message or risk becoming an obsolete counterpublic. In 1950–51 CORE took the time to change its strategy and worked to integrate Stix from the outside.

Abandoning Stix, CORE immediately went to work on desegregating lunch counters at F. W. Woolworth, Sears Roebuck, and the Greyhound bus terminal in early 1950. These locations were invaluable for small-scale operations because their cafeterias were relatively smaller in size and CORE "had a very small group of people . . . all in all about 25–30 people."[37] Therefore integration seemed far more achievable because CORE's presence was more noticeable and had a far greater effect on the economic operations. Additionally CORE's movement from the Stix lunch counter to other lunch counters helps to theorize the public sphere as both layered and hierarchical. Much like other areas of culture, an intrinsic hierarchy exists within the public sphere. To wield influence at the top levels of that hierarchy, CORE recognized that its strategies would first have to prove the ability to influence policy changes in smaller, less powerful arenas. When activists left Stix, they were not leaving the public sphere but rather relocating their efforts to areas within the public sphere where they felt they could leverage more power and, perhaps, generate more sensational responses. CORE did this because they essentially had two problems. One problem was that Stix was too economically powerful for CORE to cause hardship. Second Stix's nonchalant, nonbrutal response did not play into the hands of the media as so many southern sit-ins did. Therefore CORE was beckoned to protest in public areas that held less economic power and where the group could also work on its tactics of generating media publicity.

Focusing on smaller eateries also enabled CORE to have more conversations with more citizens throughout the city. Instead of just speaking with folks at Stix, CORE spoke with folks at several St. Louis eating establishments. This moment of decentralized activism marks an essential moment in understanding the Stix sit-in as an emerging counterpublic. Since the City of St. Louis already integrated state buildings in 1944, the integrationists and the segregationists were at odds not with the state but with two competing public visions. Some St. Louis citizens wanted private businesses to remain segregated, while some citizens wanted them integrated.

This type of paradox creates a problem for the public sphere. Obviously the state cannot satisfy conflicting public visions. If the state is willing to enforce new statutes based on the will of the people, then whose vision gets priority when there are conflicting visions? Unfortunately Habermas's public sphere is limiting in that it theorizes how a united public voice rises against an oppressive state policy. Furthermore it assumes that the public sphere is inclusive and that through this inclusivity shared public concerns arise. Therefore conflicting public concerns makes it difficult to reach an egalitarian consensus. Additionally the inclusivity of the public sphere is called into question when some citizens are not allowed into public spaces where political decisions are being made.

Critiquing Habermas, Nancy Fraser raises these concerns by claiming that the public sphere is more hegemonic than egalitarian.[38] In contrast to the public sphere, Fraser offers counterpublics as a way to theorize how decentralized voices work to persuade other citizens through various avenues of public engagement and recognize the "multiplicity of dialectically related public spheres rather than a single, encompassing arena of discourse."[39] In short counterpublics create a framework where more voices are given an opportunity to speak because a public consensus does not need to be reached before challenging the status quo. Counterpublics also attack policy on both a legal and social front. Whereas Habermas's public sphere primarily focuses on citizens challenging the legality of the state, counterpublics create a framework where citizens challenge the social values and beliefs of other citizens: for example, persuading private citizens and businesses that segregation is morally reprehensible. The extension of counterpublics produces a space for historically silenced voices and helps fill a void within the public sphere by highlighting the multiplicity of opinions and by noting that sometimes public visions civically compete with one another.[40]

Given the absence of CORE's ability to achieve full political engagement because its vision of integration conflicted with the status quo, the group decentralized its efforts and its leadership in 1950. Decentralizing its efforts allowed CORE to canvass more areas and engage in several small political dialogues instead of one large dialogue, which was proving to be ineffective. This new strategy played out as follows: the more lunch counters CORE confronted, the more likely the group would be able to achieve small victories throughout the city. While small integration victories could not bring the type of media attention that a Stix, Baer and Fuller department store victory could bring, CORE members held fast to the idea that organizing from the bottom up would soon harvest rewards. Another reason why confronting smaller-scale lunch counters was desirable was because CORE "[had] had a terrific slump in the number of people attending meetings."[41] Understandably the six-year campaign wore on people, and some members left when efforts seemed futile. To keep the members engaged after the Stix campaign first failed in 1949, CORE drafted a policy that "held frequent officer elections in order to give everyone the opportunity to serve as a leader and learn about leadership."[42] Notably some scholars have interpreted this policy in more egalitarian terms as a way to demonstrate "the group's community orientation and its commitment to developing organizational and leadership skills."[43] However frequent elections were also a strategic move, as CORE looked for a way to maintain their dwindling membership. According to Billie Ames: "Often a person willing to work along with CORE is hesitant about taking on responsibility—particularly such responsibility as being chairman or secretary. In St. Louis we have adopted the plan of electing officers every three months. We find people will take on responsibility for a short period and also find this a good way of getting participation from a number of people."[44]

With stabilizing numbers, veteran leadership, and growing experience with smaller stores, CORE reignited its negotiations with Stix in November 1951.[45] Beyond the usual weekly sit-in strategy of taking up lunch counter space and speaking with management, CORE also ramped up its efforts of reaching out to white patrons by passing out leaflets. In their unique way, the leaflets added to the growing layers of rhetorical tactics aimed at affirming the common beliefs held among the integrationists, the segregationists, and the indifferent citizens. Exemplifying these beliefs was the propensity of CORE's leaflets to carry overtly patriotic messages. Similar to Fredrick Douglass's 1852 speech "What to the Slave Is the Fourth of July?,"[46] CORE's leaflets spelled out the beauty of America's founding documents while simultaneously asking why the United States would not live up to her ideals of equality. For example, two of the leaflets read, "[America] The Grand Leader—in Everything but Democracy" and "Does the Declaration of Independence Read Like This? 'We hold these truths to be self-evident, all men, *except Negroes,* are created equal.'"[47] Drawing attention to America's principles, as well as the Bible, was a useful strategy in making segregationists and indifferent white citizens confront the paradox of supporting a separatist system that essentially mocked two of their most sacred idols: America's founding fathers and the word of God.

As the reignited movement gathered steam, CORE began to witness some long-awaited results when smaller eateries around St. Louis began to integrate in 1951 and 1952. Not wanting to lose any momentum with Stix, CORE "had a wallet sized card printed with the names of the restaurants, where blacks could eat, and that was a real achievement."[48] By publicizing their victories and handing out these wallet-sized cards, the group not only highlighted its achievements but publicly placed additional scrutiny on Stix's management finally to give in to CORE's request. This was the inevitable moment when Stix would have to succumb to the social, political, and economic pressures that surrounded St. Louis's business community. CORE attempted to speed up this process by introducing the "Plan for Establishing Equal Restaurant Service in St. Louis Department Stores" in 1952.[49] This agreement was not a legal document but was envisioned as a voluntary pledge among businesses in the St. Louis area. The notion was that if CORE could persuade enough influential business owners to sign a pledge for integration, then a line would have been drawn and all businesses would have had to choose sides in the integration debate. Even though the plan failed to materialize on paper (likely because even integrated businesses did not want to appear political and risk losing clientele), the "Equal Restaurant Service" plan did spark an internal dialogue among business owners about the fate of the St. Louis business community. After engaging in these discussions for two years, Stix, Baer and Fuller finally acknowledged the direction that St. Louis's business community was heading and sheepishly integrated its lunch counters in 1954 "without a word to CORE and with no public notice."[50]

Strategies Learned and Broader Implications

After Stix integrated its lunch counter, integrationists would have to wait seven more years before the city government finally passed a bill in 1961 that prohibited segregation in all St. Louis businesses. Although the vast majority of businesses were already integrated at this point, having its stance legally recognized was a big accomplishment for CORE and its members. In working toward the prohibition of segregation, CORE simultaneously was obliged to become more aggressive in city politics. During this time the group more fully transitioned from a marginalized counterpublic into the public sphere, where it was afforded more political voice and recognition from social leaders and policy makers.

As Oldham recalled CORE's ramped-up political action, she said, "We worked very hard to get the aldermen to vote to change the Public Accommodations Laws. We were not successful until we began getting black aldermen elected."[51] Oldham's statement indicates that the seven years of perseverance following Stix's integration held both immediate and long-term impacts. The immediate impact was obviously CORE's success at integrating Stix's lunch counter. Regarding the long-term impact, CORE utilized its strength of mobilizing members to develop a lasting political strategy for organizing campaigns and electing African American candidates who identified with the group's position on civil rights. These city-wide elections impacted more than just the lunch counters of the 1950s and placed CORE's influence in the St. Louis city council for the barrage of civil rights issues to come throughout the 1960s and 1970s. By maintaining the momentum of the movement after its initial lunch counter campaign, CORE injected itself into the heart of city politics and created a platform that allowed its voice to become more influential within St. Louis's public sphere.

The rise of CORE to the top echelons of St. Louis politics illustrated the power a counterpublic movement can have in the public sphere when a sufficient amount of economic and social capital is acquired. In the beginning CORE "chose places that were inexpensive . . . so alienating your customer would be a problem to the management . . . places that poor people could afford, not the upstairs tearoom but the downstairs lunch counter."[52] Understanding the need to tie economic influence to political agenda directly reflects Habermas's notions about the public sphere: people who hold private capital can impact policy because they can choose where to invest their resources.[53] Of course less capital elicits less impact, and more capital elicits more impact. At first CORE was limited to places that were inexpensive because the group had few members and virtually no economic influence and was not a part of the political class. Therefore the strategy to protest in places that poor people could afford made sense. If a few CORE protesters could successfully persuade a modest amount of white customers not to spend money at less expensive locations, then CORE would have a sizable economic impact on those businesses, as opposed to protesting expensive eateries that could have absorbed the lost income or used wealthy connections to remove the protesters.

In the 1940s and early 1950s, CORE's capital enabled them to boycott a limited number of small businesses. However as the group began to tangle with the political and economical elites in the late 1950s and early 1960s, it widened its influence on the plutocratic class and fought discrimination among wealthier establishments. Over time CORE was able to wage larger political campaigns, because its economic and social capital could influence more public policy and, therefore, commanded more attention in the public sphere. CORE may have started as a penniless counterpublic campaign in the 1940s, but the compounding effects of growing economic and social capital among African Americans has been felt well into the twenty-first century. The model that CORE helped to develop relied heavily on its ability to disrupt the economic goals of businesses. In the aftermath of the sit-ins, various civil rights organizations have successfully used this economically driven model to lead boycotts against Budweiser in the 1980s,[54] Coca-Cola in the 1990s–2000s,[55] the state of Florida in 2013,[56] and and television personality and restaurateur Paula Deen that same year.[57] Reportedly Deen "lost as much as $12.5 million" after she admitted to using the word "nigger."[58] Boycotting a successful white woman out of $12.5 million would have been impossible in the 1950s, because African Americans had neither money nor influence. African Americans had that kind of capital in 2013, and thus there is good reason to believe Habermas's premise about private capital having a direct link to democratic engagements.

In addition to learning about the relationship between economics and political influence, these long-suffering public policy campaigns were also drawn-out lessons in patience and persistence. Many of CORE's members were initially naive with respect to the idea that the Stix sit-in "would take six years to complete."[59] In hindsight this youthful naïveté probably aided CORE's early recruitment and excitement for the cause in 1948. Some members, had they foreseen a six-year campaign, would have likely dropped out early for lack of expedient results. As the years dragged on between 1948 and 1954, some CORE members became determined to the point of stubbornness. Ames recalled the tough days of the protest: "There have been many times when fewer than ten people carried the load of work of our group."[60] Relying on the convictions of such passionate members allowed CORE to carry on its agenda during moments of desperate doubt and dwindling numbers. These lengthy droughts that yielded no progress also allowed the group to tighten its organization and increased its maturity. Members began to understand "that it is better to test for several months or even a year and end up with a complete change in policy than it is to have 18 months of demonstrations . . . and end up in complete defeat."[61] Consequently the implicit knowledge CORE communicated was that political action required a solid foundation of supporters who were able to adjust to the changing circumstances within the public sphere and who could weather the storms of uncertainty and waning faith.

One example of commitment is seen in the work of Marion O'Fallon Oldham. Oldham's life became a testament to the amount of patience, passion, and development that must be present within a counterpublic political campaign to foster tangible results. Oldham may have joined the group as a schoolteacher with no political connections, but for fifteen years CORE "became [her] life": "I was very active in hundreds and hundreds and hundreds of demonstrations; hundreds and hundreds and hundreds of sit-ins; hundreds and hundreds of what we call 'tests,' where we would go in and see if we would be served. Made a lot of speeches to a lot of groups; went to a meeting every Tuesday night. St. Louis CORE met every Tuesday night, and I don't think I missed a dozen Tuesday nights in all those years."[62] When weighing all of the rhetorical strategies used by CORE during the Stix sit-in, perhaps one of the most important strategies revealed by Oldman's statement is consistency. The Stix sit-in was a rocky endeavor: membership numbers were up and down, CORE dismantled its direct efforts against Stix at least once in December 1949, and the group failed to create a negative economic impact on the store for six years. However CORE was willing to change its methods of protest when needed, and the creative ways it communicated its message were always evolving. For instance members experimented with public demonstrations, sit-ins, handing out leaflets, writing newsletters, and giving speeches. These methods of communication ebbed and flowed based on whether the messages were reaching an audience and whether that audience was being persuaded. The one aspect of the group's mission that did not change was its consistent ideological message that segregation was wrong and that integration was right. This consistent message was what kept CORE relevant, visible, and audible in political debates and eventually led to public policy changes as well as carved out a permanent space for African American voices within the public sphere.

Strategic Summary

The Stix sit-in spoke volumes about equal access to citizenship, democratic inclusion, political voice, and the strategies that are sometimes needed to enter the public sphere. CORE members strategically found their opening into the public sphere by using the momentum of the 1948 *Shelley v. Kraemer* decision regarding housing discrimination. While some St. Louis residents were content with the racist status quo, integrationists understood that it was imperative for African Americans to have their political opinions heard in the public sphere through civic engagement if they were ever going to be afforded any of the privileges that came with full citizenship. The *Shelley* case indicated that St. Louis was ready for these types of discussions about racial equality, and activists latched onto the emerging counterpublic that challenged racism by organizing a sit-in campaign to bring attention to lunch counter discrimination.

In leading these challenges, CORE used several key rhetorical strategies to desegregate Stix, Baer and Fuller's lunch counter. First the group insisted that its efforts be rooted in nonviolence and interracial solidarity. Forming a nonviolent interracial alliance conflicted with the ideologies of some white racists as well as some black separatists who used violence as a means of communicating their political objectives. However CORE had the foresight to realize that interracial solidarity was the only way America could move forward. Thus working across racial differences helped heal the wounds of racism and strengthened America's unity. Second CORE worked to highlight the ideological similarities African Americans shared with segregationists and indifferent white citizens through its open use of the Bible during the sit-in as well as its reliance on America's founding principles when creating leaflets. Finally the group had to make its protest as visible to the public as possible. This required a strategy that took into consideration the size and scope of the protest and accounted for shifting conversations within the public sphere. When the first Stix sit-in disbanded in December 1949, CORE did not deviate from its ideological beliefs of nonviolence, interracial solidarity, and integration. Instead members looked for lunch counters that would feel the economic impact of a sit-in. By recognizing the importance that economics played in a successful protest, CORE created a framework that illustrated how African Americans could use the economic and social capital to inject themselves into the public sphere to vocalize political beliefs and impact public policy.

Conclusion

In 1997 Robert Archibald, the former president of the Missouri History Museum, remembered St. Louis of the civil rights era "and its downtown, despite historical inequities and failures, [as] places where we intermingled. . . . It was a place that could make us realize that to get along we must be civil and observe common standards of behavior and that we must accept a shared responsibility for the health and welfare of the civic enterprise."[63]

These remarks help to capture the wide-ranging significance and spirit of the Stix, Baer and Fuller sit-in as well as the larger St. Louis community. The 1948 *Shelly* decision revealed St. Louis as a community ready for debates regarding equal treatment, economic autonomy, and the thwarting of the plague of racial segregation. Over the next six years, blacks and whites fought over the question of lunch counter segregation; in working toward these objectives, CORE's tactics were nonviolent, and activists were confronted with nonviolence. In all it can be argued that St. Louis in the late 1940s and early 1950s was ready for integration because both integrationists and segregationists were willing to engage each other civicly through a nonviolent democratic process. The willingness of St. Louis citizens to engage in public debates about segregation is what made it possible for the St. Louis lunch counters to be integrated in 1954 without violence. This was a full six years before the violent start of the famous Greensboro, North Carolina, F. W. Woolworth sit-in in 1960.

While the St. Louis activists were not met with violence, civic engagement in the public sphere still proved to be a hard-fought struggle. CORE's six years of sit-ins and marches on behalf of democratic inclusion highlighted the enormous amount of sacrifice required to disband the racist status quo and welcome a world that embraced open policy debate, dissenting voices, and an integrated public sphere. Through it all CORE stayed faithful to its foundational belief that integration was a righteous cause. Notably the group's political tactics were not always fruitful, and therefore sometimes CORE changed its strategy to convince segregationists that public discrimination was a great societal ill. By constantly working to communicate the American principles of equality and liberty, CORE amplified the similarities between the civil rights activists and the staunch segregationists and made it difficult for the segregationists to defend their racist position. Reflecting on the efforts of the nationwide sit-in movement, James M. Lawson Jr., former member of the Student Nonviolent Coordinating Committee (SNCC), wrote in 1960 that "the major defeats have occurred when we have been unable to convince the nation to support or implement the Constitution. . . . A democratic structure or law remains democratic, remains lawful only as the people are continuously persuaded to be democratic."[64] Civil rights activists knew that they were on the right side of history.

The Stix, Baer and Fuller sit-in illustrated how marginalized people organized as a counterpublic against prevailing practices of the day to participate in a democratic society. As Lawson notes, the sit-in "symbolizes both judgment and promise. It is a judgment upon middle-class conventional, half-way efforts to deal with radical social evil. It is specifically a judgment upon contemporary civil rights attempts. As one high school student from Chattanooga exclaimed, 'We started because we were tired of waiting for you to act.'"[65]

This statement describes the frustration that catalyzed some freedom fighters into political action. With relatively few members and little experience, CORE used the energy of the *Shelley* decision to grow into a decades-long movement that changed the racial policies of St. Louis. As the movement grew over the years, members gained leadership experience, learned new protesting tactics, increased their economic and social influence, and found their political voices in a sea of naysayers who did not believe that a group of average citizens could make a difference. However during six years of public demonstrations, interviews, news reports, leaflets, and sit-ins at the Stix, Baer and Fuller Department Store, CORE forced the public to engage in a political debate about race, citizenship, and Americans' ability to live together across differences. Through the efforts of these citizen activists, this emerging counterpublic successfully ended lunch counter segregation and finally found its voice in the public sphere.

Notes

1. Du Bois, *Souls of Black Folk.*
2. Lang, "Black Power on the Ground," 69.
3. Ibid.
4. Wright, *Discovering African American St. Louis*, 14.
5. Ibid.
6. Corbett, *In Her Place*, 228.
7. Ibid., 264.
8. Wright, *Discovering African American St. Louis*, 14.
9. Habermas, *Structural Transformation of the Public Sphere*, 27–28.
10. On the expansion of the public sphere, see, e.g., Calhoun, *Habermas and the Public Sphere*; Warner, *Publics and Counterpublics*; and the Black Public Sphere Collective, *Black Public Sphere.*
11. Fraser, "Rethinking the Public Sphere," 59.
12. Loehwing and Motter, "Publics, Counterpublics, and the Promise of Democracy."
13. Dowden-White, *Groping toward Democracy*, 7.
14. Kimbrough and Dagen, *Victory without Violence*, 42.
15. Ibid.
16. Meier and Rudwick, *CORE*, 54.
17. Ibid., 55.
18. "All About CORE," 83.
19. Jolly, *Black Liberation in the Midwest*, 21.
20. Oldham, "Marion O'Fallon Recalls the CORE Lunch Counter Protests."
21. Stix, interview by Missouri Historical Society.
22. "All About Core," 83.
23. Oldham, "Marion O'Fallon Recalls the CORE Lunch Counter Protests."
24. Kimbrough and Dagen, *Victory without Violence*, 48.
25. Meier and Rudwick, *CORE*, 55.
26. Lang, *Grassroots at the Gateway*, 82.
27. Kimbrough and Dagen, *Victory without Violence*, 48.
28. Swarthmore College, "St. Louis CORE Campaign for Lunch Counter Desegregation, 1948–52," http://nvdatabase.swarthmore.edu/content/st-louis-core-campaign-lunch -counter-desegregation-1948–52 (accessed 29 November 2013).
29. Kimbrough and Dagen, *Victory without Violence*, 48.
30. Ibid.
31. Jolly, *Black Liberation in the Midwest*, 23.
32. Kimbrough and Dagen, *Victory without Violence*, 47.
33. Ibid., 46.
34. Ibid., 45.
35. Meier and Rudwick, *CORE*, 54.

36. Warner, *Publics and Counterpublics,* 48.

37. Oldham, "Marion O'Fallon Recalls the CORE Lunch Counter Protests."

38. Fraser, "Rethinking the Public Sphere."

39. Asen and Brower, "Introduction," 6.

40. Ibid., 25.

41. Meier and Rudwick, *CORE,* 56.

42. Jolly, *Black Liberation in the Midwest,* 21.

43. Ibid., 22.

44. Qtd. in Meier and Rudwick, *CORE,* 54.

45. Swarthmore College, "St. Louis CORE Campaign for Lunch Counter Desegregation."

46. Douglass, *Great Speeches,* 26–47.

47. Kimbrough and Dagen, *Victory without Violence,* 45.

48. Oldham, "Marion O'Fallon Recalls the CORE Lunch Counter Protests."

49. Kimbrough and Dagen, *Victory without Violence,* 54.

50. Ibid.

51. Oldham, "Marion O'Fallon Recalls the CORE Lunch Counter Protests."

52. Stix, interview by Krishna Murali.

53. Habermas, *Structural Transformation of the Public Sphere,* 28–31.

54. John Kass, "Jackson's Role As King of Beers: Wasssup?," 6 February 2001, https://www.chicagotribune.com/news/ct-xpm-2001-02-06-0102060222-story.html.

55. Ralph Nader, "Coke's Alleged Racism: African American Employees Rally, Call for Boycott," *Common Dreams,* 1 May 2000, https://www.commondreams.org/views/2000/05/01/cokes-alleged-racism-african-american-employees-rally-call-boycott.

56. Valerie Richardson, "Prominent Black Leaders Split on Trayvon Verdict, Calls for Florida Boycott," 21 July 2013, www.washingtontimes.com/news/2013/jul/21/rep-donna-edwards-economic-boycott-florida-over-zi/?page=all.

57. Elizabeth Lazarowitz, "Paula Deen Has Lost as Much as $12.5 Million in Earnings over N-Word Controversy," 28 June 2013, www.nydailynews.com/entertainment/tv-movies/deen-lost-12-5-million-experts-article-1.1385469.

58. Ibid.

59. Meier and Rudwick, *CORE,* 55.

60. Ibid.

61. Ibid., 56.

62. Oldham, "Marion O'Fallon Recalls the CORE Lunch Counter Protests."

63. Archibald, "Life in the City."

64. Lawson, "From a Lunch-Counter Stool," 73.

65. Ibid., 74.

FROM "DEAD WRONG" TO CIVIL RIGHTS HISTORY

The Durham Royal Seven, Martin Luther King's 1960
"Fill Up the Jails" Speech, and the Rhetoric of Visibility

Victoria J. Gallagher, Kenneth S. Zagacki & Jeffrey C. Swift

This essay focuses on an early example of direct action: a sit-in at the Royal Ice Cream Company in Durham, North Carolina, in June 1957, led by Rev. Douglas Moore. Despite the fact that Moore chose an ice cream parlor located in the middle of a black community, and despite his connections to Rev. Dr. Martin Luther King Jr., this initial attempt at a sit-in campaign in North Carolina was thwarted, and Moore and his companions were given scant support by the local black community after their arrest. The actions of the "Royal Seven" functioned rhetorically to make visible public knowledge about the conditions of life in the segregated South and to illustrate the moral challenges facing its citizens. The far-reaching rhetorical consequence of this groundbreaking attempt at direct action may be seen in Reverend King's Durham speech in February 1960, in which King, at Moore's invitation, first endorsed sit-ins and other forms of direct action. The chapter describes and analyzes this initial attempt visibly to provoke new ways of thinking about the nature of democratic citizenship, illuminating the causes and implications of its initial less-than-positive reception and its actual consequence.

On June 23, 1957, nearly three years before the famous sit-in at the F. W. Woolworth store in Greensboro, North Carolina, Rev. Douglas Moore, the pastor of Asbury Temple United Methodist Church in Durham, organized a protest at the Royal Ice Cream Company. Accompanied by six fellow church members, all of African American descent, Moore and his group, who came to be known as the "Royal Seven," entered the ice cream parlor located in a building on the corner of Roxboro and Dowd streets in Durham. They sat down together and ordered ice cream in the section of the establishment posted as "whites only." The owner called the Durham police, who arrested the seven protesters for trespassing. Ultimately an all-white jury found them guilty, and the presiding judge levied fines totaling $433.25. Challenged all the way to the U.S. Supreme Court—which refused to hear the case—the charges were upheld and reaffirmed in subsequent North Carolina State Supreme Court rulings.[1]

While historians and other commentators credit the Woolworth sit-in in Greensboro with helping to launch the civil rights movement, a controversy erupted in 1979 over which North Carolina sit-in had occurred first and the extent to which the earlier sit-in in Durham had impacted the civil rights movement. The controversy ensued after requests were made to the North Carolina Historical Marker Advisory Committee to install a sign commemorating the Greensboro sit-in. Guilford College professor Alexander Stoesen, who submitted the Greensboro marker request and who had heard of the earlier sit-in at the Royal Ice Cream Company, told the *Durham Morning Herald* that "our claim was not the first, but the sit-in in Woolworth's on Feb. 1, 1960, was the beginning of a movement, the beginning of an era."[2] Eventually in 2007 the North Carolina Highway Historical Marker Program created a marker for the Greensboro sit-in as well as for the Royal Ice Cream sit-in, though it still credited the 1960 Greensboro protest with sparking "a national movement." Of the Durham sit-in, the marker website states: "Individual and group protest actions prior to 1960, generally isolated and often without wider impact, took place across the state and region. A protest in 1957 in Durham had wider consequence, as it led to a court case testing the legality of segregated facilities."[3]

The dispute over "wider consequence"—and over which sit-in, by coming first, ignited the larger civil rights movement—overlooks how each event, as well as countless other "minor" acts of protest that have gone largely unnoticed or unrecorded, nonetheless made visible, in important ways, the challenges and struggles of African Americans. It also fails to take note of the trajectory of Reverend Moore's activism and how his protest strategies and tactics contributed to making visible the struggle over civil rights both then and up to the present day. According to Gallagher and Zagacki, many different rhetorical acts, including sit-ins, demonstrations, and paintings and photographs, "worked rhetorically to . . . make visible people, attitudes, and ideas in the context of the struggle over civil rights in America."[4] Such rhetoric can work both "to articulate and to shape public knowledge through offering interpretive and evaluative versions of who does what to whom, when and where."[5] And as Leland Griffin pointed out long ago, the inception of social movements occurs when "the roots of a pre-existing sentiment, nourished by interested rhetoricians, begin to flower into public notice, or when some striking event occurs which immediately creates a host of aggressor rhetoricians and is itself sufficient to initiate a movement."[6] While for some commentators the Greensboro sit-in represents just the sort of "striking event" and moment of "flowering" described by Griffin, it seems clear that many other activities and modes of protest, some of them at first perhaps unacknowledged by individuals who later coalesced into a social movement proper, served their own significant role in "nourishing" sentiment and in creating "aggressor rhetoricians." As Griffin suggested, the precipitating factor is undoubtedly less important than the rhetorical strategies and tactics—what he called "the crystallization of fundamental issues, the successive emergence of argument, appeal, and the sanctions" invoked by oppositional forces[7]—that emerge and the forms of rhetorical consciousness they engender.

This essay, then, eschews questions about historical causality, instead considering the extent to which the Royal Ice Cream Company sit-in, as well as events associated with it, worked to make visible the struggle for civil rights and, in so doing, became part of a larger trajectory. The Royal Seven drew upon and reinterpreted an emerging tradition of protest and dissent, what Griffin once called a "rhetorical trajectory." According to Griffin, a rhetorical trajectory is "something akin to the phenomenon that Burke discusses under the heading of 'qualitative progression.' It is the salience and/or frequency of god and devil terms in a body of discourse suggestive of the qualities, motivations, or state of mind of a speaker or writer, 'a state of mind which another state of mind can appropriately follow.'"[8] Actions, in addition to terms, images, and discourses, may function in a manner similar to what Burke describes, and the Royal Ice Cream Company sit-in and the controversy surrounding it represent pivotal moments in the development of an emerging rhetorical trajectory that helped to mold the larger civil rights movement. More specifically, by protesting as they did, the Royal Seven made visible and concrete the sorts of "qualities, motivations, and state of mind" necessary to challenge the racial status quo. The sit-in did not create new images for display in national newspapers or magazines, particularly since there does not seem to have been any photographs taken of the actual sit-in itself. Rather this sit-in and the events that emerged from it add additional rhetorical significance to images and visual memories already in existence as well as those yet to come. The barriers creating segregated facilities had been breached, so for many people familiar with their (and other such) actions, the next trip to a segregated restaurant or school would be altered by what the Royal Seven did in Durham. In other words they helped to "shape" rhetorically and materially the context in which civil rights were beginning to be understood and enacted by many different audiences in Durham and across the country. They drew upon existing rhetorical measures, some of which had been tested and others that were still in the making. Like earlier advocates for civil rights and those protesting at roughly the same time, the Royal Seven spread the seeds of dissent locally even as they tried to enact things shared by all races so that a larger movement could eventually take hold and a particular kind of human consciousness could be enacted. More recent efforts by surviving members of the Royal Seven and other spokespersons to have the Durham sit-in commemorated are yet further developments in the rhetorical trajectory, the path of which waxes and wanes but continues to play a critical role in how societies and individuals move forward into the future and simultaneously preserve the past.

That Moore and members of his group recognized that they were involved in something much greater seems evident in their accounts of how they approached the sit-in. While they initially denied, after their arrests, that their trip to the ice cream parlor was planned—they claimed only to be interested in eating high-quality ice cream on what they remembered as a very hot day—Moore and other members of the Royal Seven later discussed their strategic selection of the ice cream parlor. Located in a largely African American neighborhood, the parlor was well regarded by the residents. Mary Elizabeth Clyburn Hooks, one of the Royal Seven, spoke highly about the quality of the ice cream served there: "I don't care where you went, the Royal Ice Cream was the best ice cream in town."[9] Moore himself was already aware of what could be described as an emerging rhetorical trajectory with which he hoped he and his group would align. He had previously challenged racial discrimination in Durham by petitioning the Durham City Council to end segregation at a public library and a city-owned theater. After those petitions failed, he moved toward nonviolent direct action, attempting to enter a whites-only swimming pool in Durham.[10] These previous failures helped convince him of the need for coordinated, nonviolent direct action focused on strategic targets—targets that would serve to help make visible, to blacks as well as whites, the problems of segregation. Virginia Williams, another of the Royal Seven, indicated that they chose their target with at least some of these goals in mind: "We could have picked from any establishment. . . . They were all segregated. The reason we chose this one was it was located in the heart of a black community."[11] Moore later spoke of the souring of his initial optimism concerning their chosen target: "I thought, surely we can win on this one. . . . Dead wrong."[12] Hence a rhetorical study of the Royal Ice Cream Company sit-in and its aftermath makes it possible to reconstruct the emerging logic of the rhetorical trajectory within which Moore and his group operated, to understand its tensions and how that trajectory evolved. Rhetorical analysis also demonstrates how the direction of social movements depends to a great extent on the states of mind, rhetorical cultures, actions, modes of consciousness, layered and conflicting strategies and tactics, and public memory used to sustain them even as time and circumstances change.

The essay is organized into four sections: (1) an account (rhetorical history) of the events, circumstances, and discourses surrounding the Royal Seven sit-in;

(2) a discussion of "visibility" as a rhetorical construct or strategy within the logic of social movements related to the concept of rhetorical trajectories; (3) an examination of the Royal Seven sit-in and related rhetorical actions, including Dr. Martin Luther King Jr.'s February 1960 "Fill Up the Jails" speech, through the framework these concepts provide; and (4) a discussion of consequences and implications of this case for rhetorical knowledge and social action.

Emergence of a Rhetorical Trajectory: Direct Action in Durham

When, on June 23, 1957 (just one year and a few short months after the end of the Montgomery, Alabama, bus boycott and the resulting desegregation of its bus system), Reverend Moore was arrested, he was accompanied by six fellow church members, Virginia Williams, Mary Elizabeth Clyburn Hooks, Claude Glenn, Jesse Gray, Vivian Jones, and Melvin Willis, who ranged in age from late teens to early thirties. These young men and women had gathered at Moore's UMC church earlier that day to discuss racial justice and left together to get ice cream. They ordered their ice cream on the whites-only side of the establishment. The server asked them to leave numerous times, and when they refused, the server called the owner, Louis Coletta. Coletta "[later] testified that he asked Moore and the others to leave. He said Moore began talking about the persecution of people throughout the world. Coletta said he told Moore 'that don't concern this place—this place is not owned by the city or the state, this place is private property.' He said Moore still refused to leave."[13] Moore told Coletta he would not leave because "he was a 'Christian and an American' and did not think he should."[14]

At this point Coletta called the police, who arrested the seven. The officer who made the arrest, Lt. W. H. Upchurch, told a local paper how he justified enforcing the owner's wishes about the offending customers: "I asked them to leave, not because they were Negroes—not because they were causing a disturbance—and not because they were disorderly. I asked them to leave because the owner wanted them out and they were trespassing."[15] The court ultimately found that "the owner of private property 'may accept or reject whomsoever he pleases and for whatsoever whim suits his fancies.'"[16]

An all-white jury found the group guilty of trespass, but the "Royal Seven" appealed the ruling. The appellate judge viewed this as a test case and somewhat jokingly threatened to throw it out to thwart Moore's plans:

> "I should throw the mess out of court right here and now," Judge Moore told William Marsh of the Negro defense counsel staff, adding that "if I allowed your motion to nonsuit this case on the ground that it is unconstitutional, then you'd have to start all over again—they'd (the defendants) have to find some other places to go into." Marsh, smiling at Judge Moore's comments,

replied: "On the contrary, your honor, I'd be very happy if you allowed my motion. You seem to infer that this is a 'test case' or something." "That's exactly what it is," Judge Moore replied, "and it's just as plain as the nose on your face."[17]

The case did indeed move on to the state supreme court, where Associate Justice William B. Rodman upheld the lower court's ruling:

> In handing down the court's ruling, Associate Justice William B. Rodman said no constitutional rights had been violated. "The right of an operator of a private enterprise to select the clientele he will serve and to make such selection based on color, if he so desires, has been repeatedly recognized by the appellate courts of this nation." . . . Justice Rodman said the 14th Amendment prohibits discriminatory actions by states but "erects no shield against merely private conduct, however discriminatory or wrongful."[18]

The Royal Seven's legal counsel, led by Floyd McKissick, attempted to take the case to the U.S. Supreme Court, but the nation's highest court declined to hear it, allowing the guilty ruling to stand.[19]

Even though (or perhaps because) this was not Reverend Moore's first attempt to challenge racial discrimination, and despite his thoughtful planning, the local community was not sympathetic. The majority of the local papers buried the story,[20] the Black Ministerial Alliance and the Durham Committee on Negro Affairs both frowned on such direct action,[21] and the resulting scandal was about the group's tactics rather than the dehumanizing and unequal effects of segregation they were attempting to make visible. Indeed the Royal Ice Cream sit-in not only provoked controversy in the white community; it also created consternation among black citizens, many of whom viewed the protesters not as freedom fighters but as troublemakers led astray by a radical young minister and an outsider.[22]

Part of the reason for this opposition was Moore's "end run around the traditional black leadership."[23] He had taken unilateral action rather than enlisting the help of local black clergy, of activist women's organizations such as the East End Betterment Society, or of members of the Union Baptist Church, which was across the street from the Royal Ice Cream Company and "a base of local black activism."[24] Moore's unilateral action was bad enough, but unilateral direct action was apparently too much for many in the community.

Despite his role in the Montgomery bus boycott,[25] this negative sentiment toward nonviolent direct action was shared, for much of the 1950s, by Rev. Martin Luther King Jr., a fellow student with Moore at Boston University. King had formed a discussion group for black students at the university, but it was decidedly not a venue for political discussions or civil rights activism. By comparison

Moore and another fellow student named George Thomas, who were at this point far more political than King, made attempts at direct action while at Boston but were unable to convince many others, including King, to join them. As Taylor Branch points out: "The mainstream Negro students considered activists like Thomas and Moore somewhat 'up in the clouds,' as one of them told King, adding that 'the world is not going to be converted overnight.'"[26] This tension was maintained and even magnified throughout the civil rights struggle, as significant numbers of African Americans opposed agitation, direct action, or violence. And indeed, for much of the 1950s, King himself focused on oratorical agitation—speeches, rallies, and petitions for redress.

Branch summarizes King's efforts to fight segregation in the 1950s as resulting in great fanfare but little substantive change: "This conversion approach had brought King the orator's nectar—applause, admiration, and credit for quite a few tearful if temporary changes of heart—but in everyday life Negroes remained a segregated people, invisible or menial specimens except for celebrity aberrations such as King himself."[27] The Royal Seven were left to fight the court battles, as well as the battle of public opinion, by themselves. The group picked up a few supporters, such as their lawyer, Floyd McKissick, but seemed to have accomplished very little else regarding making visible the injustices of segregation.

McKissick and Moore were surprised when, on February 1, 1960, students in Greensboro started a firestorm by sitting at the "wrong" (whites only) lunch counter. McKissick, Moore, and a few others drove to Greensboro the evening after these sit-ins started, held training sessions, and began developing a strategy to help the sit-ins spread.[28] Moore reached out to King, and on February 16, with the sit-ins dramatically raising visibility and showing potential to have a national impact, King accepted Moore's invitation to put his blessing on the movement.[29] According to Branch, by that point King begrudgingly acknowledged that direct action was the best way to move toward desegregation: "Race was too intractable to be repaired by the inspiration of any orator. Only by slow, wrenching concession could someone like King admit that eloquence was weak even when buttressed by rank and education."[30] King's speech in Durham, held at the White Rock Baptist Church, was titled "A Creative Protest" and came to be known for his groundbreaking endorsement of nonviolent confrontation: "Let us not fear going to jail. If the officials threaten to arrest us for standing up for our rights, we must answer by saying that we are willing and prepared to fill up the jails of the South. Maybe it will take this willingness to stay in jail to arouse the dozing conscience of our nation."[31] The jails were soon filled with protesters devoted to nonviolent direct action, and the rhetorical strategy of evoking common humanity through showing in addition to telling helped move the country toward significant change.

The tale of the Royal Seven does not end there, however. In the excitement and activist spirit of the early 1960s, a large boycott in Durham focused on some segregated establishments, including the Royal Ice Cream parlor. The parlor was eventually desegregated, but more by default than on principle: "Not until spring of 1963 was discrimination abolished at Royal Ice Cream: Louis Coletta simply sold the establishment to a local dairy company, which reopened it without any seating at all."[32] More recently the parlor was torn down to make room for a church parking lot. Efforts began in the early 2000s to commemorate the protest, but early proposals were rejected due to an inability to demonstrate its significance. Eventually, on the third try, the historical marker was approved and was dedicated in 2008.[33]

It is easy to suggest that the Royal Ice Cream parlor sit-in was a failure, rhetorically and politically, given the lack of community support, the relative lack of historical significance and recognition given to the event, and its failure to advance the legal case for desegregation. In fact there is some evidence to suggest that the Durham sit-in and resulting court case served to solidify the "private property" approach that would allow the white establishment legally to justify the arrest and jailing of anyone who participated in "sit-downs" in privately owned establishments.[34] However Eddie Davis, a key advocate for getting the 1957 sit-ins recognized with a national historical marker in Durham, believed differently: "Some people think that even though they were unsuccessful and . . . were found guilty along the way and did not have the guilty verdict overturned at any stage, it still raised the national consciousness within civil rights organizations. . . . So I think people recognize that even though they were unsuccessful, it still indeed helped to dismantle segregation."[35] North Carolina state senator Floyd McKissick Jr., the son of Moore's Durham compatriot, agreed, calling the Royal Ice Cream sit-ins the "seed that helped fertilize all the activity in the Piedmont of North Carolina."[36]

Visibility and Rhetorical Trajectories

Rhetorical scholarship on the civil rights movement of the 1950s and 1960s initially focused, as did many of the movement's leaders, on public, political discourse(s), namely, the public speeches and sermons, the key legal cases and legislation (e.g., the Voting Rights Act), and the writings and letters of the movement's prominent spokespersons. However in recent decades the focus of such scholarship has shifted to a consideration of the visual and material cultural artifacts, images, and events of the movement and its commemoration/commemorative practices. These artifacts, images, and events played an equally important role in crystallizing the movement's fundamental issues, arguments, appeals, and sanctions and in constituting the movement's rhetorical trajectory.

This shift is consistent with two related trends. First there has been an expanded understanding of the scope of rhetoric, which has entailed a move from understanding and theorizing rhetoric as largely public, political, symbolic, and concerned with effect to an understanding and theorizing of rhetoric as materially enacted and/or instantiated and concerned with consequences.[37] Second, as political scientist Richard Merelman notes, there has been a shift in how power struggles within the United States are enacted, particularly struggles involving dominant white and subordinate nonwhite racial groups. Merelman argues that these struggles are increasingly taking on a "*cultural* dimension, as opposed to traditional forms of economic struggle (over, say, the distribution of income) or political struggle (over, say, the distribution of elected representatives)."[38] Scholarship that takes these trends into account when examining aspects of the 1950s–60s civil rights movement is providing an expanded sense of how and why the movement developed as it did, why some things were particularly successful at the time but less so in hindsight, and also the reverse, as is the case with the Royal Seven's sit-in. This scholarship also opens up a way of seeing and understanding continued racial tensions and conflicts in our own time. One of the important concepts emerging from this scholarly work is rhetorical visibility, or the way in which rhetoric, as it is delimited and enabled by material circumstances and history, functions to make things visible. Artifacts, images, and events do this by bringing before the eyes, as it were, the material conditions under which different people, people who are nonetheless fellow citizens, live within and experience democracy in the United States differently from one another.

Indeed in the essay "Visibility and Rhetoric: Epiphanies and Transformations in the *Life* Photographs of the Selma Marches of 1965," Gallagher and Zagacki note that, in the late 1950s and early 1960s, the time period of the Royal Seven and Greensboro sit-ins, "if the idea of democracy was taken for granted by whites for whom democratic participation remained largely unproblematic, the situation was vastly different for blacks. Many whites had come to understand democracy as a non-controversial concept at work."[39] However visual images of violence enacted by whites against unarmed blacks simply walking into school, marching together (often accompanied by other whites), or sitting at lunch counters "reminded viewers that a large gap existed between abstract political concepts like democracy and what was occurring in American streets and places of business."[40] Images such as these became part of the prevailing rhetorical trajectory and therefore challenged the aforementioned taken-for-granted assumptions by showing that concepts such as democracy were "always relative to the individual or groups whose lives were most directly influenced by their presence or absence."[41] Gallagher and Zagacki posit three significant aspects of the rhetoric of visibility illustrated in these types of visual images:

disregarding or replacing established caricatures (cultural projection), creating recognition through particularity, and making abstract concepts knowable.[42]

While not documented through photographic images or artistic artifacts, it is useful to consider the extent to which the events and discourses related to the Royal Seven and their nonviolent activism may have had a similar rhetorical function regarding visibility. Upon first glance it might seem that this particular sit-in did not do much to accomplish or raise visibility. As indicated earlier the Royal Seven won little support and ultimately lost every court case and appeal. The issue may be reframed, however, as follows: did the actions of Reverend Moore and his fellow congregants demonstrate how not to achieve civil rights victories, or did their actions raise visibility for rhetorical strategies of enactment and embodiment that were eventually essential to achieving civil rights and that thereby constituted a type of victory in its own right?

Disregarding or Replacing Established Caricatures

The *Life* photographs discussed by Gallagher and Zagacki were published at a time during which white or dominant culture actively caricatured black Americans. The photographs reframed those caricatures in such a way that they made visible the common humanity of Americans "by interrogating established caricatures and overturning inferior, threatening, or otherwise demeaning character tropes."[43] A white person who viewed the *Life* photojournalism would be exposed to a vision of African Americans that was far different—and far less demeaning—than the images commonly distributed in the culture.

While it is difficult to argue that the Royal Seven sit-in successfully replaced established caricatures initially—even in North Carolina—it did illustrate how to address a stereotype and overturn a character trope among African Americans. In 1950s America a good citizen did not cause trouble. The good citizen, as might have been embodied by Andy Griffith in the popular television series *The Andy Griffith Show,* quietly went to work in Mayberry, kept things orderly, and made it home in time for dinner. In the face of this white middle-class male caricature, and even despite the recent successes of the Montgomery bus boycott, the "good" African American citizen was expected not to make waves, and the immediate response in the black community to Reverend Moore demonstrated this understanding: this "radical" young pastor and his followers took actions that flew in the face of images of ideal black citizenship of the time.[44] As Wilson explains, whites assumed "a 'good Negro' was someone who knew her place, who accepted the system and worked within it to achieve the status allowed to her by segregation and those who controlled it."[45] Even King himself, while at Boston University, tried to keep Moore and others like him from stirring things up, preferring instead to bring about change by finding ways to thrive within or despite the system rather than challenging it directly in any way.[46] Inasmuch as existing rhetorical modes of action accounted for such misgivings about more aggressive rhetorical strategies and tactics, one might suggest that, by challenging this long-standing caricature through the placement of their bodies in the whites-only section, the Royal Seven at the very least expanded the possibilities for rhetorical action and, ultimately, shaped future interactions.

The Royal Seven did this by inviting others, through their enactments in material space, to reimagine the social uses of even "private" spaces and to contest stereotypic views of blacks who might make use of those spaces—views held by both blacks and whites. By centering their protest on a site of pleasure once open only to whites, the Royal Seven undermined the stereotype of the "good" black, who never caused trouble and submitted to second-rate status or to being dominated by whites. This is probably the main reason blacks in Durham criticized the Royal Seven—they found it more tolerable to endure the indignities associated with this stereotype than to face the additional persecution brought about by a small group of agitators and the visible methods of challenging the status quo they employed. Indeed the actions of the Royal Seven risked reaffirming existing stereotypes held by many whites that blacks who openly challenged segregation were overly aggressive or a menace to the prevailing social order. While the Royal Seven sit-in revealed that blacks were willing to act in highly visible and concerted ways to agitate for civil rights, it also made visible that blacks were in an important sense no different than whites—that is, they desired and enjoyed the same simple pleasures as whites, no matter the space in which these pleasures were experienced. As Griffin might argue, the sit-in crystallized the fundamental issue of who was allowed to experience basic pleasures and of when and where this could occur. In this manner the Royal Seven problematized existing stereotypes by making visible the tension between acceptable civil disobedience, social cohesion, and the right to enjoy certain pleasures in concrete but contested urban spaces. They also problematized the relationship between public and private spaces and the appropriate balance of public and private space within a democratic society. For the Royal Seven, the right to one's basic humanity, as demonstrated in the sit-in, should have been open to people of all races, regardless of whether or not the space in which one acted was designated private property or something else.

Stated somewhat differently, when Reverend Moore and his six allies calmly sat down and requested to be served ice cream, they were doing more than getting themselves arrested. They filled up most of the booths, one protestor per booth, and waited, boldly proclaiming through the placement of their bodies within the space that in a time of blatant racial inequality, the caricature of the passive African American was threatening and demeaning to human dignity.

Regardless of the outcome of the court cases, and even if the Royal Ice Cream sit-in saga had ended right after the seven were arrested, the caricature of passivity and indirectness, but perhaps also of otherness, was challenged in the most visible of ways, and the process of overturning it had begun. These men and women were making waves by daring to act differently to gain access to what whites took for granted, standing up for themselves (by sitting down) in the face of segregated practices, injustices, and abuses that the vast majority of their brothers and sisters suffered on a daily basis. However the fact is the Royal Seven saga did not end then. It eventually culminated in a public admission by King that nonviolent direct action was appropriate and even necessary to advance the cause of equality and freedom for all. King's embrace of nonviolent direct action, in Moore's city and at Moore's request (and not in Greensboro, the location of the then-current sit-ins), was a significant event in the efforts to overturn this caricature and to replace it with a new, more progressive image or cultural projection, as Merelman would refer to it, and certainly marked an important development in the rhetorical trajectory of the movement. Indeed King's speech both "received" and acknowledged the transformation of the rhetorical trajectory made up of local history (the Royal Ice Cream Company sit-in as well as the Woolworth lunch-counter sit-ins) and private conversation (his interactions with Reverend Moore) by specifically celebrating those participating in the sit-ins for their role in challenging the caricature and its related assumptions: "You have given an additional death blow to the once prevalent idea that the Negro prefers segregation. You have also made it clear that we will not be satisfied with token integration, for token integration is nothing but a new form of discrimination covered up with the niceties of complexity. Separate facilities, whether in eating places or public schools, are inherently unequal."[47]

Creating Recognition through Particularity

It is much easier to remain a good citizen in the face of inequality when that inequality is abstract or distant. The *Life* photographs, as described by Gallagher and Zagacki, made their subjects into real people rather than distant masses of oppressed unknowns. The viewer could see and recognize the expression on a face or the bloodstain on a T-shirt he or she might have considered purchasing at the local department store. As Gallagher and Zagacki argued, through these pictures "Negro people became visible in their particularity—they were no longer simply a removed abstraction, but were clearly individuals engaged in the social world."[48] This particularity was powerful in that it made the sufferers into real people, the oppressed into neighbors. This in turn represented an important advancement in expanding and transforming the rhetorical trajectory. Images such as these illustrated how the actions of ordinary people, dealing with what was for many individuals relatively ordinary circumstances (e.g., gaining a nonrestricted seat at an ice cream parlor), could be marshaled together into significant rhetorical and material transformations.

In this sense the Royal Ice Cream sit-in did not do much to humanize the oppressed, especially among Durhamites. Citizens of this community knew that African Americans were treated differently and faced this reality every day as they shopped, went to school, watched sports, or bought dessert. These were literally neighbors and friends. As challenging as it is to increase the visibility of distant and abstracted oppression, it is even more difficult to make visible the mundane indignities of everyday life. Considering the Royal Seven from the perspective of the larger rhetorical trajectory of the civil rights movement, then, they begin looking less like rhetorical failures and more like rhetorical catalysts for change.

When Moore and his friends chose the Royal Ice Cream Company, they succeeded in giving oppression a material face and address in local, particularized downtown Durham. The face—Louis Coletta—was not that of an especially vindictive or hateful kind of oppression, nor was the Royal Ice Cream Company necessarily more segregated than any of the other shops in that neighborhood. However in the choice of that location, oppression became visible in its particularity (and in its banality) rather than an abstract evil divorced from everyday life. Moreover, focusing protest on a site of pleasure available to whites only made visible the possibilities of experiencing the world differently in a particular kind of place, of engaging structures of feeling and communicating denied or deemed appropriate only within certain spatial boundaries. As Michel Foucault might have described it in *The Archaeology of Knowledge,* the rules governing interaction that occurred in the "whites only" section of the parlor represented a "discursive formation," which specified the form that discourse, and the emotions associated with it, could assume.[49] Only a particular kind of knowledge and set of feelings were allowed by this discursive formation—that is, by virtue of stereotypic assumptions about them, blacks were forbidden to be there, whether being included sitting, ordering ice cream, or enjoying a conversation with each other. The white establishment's reaction to black resistance within this privately owned space was to expel (forcefully, if necessary) them from it—and all of this reaction to resistance was legitimized by the state and its legal institutions. One can recall the North Carolina Supreme Court ruling on this point, upholding "the right of an operator of a private enterprise to select the clientele he will serve and to make such selection based on color, if he so desires." By being in this space in a highly visible manner, however, the Royal Seven problematized the rules that characterized the space as an exclusionary site of social discourse. In the process they attempted to reframe the meaning of the context in which ordinary acts took place, changing the ice cream parlor itself from a private and exclusionary space to an open and inclusive one.

The immediate response to the sit-in did not need to be supportive, nor did this sit-in need to spark hundreds of others to be effective or to have material consequences. It was a success to the extent it created an image of a concrete and particular instance of oppression. More specifically it demonstrated how difficult it was for African Americans to participate in ordinary activities—to take pleasure in ordinary events—that whites took for granted. Even those in opposition at the time had an image in their minds, one that might have eventually gained salience as caricatures were overturned and moral ideals were made visible and concrete.

As Griffin would suggest, the rhetorical trajectory emerging from the Royal Ice Cream parlor and the Woolworth lunch counter sit-ins provided King with many resources for rhetorically creating networks of particularized grievances and linking them to other protests, events, and aims. In using his speech at White Rock Church to do so, he also, in turn, nurtured and catalyzed the emerging movement. For instance King addressed the issue of particularity and its significance to successful direct action as follows: "You have rightly chosen to follow the path of non-violence. As we protest, our ultimate aim is not to defeat or humiliate the white man but to win his friendship and understanding. . . . We have a moral obligation to remind him that segregation is wrong." Further, in a passage understood to be a direct reference to the Woolworth Greensboro sit-in but in which (based on this rhetorical history of the events and discourses that led to Moore's invitation to King to give the speech in Durham at the White Rock Baptist Church) King might also have been referring to the Royal Seven, he exhorted his audience: "Let us protest with the ultimate aim of being reconciled with our white brother. As we sit down quietly to request a cup of coffee, let us not forget to drink from that invisible cup of love." King urges his listeners to see the people with whom they struggle as persons to be respected and loved even as they diligently request, by their nonviolent direct actions, to be respected and treated with love in return: "And so I would urge you to continue your just struggle until the people with whom you trade will respect your person as much as they respect your dollar."[50] Thus King, whose speech employs what were heretofore nascent possibilities within the rhetorical trajectory, provides a rhetorical blueprint for acknowledging and making visible particularized grievances of individual citizens along with possible ways of sharing and acting together in social space and merging them into a kind of unified trajectory—what Griffin might have referred to as a crystallizing moment and a flowering of the movement.

Making Abstract Concepts Knowable

Gallagher and Zagacki argued that the *Life* photographs help people see, for the first time, the gaping chasm separating their view of the world from the realities of social experience. The photographs could do this, they argued, because they were so recognizably American in their depiction of un-American persecution: "the familiarity of the setting, the fact that it was daylight, all suggested that the very basic conditions of democracy in a capitalist society, in which people were free to buy burgers and gas in peace without fear of unprovoked persecution, had been violated."[51] The vision of free and open capitalism, of egalitarian and inclusive democracy, was jarringly replaced by views of reality that looked more like police batons and fire hoses turned on peaceful civilians. Indeed, as Griffin might argue, god and devil terms in one rhetorical trajectory may be reversed in another. These photographs showed white audiences how what they largely understood to be god terms (such as *democracy* and *capitalism*) were being corrupted for black citizens.

Much in the same way, the Royal Seven sit-in helped make the abstract ideal of standing up for oneself, of advancing the cause of freedom, more concrete and recognizable while at the same time exposing the bankrupt nature of America's god terms and material conditions related to capitalism and democracy. Certainly direct action on behalf of civil rights, especially sit-ins, had been occurring for some time and across vastly different communities and geographic distance. Also the NAACP Legal Defense Fund's work was largely rhetorical but not essentially oratorical. So all of these instances demonstrate moments where abstract concepts were made concrete. However these moments did not occur simultaneously, nor did they constitute a global, organized rhetorical trajectory that had been applied to every local context. Moreover, up to that point in 1957, while many different protests were popping up all over the nation, oratory was still the preferred means of civil rights protest. Perhaps this is because the evolving rhetorical trajectory circumscribed rhetorical practice in this way. Indeed King and other leaders were traveling the country giving speeches and advocating for legislative change, so the majority of African Americans could participate only by attending a speech or a rally. Disgruntled students might not have known what to do to move the cause forward. In fact the debates among students at Boston University when King was there were mostly limited to such questions as whether it was appropriate to mention race in term papers.[52]

In any event whatever else had been or was occurring around the rest of the American South, in Durham abstract understandings needed to be concretized around specific, familiar actions and events. The Royal Seven sit-in (and the Montgomery bus boycott and the Greensboro sit-in and the others that preceded and followed them) drew from extant strategies and tactics largely left untested or unsettled. The sit-in did so by rhetorically enacting what democracy meant or what democracy did not mean for African Americans in North Carolina, where the ideal of democracy fell well short of the practice. The sit-in showed these realities, made them visible, in addition to talking about them. As King noted, "In this period when civil rights legislation hangs in an uncertain balance in the congress—when the recalcitrance of some public officials in the South instills us with frustration and despondency, the spectacular example of determined and dedicated young people demanding their rights" made all the difference. Indeed he exhorted them as follows: "You have taken hold of the tradition of resolute non-violent resistance and you are carrying it forward toward the end of bringing all of us closer to the day of full freedom."[53]

On the other hand, an important element of the visibility explored by Gallagher and Zagacki in the *Life* pictures is the transition and translation of indefinable concepts to everyday life or, as they put it, "the evocation of humanity by moving beyond abstract or idealistic categories to depictions of social experience that are recognizable to common audiences and that add moral import to the decisions or developments before them."[54] When the Royal Seven were arrested, they moved beyond abstract ideals of freedom or equality and added concrete moral import to a banal, everyday decision: where to sit while eating ice cream. There is not a record of what happened at the ice cream parlor when the next African American customers entered the restaurant. However if personal conversations along with other discursive forms and enactments are important in the development and impact of a rhetorical trajectory, it seems entirely possible that some customers might have known what had transpired there just a few hours or days earlier. Possibly some of them began to question whether all Americans had open and equal access to goods and services. Perhaps the owner let out a sigh of relief when they obeyed the "whites only" sign, or more important, perhaps he experienced regret at having to rely on the thin, paltry excuse for denying the Royal Seven's request. At that point such obedience had an additional layer of moral import, an overt embrace of the status quo.

It is worth mentioning again that the Royal Ice Cream Company was targeted by boycotts and protests throughout the 1960s. At some point after the Royal Seven's direct actions, the community recognized the moral gauntlet that had been thrown by that initial protest. At some point the action of ordering ice cream on the other side of a segregation wall became a moral statement, an indictment of freedom and equality as presently constituted and at the same time a (re)enactment of these concepts—the Royal Seven undermined accepted beliefs about these terms even as they reinfused and restored them with new meanings. Moore and his fellow protesters might not have made that change all by themselves, but their actions were the first in that community to encourage others to see the abstract in the everyday acts of segregation that had been overlooked for too long.

The Royal Seven sit-in, considered together with King's speech, shows how different aspects are shaped by, and also shape, a rhetorical trajectory. Such rhetorical analysis illuminates the materiality and tensions of democracy and shows how they applied to African Americans while also revealing the types of arguments that are likely to (and did indeed) emerge about the means by which to change things. Their (the Royal Seven, the students in Woolworth, the Montgomery boycotters, and, eventually, King himself) participation in these events represents the enactment of protest and the constitution of a rhetorical trajectory.

Conclusion

While a historical examination or account of the Royal Seven sit-in would likely focus on its chronological relation to other major events in the civil rights movement, the present rhetorical examination, as demonstrated above, uncovers and illuminates a somewhat different set of functions and significance. First, employing the concepts of rhetorical visibility and rhetorical trajectory to an examination of these events focuses attention on the material, performative aspects of the movement and of the day-to-day lives of those who lived in and through the movement. Instead of looking for significant causal-historical relationships or immediate legal or legislative successes—standards the sit-in failed to achieve in the short term—this approach makes it possible to explore the visibility the sit-in created and the trajectories it opened and reconfigured and shaped. With this sit-in the seemingly inconsequential everyday oppression endured by Moore and his fellow ice cream shop customers became a particularized example of systematic racial oppression. To the extent their actions functioned rhetorically to make visible the everyday consequences of segregation, including the feelings of pleasure and the sites of pleasure denied, the rhetorical trajectory of a larger movement was opened as a network of particularized grievances began to be recognized as a growing and connected trajectory toward (and movement for) freedom. Additionally the rhetorical consequence of the sit-in, when taken together with King's subsequent speech and the efforts to site a historical marker, indicate the impact of these events and efforts on the development of the larger rhetorical trajectory. It becomes understood that the rhetorical trajectory of the movement plays a role not just in informing the present but in commemorating the past, not simply helping to strategize from within it but also providing a kind of lived experience of the past and its various discourses and images that can inform present actions.

A rhetorical analysis of the sit-in and the rhetorical trajectory reveals additional functions and significance. It may well be the case that the cumulative impact of rhetorical tactics such as sit-ins was to disrupt entrenched discursive formations and the use of social space and range of allowable emotions, pleasures, and feelings dictated by them. Clearly the employment of these tactics risked exasperating the divisions already experienced by blacks and whites, which had become materially embodied in everyday social (not to mention legal and political) practice. Yet, as Kenneth Burke might put it, the Royal Ice Cream Company sit-in was not so much an act of division as it was an effort at identification—or, more specifically, of enacting a way of life in which people could act (e.g., dine) together in a single, nonsegregated material space. As Burke explained in *A Rhetoric of Motives,* "in acting together, men have common sensations, concepts, images, ideas, attitudes that make them *consubstantial.*"[55] For Burke consubstantiality is the root of or grounding condition for identification. For King simple acts of sipping coffee together and of exchanging goods and services (that is, acts of "trade" that occurred in common places such as lunch counters) built upon one another, ultimately becoming the means by which individuals could come to share and respect each other's humanity. Similarly Moore and the rest of the Royal Seven were attempting to visualize these commonalities as a first move toward yielding an entirely different cultural fabric in which blacks and whites, linked by their shared desires, pleasures, and so on, could act together in the same material spaces. As a rhetorical trajectory—and in the words of Griffin—their sit-in embodied "the qualities, motivations, or state of mind" of Moore and his group. Hence it made visible a way of being in the world that others could "appropriately follow." In many ways the early history of the civil rights movement is a history of the tension between Martin Luther King Jr.'s goal of peaceful coexistence and nonviolent protest and the inevitability and perhaps necessity of political strife and aggressive resistance. The present analysis reveals this dialectic at work.[56]

This essay, therefore, serves to reinforce and demonstrate the usefulness of concepts such as rhetorical visibility and rhetorical trajectory for students and scholars who wish to understand and explore the relationship between rhetoric's symbolicity and materiality in the context of social movements. The concept of the rhetorical trajectory creates a way of bridging the traditional binaries of saying and doing, of discursive and nondiscursive, by creating the potential for local and situated rhetorical actions to be seen as related and significant. Rhetorical visibility provides a way of thinking about and organizing a set of rhetorical functions so that they can guide and be used to evaluate social actions and images in addition to discourses. Analysis guided by these functions reveals "the power of rhetoric to create a truth and falsity that contradicts our basic 'knowledge'" of things like freedom and oppression.[57] It also demonstrates how visibility can provide access to a public voice and a public presentation of lived (rather than caricatured) experience for those previously denied such access by law and by practice—a voice and a presence that evokes the moral conscience of those who witness it or learn of it through conversations, accounts, and images.

Notes

1. "Negroes Lose in Trespass Case Appeal."
2. Lloyd Little, "Greensboro's Sit-In Marker Won't Read 'First.'" *Durham (N.C.) Morning Herald*, 13 January, 1980.
3. North Carolina Office of Archives and History, "North Carolina Historical Marker Program."
4. Gallagher and Zagacki, "Power of Visual Images," 177–78.
5. Gallagher and Zagacki, "Epiphanies and Transformations," 115.
6. Griffin, "Rhetoric of Historical Movements," 186.
7. Ibid.
8. Ibid., 186.
9. Qtd. in Milliken, "Civil Rights History Marked."
10. Rossi, "Sons of Ice Cream Shop Owner."
11. Rickard, "Sit-In Site Will Get State Marker"; see also West, "Protestors from Royal Ice Cream Parlor"; Khanna, "50 Years after Sit-In."
12. Khanna, "50 Years after Sit-In."
13. "Negroes Fined in Dairy Bar Case."
14. "Going to High Court."
15. Stunte, "'Ice Cream Parlor' Negroes."
16. "State High Court Backs Local Setup."
17. Barbour, "Judge Won't Drop Store Trespass."
18. "Negroes Lose in Trespass Case Appeal."
19. "7 Negroes Pay Fines."
20. Gregg, "NC Finally Recognizes Pre-Woolworth Sit-Ins,"
21. Ruyter, "African Americans Sit-In."
22. "Galleries."
23. Greene, *Our Separate Ways*, 67.
24. Ibid.
25. In his own efforts to explain the larger rhetorical trajectory surrounding King's 1955 speech about the Montgomery bus boycott, Kurt H. Wilson argues that King's address drew upon an evolving discursive field "comprised of local history, folklore, private conversations, and public rhetoric." His address interpreted "that discursive field to unify the black community and constrain the mode of its protest" and rearticulated it "into a rhetoric that established the [rhetorical] trajectory of King's philosophy and oratorical practice" for years to come. Wilson, "Interpreting the Discursive Field," 301.
26. Branch, *Parting the Waters*, 92.
27. Branch, *Pillar of Fire*, 24.
28. Davidson, "Martin Luther King, Jr."
29. Ibid.
30. Branch, *Pillar of Fire*, 24–25.
31. King, "Creative Protest," 368.
32. Greene, *Our Separate Ways*, 69.
33. Hartness, "Marker Commemorates Pioneering Durham Sit-In."

34. For example, in 1960 a Durham District Solicitor running for U.S. Congress, when the Greensboro sit-ins began, told a Durham newspaper that "students who took part in the sit-down strikes could be arrested and charged with trespass if they refused to leave when asked." He went on to explain that the question of service at eating establishments had been settled by the State Supreme Court in January 1958 in the case involving the Royal Seven: "Incidents of this nature (such as the student strikes) can be avoided legally by the operators of the business themselves by merely ordering the 'undesirables' to leave the premises." See "Politics Enter Strike Picture as Candidate Reviews Laws on Cafes." *Carolina Times*, 13 February 1960, 1A.

35. Qtd. in Milliken, "Royal Ice Cream Sit-In"; see also Greene, *Our Separate Ways*, 67.

36. Qtd. in Ferreri, "Civil Rights Protest Finally Gets Its Due."

37. Blair, "Contemporary U.S. Memorial Sites."

38. Merelman, *Representing Black Culture*, 26.

39. Gallagher and Zagacki, "Epiphanies and Transformations," 117.

40. Ibid.

41. Gallagher and Zagacki, "Epiphanies and Transformations," 118.

42. Gallagher and Zagacki, "Epiphanies and Transformations"; Gallagher and Zagacki, "Power of Visual Images."

43. Gallagher and Zagacki, "Epiphanies and Transformations," 121.

44. "Galleries."

45. Wilson, "Interpreting the Discursive Field," 301.

46. Branch, *Parting the Waters*, 92.

47. King, "Creative Protest," 367–68.

48. Gallagher and Zagacki, "Epiphanies and Transformations," 125.

49. Foucault, *Archaeology of Knowledge*, 41–44.

50. King, "Creative Protest," 368.

51. Gallagher and Zagacki, "Epiphanies and Transformations," 128.

52. Branch, *Parting the Waters*, 91.

53. King, "Creative Protest," 367.

54. Gallagher and Zagacki, "Epiphanies and Transformations," 127.

55. Burke, *Rhetoric of Motives*, 21.]

56. The Royal Seven were somewhat like the urban streetwalkers in Michel de Certeau's *The Practice of Everyday Life*, who in their everyday social roles were subjected to the repressive rules and structures strategically imposed upon them by the organized state. At the same time, Certeau's subjects worked tactically, through their routine activities of walking, talking, reading, dwelling, and cooking (i.e., Certeau's "arts of doing"), to resist these restraints creatively. The Royal Seven, also operating at the street level—in their case as customers and, eventually, as defendants—deployed their own routine actions tactically and in ways that were never fully determined by the strategies of local businesses, government, and state institutions. And yet, importantly, they sought to be part of those organized structures by first making visible the restrictions placed on customer's activities if those customers were black. Certeau is mentioned in passing because he also recalls the extent to which rhetorical trajectories can reframe the radical significance of seemingly "ordinary" activities while at the same time downplaying their radicalness.

57. Gallagher and Zagacki, "Epiphanies and Transformations," 129.

THE NASHVILLE SIT-INS

Successful Nonviolent Direct Action through
Rhetorical Invention and Advocacy

Judith D. Hoover

"I came to Nashville not to bring inspiration, but to gain inspiration from
the great movement that has taken place in this community."

Rev. Dr. Martin Luther King Jr., Fisk University,
Nashville, Tennessee, April 20, 1960

This quotation stands today etched in glass as a part of the Nashville Public Library's civil rights display, just above a replica of the W. T. Grant lunch counter that was fully desegregated on May 10, 1960. The key to success in Nashville, Tennessee, lay in the extensive training in nonviolence received by the young civil rights movement participants. They not only heard the words and philosophies of Rev. James Lawson and others but also developed through rhetorical invention the strategies that could help change attitudes. Student leaders such as John Lewis and Diane Nash came to embody the nonviolent philosophy through the rhetorical advocacy modeled by the sit-ins.

The Nashville sit-ins illustrated the worth not only of training but also of discipline and planning, as well as shared leadership—an innovation in the top-down world of the 1960s. According to Lewis, the members of the Nashville movement had a "deeper understanding of nonviolence and a deeper commitment to the beloved community" than those in other cities.[1] They helped create, if even for the short time they were together, the "Beloved Community" that was so vital a part of the nonviolent philosophy, and they went on to lead other significant organizations such as the Student Nonviolent Coordinating Committee.

Although the first recognized sit-in in Nashville occurred on February 13, 1960, nearly two weeks after the famous Greensboro, North Carolina, F. W.

Woolworth lunch counter sit-ins, two "test" sit-ins had happened earlier—the first on November 28, 1959, at Harvey's department store's lunch counter, and the second on December 5, 1959, at Cain-Sloan department store's counter. On both occasions those who sat in were politely asked to leave and did so. Targets, methods, and responses would soon change, but the commitment to nonviolence would be retained, at great cost to those sitting in.

Workshops for training in the art of nonviolent direct action had been underway in the basement classrooms of the Clark Memorial United Methodist Church since the fall of 1958. This essay explores the historical events that resulted in the desegregation of the first major southern U.S. city; the organizations, institutions, and processes that allowed it to happen (or tried to stand in the way of its happening); the cast of characters who participated; the events themselves; and the significance of this movement for the future of the civil rights struggle in America.

The most important findings, however, lie in the rhetorical strategies invented during the training sessions and then in the heat of the sit-in battle itself and the rhetorical advocacy of change in attitudes of the segregated South. Those who had previously been a culturally invisible group of idealistic college students invented for themselves an identity as a social movement. They became a visible public that overturned cultural assumptions of the rightness of segregation as the only solution to the problems perceived as inherent in racial difference.

Preparation for Nonviolent Direct Action

In 1958 the Reverend Kelly Miller Smith, pastor of the First Baptist Church Capital Hill, also known then as the First Colored Baptist Church, founded the Nashville Christian Leadership Conference based on his participation in the formation of the Southern Christian Leadership Conference a year earlier. This group also included the Reverend C. T. Vivian, who would become a significant figure in the months to come. In the fall of 1958, Smith invited James Lawson, a doctoral student at Vanderbilt Divinity School and representative of the Fellowship of Reconciliation, to speak on "the basics of passive resistance and nonviolent action as tools for desegregation."[2] John Lewis, himself a young student at American Baptist Theological Seminary in Nashville and soon to become a sit-in leader, saw "something special" about Lawson, an "inner peace and wisdom that you could sense immediately." As an eleven-year-old child, Lawson had fought back against name-calling, but his mother insisted that instead he should practice "Christian love." Lewis notes that it was "a conversion experience" for Lawson, who became "committed to what he called New Testament pacifism."[3]

Earlier in 1958 Lawson had met with the children who had integrated Central High School in Little Rock, Arkansas, and had learned, to his dismay, that they were not prepared for the violence of the Ku Klux Klan or the White Citizens' Council nor were they given any training, other than being told "not to fight back." His response was to offer them advice that "you fight back but not imitate the enemies who are trying to drive you out of the school." Instead, he told them, they could use their "minds, [their] wit, and [their] courage" and be "more effective than if [they] swing [their] fists." When he asked about the worst things that happened to them on a typical school day, one student replied with the example of "bombing," which involved "wrapping a marble or a stone in foil and throwing it at her." She later reported that the last time it had happened, she picked up the marble and laid it on the desk of the boy who had thrown it and smiled at him. Though he was only one of many angry white students, his bombing of her stopped that day.[4]

Lawson's Workshops

Lawson, who had studied in India, brought his message of nonviolent direct action to the college students of Nashville through a series of workshops beginning in the fall of 1958. He had begun reading and studying the principles of Mahatma Gandhi in 1947 and had come to appreciate nonviolence as "an ancient wisdom" that is "always connected to strategies for change." Indeed it is "not powerlessness" but the "power of resistance." Through "action," he counseled, the students could become "new people," who would be willing to "step forward" and be "confirm[ed] . . . in a different way of life and a different way of thinking."[5]

Lawson's earlier workshops in Nashville had attracted only adults, and it was through the women who attended that he learned the details of the segregation situation that caused him to target downtown businesses for the sit-in campaign. The women complained that, although they could shop downtown, they had no place to sit down or to eat, or even to have a cup of coffee. They spoke of trying to buy shoes for their children and hats and clothes for themselves, which they were forbidden to try on.[6] Harvey's department store featured a carousel on the children's clothing floor, where their children were not allowed to play.[7] Restrooms in the department stores were designated as "white ladies, white gentlemen and colored." At first the goal was simply to get rid of the offensive "signs that divided."[8] John Seigenthaler, a white journalist at the *Tennessean* newspaper and later assistant to U.S. Attorney General Robert Kennedy, said that "Nashville was as segregated as South Africa at the height of apartheid— those signs were everywhere telling people what they could do and what they could not do and where they could go and where they could not go."[9]

Once the students began attending, more details emerged, particularly from leaders such as Diane Nash, a transfer student at Fisk University from Chicago, Illinois, who felt that segregation was "dehumanizing" and an "attack on [her] dignity." She spoke of seeing adults as well as children sitting on street curbs eating their lunch because they could buy only takeout food at the lunch counters.[10] Lawson's concentration on justice appealed to Nash as well as to other students who soon became leaders: Lewis, James Bevel, Marion Barry, and Bernard LaFayette. These four had been recruited and encouraged to take leadership roles by both Lawson and Smith with the result being that there was no sense of competition between the adults and the students. As time passed and situations changed, the adults might urge caution but still supported the students as they took the dangerous paths that the sit-ins, and certainly the Freedom Rides, became.[11]

Workshop Philosophies

The workshops' curriculum began with an overview of the great religions and philosophies of the world. They studied Gandhi's philosophy in depth, "from his concept of *ahimsa*—the Hindu idea of non-violent passive resistance—to *satyagraha*—literally, 'steadfastness in truth,' a grounding foundation of nonviolent civil disobedience, of active pacifism." They moved on to the difficult concept of "redemptive suffering," that "there is something in the very essence of anguish that is liberating, cleansing, redemptive."[12] John Lewis explains that "unearned suffering" and one's response to it "opens us and those around us to a force beyond ourselves, a force that is right and moral, the force of righteous truth that is at the basis of human conscience." Those who are suffering, however, must "hold no malice" and, indeed, must love those "who would raise their hand against us, those we might call our enemy." This "capacity to forgive," Lewis maintains, is the "essence of the nonviolent way of life" that Lawson taught them. To see one's attacker as "a victim of the forces that have shaped and fed his anger and fury" puts one on the path to "the nonviolent life."[13]

The concept of the Beloved Community, which Lewis calls the "fulcrum of all that Jim Lawson was teaching us," also represents ancient wisdom as practiced by Lawson as well as Rev. Dr. Martin Luther King Jr. and sought throughout human history. Lewis, who later became a member of the U.S. Congress from Georgia, received the John F. Kennedy Profile in Courage Award in 2001 and defined this community in his acceptance speech. He said, "In building a new America, we saw a vision then as we do now of the Beloved Community. . . . 'Beloved' means not hateful, not violent, not uncaring, not unkind. And 'community' means not separated, not polarized, not locked in struggle."[14] This community required that nonviolence be practiced not as a tactic but as a true and lasting way of life.

Workshop Activities

Once the students had absorbed the religious and philosophical aspects of nonviolence, it was time to learn how to use them. The workshops now consisted of role-playing activities, or "sociodramas," as Lewis termed them. First came lessons on how to protect themselves from serious injuries, such as "how to curl our bodies so that our internal organs would escape direct blows." Lawson saw maintaining eye contact as a "viscerally disarming thing," so they were advised to look at their attackers directly. They learned to put themselves between an attacker and anyone "taking a beating." They took turns playing attackers and demonstrators, complete with name-calling.[15] "To use a religious term," Lewis argued, "we were ready to be baptized because we believed in what we were about to do. We were willing to die for this cause, for this movement."[16]

Diane Nash said that role-playing conditioned them "to resist the impulse to run or fight back."[17] Lewis in his memoir notes the incongruity of white activists who attended the workshops screaming "nigger lover" at black activists and black activists screaming "ape" or other racist epithets at white activists.[18] Analysis sessions always followed the role-playing, with Lawson ready to offer critiques and suggestions and to insist that although careful planning had to be done, spontaneous or "creative" solutions might need to be invented on the spot. Still they must not forget the principles of nonviolence they had learned, for that was the only way to achieve the social change they so hoped for.[19]

Nashville Student Movement

Earlier in the fall of 1960, the students had organized themselves into the Nashville Student Movement with a central committee "who would represent the others in terms of decision-making and speaking for the group." Deciding early on that there would be shared or rotated leadership to promote "group effectiveness and responsibility, not individual power," the movement discouraged those who only wanted to gain popularity or political power on their campuses.[20] As Lewis notes, they took turns "at everything from chairing the committee, to being beaten, to going to jail."[21] Their first two chairs resigned after serving just one week apiece, since there would be no personal glory attached but only the promise of personal pain. Diane Nash became the third chair and rotated into that position often.

As noted above, the first test sit-in occurred on November 28, 1959, at Harvey's department store. This first group included Lewis, Nash, Barry, and a few others, all of whom dressed up to set a precedent for behavior. As Lewis maintains, "No issues would be forced, no confrontations created." Each made a purchase and then met at the lunch counter, spacing themselves out so that other customers could be served. A waitress politely said that she could not serve them. Nash, who had been chosen as the spokesperson for the day, asked calmly, but firmly, if they could speak with the manager. The manager appeared and said that it was store policy not to serve them, nor even to serve the white students who were with them. Diane thanked the manager, and they all departed with "no harsh words, no violence."[22]

One week later, on December 5, 1959, a group of eight again dressed carefully and set off for Cain-Sloan department store, which was "a bit more upscale . . . with higher prices and a much smaller black clientele." Before they had a chance to sit down, a waitress announced that they did not "serve colored people." Lewis, that day's spokesperson, asked to see the manager, who politely said that store policy prevented him from serving them. They thanked the manager and left "without incident."[23]

Expanding Preparations

By January 1960 hundreds of volunteers had joined the workshops, but many realized that they just might not be able to take ill-treatment without fleeing or responding with rage. These, however, could serve the movement differently, organizing rides, carrying messages, finding food, or working with the media.[24] Some lapses would occur once the "real" sit-ins began, with fear or anger replacing philosophy even among the best-trained and most committed of the students. Nash, for instance, explained later to an interviewer how fear had overtaken her after hearing five or six young white men saying, "That's Diane Nash. She's the one to get." At that point she gave herself a time limit either to "get myself together, or go back to the church . . . and resign [as chairperson]." Fortunately for her future role in desegregating Nashville, she did not resign, saying, "By that time limit, I was able to function."[25] Another instance pitted a student against a bouncer at a local restaurant. Seeing the student's anger building, Reverend Vivian told him to "get back to the church and renew yourself to nonviolence," which he did.[26] Lawson continued to train as many as possible for the days ahead, not knowing that in Greensboro, North Carolina, four college freshmen would take the first big leap on February 1, 1960, with no formal training at all.

From Practice to Reality

After Greensboro the concept of sitting in spread rapidly across the South. Nowhere else but Nashville, however, had students been trained in both strategically planning for and following through with nonviolent direct action and been psychologically prepared for the wrath that would inevitably follow. After a brief sit-in on February 6, 1960, designed to sympathize with those in Greensboro, Lawson began abbreviated training sessions for the hundreds who came forward. For the next several days, the groundwork was laid for the first official sit-in. According to Lewis behavioral rules were invented, especially since not everyone had experienced months of training. There would be "no aggression. No retaliation. No loud conversation, no talking of any kind with anyone other than ourselves." They should all "dress nicely, bring books, school-work, letter-writing materials." They should not slouch or nap. They should "be prepared for arrest."[27] Although the adult leaders tried to persuade the students to wait, the time had come to act, they argued, and so they did.

February 13, 1960

The city of Nashville woke up to several inches of snow on the morning of the first official sit-in. To John Lewis it seemed an omen. "Everything felt so soft, so hushed, almost holy. Pure as the driven snow. Clean. Innocent. That was the setting. That was us," he writes.[28] "The most important strength we had was the 'element of hope' that sustained us," Lewis recalled in an interview.[29] Just before lunchtime 124 students walked through the snow, two by two, toward the down-town lunch counters. Dividing into groups, each person bought something small and then proceeded to his or her assigned counter. Lewis as spokesperson asked if they could be served, and the waitress's response was "We don't serve niggers here." The counter was closed, the lights were turned off, and, as Lewis described, "there we sat, in semi-darkness, alone." They remained at the counter all afternoon, until at 6:00 P.M. a message came from the Baptist Church that it was time to go, so they did.[30] Lawson said that after this first sit-in, the students "came back exalting in the fact that they sat in and their fears were vanquished."[31] Lewis said that it was "sheer euphoria, like a jubilee."[32]

February 18, 1960

The second sit-in proved as uneventful as the first. This time there were two hundred participants; again service was refused and counters were closed, and after four hours the students returned to the church. Lewis explains this situation by noting that "white Nashville was just not ready for this. It had never had to deal with black people this way. These waves of well-dressed, well-behaved young black men and women were something no one had seen before." He hoped that people would see them "as we were, not as something in their minds, in their imaginations."[33]

February 20, 1960

By the third sit-in, the downtown merchants began to fight back, placing objects on the counters to keep the students from using them to read or write to fill the time during their virtually silent protests. White customers were beginning to complain about the lack of places to eat lunch. That evening the business owners asked for a moratorium to give them time to come up with a proposal, to which the students agreed temporarily. By the end of the week, however, the sit-ins resumed amid rumors that arrests would be made and attacks would occur.[34]

February 27, 1960

On the evening of February 26, Lewis composed a list of dos and don'ts for the hundreds of protesters and made five hundred copies for distribution. The leaflet made its way into the *Nashville Tennessean*, a liberal newspaper whose readers would see the sort of values that motivated these students. The article itself said that the students were "armed only with mimeographed leaflets which stressed non-violence and passive resistance." The list included the following:

DO NOT: 1. Strike back nor curse if abused.
DO NOT: 2. Laugh out.
DO NOT: 3. Hold conversations with floor walker.
DO NOT: 4. Leave your seat until your leader has given you permission to do so.
DO NOT: 5. Block entrances to stores outside or the aisles inside.
DO: 1. Show yourself friendly and courteous at all times.
DO: 2. Sit straight; always face the counter.
DO: 3. Report all serious incidents to your leader.
DO: 4. Refer information seekers to your leader in a polite manner.
DO: 5. Remember the teachings of Jesus Christ, Mahatma Gandhi and Martin Luther King. Love and nonviolence is the way.
May God Bless Each of You.[35]

The February 27 sit-in was marked by the sort of violence that Lawson had prepared demonstrators for and more. Taunts, shoves, kicks, and name-calling commenced as they approached downtown. Besides the racial epithets, they were called "chicken" for not fighting back, and not fighting back further enraged the crowd of young white men. As they tried to take their seats at the lunch counters, they were burned with cigarettes, dragged to the floor, beaten, and kicked. They had hot coffee poured down their backs and cigarette ashes, mustard, and ketchup poured on their heads; finally, after the crowd had done its worst, the police stepped in, and they were arrested for disorderly conduct. A white student, Paul LaPrad, slammed to the floor and beaten by several in the crowd, was filmed by an NBC news crew as he crouched on the floor covering his head while whites stood over him, daring him to get up.[36] The *Tennessean* ran a photograph of that moment on its front page the same day.[37]

In an interview with Robert Penn Warren, Lawson explained his view that the power structure in Nashville made sure that sometimes the police would act to prevent violence and sometimes they merely waited long enough for the violence to take its toll on the students. White bystanders who witnessed the beatings might yell out that the police were arresting the wrong people, but such comments served as no deterrent. Sometimes, Lawson claimed, the police themselves became the mob.[38]

On February 27, as one group of students was marched to the paddy wagons singing "We Shall Overcome," another group took its place. They came in waves all afternoon, until finally it was announced that the jail was full and no more would be arrested that day. They refused to pay bail, even though it had been reduced to five dollars apiece, because, as they said, they would gladly leave if released but they would never pay their way out. This practice became known as the "jail, no bail" strategy. After six hours they were released that night into the custody of Fisk University president Stephen Wright.[39]

Two days later they appeared in court, represented by Alexander Looby, whom the judge refused to acknowledge, even turning his back as the attorney spoke. The judge simply pronounced them all guilty, offering the choice of thirty days in the county workhouse or a fifty-dollar fine each. Nash spoke for them all, saying, "We feel that if we pay these fines, we would be contributing to and supporting the injustice and immoral practices that have been performed in the arrest and conviction of the defendants." From the workhouse they were sent out to shovel snow and collect trash, and with images of their labors shown on national television and newspapers, they began receiving letters from supporters such as Eleanor Roosevelt and Harry Belafonte.[40]

Subsequent Events

Biracial Committee

On March 1 David Halberstam reported in the *Tennessean* that "whites were ready, gathered in small groups, circling inside the stores and driving by in open convertibles. Woolworths had sealed off its mezzanine lunch counter. McClellans had not only closed its counter at 2:30 PM, but dismantled its seats as rumors spread that 2000 Negroes would march on the lunch counters."[41] None of this came to pass, and on March 3 Mayor Ben West named a biracial committee to seek a solution and asked for a moratorium on the sit-ins.[42] Alexander Looby, the attorney for the students, agreed to the moratorium but pointed out that he had "no control" over them. The *Banner,* Nashville's conservative paper, quoted Looby and listed the names and schools of all 145 who had been arrested.[43]

The students did abide by the moratorium but decided to challenge a federal law requiring desegregation of facilities engaged in interstate commerce by attempting to be served at the Post House, the Greyhound bus terminal lunch counter. Diane Nash and three others were unexpectedly served lunch, although two weeks earlier forty-five students had been arrested there. Nash responded that it represented "a very important first step forward because it is a breach in the opposition."[44] By March 20 a backlash had occurred against Greyhound. Two explosive devices were found in the men's room at the bus terminal where the students had been served.[45]

Some progress was being made among Nashville's religious communities. A group of 160 white and black ministers had "urged downtown businesses to desegregate their lunch counters," noting also that "143 Negroes had been arrested, but no whites."[46] The United Church Women of Nashville and Davidson County published a statement that said, "We grieve that our own community has for so long remained insensitive to the simple human rights of some of its citizens. We commend those who have taken a stand for social justice and rejoice in the establishment of the mayor's biracial committee."[47] Rumors were flying that an "unofficial word-of-mouth boycott" of the downtown might be looming.[48]

Expulsion of James Lawson

On the same day the biracial committee was formed, March 3, Vanderbilt University's chancellor and Board of Trustees required the dean of the Divinity School to expel James Lawson for his assistance to the students in their desegregation efforts. Two days earlier Lawson and other black leaders had met with the mayor and revealed the nature of his workshops. On March 4 the *Nashville Banner* editorialized that Lawson was a "flannel-mouthed agitator."[49] It can be no coincidence that the publisher of the *Banner,* James Stahlman, was a member of the board at Vanderbilt University.

According to John Seigenthaler of the *Tennessean,* Stahlman had introduced the motion to expel Lawson, who had finished all of his coursework for his doctorate. Seigenthaler said that this action resulted in "mass . . . a flood . . . of resignations from the Divinity School faculty who considered the expulsion as an affront to academic freedom."[50] One hundred eleven faculty members, including twelve department heads, said in a prepared statement, "We deplore the intolerance that is the fundamental cause of the Nashville disturbances."

However the undergraduate student senate unanimously passed a resolution supporting the university's action in expelling Lawson because of his "strong commitment to civil disobedience."[51] Once the chancellor realized that "the world was watching, he rescinded the expulsion, but Lawson declined" to return, deciding instead to finish his work at Boston University.[52]

Statement from the Federation for Constitutional Government

In early April the *Nashville Banner* carried the complete statement of a group in Nashville that opposed desegregation. The statement read in part:

(1) We believe in segregation, not only as the traditional way of life in the South, but as the only feasible way of life here at this time.

(2) We deplore the so-called sit-in as a disruptive movement which has served only to create tension, provoke violence and breed racial ill will.

(3) As an organization dedicated to Constitutional government, we believe that the only rights involved here are the rights of private business to operate as it sees fit, under the law, and to choose its own patrons. No one has a right—moral, Constitutional or otherwise—to force himself into a privately owned and operated business and to remain there when denied service and asked to leave. Tennessee law clearly states the rights of the owner of any restaurant or other such place to admit or serve only whom he pleases. Said law just as clearly states that no person denied admittance or refused service shall have any recourse in the Courts.[53]

The law in question had been passed in Tennessee in 1901 and illustrated what the students were up against as they continued their desegregation efforts.

Downtown Boycott

According to Seigenthaler, "some in the business community said privately that if they could just wait it out till summer, these kids would go home. Some would graduate and it would be over with." However, in late March 1960, a silent boycott of Nashville's downtown business district began. Vivian Henderson, an economist working with the movement, proposed an Easter boycott, which, Seigenthaler asserted, "absolutely brought the business community to its knees."[54] The black churches led the way with the slogans "Don't Buy Downtown" and "No Fashions for Easter." Lewis notes that blacks in Nashville spent an average of $60 million per year, and with white shoppers moving out to new shopping centers, the black shoppers were highly valued. The streets and stores were now empty, with one merchant saying he could "roll a bowling ball down Church Street and not hit anybody."[55] A way out was needed on all sides.

Highlander Folk School Workshop

Meanwhile, on April 1, 1960, a student workshop on the topic "The New Generation Fights for Equality" was held at the Highlander Folk School in Monteagle, Tennessee. This school, founded in the 1930s and committed to improving the lives of people in the South, focused at first on labor organizing, then on literacy, and then on civil rights. At this meeting half of the seventy students attending were black out of a total of eighty-two participants. The largest contingent of those was the battle-hardened veterans of the Nashville sit-in movement. Though the philosophy of nonviolence was difficult to grasp by those from elsewhere, the Nashville students made their case that it was a way of life and not just a tactic or technique. Still a committee, in an attempt to capture the philosophy, constructed a statement that was phrased in exactly the opposite way from Lawson's teachings. It said, "We believe in democracy. We are Americans seeking our rights. We want to do something. We are using nonviolence as a method, but not necessarily as a total way of life. We believe it is practical."[56]

In the next few days, discussions were held regarding the participation of whites in sit-ins and the variations being held across the country, such as "swim-ins" in Saint Louis. The groups also discussed Lawson's removal from Vanderbilt University and what that meant to the future of the movement. A significant amount of time was spent in discussions about the relationships between established adult civil rights leaders and their organizations that counseled legal approaches to desegregation and the young students who wanted immediate action.[57] The two white-owned Nashville newspapers reported on the Highlander meeting with virtually the same story, except that the *Banner* referred to the school as a "controversial interracial folk school."[58]

Indeed Highlander had been and continued to be controversial. The fact that Martin Luther King Jr. and Rosa Parks had both visited there made it suspect, especially to J. Edgar Hoover and his Federal Bureau of Investigation. The FBI "vault" contains nineteen files holding hundreds of documents on the Highlander School alone. One example, a newspaper article from the *Atlanta Journal-Constitution,* seemed designed to paint Highlander as a training school for communists. Calling Highlander a "race-mixing center" engaging in the "same field" as the Communist Party, the article gave details of a report by a "Georgia Commission set up to preserve segregation." The report concluded that "persons connected with Highlander were connected with those labeled as 'communist fronts' by the House Un-American Activities Committee." In response Miles Horton, founder and director of Highlander, said that "they [communists] say they're interested in social equality. We're interested in social equality," and let it go at that.[59]

Partial Integration/Partial Segregation

On April 5 the students came home from Highlander to the news that the mayor's biracial committee had decided to accept a proposal from the downtown business owners. They agreed to "serve blacks separately in designated sections of the formerly whites-only restaurants" for a three-month trial period. As Lewis points out, this was a return to the "separate but equal" doctrine that had been ended in 1954 with the *Brown v. Board of Education* Supreme Court decision. He wondered why they could not see "that this was not about sandwiches and salads. It was not about being allowed to sit separately at a counter. It was about nothing less than being treated exactly the same as the white people with whom we shared citizenship in this country."[60]

To make matters worse for the students' morale, on April 6 Thurgood Marshall, counsel to the NAACP and one day to become the first black Supreme Court justice, told an audience of four thousand at Fisk University that they should not stay in jail but should do what "the black power structure" had been doing all along: rely on the courts.[61] To Lewis this was one of those "times in history . . . when more immediate, more dramatic means are called for, when the people themselves must be asked to put their own bodies and hearts and spirits on the line."[62] John Seigenthaler agreed. He said, "Thurgood Marshall, good man that he was, put his reliance in the courts, but without the movement, we would still be in court to this day."[63]

Shaw University Conference

With sit-ins resumed, John Lewis remained in Nashville while Diane Nash, Bernard LaFayette, Marion Barry, and James Lawson attended a conference at Shaw University in Raleigh, North Carolina, which had been organized by Ella Baker of the Southern Christian Leadership Conference. With advice from Lawson and Baker about the need for student-led action rather than the more conservative path of reliance on laws and courts, the students at this conference formed an organization titled the "Continuations Committee," which was quickly changed to the Student Nonviolent Coordinating Committee, SNCC for short, commonly pronouced "Snick."[64]

A Bomb, a March, and a Counter

The Sunday night of the students' return from Raleigh marked the end of the first round of sit-ins in Nashville. Early Monday morning a bomb was thrown that destroyed much of Alexander Looby's home. Fortunately the family was not harmed, but a powerful message had been sent that required a powerful response. As word spread, students began to gather at Tennessee State University for an eerily silent march, gathering more marchers as they passed by Fisk University and American Baptist College and on to City Hall. Estimates range from two thousand to five thousand, but the Legislative Plaza was packed once they reached Mayor Ben West on the steps of City Hall. March leaders had sent him a telegram, so he was prepared for the confrontation.[65]

As the mayor began speaking, C. T. Vivian interrupted him with an indictment of his leadership. The mayor argued that he had no control over lunch counters, except for the one at the airport, which was desegregated. Vivian said that he went to the airport not to eat lunch but only to fly, and that the mayor had not desegregated it, the federal government had. Seigenthaler claimed that Vivian's tone was "not uncivil, but was very assertive."[66] As the argument heightened, Nash stepped in to ask a few questions. She asked if the mayor would use the prestige of his office to appeal to the citizens to stop racial discrimination, to which he said, "I appeal to all citizens to end discrimination, to have no bigotry, no bias, no hatred." She then asked about the moral rightness of segregation. When the mayor agreed that it seemed not morally right and that he recommended that the lunch counters be desegregated, that became the next day's headline in the *Tennessean*: INTEGRATE COUNTERS—MAYOR.[67] James Lawson praised the mayor, saying that he was a "moderate and had the courage to say so." Reverend King arrived that night and proclaimed Nashville is a "model movement" that had "carved a tunnel of hope through the great mountain of despair."[68] The way out had been found, at least temporarily, as the civil rights movement would continue for the next four years to integrate other establishments such as movie theaters with "stand-ins" and hotels with "sleep-ins."

Role of the Media

Both CBS and NBC television networks came to Nashville to film documentaries on the sit-in movement and used some footage from the workshop role-plays to dramatize the preparations. When the sit-ins began in earnest, they filmed the brutality as it happened. NBC's *White Paper*, broadcast on December 20, 1960, with Chet Huntley as narrator, was able to show both the "shame and glory" of Nashville, the "Athens of the South," counterposed against segregation signs posted throughout the city. Mayor West described the city as having "small townish ways." A young woman insisted that it violated her civil rights if "Negroes must be served." A white man said that "breaking bread is a family custom—almost a sacrament," that should not be interrupted. Once the economic boycott took hold, Huntley said, "You could see the city slowly destroying itself." After the bombing of Looby's home, West said, "I had to act. I felt outraged along with them. The thinking majority of white people were outraged, too." Nashville's successful integration of lunch counters marked a turning point, Huntley said, since it was the first city in the South to allow whites and blacks to sit together.[69] Both the NBC documentary and a CBS documentary that was similarly structured and narrated by Douglas Edwards brought national attention to desegregation campaigns in the South. Tennessee's governor, Buford Ellington, outraged by the news coverage, blustered to reporters that "these sit-ins are instigated and planned by and staged for the convenience of the Columbia Broadcasting System."[70]

The two white city newspapers took many different approaches to the sit-in movement and civil rights issues themselves. According to John Seigenthaler, the *Nashville Banner,* for instance, published oppositional pieces from both the ministers of the more prominent white churches, who "couched arguments in philosophical and Biblical terms," and from the ministers of white working-class churches, who used "almost racist language." Seigenthaler explained that the *Tennessean*'s coverage was "not slanted, but provoked questions." The publisher of his paper assigned a team to cover the civil rights issue. Wallace Westfeldt covered Vanderbilt Divinity School, David Halberstam was "on the street," where he had a "great line of communication with Kelly Miller Smith and James Lawson," and Seigenthaler "covered the City Desk."[71] As noted above, James Stahlman of the *Nashville Banner* made the motion to have Lawson dismissed from Vanderbilt University.

When asked about editorials during the sit-ins, Seigenthaler said that the *Tennessean* did editorialize but that they were not "dripping with hearts and flowers." He said, "We pointed out that *Brown v. Board of Education* was the law of the land and that separate but equal was defeated. We ran moderate editorials, called on the public to end the assaults on those sitting-in, but we never called for an end to the sit-ins. We suggested that the police do their duty and that the arrests and imprisonment of the kids were uncalled for." He said they received outraged phone calls and as the one assigned to the city desk, he took the calls. One call in particular was memorable. "A lady gave us hell for 'kowtowing' to these kids, these troublemakers, but when I said, 'Pardon me lady, are you black or white?' she slammed down the phone."[72]

The *Nashville Globe and Independent,* a weekly black-owned newspaper that referred to itself as a a "Progressive Journal of the New South," had called for "advocates of integration to possess themselves with patience" and to seek "the very best of the advice" from established leaders "rather than make a frontal attack upon the enemies of integration" in an editorial published a few months before the sit-ins began but nearly a year after the start of Lawson's workshops.[73]

Just after the test sit-ins, the paper briefly noted that members of a group, the Nashville Christian Leadership Conference, were seeking to desegregate restrooms and restaurants in Harvey's and Cain-Sloan department stores.[74] One week later the newspaper praised Thurgood Marshall, director and counsel of the NAACP Legal Defense and Education Fund, for his support of "effective leaders" who had yielded to "'token' school integration."[75]

On March 4, just after the sit-in students were attacked by a white mob on February 27, arrested, and then brought before a judge on trespassing charges, the newspaper finally came around to their side, although it labeled them "militant" in a headline. The article noted that the students were "not dismayed by these attacks and arrests. As soon as one bunch was hustled out, another would come in to take their places. At the city jail, the students were smiling, singing, and praying."[76] In a second article, the newspaper praised the students as "well organized and well disciplined."[77] In an editorial on the same day, the newspaper called the actions of the police who arrested no whites a "mockery of democracy," a "miscarriage of justice," and a "flagrant disregard for human dignity." The writer was "dumbfounded, confused, and [could] hardly realize" that these actions "could happen in Nashville, the so-called Athens of the South."[78]

Analysis of the Nashville Sit-Ins

These materials could be analyzed in any number of ways. However David Zarefsky urges scholars to avoid standard approaches but instead to "illumine the text."[79] The text here consists of episodes from American history, of young people veering off the well-worn path so patiently trudged along by their ancestors and their elders and striking out for parts unknown. Perhaps the best way to examine these events is through the lens of the rhetorical tradition, since their goals had persuasion at their heart. In many instances, as noted, they faced disapproval from members of the African American community, who counseled patience and reliance on courts rather than direct action. Such disapproval may have been even more distressing than the snarls and vitriol from the white community, yet they never wavered.

Looking at this cast of characters scattered along a treacherous timeline causes one to ask questions: How did they expect success in the face of such prejudice and such caution? What made them think it would work? Why did it work? The paradox here, as John Seigenthaler pointed out, is that "nonviolence is countercultural in a violent society such as ours." Despite that truism, he said that "it only could work with the commitment to nonviolence. There were not enough guns or clubs in the hands of these kids to have worked. But as they said, nonviolence became a weapon."[80]

Rhetorical Invention and Advocacy

If we look for rhetorical answers, we must perceive rhetorical invention not as a search for persuasive arguments by a single orator, as conceived in ancient times by Cicero. Instead invention must be acknowledged as a social construction in which groups of people discuss issues and devise strategies to achieve social goals. During these deliberations they bring up their life experiences as evidence, they collaborate to find solutions, and along the way they create an identity that reinforces solidarity.[81]

The time spent together in Nashville's church basements, in debriefing sessions after the sit-ins, in workshops at the Highlander School, and in the city jail gave opportunities for trying out ideas, accepting the ones that worked, and rejecting those that failed. By the time the February sit-ins occurred amid violence and intimidation, these students had acquired the discipline necessary to persist as they sought nonviolence as a way of life. They knew what to do when Looby's house was bombed, although their potent silent march through the city could not have been planned.

So what did these students invent that was unique to the civil rights movement? Although they did not invent nonviolence as a political tool, they overwhelmingly embraced the concept and practiced it faithfully. Their code of conduct, their lists of dos and don'ts, all reflected nonviolence. Their use of collaboration and shared leadership, their commitment to civility in the face of determined incivility, their decision to sit-in in waves and simply replace one another at the lunch counters and then the jail, their choice of "jail over bail" all represent the Nashville model.

Rhetorical advocacy comes in many forms, such as public relations, issue management, and image management.[82] Here, to reach not only the immediate goal of integration of Nashville's lunch counters but also a long-held wish for a change in attitudes, a first step had to be a change of image. As John Lewis noted, they wanted to be accorded the simple human freedom to eat a meal in dignity as other citizens could do. In the background loomed persistent attitudes of racial inferiority linked with white privilege that had been a part of southern society since the days of slavery. These attitudes had resulted in the "taken-for-granted cultural practice" of segregation that the students needed to "interrupt."[83]

To achieve the goal of persuading white Nashville to see them differently, their first invention was a dress code. Looking nothing like today's college students in cut-offs and tank tops, or even yesterday's hippies adorned with long hair and love beads, these students dressed in their best clothes. Lewis is shown in every photograph wearing a trench coat over a suit. Their rules of behavior, their lists of ways to behave while sitting in, their insistence that everyone bring schoolwork to do and that they not laugh or nap at the lunch counter all added to their image as serious and well-behaved young people. Their speech was invariably polite. Even on the morning of the bombing of their attorney's home, Nash spoke assertively but not aggressively to the mayor.

Of course the combination of philosophy and economics changed many minds. The merchants' tills were emptying day by day, and no amount of hatred or brutality would bring back the flow of profits. Only when the white shoppers could feel safe coming back downtown and the black shoppers were welcomed would the deadlock end. The sound of thousands of feet marching toward a showdown became too loud for Mayor West to bear, so he provided the excuse for desegregation to begin. The old displays of intimidation no longer worked to stop this group of young activists who willingly put themselves in harm's way in the name of justice.

The group from Nashville soon faced worse violence as they volunteered to restart the Freedom Rides that had been discontinued when the first bus was firebombed in Anniston, Alabama, and the second was stopped in Birmingham and the riders beaten. Seigenthaler himself soon became part of the scene as the assistant to Attorney General Robert Kennedy, who sent him to Montgomery, Alabama, to observe the arrival of the Freedom Riders in that city. There he was beaten unconscious along with the riders for trying to help two of the women escape the mob that awaited them. These events helped involve the federal government in the civil rights struggle, though years would pass before concrete change could be claimed in the South.

What can be said about the achievements of the students who sat in in Nashville? Their recognition by Reverend King as having created a model movement speaks for itself. They illustrated the worth of training, discipline, and planning. They practiced shared leadership. The fact that more than one of them was able to practice the leadership skills they were learning enhanced the organizations, such as the Nashville Student Movement, the Nashville Christian Leadership Conference, the Southern Christian Leadership Conference, and certainly the Student Nonviolent Coordinating Committee, that they served at that time and far into the future. According to Lewis, they had "a circle of trust—we were a true band of brothers and sisters in Nashville."[84] Each of these leaders continued the commitment to civil rights throughout their lives, and James Lawson even received an apology from and was awarded a distinguished professorship at Vanderbilt University, the school that expelled him. These students may have helped create, if even for a short time they were together, the Beloved Community that was so vital a part of the nonviolent philosophy.

Notes

1. Lewis, Hoover interview.
2. Lewis, *Walking with the Wind,* 74.
3. Lewis, *Walking with the Wind,* 74–75.
4. Lawson, "Lunch Counter Sit-Ins in Nashville."
5. Ibid.
6. Ibid.
7. Lawson, Barnes interview.
8. Lawson, "Lunch Counter Sit-Ins in Nashville."
9. Seigenthaler, Hoover interview. 23 August 2012. Transcript available from Judith Hoover.
10. Nash, Smiley interview.
11. Lee, "Nashville Civil Rights Movement," 135–37.
12. Lewis, *Walking with the Wind,* 75–76.
13. Lewis, *Walking with the Wind,* 76–77.
14. Lewis, "Acceptance Speech."
15. Lewis, *Walking with the Wind,* 85.
16. Lewis, Hoover interview.
17. *Nashville: We Were Warriors.*
18. Lewis, *Walking with the Wind,* 91.
19. *Anatomy of a Demonstration.*
20. Lewis, *Walking with the Wind,* 85.
21. Lewis, *Walking with the Wind,* 85–86.
22. Ibid., 86–88.
23. Ibid., 88–89.
24. Ibid., 91.
25. Nash, "She's the One to Get."
26. Powell, Bennett interview.
27. Lewis, *Walking with the Wind,* 93.
28. Ibid., 94.
29. Lewis, Hoover interview.
30. Lewis, *Walking with the Wind,* 94–96.
31. Lawson, "Lunch Counter Sit-Ins in Nashville."
32. Lewis, *Walking with the Wind,* 96.
33. Ibid., 97.
34. Ibid., 97–98.
35. Ibid., 98; "Rules . . . That Led to Jail."
36. "Sit-In Halt Advisable."
37. Talley, "75 Students Arrested Here."
38. Lawson, Warren interview.
39. Lewis, *Walking with the Wind,* 100–102.
40. Ibid., 99–103.
41. Halberstam, "Fifth Avenue Tense as Rumors Fly."
42. "Mayor Names Biracial Group to Seek Peace."
43. "Sit-In Halt Advisable."
44. Halberstam, "Negroes Served at Bus Terminal."
45. "Ministers Urge Lunch Freedom."

46. Ibid.

47. "Ohio College to Aid Sitters."

48. "Ministers Urge Lunch Freedom."

49. Lewis, *Walking with the Wind*, 104.

50. Seigenthaler, Hoover interview.

51. "Vanderbilt University Group Urges Race Tolerance."

52. Seigenthaler, Hoover interview.

53. "Federation for Constitutional Government Issues Statement."

54. Seigenthaler, Hoover interview.

55. Lewis, *Walking with the Wind*, 105–6.

56. Glen, *Highlander*, 146–47.

57. Highlander Folk School Audio Archives.

58. "Highlander Delegates Propose Expanded Desegregation Drive."

59. Nelson, "Race-Mixing Center Under Fire."

60. Lewis, *Walking with the Wind*, 106.

61. "NAACP Backing Them, Sitters Told."

62. Lewis, *Walking with the Wind*, 107.

63. Seigenthaler, Hoover interview.

64. Lewis, *Walking with the Wind*, 107–8.

65. Seigenthaler, Hoover interview.

66. Ibid.

67. Lewis, *Walking with the Wind*, 109–10.

68. Lawson, Conversation with James Lawson."

69. "Sit-In Halt Advisable."

70. Lewis, *Walking with the Wind*, 105.

71. Seigenthaler, Hoover interview.

72. Ibid.

73. "The Best Strategy." *Nashville Globe and Independent*, 21 August 1959.

74. "Local Group Seeks Non-Segregated Facilities in Downtown Stores."

75. "Thurgood Marshall Hails Progress."

76. "Nashville Citizens Rally to Efforts of Militant Students."

77. "Editorial: A Mockery of Democracy."

78. "79 Abused Arrested in Downtown Stores."

79. Zarefsky, "Interdisciplinary Perspectives on Rhetorical Criticism," 385.

80. Seigenthaler, Hoover interview.

81. See Murphy, "Civil Society"; Hauser, *Vernacular Voices*.

82. See Hoover, *Corporate Advocacy*, 3.

83. See Farrell, *Norms of Rhetorical Culture*, 258.

84. Lewis, Hoover interview.

2

CONFLAGRATION

The Spread of the Sit-Ins across the South

In her fascinating study of the Student Nonviolent Coordinating Committee, Wesley C. Hogan notes that

> in an orderly and logical world, the great wave of student sit-ins that washed across the South early in 1960 should have flowed outward from Nashville. They did not, of course. The source of the momentous sit-ins was Greensboro, North Carolina, and the students were from North Carolina A&T State University—not Fisk, or American Baptist, or Meharry. Though the Nashville students had planned to start their sit-in in January 1960, [James] Lawson recalled that they "lolly-lagged" and had trouble getting back together after the Christmas break. Lawson himself had been preoccupied with final exams and traveling for the Fellowship of Reconciliation. "February 1 [1960] happened, and woke us up."[1]

As the foregoing section reveals, Nashville was by no means as given a starting point as Hogan suggests, but she is right to note that Greensboro's sit-ins, unlike those before, ignited something unpredicted and unprecedented. Greensboro fired not only James Lawson and his Nashville students but also, in such rapid succession that exact numbers are lacking, students across North Carolina, then those in Virginia, South Carolina, Tennessee, Maryland, Kentucky, Alabama, and beyond. By mid-April the movement had reached the last southern state, Mississippi.[2]

Estimates of sit-in activism in the period range from fifty thousand[3] to seventy thousand participants in at least 150 communities across all of the southern states.[4] Participants were predominantly young high school and college students and often were new to direct-action protest. Their sudden activity, as Lynne Olson makes clear, "caught the country completely by surprise." She suggests that

> American college students, for the most part, were seen as politically apathetic, interested more in the material trappings of success than in changing the world. That was as true for black students as for white, with most black schools encouraging their students to conform to the values of white society, to aspire to middle-class respectability. Many African-American students in the late 1950s and early 1960s represented the first generation of their families to go to college, and their attendance often came as a result of great sacrifice by their parents. Theirs was a generation with the potential

to become doctors and lawyers and professors, so when they sat in at local lunch counters, when they risked arrest and expulsion from school, they were also putting their futures at risk—the futures in which their parents had invested so much.[5]

Throughout the first year of the sit-in movement, students added considerably to the twin themes of sacrifice and risk: their determination, perseverance, and endurance were frequently noted in the regional and national press, and their stoicism and general (though not universal) commitment to nonviolence gained them important though distant allies.[6]

Taking the risk paid off in other ways as well, ways almost no one could have foreseen. The most obvious of these were the U.S. Supreme Court and other federal court decisions that arose out of the sit-ins, as well as the shape and content of the Civil Rights Act of 1964 and the Voting Rights Act of 1965.[7] There were also ill-defined but nonetheless important psychological gains, as Clayborne Carson has observed. Carson notes how student leaders became, over the course of the sit-ins, "increasingly self-confident, able, and resourceful," able to "initiate a social struggle without the guidance of older black leaders."[8] This self-confidence and resourcefulness, in turn, led to important developments in the larger civil rights movement. Sit-in successes (and sometimes even failures) galvanized others into activism, swelling the ranks of direct-action protests as never before. As activist Anne Braden put it, "The sit-ins brought back the life-blood of citizen participation that had been scared out of our parents by the witch hunts and McCarthyism."[9] Increased activism found its voice in new organizations. Most notable of these was, of course, the Student Nonviolent Coordinating Committee, which gave students a voice independent from the NAACP, Martin Luther King's Southern Christian Leadership Conference, and CORE, more established civil rights groups with an older cadre of leaders. Moreover the sit-ins facilitated the emergence of women leaders such as Diane Nash, who continued in very visible leadership capacities through the Freedom Rides of 1961, the Birmingham, Alabama, desegregation campaign of 1963, and the Selma, Alabama, voting rights campaign of 1965,[10] as well as those who laid the foundations of second-wave feminism, including Casey Hayden, Mary King, and Bernice Reagon.[11]

Largely unnoticed, however, were the profound changes in the very nature of protest. Andrew Lewis gets closest to them when he notes that the sit-ins rewrote the rules of protest, arguing that they "represented a profound ideological shift" in that they were deeply "democratic and egalitarian."[12] He is right that the sit-ins did not rely on elites—and in most cases relied on the "common person" as protester—and were anything but centralized. There was more to it, however, and the authors in this section, as did those in part 1, highlight the markedly rhetorical aspects of the sit-ins. Rhetoric, as the late Michael Leff taught, is always radically situated, recognizing the distinct and sometimes unique aspects of (in these cases) each segregated community, each clan of diehard segregationists, each town's local and regional media, and each region's religious, political, legal, and economic rituals of racism.[13] As the essays in this section continue to illustrate, the sit-ins crafted new pedagogies for nonverbal rhetorical action; took widely accepted tactics and strategies and adapted them to particular circumstances and situations; created stunning visual images juxtaposing calm, peaceful, youthful bodies with the brutal physical violence against them; massaged media coverage and helped extend that coverage far beyond the South; and used the very spaces and places they were denied to fashion the vast and sweeping fires of change.

Notes

1. Hogan, *Many Minds, One Heart*, 26–27.

2. On this succession see especially Carson, *In Struggle*, 9–11.

3. See Lewis, *The Shadows of Youth*, 65; Olson, *Freedom's Daughters*, 147. See also Southern Regional Council, "Special Report: Student Protest Movement, Winter, 1960."

4. Farber and Bailey, *Columbia Guide to America*, 16; Fairclough, *Better Day Coming*, 242.

5. Olson, *Freedom's Daughters*, 147–48. But cf. Chafe, *Civilities and Civil Rights*, 98, for an argument that the Greensboro sit-in was a "dramatic extension of, rather than a departure from, traditional patterns of black activism in Greensboro."

6. See, e.g., Sitton, "Negro Sitdowns Disquiet South"; Halberstam, "Good City Gone Ugly"; and Salisbury, "Fear and Hatred Grip Birmingham."

7. See our discussion of these in the introduction to part 3, "Embers," nn. 1, 2, and 7.

8. Carson, *In Struggle*, 17–18.

9. Qtd. in Olson, *Freedom's Daughters*, 33.

10. A good biography of Diane Nash has yet to be written. The brief chronology of Nash's many civil rights campaigns comes from a personal conversation with Sean Patrick O'Rourke in Greenville, South Carolina, on 29 January 2013.

11. Olson makes these connections in *Freedom's Daughters*, 231–34.

12. Lewis, *Shadows of Youth*, 65.

13. Leff states, "So also is rhetoric a universal activity that finds its habitation only in the particular." See Leff, "Habitation of Rhetoric," 160. See also de Velasco, Campbell, and Henry's introduction in the same volume (*Rethinking Rhetorical Theory, Criticism, and Pedagogy*), ix.

READING BODIES, READING BOOKS

A Rhetorical History of the 1960 Greenville, South Carolina, Sit-Ins

Sean Patrick O'Rourke

Many of the sit-ins that occurred after the Greensboro, North Carolina, protests of February 1, 1960, followed the pattern of college students targeting segregated lunch counters. Always and everywhere at considerable risk when protesting segregation, college students, especially those studying away from home, nonetheless risked fewer reprisals against family members when they protested. And lunch counters were, after all, some of the most visible sites of segregation, for they highlighted the egregious inequities of the system: black customers were welcome to shop in the store but were not allowed to dine with other customers. Shopping, it seemed, was impersonal (and profitable) enough to tolerate a black presence, but the communal act of breaking bread was too intimate, too tied to friendship and family and home, to be done together. Blacks who wanted to eat out were required to do so "out back," away from white customers and public scrutiny.

In Greenville, South Carolina, however, the pattern did not hold. The sit-in movement there began with ministers and high school students and focused its initial attention on the public airport and library, gradually expanding to include lunch counters, churches, swimming pools, skating rinks, and more. It was the result of a combined, multigenerational effort of students and teachers, congregants and ministers, protesters and lawyers, reporters and photographers. Greenville's sit-in movement traced a dynamic, multifaceted rhetorical trajectory, one that arced across nearly three years and moved against a long-standing culture—with all that the term implies—of segregated cohabitation.

To say that it was multifaceted is to suggest that a protest movement, like a rhetorical text, can exhibit what Edwin Black some years ago called "prismatic" qualities,[1] offering those who engage it a complex, many-sided, multimodal persuasive appeal, a type of appeal long recognized as a central characteristic of rhetoric in controversy.[2] In practice and over time, a movement provides a *multiplex ratio*—a constellation of many reasons—for change, and the "reasons" proffered to desegregate Greenville were both verbal and kinetic: traditional speech and somatic rhetoric. To say that the movement had a "rhetorical trajectory" is to suggest that the Greenville sit-in movement is open to study from the perspective of rhetorical history generally[3] and as a complex of strategic rhetorical adaptations over time to "a series of rhetorical problems," fluid, multiple, and mutable "situations that call[ed] for public persuasion to advance a cause or overcome an impasse" more specifically.[4] Examining the rhetorical trajectory of the Greenville sit-ins by attending to the prismatic qualities of the movement reveals that it was no mere copycat protest but rather an organic, homegrown rhetorical movement in constant, considered flux as it adapted to changing conditions over the course of its existence.

I begin by considering Greenville's culture of segregation as the 1950s became the 1960s, with special attention to the physical and rhetorical construction of an apartheid city under the guise of harmony. I then look at four phases of the movement: the initial march and stand-in at the airport on the first day of 1960, the library sit-ins of March and July of that same year, the expansion of protests to lunch counters, churches, swimming pools, and skating rinks as the movement developed, and finally the culmination of protest efforts in the courts. I conclude with a few thoughts on Greenville's sit-in movement and some larger issues the study raises.

Greenville's Culture of Segregation

Greenville, the third-largest metropolitan area in South Carolina, is an old textile town located in the Upstate, fifty-five miles south of the North Carolina border, now on the I-85 corridor and Amtrak line between Atlanta and Charlotte. In the wake of the Supreme Court's decisions in *Brown v. Board of Education* (consolidating four separate cases, one of which, *Briggs v. Elliott,* was on appeal from South Carolina),[5] *Life* magazine ran a series of articles on race relations in five southern cities. Greenville was featured in the September 17, 1956, issue, in which Mayor Kenneth Cass claimed that "there's always been a good feeling in the race situation" in Greenville and predicted that the good relations between blacks and whites would remain unless an outside agitator "comes in and stirs it up."[6] The truth, however, was that these three themes, good relations, minimal local discontent, and outside agitation, were a thin veneer, a stable and useful cover of what was, physically and rhetorically, a thoroughly segregated city.

Like other southern cities in 1959, Greenville was still physically segregated in almost every conceivable way. Public transportation, swimming pools, skating rinks, bathrooms, drinking fountains, libraries, and schools were all segregated by race, as were the lunch counters on Main (and every other) Street and the waiting rooms in the bus and train stations. Even institutions founded and nurtured by the black community—such as the Phillis Wheatley Association, a community center founded in 1919, and the Sterling Industrial School, a "Negro" school founded in 1902—were eventually taken over by the white establishment and, ironically in light of today's dominant southern political ideology, converted from private centers of black empowerment to white-controlled public or quasi-public institutions.[7]

Segregation was rigorously enforced by city, county, and state law enforcement officials and, equally important, by a structure of extralegal organizations. Most notorious of these was the Ku Klux Klan. Organized regionally just after the Civil War, the KKK terrorized black citizens—especially black voters—during Reconstruction but disbanded in the 1870s, only to rise for a "second coming" in the 1920s.[8] In Upstate South Carolina, the KKK was especially strong, often "aiding" police in their investigations and aggressively and sometimes brutally opposing labor organizers, voter registration drives, and individual black citizens it thought posed a danger.[9] The threat and reality of physical violence was a fact of life for black citizens of Greenville in the middle of the twentieth century. The city saw five lynchings between 1905 and 1933, and the 1947 lynching of Willie Earle received international notoriety.[10]

In many ways more powerful than the KKK, South Carolina's version of the White Citizens' Council, the South Carolina Segregation Committee (known informally as the Gressette Committee after the group's chair, Marion Gressette), sought to lead and control the effort to maintain segregation. Comprising white business, civic, and political leaders from across the state, the Gressette Committee warned, as Steve O'Neill has noted, of the bad press the KKK could give to segregation and sought to maintain the long-standing culture of segregated cohabitation by putting a professional face on it, one that spoke of racial harmony, prosperity, and cooperation.[11]

Greenville's physical segregation was buttressed by a more nuanced rhetorical segregation. The rhetoric of segregation drew upon debunked scientific theories of racial inferiority, Jim Crow–era constitutional interpretations of the Fourteenth Amendment, and fundamentalist readings of the Bible to propagate an "intellectual" opposition to desegregation. This rhetoric was potent and pervasive.[12]

The South produced a series of books in the mid-twentieth century that, taken together, perpetrated this cult of segregation. The more anthropological of these were only one small step removed from their intellectual forebears, works such as Samuel Morton's *Crania Americana* (1839) and Samuel Cartwright's "Diseases and Peculiarities of the Negro Race" (1851).[13] In their popular books, Stuart Landry (1945) and Theodore Bilbo (1946) refurbished these antebellum racial theories to stress the intellectual and ethical inferiority of blacks for a New South eager to continue to justify segregation.[14] Similarly Tom Brady's *Black Monday* (1955)[15] and the congressional "Southern Manifesto" (1956) used the constitutional theories of the Jim Crow era to attack the Supreme Court's 1954 *Brown* decision as unwarranted judicial activism at best and social engineering wrapped in a judicial coup at worst.[16]

This segregationist thought was aggressively supported and disseminated by local Greenville media, especially the rhetorical efforts of Wayne C. Freeman and William D. Workman Jr. of the *Greenville News*. Freeman was editor of the *News* and also served as an officer of the Gressette Committee. Over the course of several years, he wrote editorials defending segregation "as morally right, legally right, and necessary for the preservation of peace and good order."[17] Workman was the *News*'s political correspondent in Columbia, who also wrote for Charleston's *Post and Courier* and Columbia's *The State* and who published the segregationist *The Case for the South* in 1960.[18] Their efforts served to embed the themes of good relations, minimal local discontent, and outside agitation into the media's coverage of civil rights protests and to wrap them in what Jennifer E. M. Hill has identified as a frame of "victimage"—the notion that somehow the South was a victim of the slander, discrimination, and violence of northern integrationists and their southern stooges.[19]

The secular media, however, were not alone. Equally powerful were the voices of the fundamentalist Protestant churches and schools. Known locally as the "Buckle of the Bible Belt," Greenville boasted numerous Christian churches in 1959 and had become home to Bob Jones University in 1947 and nearby North Greenville Junior College in 1950, two conservative Christian universities. Conservative white ministers preached a gospel of segregation, rooting their views in Old and New Testament accounts of slavery, race, and Christian duty. Perhaps most influential of these was Bob Jones, founder of the university bearing his name. On April 17, 1960, he delivered a radio address titled "Is Segregation Scriptural?" and published a pamphlet version of it shortly thereafter.[20] Speaking to and for "Bible-believing Christians," Jones argued forcefully in favor of segregation just after the Greenville sit-in movement had begun in earnest. In strikingly contradictory terms, Jones acknowledged that "no race is inferior in the will of God" and yet claimed that segregation was God's "established order" and that desegregation, an effort to "run over God's plan and God's established order," would cause only "trouble."[21] Similar arguments are evident in the contemporaneous *Essays on Segregation,* a slim volume of seven essays by white, southern Protestant preachers, including four from the Carolinas.[22]

The culture of segregation presented civil rights activists with enormous challenges. That culture said that segregation led to good relations and minimal discontent, while desegregation was evidence of outside agitation. Segregation was law and order; desegregation was illegal disruption of that order. Segregation was natural and scientifically justified; desegregation went against science and the natural order. Segregation was Christian for it was God's will; desegregation was unchristian and defied God's will. And in 1959 defiance of that culture brought punishment: lynchings were well within living memory, and protesters bucking the segregationist white power structure in the Cold War–era South risked loss of jobs, denial of credit, and the noxious labels of "communist" and "socialist."[23] Opposing the segregated South was dangerous business, and civil rights advocates therefore had to invent rhetorical strategies that countered the racist claims of intellectual and ethical inferiority, placed them and not segregationists on the side of good relations, made segregationists instigators of local discontent, and contrasted black Christian virtue with white Christian hypocrisy.[24]

Ministers at the Airport

"Beginnings" are usually elusive, of course, but Greenville's public civil rights protests began on January 1, 1960, and focused on the city's segregated public facilities.[25] They were prompted by the arrival of two visitors in February and October 1959. The February visitor was Richard Henry, a civilian Air Force employee from Michigan who sought to fly out of Greenville's downtown airport. When he entered the airport, he was told that he had to sit in the "Negro" waiting room, a room less comfortable and more poorly appointed than the "white" waiting room. When Henry complained, he was told he could fly out of another airport if he wanted to. Henry filed complaints with the U.S. Air Force, the national NAACP, and local airport authorities. With the help of the NAACP Legal Defense fund, he filed suit in federal court, claiming discrimination and denial of the equal protection of law guaranteed by the Fourteenth Amendment.[26] Little was done locally, however, before the second visitor arrived in October.

On October 25, 1959, as Henry's case was making its way through the federal court system, Jackie Robinson, Major League Baseball's first black player, flew into Greenville to address a meeting of the South Carolina NAACP. A small group including Robinson's colleague Gloster Current and local black leaders Willie T. Smith Jr., Rev. H. P. Sharper, and Billie Fleming waited to greet him. They were told to leave the white waiting room. Later that day Robinson returned to the airport to fly home, and once again he and his companions (among them the Reverend and Mrs. James S. Hall) were harassed by airport officials and threatened with arrest. This time, however, Robinson was accompanied by a contingent of Greenville's most prominent black civic leaders, including the local NAACP president, several ministers, and at least one lawyer. Robinson himself was well connected, and he fired off two letters to Thurgood Marshall, urging the NAACP Legal Defense team to take action.[27]

Marshall refused on the grounds that the issue was already in the courts (Richard Henry's case) and another action would be redundant and therefore a waste of limited resources. For the local black community, Greenville's segregated municipal airport had long been a sore spot. All too often national and international visitors' first impression of their community was of the airport's segregated waiting rooms, visible reminders of Greenville's flagrant disregard for the Supreme Court's 1954 declaration that "separate is inherently unequal" and the Court's 1955 order to desegregate with "all deliberate speed." Such contempt was all the more maddening because the U.S. Constitution gives the federal government, not state or local officials, clear authority over interstate commerce.[28] Embarrassed by the Robinson incident and upset by the lack of progress, Greenville's black leaders decided to act. They organized a protest march and prayer vigil on Emancipation Day, January 1, 1960.

In Greenville it was the pebble that started an avalanche, the trickle that became a flood. The march and prayer vigil were the first organized, overtly public acts of Greenville's civil rights movement. Organizers and participants indicate that the march included between 1,000 and 1,500 marchers, who drove cars and then trudged in a bitingly cold, icy sleet and rain from Springfield Baptist Church downtown out to the airport.[29] The Reverend Hall called their march a "prayer pilgrimage." Outside the terminal the group sang "America" as fifteen of them, led by Hall, entered the airport. The Reverend H. P. Sharper of Florence asked for blessings on "our friends" and "mercy on our enemies" and prayed "that history might be made here." The Reverend Matthew D. McCullough of Orangeburg read a five-point resolution condemning "the stigma, the inconvenience, and the stupidity of racial segregation," a system that made blacks "second-class citizens." He urged that no one should acquiesce to the "degradations" of "Southern tradition" or be satisfied with the mere "crumbs of citizenship." The resolution characterized the march as "an expression of patriotism" and declared that "with faith in this nation and its God we shall not relent, we shall not rest, we shall not compromise, we shall not be satisfied until every vestige of racial discrimination and segregation has been eliminated from all aspects of public life."[30]

A close reading of the words of the airport protest indicates a keen attentiveness to the dynamics of Greenville's culture of segregation. The singing of Rev. Samuel F. Smith's "America," one of the oldest hymns in the American songbook and one that, in the 1950s, was considered less edgy than Woody Guthrie's "This Land Is Your Land," invited listeners to see the protest less as a radical event and more as an attempt to reclaim a right due to all Americans. The description of the event as a "prayer pilgrimage" and the opening Christian prayer inoculated against charges of anti-Christian protest, and the call for "blessings" and "mercies" countered the good relations trope of segregationist rhetoric. Reverend McCullough's five-point resolution, while strongly worded, mediated against the presumption of intellectual and ethical inferiority by its calls for citizenship, patriotism, and the best in southern traditions; its elegant language; and its anaphoristic power. And while the protest most certainly evidenced discontent, all participants were long-time South Carolinians and in no way outside agitators.

The words, however, were only a part of the protest. When protests are at least in part nonverbal, as is the case with marches and sit-ins, they become instances of rhetorical somatics, the rhetorical use not of words but of the very bodies of the protesters.[31] Protestors place their bodies where they are not supposed to be and, through this juxtaposition of black bodies in "white" places, offer a vision of a new, different, desegregated South. In the Greenville Airport march, the protesters used their bodies to deploy the visual rhetorical figure of *enargia,* the generic name for a family of figures devoted to vivid description, figures that lend themselves to the visualization of places, faces, characters, and actions. Two figures in this family, *chronographia* and *pragmatographia,* were particularly important, for they functioned to represent vividly certain historical or recurring time and the action within it (waiting time or traveling time) to depict a different reality—black travelers waiting where and when they wanted to.

The images of the stand-in reinforced the words of the protest. All fifteen who entered the airport were members of the black middle class—professionals, mainly ministers—and defied in every way the negative images of black Americans evoked by segregationist rhetors such as Landry, Bilbo, and Brady. Their presence in the airport terminal caused no disruption of service, no "trouble," and reinforced the idea that good relations in Greenville did not depend on segregation.

As is the case with any form of rhetorical argument, however, these claims could be contested. Because the argument was verbal and visual, the newspapers used reports with photographic texts to deflect the thrust of the argument and to suggest a different set of conclusions. In one sense the newspapers deployed the same figures but created narratives that supported their versions of protest.

The morning paper, the *Greenville News,* ran a brief article announcing the intended demonstration in its January 1 edition. The article noted the scheduled time of the march as well as the leaders associated with it, Reverend Hall of the Congress of Racial Equality and Reverend T. B. Thomas, president of the Greenville Ministerial Alliance, which the paper called the "Greenville (Negro) Ministerial Alliance."[32] The next day the *News*'s description of the march invited readers to consider the protest as less threatening and less important than it clearly was. Downplaying the numbers, the *News* claimed that "about 250" participated in the march on the airport, an estimate that was a quarter of the most conservative estimate of those involved in the march. The *News* also indicated that most of the protesters "sang outside the . . . Airport terminal" for about "5 minutes," while "15 of their number entered the terminal without incident to present a resolution." But there was nothing to fear, the *News* implied, because the real focus of the story was on the law enforcement that had matters under control: "An air of tense expectancy prevailed at the airport as a crowd waited, some for several hours, for the Negroes to arrive, but the large number of city, county, and state law enforcement personnel gave the impression that the situation was well in hand. The tension seemed to disappear." The story was accompanied by a single photo of four black ministers reading the resolution while three more look on—a total of seven black protesters.[33]

The evening *Piedmont* provided a less neutral and more inflammatory narrative. "Airport Protest Is Held," read the small notice—on page 13—of the January 1 paper.[34] The next day's edition carried more extensive coverage on page 2, where the march was deemed "peaceful" and "march" was placed in quotation marks, suggesting somehow that the paper disagreed with the protesters' (and the rival *News*'s) description of the event. That assumption is borne out by the rest of the report, which was dominated not by the march but rather by remarks made by Ruby Hurley, NAACP field secretary in Atlanta. In a striking use of *pragmatographia,* the paper depicted Hurley as antiwhite ("the only thing Whites have done for the Negro is to brainwash him"), anti-American ("America will not be able to convince a single person in Asia or Africa that it means right when 17 million colored people are 'enslaved'"), anti–South Carolina ("South Carolina has not produced a single statesman in all its history"), and anti-education ("Closing schools might be a good thing because then White folks and colored could grow up in equal ignorance"). The *Piedmont*'s small coverage of the airport march was limited to a reading of the resolutions the pastors presented at the airport. Two photos accompanied the story. In one, two black ministers are shown at the airport, one giving the benediction. In the other photo, a line of black marchers is depicted walking single file between law enforcement officers, supporting the story's contention that officials had warned marchers that "no disturbance was expected and none would be tolerated."[35]

The description of the actual events in time, *chronographia*, follows the *pragmatographia*, which perhaps unwittingly apes the use of the figure in classical drama by describing events occurring offstage—Hurley's comments were used to imply that the real motives and thoughts and actions were nothing like what was being represented in the march. The result, of course, was a subtle suggestion that what the marchers were doing was not to be trusted: their appeals to God and to American values and to peaceful coexistence served simply as the pretty public face that covered a deeply cynical and antagonistic reality.

The rhetorical contest was engaged but not resolved. The airport, after bouncing between federal courts in a series of appeals and remands, was desegregated by court order on February 20, 1961. In the winter of 1960, however, the city of Greenville was a city on edge—everyone knew the airport stand-in was a beginning, not an end. No one knew what was next.

Students in the Library

Nearly two months after the airport stand-in, sixteen-year-old Ben Downs was sitting at his desk waiting for class to begin at Sterling High School. His friend Hattie Smith approached him and quietly told him that she thought he should join her in sitting in at the main branch of the Greenville Public Library. "I asked her," Downs said, "'You mean the white library?'" "Yes, I do," Smith replied. "OK," Downs said. Years later, when asked why he agreed to break the law so readily, Downs, a straight-A student, said, "Well, first of all, it was Hattie asking, and you don't say no to Hattie. And second, exclusion from that library and other good libraries always bugged me."[36] Downs's sentiments were shared by others in the black community, especially students. By the middle of the twentieth century, American public libraries had become important sites of literacy and learning for many and an increasingly rhetorical space for some.[37] They had also become symbols of privilege, signifying access to and exclusion from education, the exchange of ideas, and civic engagement.[38] And from at least 1939, libraries had been contested.[39]

The main branch of the Greenville Library was at the time located on North Main Street. It was off-limits to the county's black community, which had to make do with the McBee Avenue location. As several witnesses have since reported, the McBee location frequently had worn and tattered books that reached their hands only after white patrons had used them for years at the main branch and had a "spotty" collection a fraction of the size found in the main branch.[40] Acquiring books on interlibrary loan was sometimes impossible and, when possible, could take weeks.[41]

As stories of the sit-ins elsewhere reached Greenville like rumors of storm, student leader Hattie Smith and Rev. James S. Hall of Springfield Baptist Church went into action. Smith organized the students, and Hall helped coordinate adult support at his church and among the teachers at Sterling High School. All knew they would eventually meet heavy resistance and that those who sat in were risking physical and verbal abuse of the worst kind—segregationists elsewhere had begun dumping hot coffee and chocolate on protesters' heads, spitting on them, yanking them from their seats, and frequently beating them. Sitting in required disciplined, passive, nonviolent resistance. And it frequently resulted in—and depended upon—arrests and jail.

The students tested both the segregated system and their own resolve on March 1. A loosely organized group of twenty to twenty-five students began walking to the main library. A few were picked up by the Reverend S. E. Kay of New Pleasant Grove Baptist Church when he responded to what he called a "hitchhiking signal" from them, and those in the car met those who had walked up North Main at the library. Accompanied by Kay, they entered the library at about 4:45 P.M., selected some reading materials, and sat quietly at tables reading. Kay reported that the head librarian, Charles Stowe, asked him to leave, as did F. Dean Rainey of the library board. When neither Kay nor the students left, the board of trustees decided to close the building for the night. At that point everyone, including the protesters, left the building. According to one of the students, they then met with Rev. Hall, who asked what had happened. When the students indicated they were told to leave or they would be arrested, they left.[42]

This first attempt to protest the library was clearly either poorly planned, improvised, or spontaneous. As Hall explained to the students, the whole point of a nonviolent sit-in was to get arrested and thereby call attention to the inequities of the library system and the city ordinances that supported them. Still the sit-in demonstrated that some Sterling High students not only had the resolve required to initiate a sit-in but also that the library was ill prepared to respond to a sit-in by orderly, neatly dressed, quiet, and studious teens. Moreover the impression left by Jack Putnam, the one white eyewitness interviewed by the *News,* was of students using the library in entirely appropriate ways. When questioned by board member Rainey, Hattie Smith had indicated that the McBee branch did not have the books they needed, and they could not always wait for books to be sent to McBee. Kay testified that "nothing out of the way was said to any white person."[43] In short, though perhaps not as well planned as activists would have liked, the March 1 library sit-in nonetheless pushed back against Greenville's culture of segregation in important ways. By targeting the library and using it as it was intended—for reading and with seriousness of purpose—the sit-in undermined segregationist claims of black intellectual and ethical inferiority and slovenly or disreputable lifestyles. It also resisted charges of disruption and outside agitation, for the students were quiet and all were Greenville residents.

The strategy of civil disobedience required arrests, however, and on March 16 seven students entered the library, sat down, and began to read. The "Greenville Seven" were, according to the *Greenville News,* Hattie Smith, eighteen; Doris Walker, seventeen; and Dorothy Franks, Blanche Baker, Benjamin Downs, Virginia Hurst, and Robert Anderson, all sixteen.[44] Librarian Charles Stowe once again told them that they "would have to use the McBee Ave. branch" for blacks. The students refused. When police arrived they found the students "sitting quietly at three tables, or standing around," and later determined that they had not "said anything to anyone other" than Stowe, with no disturbance of the peace.[45] One officer said, "It was the nicest sort of thing. They were polite, quiet, and did as they were told."[46] When the police asked them to leave, the students indicated that they were in a public library, their parents paid taxes, and they had every right to be there. They were promptly arrested, booked, and released on bond after spending "about an hour" in jail, where the first song they sang was "America."[47]

The second library protest relied on and drew attention to its connections to the airport and first library protests but also shifted to new strategies, revealing different facets in the Greenville sit-ins' rhetorical trajectory. By singing for the short time in jail and making their first song "America," the students drew attention to their solidarity with the ministers at the airport. They also continued to undermine the segregationists' misanthropic vision of the black community by dressing, sitting, standing, and otherwise behaving in ways that not only put the lie to the charges of social disruption, careless lifestyles, and sloth but also contributed to the impression of intellectual and ethical integrity, just as they had on March 1. But the students had also changed strategies. By voluntarily giving up their bodies for incarceration, they began to enact a complex somatic rhetoric of the law. Peter Goodrich explains that

> imprisonment implicitly renders the body docile and so amenable to instruction (*docere*) or inscription of law. The body is both the site and the conduit of submission of the soul to the "will of the law": arrest deprives the person of will so as to replace it, to bind it, to the meaning and form of law. While in one sense the superimposition of a collective intentionality upon the itinerant form of the person is unexceptional, there is also a more complex play of person and will, body and soul that deserves expansion. The law is staged through the body, and it is through corporeality, through the characteristics and qualities of the body and its movements, that the most profound substrates of law are to be read.[48]

By allowing themselves to be arrested, the students surrendered their bodies in the conventional sense and most certainly in the eyes of the public, black as well as white. However they also precipitated a new action, allowing the law to be staged and challenged through their bodies—demanding, in a sense, that the legal question raised by their sit-in—is segregation lawful?—become, through the complex play of body and soul, should segregation be lawful? Put another way, the students' willingness to be imprisoned was the necessary first step of the legal battle to come: Was Greenville's inscription of segregation on the black body forbidden by a higher law?

Later that year returning college students brought additional energy and determination to the youth movement, and on July 16 eight more students entered the library. The Greenville Eight were (again according to the *News,* with errors corrected in brackets), Benjamin Downs, seventeen; Elaine Leans [Means], Hattie Smith, Jeff [Jesse] Jackson, Joan Mattison, Doris Wright, Margaret [Margaree] Seawright, all eighteen; and Willie Wright, twenty. These students were also arrested, jailed for forty-five minutes, and released on bond. As in the March 16 sit-in, the students were "neatly dressed. The girls wore high heel shoes, and one of the boys wore a coat and hat. The others were clad in sport clothes."[49] By submitting their bodies to the law, they too joined the action precipitated by the March 16 sit-in, pushing the question of segregation's legality in the face of a higher law to the fore. The media coverage of this sit-in, the first to include a young Jesse Jackson, home from college for the summer,[50] included a photo of the students walking on Main Street and two more depicting them at the police station being booked. As received by the public, the July 16 sit-in was almost entirely somatic—few words were quoted, and the focus in the newspapers' accounts of the protest and arrest and in the photos that accompanied the stories was on their bodies—sitting, reading, walking, and surrendering themselves to the law.

Two days later the sit-ins moved to the lunch counters of Greenville's Woolworth, Green, Grant, and Kress variety stores, but the importance of the library sit-ins to Greenville's civil rights movement bears some mention. Libraries were sacred and symbolic public places, all the more so because they represented, to the great-grandsons and great-granddaughters of slaves, a break from the last vestiges of the slave code's abhorrent literacy bans and an important step to full citizenship. On July 28 Robert Anderson and his father filed suit in federal district court, arguing that segregated public libraries violated the Fourteenth Amendment's equal protection guarantee. In response the library board voted to close all branches. On September 19, however, after weeks of anxious and agonized meetings of city officials—and perhaps seeing the future—they reopened as nonsegregated facilities, open to, in the words of Mayor Cass, "any citizen having a legitimate need for the libraries and their facilities."[51] Somehow they had won the struggle for the library. Like black letters on a white page, the actions of these students—and all who followed their lead later that spring and summer—were read as invitations to reexamine not only the law but also the system of segregated public places the law supported.

Citizens at the Lunch Counters
(and in the Churches and Skating Rinks)

Those involved in the Greenville sit-ins could not have known in the middle of July 1960 that a victory at the public library was two short months away and that the mere threat of federal action and more sit-ins would be enough to integrate the library by September. Their apparent willingness to subject themselves to arrest and imprisonment—to the authority of a law with which they disagreed—and their refusal to allow their dynamic and multimodal rhetoric to fall into any of the old segregationist traps frustrated the white establishment and encouraged the protesters. As Dorothy Franks and Ben Downs confirmed in a 2014 conversation, they felt "momentum building."[52]

The time felt right, but what was the next step? What strategic adjustments did the moment demand, and what direction should their rhetorical trajectory take? And what new challenges would they face?

As it turned out, they did not have (or take) long to think about these questions. On July 17, after attending the police court hearing for the Greenville Eight and feeling disappointed that the trial had been postponed to give time to have the jury trial requested by the city, activists staged sit-ins at Woolworth, Grant, and Green department store lunch counters. Violence soon followed. Charles Helms, a twenty-four-year-old white ministerial student from Atlanta, was "slapped around" and "roughed . . . up" outside the Grant store by "a group of White men," sit-in attorney Donald L. Sampson received bomb threats at his home, and the police received two anonymous calls, one of which predicted that there would be "bloodshed in Greenville before the night."[53]

Some have argued that nonviolent protest relies on a violent response for its effect, and certainly there are instances of this in the national sit-in movement. In Greenville, however, several key factors obviated against such a result. The national media were not in Greenville to cover the violence and local media were far less inclined to show white violence against nonviolent, nonresponsive black activists. Additionally the chain department stores in Greenville had taken time to learn from their sister stores in cities where the sit-ins had hit the lunch counters first and simply closed the restaurant portion of the store and cleared everyone—black and white—out before violence arose. Finally—and this is crucial—violence only advances nonviolent protests as long as they stay nonviolent.

The Greenville sit-ins did not. Less than a week after the sit-ins moved to the lunch counters of Main Street, the headlines blared, "Whites, Negroes in Street Battle."[54] The stories depicted a street fight that consumed an entire city block and involved at least thirty people, most of them youths. At least one source reported that the fights had broken out when "one in a group of White youths following the Negro demonstrators down Main St. leaped on one of the Negro youths from the back."[55] A lengthy fight ensued, ending only when local police and members of the South Carolina Law Enforcement Division (SLED) stepped in and arrested three local white students. A few days later, another fight broke out, this time in the parking lot of a "Kash and Karry" store. Police reported that the clash involved more than "200 teen-agers" and that "several shots" had been fired, but no one had been wounded.[56] A day later more fights broke out in downtown Greenville, and "half a dozen" blacks and whites were arrested. More shots were fired, and this time the media placed blame squarely on the black community.[57] In an effort to "ease racial unrest," the Greenville City Council imposed a 9:00 P.M. curfew on all "persons 20 years old and younger."[58]

The sit-ins continued into August 1960 and so did the violence, which involved rocks, bottles, fists, and occasionally guns and knives. Most of the activists and segregationists were young. Parents, apparently, favored the continuing curfew, but the young people in the center of the things did not.[59] The curfew remained in place for most of what remained of that long, hot summer, and police continued to issue citations to young people involved in the fights, violating the curfew, and sitting in at lunch counters.[60] On August 9, 1960, fourteen young black men and women staged a lunch counter sit-in at Greenville's S. H. Kress store and were arrested. Local news reported that they were the "first to be arrested" since the protests moved to the lunch counters. The ten who were sixteen or older were charged with trespass, jailed for several hours, and then released on bond.[61] They were convicted in Greenville's General Court of Session and appealed their case to the South Carolina Supreme Court.

While their case played out over the course of the next few years, Greenville's sit-in movement continued. During the 1960–61 academic year, black students made concerted efforts to integrate the city. Several students sought to integrate all-white churches with a series of "pray-ins" at First Baptist and other downtown churches. The church struggle was more difficult in the wake of the violent summer and in a town known for its numerous Christian churches, both black and white. And yet the very multitude of churches yielded part of the rationale for integration—churches, activists believed, were places in which a good deal of the city's business and politics were discussed, and exclusion from church meant exclusion from the conversation. Black students stood on the steps of the churches, talking with white congregants about their shared Christian faith and asking to pray together. Whites often ignored them, but occasionally a few engaged them in conversation. Eventually many white churches invited them in and allowed them to pray with willing white congregants.[62] In early 1961 other students sought to desegregate the local all-white skating rink operated by the city. Several students were arrested, and the city closed the rink rather than desegregate.[63]

As in the earlier phases of the movement, activists involved in the sit-ins of the late summer and fall of 1960 and the winter and early spring of 1961 once again shifted strategies. The most significant shift was one of place, as they moved their direct-action protests from fully public facilities and institutions to those that might be deemed quasi-public and others that were most certainly private. Churches, for example, enjoy tax-exempt status and also enjoy First Amendment freedom of religion protections. Lunch counters at variety stores were a different matter. While privately owned, they were not entirely segregated—blacks could shop but not eat in them—and the city's segregation ordinances allowed private owners to exclude blacks from the lunch counters if they wanted to.

The protesters—or at least some of them—also abandoned nonviolent modes of action and engaged those who physically accosted them. This move, while by no means unique in the larger civil rights movement, took away one aspect of their somatic rhetoric. Arrests for violent behavior could no longer represent a willing surrender of the body to the rule of law and the precipitation of an examination of the unjust law. In cases in which activists were charged with disturbing the peace, assault, or other violent acts, the law in question was not segregation. In cases of trespass, segregation was at issue and, as we will see, offered momentous opportunities for the kinds of change advocates most desired. In addition violent behavior played into the segregationist rhetoric of black shiftlessness and ethical carelessness and allowed segregationists an opportunity to reclaim the moral high ground—the disturbance of good relations, after all they said, was triggered by black integrationists attempting to change the long-accepted racial order and was perpetrated against law-abiding Christian business owners. Finally out-of-town activists' participation in some of the sit-ins and some of the violence opened rhetorical space for segregationists' argument about the baleful influences of outside agitators on what had been, they said, a community of racial harmony.

Nonetheless by the summer of 1961, Greenville's white establishment began to worry about the effect the sit-ins and the growing racial disturbance would have on business in the city and state. They held conversations throughout the year and considered changes, in part due to their perception that the federal government would intervene and force the city and state to change public elements of its culture of segregation and in part due to the seemingly relentless pressure put upon communities by the sit-in protests. These changes coalesced in a speech given by prominent Greenville businessman Charles E. Daniel at the Hampton, South Carolina, Watermelon Festival on July 1, 1961. In "The Watermelon Speech," Daniel warned of the deleterious effects of a stubborn refusal to change and urged white South Carolinians to "forsake some of their old ways" and to take care of the segregation issue themselves before the federal government took even that choice away from the state.[64] His remarks were more timely than he knew, because, as he was delivering the speech, one of the legal cases involving Greenville's sit-in protesters was making its way through the South Carolina courts, heading to the federal government in the form of the U.S. Supreme Court.

Lawyers (and Judges) in the Courts

On March 22, 1960, just after the second library sit-in, the *Greenville News* ran an op-ed by syndicated columnist Ray Tucker. Titled "Negroes' Sitdowns Stir New Discord," Tucker's piece noted that neither President Eisenhower nor Vice President Nixon had "ever expressed an opinion on the question of Negroes' admission to privately owned facilities, where the management has a segregation policy and where local law does not require mixing of the races." He went on to note, correctly, that the "Supreme Court, in all its recent rulings, ha[d] not passed on this question," either.[65] He was correct—it had not. But it was about to.

The Greenville sit-in movement gave rise to many legal actions. As is often the case in American controversies, the rhetorical trajectory of a contested right, duty, privilege, concept, space, term, or condition of existence often includes or culminates in the legal forum. Part of this may be accounted for in the distinctly American tradition of judicial review of constitutional questions, part in our preference for rational, discerning judgment, and part, one might posit, in our very litigiousness. Whatever the explanation, the last phase of the Greenville sit-ins occurred in court.[66]

Several legal actions prompted resolution outside the court of the questions raised inside or were decided, settled, or dismissed as events unfolded. Richard Henry's case against the Greenville airport initially went against him in the federal district court when Judge George Bell Timmerman found that the "custom" of separate waiting rooms for blacks and whites at the airport did not amount to "state action" as required by the Fourteenth Amendment.[67] However, Henry appealed the case and eventually won in the Fourth Circuit Court of Appeals, where the court concluded that any action by the airport commission clearly constituted state action.[68] The library case, filed on behalf of the Greenville Seven,[69] was dismissed by federal district judge C. C. Wyche after city officials decided to close the library. Wyche ruled, as one reporter wrote, "that a nonexistent library cannot be integrated."[70] Still the case functioned as the student protesters wanted, for it pressured the city into reopening the library as an integrated facility. A third case, filed on behalf of the students who sought to integrate the city's all-white skating rink, was handled similarly by Judge Wyche, who dismissed the case as moot when the city closed both of the city's skating rinks—one for blacks and one for whites—permanently.[71] Unlike the library case, however, the city did not move to reopen the skating rinks after the case was dismissed.[72]

However *Peterson v. City of Greenville,* the case that grew out of the August 9, 1960, lunch counter protests and arrests at Kress variety store, is a different matter altogether. *Peterson* raised the issue of whether the denial of service to black patrons, by an essentially private business, on the basis of their race, met the "state action" requirement of the Fourteenth Amendment and accordingly violated the amendment's guarantee of equal protection of the laws.[73] The question was of considerable import before the passage of the Civil Rights Act of 1964 because it was an open question. "State action," required by part 1 of the amendment ("No state shall . . ."), was litigated in all of the cases above, and in *Henry* the federal district court and the Fourth Circuit Court of Appeals disagreed vehemently on whether actions by the Greenville Airport Commission rose to the level of "state" action. *Peterson* tested how far the Warren Court was willing to extend the theory of state action.

The facts of the case presented each party with a bit of argumentative purchase. On the one hand, the store manager had testified that he had asked the protesters to leave because to serve them would have been "contrary to local customs," strengthening the city's case that, if any discrimination took place, it was a private business decision and not a state action. On the other hand, the store manager also mentioned the Greenville city ordinance requiring separation of the races in restaurants.[74] At stake was an enormous slice of American urban and suburban life and a great deal of the culture of segregation.

Formally the sit-in protesters had been arrested and charged with trespass when they refused to leave the lunch counter when asked. At trial in the General Sessions Court of Greenville, special county judge James H. Price presiding, the defendants were convicted. They appealed to the South Carolina Supreme Court, which affirmed the lower court's ruling on November 10, 1961. Chief Justice Taylor wrote the opinion and was joined by Justices Oxner, Legge, Moss, and Lewis. Taylor dismissed the Fourteenth Amendment arguments by asserting that the defendants had been arrested and charged because they had remained in the restaurant after it had closed; all other patrons had left as requested, they had been asked to leave, and they had not. Taylor granted that the lower court record revealed that the restaurant was closed to follow its custom of serving whites only but stressed that the state law of trespass under which the defendants were convicted made "no mention of segregation of the races" and therefore the decision to have them leave was a merely private one. He argued that "the Fourteenth Amendment erects no shield against merely private conduct, however discriminatory or wrongful, . . . and the operator of a privately owned business may accept some customers and reject others on purely personal grounds in the absence of a statute to the contrary."[75]

The protesters appealed, and the U.S. Supreme Court granted certiorari to "consider the substantial federal questions presented by the record."[76] The brief for petitioners was filed on September 19, 1962, and the brief for respondents on October 19, 1962. The Court heard oral arguments in the case on November 6–7, 1962.[77]

The protesters argued on Fourteenth and First Amendment grounds. On Fourteenth Amendment grounds, they argued that their exclusion from the lunch counter, along with their arrest and conviction, was required by a Greenville city ordinance that compelled segregation in eating facilities, and the exclusion, arrest, and conviction violated the Fourteenth Amendment's Equal Protection Clause.[78] In addition enforcement of segregation by the police and the courts of South Carolina, even in the absence of a law and the presence of custom, nevertheless still constituted state action.[79] Petitioners also asserted that the state's licensing and regulatory powers involved it deeply in the segregation policies of the stores and restaurants it licenses and regulates, again constituting state action, and that no essential property right of the Kress store was at issue.[80] The City of Greenville argued the proprietor of a privately owned restaurant has the right to serve only those whom he chooses and to refuse to serve those whom he desires not to serve for whatever reason he may determine and that there was no state action and consequently no denial of equal protection.[81]

The Court issued two opinions, a majority opinion authored by Chief Justice Earl Warren and a concurrence by Justice John Marshall Harlan II. Warren's majority opinion is stunning in its brevity and its dismissal of extraneous issues. After a review of the facts and a tight summary of the issues raised, he cut straight to the sole question the Court must answer: "Petitioners . . . assert that they have been deprived of the equal protection of the laws secured to them against state action by the Fourteenth Amendment."[82] Warren's tightly worded syllogistic argument has three parts: first, that the record demonstrates "beyond doubt that the Kress management's decision to exclude petitioners from the lunch counter was because they were Negroes";[83] second, that "the City of Greenville, an agency of the State, has provided by its ordinance that the decision as to whether a restaurant facility is to be operated on a desegregated basis is to be reserved to it," and the "Kress management, in deciding to exclude Negroes, did precisely what the city law required";[84] and third—and as a consequence— the convictions of the petitioners cannot stand, "even assuming, as respondent contends, that the manager would have acted as he did independently of the existence of the ordinance." The result, he held, was a "palpable violation of the Fourteenth Amendment [that] cannot be saved by attempting to separate the mental urges of the discriminators."[85] It is a hypothetical deductive argument: If there is state action that discriminates on the basis of race, that action violates the Fourteenth Amendment. There is state action that discriminates on the basis of race. Therefore that action violates the Fourteenth Amendment.

Justice Harlan's concurrence is more nuanced. Though he reached the same conclusion in *Peterson* (there were five cases consolidated in *Peterson*, and Harlan did not reach the same conclusion as the Court in all five), he warned against assuming state action just because the ordinance existed. The central question, he believed, was whether the proprietor of a private business was acting of his or her own accord, based on private convictions and choices, or was coerced or influenced by the city ordinance. Because the manager's testimony at trial indicated both the restaurant's private choice and an acknowledgement of the city ordinance's demands, Harlan came down on the side of the protesters.

Peterson represents the last shift in the rhetorical trajectory of the Greenville sit-in movement. Far from the airport and the libraries, the lunch counters and the churches and the skating rinks, the movement's legal representatives took the protesters' bodies and their questions to the Supreme Court. In response to the question of whether Greenville's inscription of segregation on the black body was forbidden by a higher law, the Court's answer was, yes, most certainly it was.

Conclusion

At the outset I suggested that Greenville's sit-in movement traced a dynamic, multifaceted rhetorical trajectory, one that arced across nearly three years and moved against a long-standing culture of segregated cohabitation. I have tried to highlight what I believe to be the most important facets—changing, multimodal persuasive appeals—and pivotal moments in the movement's course and to show how the movement adjusted to meet the shifting demands placed upon it not only by its circumstances and opponents but also by its own miscues and mistakes.

This study offers but one approach to protest movement rhetoric, but perhaps it offers some insight for the study of protest movements generally. For instance it seems to confirm Kendall Phillips's notion that, in our study of controversy, we might profitably focus on the intersection of moments of opportunity and specific sites of discourse instead of assuming a more or less static relationship between the public sphere and the controversial.[86] The Greenville sit-in movement progressed by seizing the opportunities presented by specific sites (and moments) of discourse and regressed by failing to seize (or perhaps recognize) other of those opportunities. In addition the study takes a decided posture in favor of case-based approaches to protest discourse and against predetermined or overly theory-laden approaches, preferring if possible to let the rhetorical strategies or discourses guide the study rather than force the study to try to corral the strategies and discourses.

Accordingly it is appropriate to end with a few words about the case at hand, the Greenville sit-in movement. Against all odds it succeeded about as well as a movement can, despite its mistakes. Martin Luther King Jr. later said about the sit-in movement generally that "as they were sitting in, they were really standing up for the best in the American dream . . . taking the whole nation back to those great wells of democracy."[87] It is fair to say that the Greenville sit-in movement, culminating as it did by breaching de jure segregation's last line of defense—"private" property—in *Peterson v. City of Greenville,* did more to advance democracy than the ministers, high school and college students, and even the lawyers involved ever imagined it could.

It did so despite succumbing to violence in the latter half of the summer of 1960. Whether justifiable or not, provoked (as it surely was) or initiated, the turn to violence did not help the movement. It gave segregationists rhetorical ammunition and gave those sitting on the fence pause. In the end it did not prevent the all-important legal case from moving forward, did not damage the case, and allowed the state's business leaders to make decisions favorable to the movement's goals. But it may have damaged the community and delayed its recovery from the turmoil. In 2000, decades after the events of 1960–63, Greenville erupted in another bitter battle, this time over recognition of the Martin Luther King holiday, and the state of South Carolina fought over the Confederate battle flag on its statehouse ground—placed there in April 1961—until it finally came down in the summer of 2015.

Still few of these difficulties can be attributed, directly or indirectly, to the Greenville sit-in movement or *Peterson v. City of Greenville.* The rhetorical legacy of the Greenville movement, like all protest movements, will continue to evolve as our understanding of it deepens and clarifies over time.

Notes

The author wishes to thank the librarians at the Greenville County Library, especially the staff of the Carolina Room and the library's generous director, Beverly James. The author also wishes to thank Jennie Hill for invaluable research assistance, Lesli Pace and Melody Lehn for helpful readings of this essay, Tierney O'Rourke and Rob Terrill for prompt and timely assistance in hours of need, and James Horner for the score of the motion picture *Glory.*

1. Black, "Gettysburg and Silence," 21–36. For further insight consider Terrill, "Rhetorical Criticism and Citizenship Education," 170–72. I am not aware of a study, other than this chapter, that considers the prismatic qualities of protest movement rhetoric.

2. Indeed it is known as Protagorean and Ciceronian *controversia* and has a rich literature. See, e.g., Mendelson, *Many Sides*; Sloane, *On the Contrary*; Conley, *Rhetoric in the European Tradition,* 37. For consideration of the larger issues found in rhetorics of confrontation and controversy, see Scott and Smith, "Rhetoric of Confrontation," and Phillips,

"Rhetoric of Controversy" (reconsidering the relationship between the public sphere and the controversial and suggesting a focus on the intersection of moments of opportunity and specific sites of discourse, issues upon which I touch at the end of this chapter).

3. The standard text on rhetorical history is still Turner, ed., *Doing Rhetorical History*. See, in particular, Zarefsky, "Four Senses of Rhetorical History."

4. Zarefsky, "Four Senses of Rhetorical History," 30. The earliest effort at studying rhetorical trajectories seems to have been Griffin, "When Dreams Collide." The current study takes added perspective from several others, including Kluver, "Rhetorical Trajectories of Tiananmen Square"; Ray, "Transcript of a Continuing Conversation"; and Dionisopoulos, et al., "Martin Luther King, the American Dream, and Vietnam."

5. *Brown v. Board of Education of Topeka*, 347 U.S. 483 (1954) (Brown I); and *Brown v. Board of Education of Topeka*, 349 U.S. 294 (1955) (Brown II).

6. "No Trouble Here Unless . . ."

7. Huff, *Greenville*, 257.

8. See Gordon, *Second Coming of the KKK*; Harcourt, *Ku Klux Kulture*; Hochschild, "Ku Klux Klambakes."

9. Huff, *Greenville*, 323–25, 357–58. See also O'Neill, "Memory, History, and the Desegregation of Greenville," 287.

10. On the lynchings between 1905 and 1933, see Huff, *Greenville*, 355–57. On the lynching of Willie Earle, see Gravely, "The Civil Right Not to Be Lynched"; and the William Gravely Oral History Collection on the Lynching of Willie Earle in the South Caroliniana Library, a division of the University of South Carolina University Libraries. It can be accessed online at http://digital.tcl.sc.edu/cdm/landingpage/collection/gravely. The international notoriety is largely due to Rebecca West, "Opera in Greenville." See also O'Rourke, "Racism's Lessons Learned in Upstate."

11. O'Neill, "Memory, History, and the Desegregation of Greenville," 288.

12. For differing accounts of white resistance generally, see, e.g., Lewis, *Massive Resistance: The White Response to the Civil Rights Movement*; and Webb, ed., *Massive Resistance: Southern Opposition to the Second Reconstruction*. For a sense of the rhetoric of this opposition, see Walker, "Legislating Virtue"; Mixon, "Rhetoric of States' Rights and White Supremacy." My account differs from these and seeks to attend to the interplay of regional and local themes.

13. Morton, *Crania Americana*; Cartwright, "Report on the Diseases and Physical Peculiarities of the Negro Race," originally published in the *New Orleans Medical and Surgical Journal* and *DeBow's Review* (both in 1851; the report was reprinted in many forms after). In his report Cartwright claimed to have discovered two diseases unique to African Americans: "Drapetomania," an illness that causes "Negroes to run away," and "Dysaesthesia Aethiopica," which is the "natural offspring of negro liberty" and accounts for the African American tendencies "to be idle, to wallow in filth, and to indulge in improper food and drinks."

14. Landry, *The Cult of Equality*; Bilbo, *Take Your Choice*.

15. Brady, *Black Monday*. The book, originally delivered as a speech to the Greenwood, Mississippi, chapter of the Sons of the American Revolution, was widely read across the South.

16. "Decision of the Supreme Court in the School Cases." For interesting reassessments of what came to be called "The Southern Manifesto," see Day, *Southern Manifesto*; and Driver, "Supremacies and the Southern Manifesto." Most agree that the manifesto was originally drafted by South Carolina senator and Upstate resident Strom Thurmond.

17. *Greenville News,* 7 June 1960.

18. Workman, *Case for the South.* This work was followed quickly by James Jackson Kilpatrick's *The Southern Case for School Segregation* (N.p.: Crowell-Collier, 1962). Kilpatrick, then editor of the *Richmond News Leader,* was a frequent visitor to South Carolina, where he eventually retired.

19. Hill, "Reframing the Victim," 45–57.

20. Bob Jones Sr., *Is Segregation Scriptural?* (Greenville, S.C.: Bob Jones University, 1960). Original copies of this tract are extraordinarily and mysteriously rare these days. I am grateful to my friend and colleague Dr. Camille Lewis for her indefatigable work tracking one down and providing public access to it. See http://www.drslewis.org/camille/2013/03/15/is-segregation-scriptural-by-bob-jones-sr-1960/. See also Lewis, "A Is for Archive."

21. Jones, *Is Segregation Scriptural?,* 8–10.

22. Ingram, ed., *Essays on Segregation.*

23. On the importance of the Cold War setting, see in particular Gilmore, *Defying Dixie* (demonstrating how radical reformers in the South made significant gains between 1919 and 1945, only to have them quashed by the second Red Scare and the Cold War). See also Egerton, *Speak Now Against the Day* (uncovering the stories of those who resisted the culture of segregation).

24. An earlier version of part of the following section of the essay was published in O'Rourke, "Circulation and Noncirculation."

25. As Jacqueline Dowd Hall has persuasively argued, neither the years 1954–68 nor even the broader frame of 1948–73 can contain the civil rights movement. See "Long Civil Rights Movement." On Greenville's civil rights struggle generally, see O'Neill, "Memory, History, and the Desegregation of Greenville"; and Hart, "Amend or Defend." For a more general view of South Carolina's civil rights history, see Lau, *Democracy Rising;* Hudson, *Entangled by White Supremacy;* and Moore and Burton, *Toward the Meeting of the Waters.*

26. *Henry v. Greenville Airport Commission,* 175 F. Supp. 343 (D.C. W.D.S.C. 1959); *Henry v. Greenville Airport Commission,* 279 F. 2d 751 (4th Cir, 1960); *Henry v. Greenville Airport Commission,* 284 F. 2d 631 (4th Cir, 1960).

27. For more details on the incident, see "Gloster Current to Robert Carter," in *First Class Citizenship,* ed. Long, 74–76. For Marshall's response to Robinson, see "Thurgood Marshall to Robinson," ibid., 79–80. For a general overview, with a sense of where the case fit in the larger national effort to desegregate airports, see Ortlepp, *Jim Crow Terminals,* esp. 36–89.

28. U.S. Const. art. I, §8, cl. 3.

29. Interview with Lottie Gibson, 19 January 2010.

30. "Negroes Conduct Orderly Segregation Protest Here." See also O'Rourke, "Greenville Airport Protest Started an Avalanche."

31. Goodrich, "Rhetoric and Somatics."

32. "Pilgrimage by Negroes Set Today."

33. "Negroes Conduct Orderly Segregation Protest."

34. "Airport Protest Is Held."

35. "Airport 'March' Peaceful."

36. Interview with Ben Downs, 19 January 2010.

37. By "rhetorical space" I mean not only sites or locations in which meaning—and motive, value, ritual, reason, and community—are performed and inscribed, but also the ways in which such locations hold and convey meanings of their own. See Middleton, et

al., *Participatory Critical Rhetoric*; Endres and Senda-Cook, "Location Matters"; Johnson, *Gender and Rhetorical Space*; Mountford, "On Gender and Rhetorical Space."

38. I am grateful to Janice Hamlet for this insight. Her unpublished draft manuscript, "Oh Mercy, There's Colored People All Over the Library" (in my possession), begins to explore some of the contours of the library as rhetorical space, and I have benefitted from her insight.

39. The year 1939 marks the date of the library sit-ins in Alexandria, Virginia. See Sullivan, "Lawyer Samuel Tucker"; "1939 Library Sit-In Anniversary." For a wider scope on public library integration in the civil rights movement, see Wiegand and Wiegand, *Desegregation of Public Libraries*; Knott, *Not Free, Not for All*; Battles, *History of Public Library Access*; Graham, *Right to Read*.

40. Judy Bainbridge reports that the main branch held 55,508 books and the McBee branch held only 11,644, "chosen, librarians said, to include those 'of most interest to Negro readers.'" Bainbridge, "Integrating Greenville's Library."

41. Interview with Hattie Smith Wright, 10 July 2010. Franks, Downs, and O'Rourke, "Communicating Civic Responsibility and Reconciliation."

42. Bainbridge, "Integrating Greenville's Library."

43. Walker, "Group of Young Negroes Enters Greenville Library."

44. Stokes, "7 Negroes Walk into Library Here." Bubbling just below the surface of the literature on the Greenville sit-in movement is a gentle jostling for history between the "Greenville Seven," high school students who sat in on 16 March 1960, and the "Greenville Eight," a mix of high school and college students who sat in on 16 July 1960. As I hope this chapter shows, both groups were important and perhaps even essential to the movement. The fact that the Reverend Jesse Jackson was a member of the Greenville Eight may account for its greater acclaim. I would point out that only two people, Hattie Smith and Ben Downs, were in both groups.

45. Ibid.

46. Ballenger, "City Library Calm during 'Sitdown.'"

47. Ibid.

48. Goodrich, "Rhetoric and Somatics."

49. Timms, "8 Negroes Sit-In at Library Here: Arrested and Jailed Briefly."

50. "The Greenville Civil Rights Movement," panel discussion at the Greenville County Library, Greenville, S.C., 22 August 2013.

51. Eberhart, "Greenville Eight: The Sit-In That Integrated the Greenville (S.C.) Library." I cannot say that I agree with the title of this otherwise fine essay. As I think my chapter makes clear, all of the library sit-ins were important, and if forced to choose a "most important," I would go with 16 March.

52. Franks, Downs, and O'Rourke, "Communicating Civic Responsibility."

53. Ballenger, "Negroes Stage Sit-Ins at City Lunch Counters"; Timms, "3 Counter Sit-Ins Held in Greenville."

54. Thompson, "Whites, Negroes in Street Battle"; Ballenger, "Violence Flares on Main Street."

55. Thompson, "Whites, Negroes."

56. "White and Negro Teen-agers Clash."

57. "Gunfire Breaks Out as Races Clash in Greenville."

58. "9 PM Curfew Ordered to Ease Racial Unrest."

59. "Parents Unanimously Approve Curfew"; "Curfew Keeps City Quiet."

60. "New Sit-Down Staged Here."

61. Stokes, "14 Young Negroes Are Arrested after Sit-In."

62. Interview with Doris "Dee Dee" Wright and Leola Clement Robinson-Simpson, 19 January 2010, and interviews with Lottie Gibson, Ben Downs, and Leola Clement Robinson-Simpson, 10 January 2010. For images of the church campaign, see Robinson-Simpson, *Greenville County South Carolina*, 76, 86.

63. Zimmerman, *Negroes in Greenville*, 25–26.

64. Edgar, *South Carolina: A History*, 537–38.

65. Tucker, "Negroes' Sitdowns Stir New Discord."

66. On this movement from conflict to constitutional question, see Zarefsky and Gallagher, "From 'Conflict' to 'Constitutional Question.'"

67. *Henry v. Greenville Airport* Commission, 175 F. Supp. 343 (D.C. W.D.S.C 1959) at 351.

68. *Henry v. Greenville Airport Commission*, 279 F. 2d 751 (4th Cir, 1960); *Henry v. Greenville Airport Commission*, 284 F. 2d 631 (4th Cir, 1960). On remand Judge Timmerman expressed his exasperation with the appellate court by writing that "appellate court rulings, with which this Court heartily disagrees, are nevertheless binding and must be followed" and ruled in favor of Henry. *Henry v. Greenville Airport Commission*, 191 F. Supp. 146 (D.C. W.D.S.C 1961).

69. Walker, "Integration Local Library Is Sought."

70. Crocker, "Judge Dismisses Library Suit Here."

71. *Walker v. Shaw*, 209 F. Supp. 569 (1962).

72. A fourth case, *Whittenberg v. Greenville* (424 F.2d 195 [1970]), also arose out of the Greenville civil rights period. It involved integration of the Greenville schools but dates from beyond the period of the sit-in movement.

73. U.S. Const. amend. XIV, § 1.

74. Code of Greenville, 1953, as amended in 1958, § 31–8:

> (a) Separate eating utensils and separate dishes for the serving of food, all of which shall be distinctly marked by some appropriate color scheme or otherwise;
>
> (b) Separate tables, counters or booths;
>
> (c) A distance of at least thirty-five feet shall be maintained between the area where white and colored persons are served;
>
> (d) The area referred to in subsection (c) above shall not be vacant, but shall be occupied by the usual display counters and merchandise found in a business concern of a similar nature;
>
> (e) A separate facility shall be maintained and used for the cleaning of eating utensils and dishes furnished the two races.

75. *City of Greenville v. Peterson*, 239 S.C. 298, 122 S.E.2d 826 (1961) at 828.

76. *Peterson v. City of Greenville*, 373 U.S. 244 (1963) at 245.

77. The oral arguments are now available at *Peterson v. City of Greenville*, Oyez, https://www.oyez.org/cases/1962/71.

78. Brief of Petitioner at 14–21, *Peterson v. City of Greenville*, (No.71) 373 U.S. 244 (1963).

79. Brief of Petitioner at 22–27, ibid.

80. Brief of Petitioner at 28–37, ibid.

81. Brief for Respondent at 3–15, ibid.

82. *Peterson v. City of Greenville* at 247.

83. Ibid.

84. *Peterson v. City of Greenville* at 247–48.

85. *Peterson v. City of Greenville* at 248. Christopher W. Schmidt reaches a somewhat different conclusion, arguing that the Supreme Court in *Peterson* reached the limit of what it was willing to do absent federal legislation. That legislation, as Schmidt shows, came in the form of the Civil Rights Act of 1964. See Schmidt, *Sit-Ins*, esp. 129–34.

86. Phillips, "Rhetoric of Controversy."

87. Martin Luther King Jr., "I've Been to the Mountaintop," text available online at the Martin Luther King Jr. Research and Education Center, Stanford University, http://king encyclopedia.stanford.edu/encyclopedia/documentsentry/ive_been_to_the_mountaintop/.

NOTHING NEW
FOR EASTER

Rhetoric, Collective Action, and the
Louisville Sit-In Movement

Stephen Schneider

On April 27, 1961, the *Louisville Defender,* Louisville's African American weekly newspaper, led with an article titled "What a Record? Louisville Leads Nation in Sit-In Arrests." The article described the 685 arrests that had occurred since February 20 of that year as part of a concerted campaign against segregation in public accommodations, a campaign that peaked with the "Nothing New for Easter" boycott of downtown businesses. However it was not only the high arrest total that made the campaign remarkable. Perhaps more surprising was that it occurred in Louisville, a city that was considered to be racially progressive in its laws and customs.[1]

This might also explain why Louisville's sit-in movement of 1959–61 is not as widely recognized as similar movements in Greensboro and Nashville. But despite its relative historical neglect, the "Nothing New for Easter" campaign and the sit-ins that led up to it provide important evidence both on the widespread adoption of the sit-in strategy within civil rights campaigns and the manner in which the sit-in as a form of direct action resonated among African Americans across the South. Sit-ins provided civil rights activists with a means of dramatizing their campaigns for integration and first-class citizenship, via the occupation of space that had hitherto been closed to them. As such sit-ins proved to be an important framing process—a means of interpreting injustice and coordinating direct action in response to that injustice.

In recognizing sit-ins as a framing practice, we might also recognize the way that sit-ins function rhetorically on both macro- and micro-mobilizational levels. Sit-ins not only dramatized injustice urgently and dynamically; they also fostered collective identity among participants and presented them with an immediate agency for collective action. Furthermore, insofar as they represent coordinated physical action, sit-ins speak both to the materiality of framing processes and to the manner in which collective action itself provides the foundation for the development of collective action frames among social movement participants.

Louisville and the "Nothing New for Easter" Campaign

Much like elsewhere in the United States, sit-ins in Louisville, Kentucky, focused on desegregating the city's public accommodations—particularly downtown lunch counters and department stores. While these sit-ins gathered momentum in 1959 and 1960, they nonetheless drew on prior efforts that extended back at least into the late 1940s. In fact, the sit-in as a strategy for desegregating public amenities in the River City had an even longer history: between October 1870 and May 1871, Louisville African Americans staged sit-ins on the city's streetcars and ultimately desegregated public transport.[2] This early campaign not only speaks to a long history of African American activism within the city of Louisville but also to the somewhat patchwork nature of segregation in Louisville—while public transport was integrated, segregation remained the custom in many other aspects of Louisville life. Nonetheless segregation was applied unevenly and to some degree unpredictably, suggesting to African Americans that it would require broad legislation on the part of city officials to eliminate racial discrimination from public facilities and accommodations.

By 1950 African Americans had already issued challenges to the segregation of public parks, golf courses, entertainment venues, and libraries. While early efforts met with important but limited success—Louisville hospitals began desegregating in 1949, as did the main branch of the Louisville Public Library, and the city's golf courses were opened to African Americans in 1952—segregation remained widespread in downtown department stores, theaters, restaurants, and lunch counters. The Louisville African American community called for legislation desegregating downtown businesses as early as 1954, with the city first considering such an ordinance in 1957.[3] Nonetheless city and state officials proved unwilling to further the cause of desegregation, citing questions of jurisdiction (uncertainty over whether desegregation was properly a city or a state issue) and the rights of private business to choose their clientele.

During the same period, Louisville's NAACP Youth Council and the Congress of Racial Equality attempted to pressure local business with sporadic sit-ins at lunch counters. Clarence Matthews, a reporter for the *Louisville Defender*, noted that African American journalists had already been testing segregation up to that point: "Some people forget this, but black reporters used to go out

and test lunch counters, even before the students did in North Carolina. . . .
I remember going in the old hotel, I think it was Fourth and Chestnut, and sitting down. And of course they refuse you, you go back and write a story about
the refusal. . . . Black reporters used to do that all over."[4]

Matthews noted, however, that early efforts did not typically occasion the
resistance leveled at later sit-in campaigns: "They just didn't serve me, that's
all. They said, 'We don't serve Negroes here.' It wasn't any confrontation 'cause
I wasn't being paid enough for that, to go to jail."[5] But whereas early test cases
involved only individual reporters, sometimes accompanied by a photographer,
the sit-ins that commenced in 1956 were a collective effort on the part of the
city's civil rights leaders and students.

Lyman Johnson, a teacher at Louisville's Central High School and the plain-
tiff in the case that led to the desegregation of the University of Kentucky in
1949, led student sit-ins at drugstore lunch counters as early as 1956. The matter
received further attention in 1958, when the visiting mayor of Kingston, Jamaica,
was refused service at a Walgreens.[6] However these sit-ins did not coalesce into
a wider movement until the Christmas of 1959 when African Americans decided to protest the opening of *Porgy and Bess* at the downtown Brown Theater.
Despite the fact that the show featured an all–African American cast, African
Americans were not permitted to attend the show.[7] The theater had, however,
made tickets available via mail order, which allowed African American activists
to organize protest actions outside the theater. Having purchased mail-order
tickets, they attempted to take their seats for the show. As Raoul Cunningham
recalls, "we already had our picket signs made. Once they turned the first group
of us away, we immediately started picketing."[8]

The protests at the Brown Theater garnered wider attention than previous
sit-ins and became a serious enough issue for the city to hold a public meeting
about desegregation on January 7, 1960. While this led city aldermen to consider another integration bill in February, the ordinance was voted down, and
action at the level of the city went nowhere.[9] In response African Americans initiated another round of sit-ins focused on downtown businesses generally and
the Kaufman-Strauss department store specifically. "In contrast to comparable
protests in communities across the South, however," Tracey K'Meyer notes,
"these demonstrations did not spark mass daily demonstrations accompanied
by nighttime rallies and arrests."[10] The protests did, however, coincide with the
organization of the Non-partisan Voter Registration Committee—which ran
widespread voter registration campaigns that summer—and local protests at
venues such as the Algonquin Manor shopping center and Stewart's Dry Goods
department store later in the year.

By 1961, however, sit-in protests were gaining momentum within the city.
The success of sit-ins elsewhere in the region spurred local high school students

and activists to once again engage in sit-ins at Kaufman-Strauss and Stewart's Dry Goods on February 9.[11] On February 20 five protestors were arrested; this, along with the increased media attention given to the latest round of protests, led to a sudden escalation of activity. The number of protestors increased to seventy-five on February 21, and sit-ins quickly expanded to more downtown restaurants, theaters, and department stores. Arrests increased as well, to a total of fifty-eight by February 24.[12] Aside from attracting the sorts of attention typically associated with civil rights sit-ins, these protests were also significant insofar as they gave birth to the "Nothing New for Easter" campaign.

"Nothing New for Easter" was intended to hit downtown businesses where it hurt in the lead-up to the 1961 Easter holidays. Protestors targeted both segregation and discriminatory hiring practices and encouraged African Americans to boycott businesses and cancel credit accounts with larger department stores. The campaign brought initial results relatively quickly, with Kaufman-Strauss and Stewart's opening negotiations with civil rights leaders by the end of February.[13] Mayor Bruce Hoblitzell likewise appointed a commission to examine the issue of desegregation and encourage dialogue between protestors and business owners.[14] But while the mayor had optimistically suggested that there might be a resolution to the issue by April 1, the failure to achieve concrete results by early March led civil rights protestors to hold a march downtown on March 10. Civil rights organizations including the National Association for the Advancement of Colored People (NAACP), the Congress of Racial Equality (CORE), the Student Nonviolent Coordinating Committee (SNCC), and the Southern Christian Leadership Conference (SCLC) also held events in support of the Louisville sit-ins, which reinforced the connection between local protests and the broader civil rights movement. In the same period, arrests continued to escalate to a total of 175 by March 15 and 685 by April 27—a number that Tracy K'Meyer notes were the highest in the nation to that point.[15]

Demonstrations were suspended during the 1961 Kentucky Derby (as much for fear of drunken reprisals against protestors as for respect for Louisville's signature cultural event) but began again soon after. Perhaps the most famous were the protests at the Fontaine Ferry amusement park, which began on June 19.[16] Protests against segregation of the park led local courts to issue an injunction against protests being held in front of the park, as well as a probation agreement with protestors that proved contingent upon them disavowing further protest activities. While the strong-arm tactics employed against the Fontaine Ferry protests attracted media and community attention, local activists also sought to organize the African American community in anticipation of fall elections. Their call for voters to vote for Republican candidates proved successful, and the elections saw many Democratic candidates suffer defeat in both mayoral and alderman races.

Continued activism by CORE and others in 1962 kept the pressure on the new city administration, and the overall efforts of civil rights activists eventually led the city on May 14, 1963, to pass an ordinance making it illegal to discriminate based on race in any public business.[17] Furthermore the Louisville sit-ins helped set the stage, along with similar protests in Lexington and Frankfort, for the eventual 1964 March on Frankfort to secure a statewide public accommodations law. While the legislation itself would not be passed until 1966, the march brought participation from national civil rights activists such as Rev. Dr. Martin Luther King Jr. and Jackie Robinson and culminated with a sit-in at the state capitol as civil rights protestors brought pressure to bear on state legislators.

Louisville's sit-in movement is noteworthy for several reasons. Not only does it speak to the widespread impact of the regional sit-in movement of 1960 and 1961, but it also highlights how sit-ins were already a recognized form of civil rights protest long before their widespread uptake during the classical period of the civil rights movement. Furthermore the "Nothing New for Easter" campaign allows us to understand better when and how sit-ins moved from being a civil rights strategy to an important movement in their own right. As I argue below, this shift also suggests a shift in how sit-ins function rhetorically, as they change from being primarily a form of public protest to also being a means of framing movement activity. Sit-ins, then, do not just provide protestors with a means of publicly communicating injustice; they also provide a means of organizing and fortifying collective action among movement participants.

Civil Rights Frames in the Louisville Sit-In Movement

It bears mentioning at the outset that the term *sit-in,* as it is encountered in descriptions of the protests in Louisville, designates a number of protest strategies: aside from sitting down at downtown lunch counters, Louisville civil rights activists also picketed theaters and bowling alleys, protested at drug stores and department stores, and boycotted segregated business in the lead-up to Easter 1961. As a result it might be asked how the sit-in movement emerged in Louisville and how that movement came to organize the civil rights struggles rhetorically within the River City in the late 1950s and early 1960s. Furthermore it might be asked how sit-ins, as a rhetorical locus for civil rights organizing, helped facilitate a shift from legal and political strategies to direct action in the fight against segregation in public accommodations.

The framing approach—an approach popular among sociologists looking at cultural and ideological aspects of social movement activity—may help understand the common identity that underpinned local forms of protest in the late 1950s. This approach examines how social movements establish various frames or "schemata of interpretation" that help movement participants understand and respond to the world around them.[18] While the term *frame* is borrowed from the earlier work of Gregory Bateson and Erving Goffman, most movement scholars use the term to describe the collective action frames that social movements attempt to establish among participants and allies. Furthermore frames function as diagnostic, prognostic, and motivational structures: frames help individuals not only to attribute injustice and causality to social problems but also to develop and pursue potential strategies for social change.[19] As such, "collective action frames are action-oriented sets of beliefs and meanings that inspire and legitimate the activities and campaigns of a social movement organization (SMO)."[20]

Nevertheless Benford expresses doubt about the utility of simply identifying and describing movement frames: not only do descriptions often identify more frames than could be used in an explanatory sense, but they also overlook how frames are created and maintained by framing processes.[21] Put another way, framing approaches also recognize that movements are involved in important "signifying work."[22] Insofar as movements are involved in framing activities, "movement organizations and actors [are] actively engaged in the production and maintenance of meaning for constituents, antagonists, and bystanders or observers."[23] Frames emerge from and are transmitted by movement discourse, even as they determine in part what shape that discourse will take. As such they are as much rhetorical structures as they are cognitive ones, emerging from the interaction of movement participants and their interlocutors. Nor are these interactions limited to language: "frames can also be communicated through nonverbal devices, such as presentation of self, tactics, and organization forms."[24]

As rhetorical structures frames highlight important dimensions of social movement activity. First, they reveal that micro-mobilization (the recruitment and organization of movement participants) is as important a movement activity as macro-mobilization (the execution of protests and direct action campaigns.) Second, movements are constantly involved in the production of movement identity and culture. Third and finally, the rhetorical aspects of a movement's activities have a direct structuring effect on its collective identity and actions. Frames, then, might appear similar to Kenneth Burke's concept of terministic screens, which likewise serve to constrain rhetorically the manner in which individuals interpret and respond to the world around them.[25] However, where Burke's terministic screens might seem to function as ideological structures that determine worldview and rhetorical action, frames are more strategic. As such they describe not an ideological structure (which we might define as a complete system of values and beliefs) but rather a strategic arrangement of terms and concepts designed to garner support and structure response.[26]

An examination of the frames established by the Louisville sit-ins might help us understand how various protest forms came to be understood as extensions of a broader sit-in movement. In its most simple articulation, the collective action frame established by the sit-in movements of the late 1950s and early 1960s might be considered an extension of the master civil rights frame. This frame focused attention on African American demands for legal, political, and economic equality; defined segregation and Jim Crow as moral and legal injustices; and asserted the dignity and justice of African American efforts to secure their rights. Civil rights frames also informed and were in turn informed by the nonviolent direct-action campaigns that attended civil rights organizing across the South.

Sit-ins focused civil rights frames in a few key ways. First, sit-in frames were focused around the desegregation of public accommodations such as lunch counters, restaurants, theaters, and department stores. Sit-in frames also typically established the right of African Americans to request and expect service, with many sit-ins following a script that began with a request for service at a restaurant or lunch counter and became a refusal to leave without service if the initial request was denied. However, as the Louisville sit-in movement reveals, sit-ins also served as a rhetorical element within civil rights frames: they focused attention on the need for direct action in response to segregation, thereby helping to facilitate a shift from legal and political strategies for the mass campaigns associated with the classical phase of the civil rights movement.

The rights frame that Louisville activists drew upon had been formed much earlier than 1957, and civil rights activity was a constant feature of the city by that point. The frame that animated the sit-ins came from three key sets of events: local civil rights campaigns focused on integrating public accommodations in Louisville; larger national efforts to secure integration; and direct action campaigns such as those found in Montgomery and Greensboro. The existence of a strong NAACP chapter and an active African American newspaper, the *Louisville Defender,* meant there was also the infrastructure needed to tie these events together as a local movement frame.

In fact the *Defender* is a rich source for examining how civil rights frames developed in advance of and during Louisville's sit-in campaigns. While it should not be regarded as the only institution that contributed to frame development (nor should the frames presented in the *Defender* be considered the sole script for local civil rights activists), the *Defender* is an important source because it presented itself as a rhetorical agency for the expression of African American political aspirations. As an African American newspaper, the *Defender* overtly adhered to the Negro Press Creed, "that America can best lead the world away from racial and national antagonisms when it accords to every man regardless of race, color, or creed his human and legal rights."[27] In an editorial commemorating the 125th Negro Newspaper Anniversary Week, the *Defender* further articulated its mission as not just "[telling] of the failures and shortcomings of Negroes" but also "[pointing] the way to overcoming these handicaps in order to reach the full stature of manhood."[28] The *Defender* thereby defined its role as the active articulation of a civil rights program that would serve and extend "the aspirations of Negros in Kentucky and America."[29]

By the early 1950s, the *Defender* had articulated its journalistic program to that of local activists. On the occasion of the paper's twentieth anniversary, its editors proclaimed that "because of their cooperation with the *Defender* and its ideas Negroes have made many openings where none existed before, they have been ready to grasp opportunities which if presented before could find no acceptable takers."[30] What the *Defender* brought to civil rights efforts in Louisville, then, was twofold. First, it provided an important vehicle for presenting local, regional, and national civil rights events, thereby aligning campaigns in Louisville with other campaigns across the country. Second, its editors provided clear interpretations of local civil rights issues as well as recommendations about how the African American community should respond. As a result they were involved rhetorically in developing local movement frames and aligning those frames with emerging national narratives about civil rights.

It also warrants mention that the *Defender* was staunchly committed to integration as the only means of achieving "first-class citizenship for all."[31] Local civil rights campaigns in the early 1950s likewise focused on the integration of public facilities. The Louisville NAACP chapter had already devoted considerable time to desegregating public libraries, schools, parks, and entertainment venues (primarily Memorial Auditorium and Iroquois Amphitheatre). In 1952 federal district court judge Roy Shelbourne ordered the integration of the city's golf courses in response to a lawsuit filed by African American dentist P. O. Sweeney. At the same time, African Americans were attempting to have segregated seating removed from Louisville's Parkway Field. By 1953, as the battle over park and amphitheater access continued alongside efforts to desegregate baseball games, the NAACP also turned its attention to the local interstate bus stations.

Buoyed by these efforts, *Defender* owner Frank Stanley wrote that "we have only scratched the surface":

> Segregation must be eradicated completely—especially in education, employment, and recreation. All public accommodations must be opened to us. There must be a Negro member of every policy-making body. Our immediate objective should be the Louisville Board of Education. Library integration should spread from the main library to all branches. Hotels, theaters, restaurants and stores should be opened to Negro patrons without restriction. In short, Kentucky should have a civil rights law that would prohibit any merchant or public accommodation from refusing service to a citizen solely because of race. In addition, we need greater collaboration on every movement designed to make democracy a live, vibrant thing for everyone.[32]

We see in Stanley's remarks a full elaboration of the civil rights frame animating the *Defender's* commentary in the early 1950s. William Gamson suggests that the basic architecture of collective action frames involves the coordination of three elements: injustice, identity, and agency.[33] Stanley hardly needed to identify the injustice associated with segregation, though he did situate it in opposition to a conception of democracy as a "live, vibrant thing for everyone." Furthermore this conception of democracy allowed Stanley to articulate African Americans' collective identity to a shared communal purpose and to efforts to define citizenship as a right not limited by race. Stanley also articulated the need for collective action, both when he exhorted readers to continue the fight against segregation and when he called specifically for "greater collaboration" in the interests of democracy. Perhaps most important, Stanley identified major sites of injustice—public accommodations, education, libraries, and representative bodies—and suggested that integration of one such site (in this case golf courses) naturally demanded integration of all of them.

It is worth noting that the collective action advocated by the *Defender* at this point was primarily focused on legal and legislative intervention—the securing of favorable rulings from judges or the election of local and national political candidates who supported civil rights legislation. For the most part, this was in keeping with the general strategies adopted by the NAACP, which remained Louisville's most prominent civil rights group until the late 1950s. Nonetheless, as the civil rights movement developed across the South and the nation, local groups came to focus increasingly on direct collective action—and the sit-in— as a complementary (or sometimes competing) strategy.

These campaigns received important rhetorical recognition when, on May 17, 1954, the U.S. Supreme Court ruled unanimously against the segregated public school in *Brown v. Board of Education* (347 US 483 1954). While the *Brown* decision had the partial effect of turning local NAACP attention toward school integration, it also provided an important master frame for local activists to align their efforts with; that the decision covered public education no doubt gave it even greater rhetorical resonance.[34] Reflecting on the importance of the case in May 1955, the *Defender's* editors concluded that the case "[gave] legal sanction to moral obligation," thereby validating local efforts to combat segregation.[35] The master frame espoused in the *Brown v. Board* decision—one embodied in the language of the court decision itself—aligned with the local frames promulgated in the *Defender*. The focus was once again on integration as the only responsible means of achieving equality and on public institutions as the crucial battleground in that fight.

During the same period, the rights frame espoused by the *Defender* began to advocate direct action alongside support for the NAACP and other legal challenges to segregation. Commenting in 1955 on the still-segregated lunch counters at the city's train stations, the editors offered a pointed if oblique warning: "Better wake up, Louisville, to the inevitability of change—It is later than you think."[36] This warning followed what the paper perceived as unnecessary and unconscionable delays in the implementation of federal and Supreme Court decisions: as Frank Stanley put it, "the only way to integrate is to integrate."[37] It also anticipated the rise of massive resistance and the lack of federal response to increased violence against African Americans.[38] With the 1955 murders of George Lee, Lamar Smith, and Emmett Till, the *Defender* lost patience with a federal government that "has yet to intervene in a concrete way."[39] In the same issue, Stanley warned that "unless this reign of terror is abated in time, serious trouble is bound to come."[40]

Bus boycotts in Montgomery, Alabama (1955–56) and Tallahassee, Florida (1956–57), provided African Americans across the South with successful examples of direct-action campaigns. Frank Stanley remarked that "the Bus Boycott in Montgomery, Alabama stands out as an intelligent, organized method of making an effective fight against segregation" and that "their example is one worthy of emulation by others who would seek to better their lot."[41] A little more than a month later, Stanley reflected on the potential effectiveness of similar actions in Louisville.[42] By November the *Defender* concluded that "accomplished achievements were obtained by militant demands. Go-slowers and conservatives notwithstanding, other advancements will come only from more constant and militant demands for our just due."[43] It is significant that Stanley viewed direct action not just as a new means for responding to segregation but also as a means of responding to the failures of both government agencies and legal strategists to offer a serious challenge to racial prejudice.

We might suggest, then, that the militant demands championed by Stanley did not just establish direct action as another potential agency within the *Defender's* rights frame; they also stood as evidence of an emergent collective identity among African Americans: "The hard facts are that Negroes no longer can be frightened on the issue of civil rights. In the case of buses some two dozen southern cities have desegregated them successfully. Moreover, in the cities of hard core resistance like Birmingham and Atlanta, Negroes are asserting their rights spelled out in recent court rulings. They can be depended upon to continue this movement irrespective of reprisals, trumped local evasion and temporary suspension of service."[44]

The *Defender's* editorials speak to the dynamic nature of the rights frame they were espousing, which remained responsive not just to broader developments within the civil rights movement but also to the interrelation of injustice, identity, and agency. When legal challenges proved successful, they provided civil rights activists with new legal definitions of citizenship that in turn animated the conceptions of identity and agency that lay at the heart of local rights frames. That collective identity, however, increasingly looked beyond legal strategies to direct action as an agency for achieving their demands.

The increased attention toward direct action coincided with a renewed attention on public accommodations. Focus had already turned to public accommodations by 1956, when the January 19 issue of the *Defender* ran the front-page headline "Lunchrooms Still Segregated Here" in reference to waiting rooms and restaurants at city train stations.[45] Clarence Matthews and Frank Stanley again returned to the topic in November 1956, focusing on segregation in restaurants, theaters, bus terminals, and hotels.[46] However the issue received sustained attention in December 1958, following the refusal of a Walgreens drugstore to serve the visiting mayor of Kingston, Jamaica. The *Defender's* editors immediately decried the event as an insult and called for a public accommodation ordinance to address the problem.[47] In the same issue, journalist Nat Tillman began what would become an eighteen-story series on the segregation of public accommodations in Louisville. The series—along with nineteen other editorials and articles devoted to segregation in Louisville's public accommodations—not only emphasized segregation as a widespread issue across downtown Louisville but also kept the subject on the *Defender's* front page until April 1959. Throughout those months the injustice posed by downtown segregation once again became a "hot cognition," a site of moral indignation that required immediate redress.[48]

It was this elaborated rights frame—one in which segregation in public accommodations became a hot cognition to be remedied by legal and protest actions—that animated sit-ins throughout 1959, first at Taylor Drug Stores and then at the American Legion and the Brown Theater.[49] It also informed Tillman's argument that "the examples set by the Committee of Racial Equality [*sic*] in its effort to break down racial discrimination have plenty of merits and could very well be utilized by other groups opposing segregatory practices."[50] Tillman drew attention to CORE sit-ins occurring in St. Louis and closer to home in Lexington and argued for similar sustained activities in Louisville. The Christmas pickets of the Brown Theater further assured that this frame would continue to have resonance as Louisville's emerging sit-in movement headed into 1960. Reflecting on the failure of city and state public accommodations ordinances, the *Defender's* editors concluded that "wisdom, therefore, dictates a consolidation of effort toward winning the battle first in Louisville, where there is some evidence of desegregated public accommodations."[51]

Remarks by Tillman, Stanley, and the *Defender's* editors prove significant insofar as they suggested the need for a shift in strategy—from legal action to direct action—and the adoption of CORE protest strategies alongside those of the NAACP. However to suggest that direct action became an increasingly central aspect of civil rights frames within Louisville is not to suggest that activists gave up on legal and political strategies. Much of the *Defender's* attention on the issue then turned to the efforts of Alderman W. W. Beckett to introduce a city public accommodations ordinance, efforts that continued without success for much of the year. (Beckett twice brought ordinances before the city council—once in February and once in March—only to have them voted down on both occasions in favor of voluntary desegregation.) Nonetheless the outrage that followed the defeat of Beckett's efforts was expressed within the context not just of intransigent city politics but also of the emerging sit-in movement. The *Defender* first noted the sit-in movement on March 3, devoting front-page space to the spread of sit-ins as a "vital force to be reckoned with."[52] A week later, an editorial titled "It Can Happen Here" linked the failure of city desegregation efforts directly to the potential for sit-in protests in the River City: "For the moment Louisville has been spared of renewed protest demonstrations. They will not be forever absent, however, if Mayor Hoblitzell, the Board of Aldermen and segregating businesses continue to underestimate the extent of Negro dissatisfaction with the 'Status Quo.'"[53]

The *Defender*'s editors recognized that the political opportunity structure surrounding the issue of public accommodations in Louisville had shifted in important ways. The city's civil rights activists had been challenging segregation of public facilities for more than a decade, and landmark federal legal decisions had served only to strengthen their resolve. Furthermore civil rights campaigns in Montgomery, Tallahassee, and later Greensboro provided activists with new protest strategies and with evidence of those strategies' efficacy. The rhetorical figure of the sit-in, alongside the material practice of sitting in, came to organize civil rights rhetoric in the River City and led activists to read events in Louisville in the context of emerging direct-action campaigns across the South. It is this shift in political context that led both to the widespread adoption of sit-in strategies by Louisville's civil rights campaigners and to the use of sit-ins across the region as a rhetorical lens for discussing local civil rights struggles.

The Sit-In as a Framing Practice

As Louisville's sit-in movement gathered momentum in the early months of 1960, CORE activist Rev. James Lawson visited Louisville to help local NAACP members coordinate their civil rights activities. Lawson advocated sit-ins as a logical means of pursuing nonviolent resistance to segregation and racial prejudice and specifically identified four key aspects to such nonviolent direct action. First, such action drew attention to segregation as an "immoral, unjust, and sinful" institution. Second, a nonviolent action brought about "Christian change" in a faster manner than legal action. Third, a nonviolent action allowed African Americans to discover "new concepts of themselves in this new spirit of disciplined unification." And fourth, nonviolence created an "atmosphere in

which social change can take place."[54] In offering these four points, Lawson not
only reflected on the theories of nonviolent resistance then developing among
CORE, SNCC, and SCLC members; he also sought to align local civil rights
frames in the River City with those developed elsewhere across the South.
These new civil rights frames—which were immediately linked to the emerging
regional sit-in movement—would, in turn, animate sit-in protests in Louisville
throughout the early 1960s.

Lawson's remarks are also important as a description of how the sit-in strategy was not only animated by civil rights frames but also an increasingly important element within those frames. Furthermore his four points suggest that
he understood sit-ins not just as a protest strategy but rather as material rhetorical structures that enabled activists to dramatize and disseminate civil rights
frames. As suggested above, the sit-in frame espoused by Louisville's civil rights
activists not only drew on earlier rights frames but also served to organize a
range of activities—from the Brown Theater pickets to lunch counter sit-ins, to
the "Nothing New for Easter" boycotts. Frank Stanley even referred to the need
for a "vote-in" in the 1961 city elections, suggesting that even more conventional
political organization could and should now be understood within the context
of local direct-action efforts. Sit-ins, then, were not simply the manifestation of
already extant rights frames; rather they were an important rhetorical agency
for developing and maintaining those frames.

Most immediately sit-ins dramatized the injustice of segregation as an
urgent issue in need of immediate remedy. In an editorial republished in the
Defender in March 1960, the *Philadelphia Tribune* argued that "the one thing
already accomplished by the demonstration of Negro students in the South is
to disprove the assertions of Southern politicians that Negroes are satisfied with
segregation."[55] Reflecting on local conditions, Stanley echoed this sentiment
when he suggested that "considerable Louisville Negro souls are tired enough
right now to rise up in righteous indignation."[56] Sit-ins became the natural
outpouring of African American demands for justice, which increasingly highlighted the lack of progress made via political or legal avenues. Indeed by 1961
the *Defender* claimed that sit-ins "were born in the persistent denial of Public
Accommodations privileges and the total lack of official leadership given to
this issue."[57] Sit-ins, then, established the kairos of the public accommodations
battle materially, in much the manner that King argued in his "Letter from Birmingham Jail" that African Americans could no longer wait for white approval
or assistance on the issue of civil rights. "The only way to obtain your rights,"
concluded the *Defender*'s editors, "is to nonviolently clamor for them."[58]

Sit-ins did not always decry the injustice of segregation in strident terms;
humor and irony proved to be just as effective in highlighting the arbitrary and
ultimately indefensible segregation policies of local businesses. The *Defender*

noted that, during negotiations over the Algonquin shopping center pickets and attempts to desegregate the center's bowling facilities, "two fair skinned Negroes . . . were completing games on one of the lanes' 72 alleys."[59] Mervin Aubespin discussed a similar set of events that occurred at the Blue Boar restaurant during downtown sit-ins in 1960 and 1961:

> A guy named Johnson owned the Blue Boar chain, and there were about three restaurants local [sic]. But there was one at Fourth and Chestnut Street. He was also president of the Restaurant Association, and a member of the Board of Education. And it was a fast place, it was a cafeteria like place that was quite popular at noon. We focused on it, because it was the type of place that all economic levels felt comfortable in, but blacks were not allowed in there. And one day, in order to show how ironic it was, and he was a hard egg to crack, we sat my mother, and a number of members of the African American community, who were extremely fair and you couldn't tell the difference. People like Marjorie Miles, who was as white as this cup with straight hair and others, but then you know, we've just got that whole rainbow thing. And there were a number of them, who were that fair, that you couldn't tell. And we had them to go, they went, and not in a group, two at a time, three here, just like they were going in. And they were seated all over the place. And then their husbands arrived to meet them. And of course, they stopped them at the door. And it made the point so beautifully: it was interesting that I never saw anything in *The Courier-Journal* about it.[60]

The Blue Boar protests highlighted the uneven application and enforcement of segregation customs in Louisville. Aubespin's reflections on the humor involved in the process also demonstrate how the protest challenged not only the arbitrary nature of desegregation but also the faulty logic underlying the use of skin color as a dividing line.

However, just as important, sit-ins did not simply articulate a goal or demand equal service; rather they established African American rights via an occupation of public space. The very nature of their demands—for a sandwich or a cup of coffee, without having to move—made any attempt at "reasonable" resistance all but impossible. By physically enacting their demands, sit-in participants also highlighted the inadequacy of calls for voluntary action on the part of business owners, who in turn claimed to be waiting for other business to make the first move. Insofar as they dramatized injustice and provoked visible responses from business owners, sit-ins proved capable of capturing the public imagination in a way that newspaper articles and legal strategies had not.[61]

The sit-in became a performative rhetorical strategy—one that dramatized the claims of civil rights activists by enacting materially the behaviors that they hoped to have protected by law. As one editorial on the May 1960

Kaufman-Strauss pickets put it: "We do not know how Vice President, Roy Gardner will determine when its Tea Room integration will be right. But it has been 'right' all along—the principle of fair play and common service to all customers alike, that is. There is no justifiable argument against the rightness of integration. It is one of those things almost everyone agrees should be done. But few do anything to achieve it."[62]

Sit-ins, then, were an attempt to achieve integration, and to do so in the faster manner identified by Lawson. However they were also an attempt to intensify the claim that integration was an indisputable moral right by enacting integration counter to legal or social custom. Sit-ins thereby begged the question—why can't everyone be served?—by dramatizing both the question and its only reasonable answer in the most urgent of terms.

The demands of local picketers were no doubt strengthened by the other local and regional efforts being made to combat segregation. Stories following the regional sit-in movement appeared on the front pages of the *Defender* alongside articles devoted to Alderman Beckett's battles with the city board.[63] Sit-ins became a means of demonstrating the shared identity of civil rights campaigns—whether focused on legal or direct action, whether local or regional in scope—and further framing local civil rights campaigns regarding shared principles. A front-page editorial published on January 7, 1960, indicates the framing potential to be found in the December 1959 pickets of the Brown Theater: "The current picketing is actually not against the Brown Theatre alone, nor is it a clamoring just to see Porgy and Bess. . . . However, the principle remains: Why cannot Negroes go to movie houses unsegregatedly in Louisville? Would it not seem that races that can swim, play, study, read, work and in some instances worship and eat side by side certainly could sit together at a movie?"[64]

Concluding that protests were necessary for the face of lingering prejudice and neglect by city officials, the editorial argued that the only actions open to "all people of good conscience" were both to join the picket line and apply pressure to city officials and theater owners.[65]

However, just as important, sit-ins provided an immediate representation of local rights frames. Commenting in March 1961 on the momentum and the achievements of the sit-in movement, Frank Stanley noted that "the manner in which Louisville Negroes are making their clamorous demands felt—the coordination of effort and the depth of solidarity all are wonderful sights to behold. The movement in itself without any real test of strength has won many white supporters."[66] What Stanley's remarks make clear is that sit-ins themselves structured and fostered collective identity, suggesting that the coordination of effort emerged from the dynamic structure of sit-in protests. However coordination—the coordination of sitting down together, picketing together, and maintaining the composure needed for nonviolent action—is just as important as the sense of shared purpose that Louisville's civil rights activists had. By engaging in the coordinated activity, activists created what Gladys Ritchie has called a "rhetoric of human action."[67] For Ritchie such a rhetoric inheres not only in the manner in which the sit-in participant's body becomes a vehicle for displaying and protesting an injustice but also in the way that participants act together: "Greensboro, 1960. Surrounded by a large crowd of white high school toughs dressed in black leather jackets and carrying Confederate flags, a group of integrated students sat-in at the Kress lunch counter. The students were very well dressed, many in suits and ties and several carried Bibles. While the young whites taunted, snarled and jeered, the students remained silent, poised, determined."[68]

What becomes important in this description is the shared activity of wearing suits, carrying Bibles, remaining silent in the same pose. These activities become an instance of what historian William McNeill has called "keeping together in time," the coordinated physical aspects of dance and drill that create in participants a feeling of solidarity and membership within a group.[69] If we acknowledge sit-ins not simply as a protest strategy but also as an instance of a coordinated physical action, then we might see similar dynamics at work within those protests as well.

If we understand sit-ins as a rhetorical practice, then Stanley's comments demonstrate the manner in which sit-ins and collective action made civil rights frames both visible and rhetorically effective. The collective action itself becomes a crucial means of cultivating collective action frames and not simply the desired output of other framing efforts. Furthermore Stanley's comments describe how the sit-in as a rhetorical practice also allowed the amplification of civil rights frames for white sympathizers. While collective action as a framing practice no doubt exists in a somewhat reciprocal relationship with extant and emerging civil rights frames, its foundational importance as a framing practice demonstrates how sit-ins worked rhetorically on both macro- and micro-mobilizational levels.

With the emergence of the sit-in movement in Greensboro and other southern cities, the *Defender* had further evidence of the efficacy of sit-in protests.[70] Efficacy, however, was framed not simply in terms of sit-ins' disruptive force, nor their dramatization of the just demand for access to public space, but rather in terms of economic impact. "Next to his ballot," stated a March 1960 editorial, "the Negro's buying power is his most potent weapon."[71] Dean Gordon Hancock, writing only two weeks later, noted that the sit-in movement was by now "the top controversy in the United States."[72] However the importance of the sit-ins for Hancock was, once again, economic: "The current sit-downs are attempts to emphasize the possibilities in making the dollar do double duty, by using it as a weapon against segregation and as a protest against restricted economic opportunities."[73] The collective identity found in sit-in protests was aligned with a collective economic identity that might have been less easily recognized. Nonetheless as boycotts continued and stores elected to shut rather than integrate their restaurants, this collective economic force became more and more apparent. As one editorial put it: "The sit-in and the economic boycott are the surest signs that a new era in race relations in the South is underway. They are signs that there is a deep convention [*sic*] among Negroes that they can wait no longer in starting programs to achieve what they consider to be their rights."[74]

The arguments found within the *Defender* also suggest that local sit-ins increasingly came to invoke the regional sit-in movement and thereby functioned rhetorically as a reference to struggles against segregation across the South. Furthermore the *Defender* aligned the rights frames of local protestors with similar frames held by individuals sympathetic to the cause of civil rights. An editorial reprinted by the *Defender* in March 1960 argued that, in the face of the escalating sit-in movement, "surely [President Eisenhower] does not consider it lawful for Negro American citizens to be thrown in jail by the hundreds and showered by tear gas bombs simply because they seek to have the same privileges enjoyed by other Americans."[75] Chastisement of the president's inaction served not only to highlight the injustice of federal inaction but also to rally those readers who agreed with the editorial's depiction of the moral character of the sit-in movement. The *Defender*'s editors likewise encouraged local African Americans to align their actions with the sit-ins underway at the Brown Theater, Kaufman-Strauss, and Taylor. This attempt at frame alignment likewise came via censure of those not boycotting protested businesses: "The very least side-line-sitting Negroes can do is to have enough self-respect to stay away from businesses that segregate."[76] Sit-ins served as a means of elaborating and disseminating local civil rights frames via collective action itself and as a means of inviting support and participating from like-minded citizens for whom the sit-ins resonated.

Sit-ins thus proved to be important forms of collective action on both macro- and micro-mobilizational levels. That they also functioned rhetorically as dynamic framing processes can be seen in the formation of the Student Nonviolent Coordinating Committee, which itself emerged in part as an expression of the collective identity that had formed between sit-in participants across the South. The centrality of the sit-in strategy even led one Associated Negro Press article to refer to the movement as "sit-downism."[77] This process of identity formation also functioned as an agency for directly pursuing social change. Frank Stanley directly linked both processes when he remarked that "all social progress—all crusades have had . . . radicals, whom I prefer to call people so endowed with a sense of freedom that they will speak up and out at all times against human injustice. These bold expressionists have now been buttressed by those who stand-in, sit-in and kneel-in."[78]

Conclusion

The Louisville, Kentucky, sit-in movement played an important role in the development of the city's civil rights movement within the River City. The protests that culminated in the "Nothing New for Easter" campaign represented a shift among local activists from campaigns centered primarily on legal and political assaults on segregation to those based on nonviolent direct action. These campaigns not only had the effect of calling into question the efforts of local and federal officials but also highlighted the existence of widespread racial injustice in a city that had been regarded as one of the more racially progressive in the South. As depicted in the *Defender,* local sit-ins gave lie to the notion that African Americans were content with their lot and dramatized the injustice they faced in restaurants, parks, sports facilities, and bus stations. Furthermore segregation was not simply a sectional problem: by aligning their efforts with those of civil rights activists across the South, Louisville's civil rights movement drew attention to racism as a problem faced by African Americans everywhere.

The "Nothing New for Easter" campaign provides a rich archive for the study of the rhetorical dimensions of sit-in campaigns. Sit-ins proved to be important rhetorical actions not just on a macro-mobilizational level (where they served to highlight and challenge directly the injustice of segregation) but also on the micro-mobilizational level (where they served to coordinate civil rights activists and foster collective identity among African Americans and sympathetic whites). But perhaps most significant is the manner in which sit-ins, as a form of coordinated activity, made coordinated collective action itself the rhetorical foundation for the creation and elaboration of civil rights frames. Far from being the simple product of prior framing activities (though the Louisville sit-ins did emerge in part from the rights frames already articulated in the *Defender* and the African American community), sit-ins became a material framing practice in their own right and made possible the broader dissemination of rights frames.

The Louisville sit-in movement also highlights the way that the sit-in functioned as a rhetorical structure to organize a range of protest activities in a coherent set of campaigns. The rhetorical role of the *Louisville Defender* in fomenting Louisville's sit-in movement, and also in interpreting and amplifying that movement's demands, further emphasizes the manner in which sit-ins worked rhetorically to extend and transform earlier civil rights frames. The arguments presented by the *Defender*'s editorial staff also make clear that the sit-in frames developed by Louisville's civil rights movement extended beyond the simple act of sitting in and provided a means of interpreting the city's civil rights history. These frames not only served as an extension of earlier frames focused on legal and political strategies but also as a pointed response to those frames. Locally sit-ins spoke to the failure of city administrations and government officials alike to achieve meaningful civil rights reforms and to the need for African Americans to assert the rights they hoped to have recognized under the law.

While it remains important to locate civil rights sit-ins within the broader historical context of the civil rights movement, and also to locate the sit-in frames constructed by the Louisville sit-in movement within the broader civil rights frames operative within Louisville's African American community, the study of these sit-ins as framing practices provides a means of better understanding how collective action operates within social movements as a form of rhetorical action. Sit-ins were able to dramatize the injustice of segregation via the occupation of public spaces to which all citizens should have access. While the coordinated collective action found in such protest strategies as marches, singing, pickets, and sit-ins always takes place within the broader context of a specific social movement, such actions remain an important means of animating, maintaining, and furthering that movement's identity and influence. Collective action not only offers a means of communicating a movement's goals and demands; it also provides a structure for creating a collective identity and deploying that identity as an agency for social change.

Notes

1. "What a Record?" See also K'Meyer, *Civil Rights in the Gateway to the South*, 91.
2. Norris, "Early Instance of Nonviolence."
3. K'Meyer, *Civil Rights in the Gateway to the South*, 80.
4. Fosl and K'Meyer, *Freedom on the Border*, 88.
5. Ibid., 89.
6. K'Meyer, *Civil Rights in the Gateway to the South*, 81.
7. Fosl and K'Meyer, *Freedom on the Border*, 92.
8. Ibid., 92.
9. K'Meyer, *Civil Rights in the Gateway to the South*, 83.
10. Ibid., 85.
11. Ibid., 87.
12. Ibid., 88.
13. Ibid., 89.
14. Ibid., 91–92.
15. Ibid., 90–91.
16. Ibid., 97.
17. Ibid., 77.
18. Snow et al., "Frame Alignment Processes," 464.
19. Benford and Snow, "Framing Processes and Social Movements," 615.
20. Ibid., 614.
21. Benford, "Insider's Critique of the Social Movement Framing Perspective."
22. Snow and Benford, "Master Frames and Cycles of Protest," 136.
23. Ibid.
24. Noakes and Johnston, "Frames of Protest," 8–9.

25. Burke, *Language as Symbolic Action,* 44–63.

26. Zald, "Culture, Ideology, and Strategic Framing."

27. "Negro Press Creed."

28. "Negro Press Is You."

29. Ibid.

30. "Our Anniversary."

31. Stanley, "Being Frank," 18 August 1951.

32. Ibid., 2 April 1952.

33. Gamson, "Constructing Social Protest," 90.

34. Bell, *Silent Covenants,* 35.

35. "Notable Anniversary."

36. "How Not to Attract."

37. Stanley, "Being Frank," 6 January 1955.

38. "Federal Intervention Necessary."

39. "Mississippi Injustice."

40. Stanley, "Being Frank," 15 September 1955.

41. Ibid., 9 February 1956.

42. Ibid., 15 March 1956.

43. "Militancy Is the Watchword."

44. "Groans from Dying Practices."

45. "Lunchroom Counters Still Segregated Here."

46. "Louisville Public Places Present Dismal Picture of Discrimination"; Stanley, "Being Frank," 29 November 1956, 6 December 1956.

47. "Ordinance Needed to End 'Accommodations' Bias."

48. William Gamson, "Constructing Social Protest," 90.

49. "Public Accommodations Bias Protest Begins"; "Wave of Protest Gets Legion Action"; "NAACP Pickets Brown Theater."

50. Stanley, "Being Frank," 20 August 1959.

51. "Better Strategy."

52. "Student 'Sit-Ins' Emerge as a Vital Force."

53. "It Can Happen Here."

54. "Sit-In Leader Advises Appeal to Moral Issues."

55. "Sit-Downs Prove Negroes Not Satisfied."

56. Stanley, "Being Frank," 21 April 1960.

57. "Crisis of Conscience."

58. Ibid.

59. "Bowling Segregation Is Cause of Disagreement."

60. Aubespin, Brinson interview, 24–25.

61. "Brown Theater Protest Points Up Bias Problem."

62. "Can't Eat—Don't Buy."

63. "Aldermen 'Kill' Human Relations Bill"; "Citizens Rally to Hear Core Leader"; "Students Win Sit-In Victory in N.C. Court"; "Sit-In Leader Lawson at NAACP Meet Here."

64. "Editorial."

65. Ibid.

66. Stanley, "Being Frank," 9 March 1961.

67. Ritchie, "Sit-In," 22.

68. Ibid.

69. McNeill, *Keeping Together in Time.*

70. "Student 'Sit-ins' Emerge as a Vital Force."

71. "It Can Happen Here."

72. "Student 'Sit-Ins' Is Top Controversy in United States."

73. Ibid.

74. "Sit-Ins, a Weapon of Choice?"

75. "Sit Downs Prove Negroes Not Satisfied."

76. "Sit-Ins, a Weapon of Choice?"

77. "Students Form Non-violence Coordination Group."

78. Stanley, "Being Frank," 22 September 1960.

SUFFER THE LITTLE CHILDREN

Propriety and Piety in the 1963 Birmingham, Alabama,
Youth Demonstrations for Civil Rights

Roseann M. Mandziuk

Late in the spring of 1963, while facing extraordinary pressures to suspend its demonstrations in Birmingham, Alabama, the strategists of the Southern Christian Leadership Conference (SCLC) and the local activists in the Alabama Christian Movement for Human Rights (ACMHR) launched one of the most controversial tactics of the civil rights movement. *Newsweek* magazine described what it called the "puzzling new adversary" that confronted Commissioner Bull Connor and his police the first day of the children's demonstrations: "They came in all sizes from kindergarten through high-school age, averaging perhaps 14. They came from all directions, thicker and faster than the police could handle them. And, when the cops caught up, they rode off to jail as cheerily as they would to a Sunday-school picnic."[1] In an action variously referred to as the "children's miracle"[2] and the "children's crusade,"[3] for six days in early May 1963, Birmingham's black children demonstrated, faced down high-pressure fire hoses and police dogs, and were arrested and incarcerated by the hundreds. While the strategy succeeded in garnering sympathy for the movement's efforts and forced the white city leaders to the bargaining table, the tactic also attracted criticism from within the movement leadership circles, the black community, and the national press.[4]

Many historical commentators look to the 1963 demonstrations and ultimate victory in Birmingham as the key turning point for the leadership of Rev. Dr. Martin Luther King Jr. and the amassing of massive public sentiment on the side of the struggle for racial equality being played out in southern communities.[5] Rhetorical studies examining this critical campaign focus upon the eloquence of King's stirring "Letter From Birmingham Jail"[6] to the exclusion of examinations of the movement strategy more generally or the children's demonstrations more specifically. Much more of rhetorical interest occurred in Birmingham than King's response to the criticism of local white ministers. Indeed while King's arrest actually did little to invigorate the SCLC's flailing efforts in the community immediately, the children's involvement ignited many flames for the civil rights cause, including drawing the necessary media attention to the movement and pressuring city officials, as well as President John F. Kennedy's administration, to come swiftly to a negotiated settlement. In particular the photographs circulated in the national news media spurred a sense of outrage and urgency and became the basis for a specific understanding of the events as a mythic struggle between good and evil.[7] Still the children's demonstrations constituted a significant rhetorical gamble on the part of the movement's leadership.[8]

The controversy surrounding the children's demonstrations in Birmingham reveals several important aspects of the rhetorical dilemmas faced by social movements, the dramatistic dimensions of such struggles, and the forces of social control in American society. Similar to other protest strategies used by the civil rights movement, such as sit-ins and wade-ins, the marching of children evokes questions of the body in protest and the materiality of the public space. As Kevin DeLuca argues, "Bodies are enmeshed in a turbulent stream of multiple and conflictual discourses that shape what they mean in particular contexts."[9] The location of a protest powerfully meshes with the presence of protestors to become "a rich intersection of bodies, material aspects, past meanings, present performances, and future possibilities."[10] When bodies enter into a disputed space, a formerly disciplined body becomes "unruly" and functions as "a rich source of argumentative force."[11] Children's bodies in the arena of public protest presented a specific and potent rhetorical challenge to the symbolic and exclusionary meanings of the public spaces of Birmingham, as their insistence on agency defied the doubled docility culturally imposed upon them both as children and as black bodies.[12]

The use of children for protest in a volatile climate such as that which marked Birmingham in 1963 especially challenged the propriety of the movement's leaders and the piety of the social system. This essay examines these rhetorical dimensions by situating the children's demonstrations within the strategic framework of the movement itself and by contextualizing the tactical choice within the larger arena of social relations. Because the campaign in Birmingham was selected by the SCLC to achieve impact for the movement on the national stage, the essay relies primarily on national press accounts and historical sources to trace how the dimming of King's reputation underscored the motivation to look to Birmingham for a clear and dramatic outcome.[13] The involvement of youth in their liberation ultimately raises significant issues regarding the ethical responsibilities of the adults who guided them to activism and the implications of choosing such rhetorical tactics.

Significantly the movement's internal conflict over the use of the children in Birmingham is a key moment when the younger generation of sit-in activists collided with the SCLC's older generation of leaders and their more cautious tactics. When James Bevel and Diane Nash, veterans of the Nashville lunch counter campaign, arrived in Birmingham in 1963, they sought to move the movement's leadership further toward increasing levels of direct engagement, including the use of youth in demonstrations and confrontation strategies. As David Halberstam argues, the sit-in generation shared "the commitment to a radical, nonviolent way to change America" and was inspired by its victories.[14] The eventual success of the 1963 children's crusade in Birmingham represented an important transition when the rhetorical strategies of the sit-ins entered into the later direct-action campaigns in the larger movement. When the lesson learned by the sit-in veterans, "that each victory they gained demanded a further step" against the totality of segregation, was embraced in 1963, the result dramatically changed the tide of the civil rights movement.[15]

Rhetorical Dimensions of Propriety and Piety

The extant rhetorical literature regarding social movements emphasizes either the functional, managerial, strategic nature of the rhetorical choices made by proponents[16] or highlights the symbolic, confrontational, dramatic nature of the movement's enjoinment with the establishment.[17] One perspective considers rhetoric as an agency for change and analyzes its strategic value for movement advocates; the other considers more broadly the question of rhetorical form and meaning in social protest. Few studies attempt to combine the perspectives to yield a critique of the internal and external rhetorical dimensions of a movement's actions. A complex event such as the children's demonstrations in Birmingham requires both perspectives to illuminate the crucial features of the symbolic interchanges and clashes that marked the six days of protest and their aftermath. Consequently this essay employs contributions and concepts from both approaches to social movement rhetoric to reach a critical understanding of the children's actions.

First, from the literature focused on the strategic and functional aspects of social movement rhetoric a key concept can be gleaned regarding the potential for a strategic choice to challenge the legitimacy of the movement, what I will call "propriety." In his influential essay on the "requirements, problems, and strategies" of social movement persuasion, Herbert Simons proposes that "to deal with pressures from the external system, a movement may lose sight of its ideological values and become preoccupied with power for its own sake. Careful, by contrast, to remain consistent with its values, the movement may forsake those strategies and tactics that are necessary to implement the program."[18] Each rhetorical act undertaken by a movement not only fulfills a strategic function, such as transforming perceptions or mobilizing members for action,[19] but it also reflects the values of the movement. Consequently each strategic choice crucially contributes to the legitimacy or illegitimacy of the movement in light of the extent to which the individual tactic is perceived as consistent with the value set that the movement espouses. The children's demonstrations contained the potential to diminish the legitimacy of the campaign in Birmingham overall as well as, more specifically, the legitimacy of King's leadership. The concept of propriety is employed in this essay to examine the internal conflicts over the children's demonstrations and the challenges to its rhetorical image this tactic generated in the public reactions to it.

Second, the concept of "piety" can be gleaned from the rhetorical studies literature focusing on confrontation as a rhetorical form in movements. In a formative essay, Robert Cathcart argues that confrontation is consummatory for movements because its challenge to the system—in essence its rejection of the authority of the establishment—"produces dialectical enjoinment in the moral arena."[20] In his discussion Cathcart draws significantly from the ideas of Kenneth Burke regarding hierarchy, order, and mystery. As Burke proposes, the hierarchical principle underlies all human behavior, such that "order, the secret, and the kill" are the three primary motives that undergird human symbolic actions.[21] For Burke it is the rhetoric of piety, the keeping of the essential secret or mystery, that holds the hierarchy in place and functions to dispel challenges to it.[22] Movements consequently must challenge this piety by seeking confrontational symbols that expose the contradictions of the system they oppose. In the case of the children's demonstrations, much of the success of the movement's campaign in Birmingham can be explained by the degree to which the tactic engendered a moral conflict and challenged the pious coherence of the white community's legitimacy. The concept of piety is used in this essay to explore the confrontational dimensions of the children's tactic conceived as a symbolic, moral negation leveled in opposition to the general support being offered to the Birmingham city officials and the pressures put upon the SCLC to suspend its demonstrations there.

Propriety: From Desperation to Triumph

Taylor Branch begins his book *Pillar of Fire: America in the King Years, 1963–65* with the statement: "There was no historical precedent for Birmingham, Alabama, in April and May of 1963, when the power balance of a great nation turned not on clashing armies or global commerce but on the youngest student demonstrators of African descent, down to first- and second-graders."[23] By all accounts, however, up to that point, the civil rights movement's efforts in Birmingham had stalled, drawing intense criticism from many quarters.[24] The victory won there ultimately depended upon the movement leadership's embarking on the unprecedented step of drawing upon the youth to achieve the Gandhian principle of filling the jails.[25] The choice to use children as the front-line soldiers in the battle of Birmingham turned the tide but also significantly challenged the rhetorical propriety of the movement leaders.

Due to their stalled efforts in Albany, Georgia, the previous year, the stakes were extremely high for King and his SCLC forces as they contemplated a campaign for desegregation in Birmingham in 1963. Although local activists considered the efforts in Albany to be a success, the movement had failed to win any real public victory; the schools remained segregated, and the public parks were closed in defiance of integration.[26] Moreover in Albany the movement had experienced the failure of their strategy to fill the jails. The tactic effectively was countered by Police Chief Laurie Pritchett, who emerged in the press as the "white knight" for his appearance of restraint.[27] In the midst of much criticism about his leadership from the national press, including *Time*'s assessment that "too much success has drained him of the captivating fervor that made him famous,"[28] King called a two-day meeting of the SCLC inner circle in Dorchester, Georgia, in January 1963. Their discussions explicitly focused on evaluating the lessons from Albany, reconsidering the structure of the SCLC, and strategizing the movement's next move.[29] King and his lieutenants sought a location for their next campaign where the outcome would be dramatic and gain crucial attention and momentum for them. The movement leaders chose Birmingham largely because of its infamous record of race relations, including its eighteen racial bombings and more than fifty cross-burnings since 1957, and its segregated schools, restaurants, and drinking fountains.[30] In his "Letter from Birmingham Jail," King describes this southern locale as "probably the most thoroughly segregated city in the United States."[31] Part of the calculation for the choice also was based on the reputation of Birmingham's commissioner of public safety, Eugene "Bull" Connor, who represented the old-style southern police brutality that Pritchett's public image departed from. As noted by biographer William A. Nunnelly, Connor served as "the perfect adversary" for the movement.[32] Additionally a local minister and activist, Fred Shuttlesworth, advocated strongly for the movement to choose Birmingham as its next target, as the city held the attraction of having an established local organization of activists and little of the national organizational infighting that had marred progress behind the scenes in Albany.[33] However King and the SCLC leadership did not recognize the limited appeal of the ACMHR among Birmingham's black middle class and business leaders due to its tradition of militant Christianity and practice of direct action.[34]

Following the Dorchester discussions, King assigned SCLC coordinator Wyatt Tee Walker the task of managing the Birmingham campaign. Walker developed a preliminary strategy that would unfold in stages, starting with small-scale sit-ins, moving to a boycott of downtown stores, progressing to slightly larger demonstrations; these original plans were not designed for provocation or mass arrest.[35] As the SCLC leadership cautiously postponed the planned start of the demonstrations from March until April to avoid beginning the activities before Birmingham's mayoral election and subsequent run-off, Shuttlesworth grew concerned about the lack of organization in the campaign and the timidity of the limited activities devised by Walker; he pleaded with the SCLC to consider a "broader scope of activities."[36] The cautionary stance taken by King and the SCLC leaders was captured by Ralph Abernathy who recalled that, while these delays were strategic, "we were also concerned about our own hides."[37]

The movement launched the Birmingham campaign on April 3, 1963, but the initially small number of demonstrators was a harbinger of the difficulties to come for the effort. King perceived "an alarming tide of opposition among activist Negroes,"[38] who along with the national press and the local city officials perceived the SCLC's efforts as ill-timed due to the defeat of Connor—who had "cowed Negroes for 23 years with hoarse threats and club-swinging cops"[39]—by racial moderate Albert Boutwell in a run-off election just the day before the launch.[40] The campaign and King's presence were criticized and resented by both the Kennedy administration and the local black business community. Branch specifically describes the difficulties that the meager early results of the demonstrations created for King's image: "Of the handicaps early in the Birmingham crisis, perhaps the most serious was King's image as a reluctant and losing crusader. He had been largely out of the public eye for eight months since his retreat from Albany. His name had faded. He appeared to be a worthy symbol from the 1950s who had overreached himself trying to operate as a full-fledged political leader."[41] The cautious admonishment of the *New York Times* captured the opposition to the SCLC's demonstrations: "We do not expect that there will be overnight rejection of all the policies that caused so much distress to the Negro community. The Rev. Dr. Martin Luther King Jr. and other leaders of the drive to break down racial barriers ought not expect it either."[42] The pressures on the movement to achieve a clear victory were intense right from the start, as was the significant attention paid to the propriety of their tactics.

The failure of several strategies employed throughout April defined the context in which the SCLC was forced to consider the use of the children to ignite the cause. Although on Palm Sunday a clash with Connor's police dogs yielded dramatic photographs that inspired Walker to consider a new "coercive nonviolent strategy," internal divisions among the SCLC, ACMHR, and local black elites put the movement into a damage control phase.[43] Following this incident, on April 10 a temporary court injunction was issued against the protest leaders "for encouraging demonstrations calculated to provoke breaches of the peace."[44] Facing legal opposition and pressure from religious, political, and local constituencies, and after generating only small numbers of jail volunteers and lackluster attendance at nightly mass meetings, the SCLC leadership was frustrated and desperate.[45] Even the Good Friday jailing of King and five other leaders on April 12 did little to inspire new adult volunteers as the movement "struggled along during the two weeks King spent in Jail and court."[46] Additionally, in hopes of garnering Kennedy administration support, in mid-April Walker shifted the movement strategy to an ill-fated voter registration drive, but the effort yielded little additional local support and no federal intervention.[47] As Glenn T. Eskew concludes, "Two deficiencies—the lack of volunteers and the lack of sensation—suggested that the movement had about run its course."[48]

Upon King's release from incarceration, at an SCLC staff meeting on April 29, activist James Bevel suggested the use of children in mass demonstrations. The ACMHR had begun a children's section two years earlier,[49] and Bevel and his wife, Diane Nash, a veteran of the 1960 Nashville lunch counter sit-ins, had been recruiting Birmingham high school students for nonviolence workshops. They began with the elite students, such as sports stars, and eventually drew large numbers of students who were "full of bravado, ready to march to jail."[50] Inside the movement strategy session, the idea of using child demonstrators alternatively created excitement and raised opposition and fears. Specifically while Bevel, Walker, and Shuttlesworth embraced the tactic, King "deliberated intensely"[51] as he and other movement leaders worried about the implications of the action for their reputations and the image of the movement's moral legitimacy. When King presented the idea to the central committee of Birmingham's black community leaders, these "middle-class locals, who theoretically got to approve all SCLC strategies, were aghast."[52] Concerns over the minimum age of the children who might be allowed to be involved were raised, as were questions about negative implications should violence result and fears that adult leaders realistically could be prosecuted for contributing to the delinquency of any minor who was arrested.[53] King was also extremely aware that national news reporters were losing interest in the SCLC's efforts and were preparing to leave town; as he proclaimed to movement insiders, "You know, we've got to get something going. . . . We've got to pick up everything because the press is leaving."[54] King's rhetorical problem of sustaining the movement while retaining its moral clarity placed him squarely in a dilemma regarding his ability to lead while remaining true to his principles.

The use of children challenged the rhetorical propriety of the SCLC leadership by placing in opposition its pragmatic and spiritual motives. In essence the movement found itself in a tactical contradiction; it was in need of a public, dramatic turning point but devoid of material and human resources among Birmingham's adult population.[55] If they risked the children and violence ensued, the damage done to their legitimacy as a moral force threatened their efficacy in future campaigns. The potential backlash could severely impact the sympathies of the press and the presidential administration, destroying the movement's ability to demand to be seen as a legitimate voice in the public discussions of race relations; yet if they did nothing, the movement would suffer another failure on the heels of Albany. The rhetorical paradoxes inherent in choosing to use child demonstrators had the potential to exact high penalties from the leadership and ultimately undermine the movement completely.

For King, in particular, the children's demonstrations threatened to destroy his legitimacy as well. Already under fire and perceived by the national press as "the Negroes' inspirational but sometimes inept leader,"[56] King remained undecided regarding the use of children but ultimately benefited from the bold leadership of those around him. King did not endorse the use of children as demonstrators publicly, but behind the scenes his inclinations were less clear; in his conversations with Bevel, he "was allowing the minimum age of jail volunteers to drift steadily downward," while Bevel suggested the simple standard that "any child old enough to belong to a church should be eligible to march to jail."[57] King tentatively approved the "D Day" gathering of students at the Sixteenth Street Baptist Church on May 2, but while Walker and Bevel prepared the children, "King wrestled with his conscience and wrangled with a contingent of black professionals criticizing him for even considering using the youngsters."[58] When King failed to appear at the church by noon, the decision to launch the children's demonstration was made by Bevel without full knowledge of the other movement leaders.[59] After two days of circulating flyers at local high schools and veiled promotions to students via a popular radio DJ who announced, "Kids, there's going to be a party at the park,"[60] the children's crusade began with young demonstrators spilling out of the church doors and into nearby Kelly Ingram Park. *Time* reported: "On the first day the demonstrations were a bit like a picnic. The youngsters clapped and sang excitedly, and when Connor's men arrested them, they scampered almost merrily into patrol wagons."[61] The numbers had overwhelmed the police and had indeed filled the jails. King's initial anger at Bevel's insubordination had vanished by the evening's mass meeting when he told the crowd: "I have been inspired and moved today."[62] Indeed by the publication the following year of his book *Why We Can't Wait,* King had fully embraced Bevel's decision, so much so as to take credit for the success of the children's actions: "I called my staff together and repeated a conviction I had been voicing ever since the campaign began. If our drive was to be successful, we must involve the students of the community."[63] Luckily for King's rhetorical image, the reverberations from the children's demonstrations lifted to new heights perceptions of him as an effective leader, even though previously his hesitancy behind the scenes indicated little of this boldness.

The challenges to the propriety of the movement's actions continued as the press, local leaders, and the larger national community reacted to the tactic with both amazement and outrage. U.S. Attorney General Robert Kennedy reinforced the point about the error in the timing of the protests and stated: "Schoolchildren participating in street demonstrations is a dangerous business."[64] Newly elected Birmingham mayor Albert Boutwell praised the restraint of city officials while criticizing the movement leaders: "Whatever our sympathies and loyalties have been in the past, whatever they may be in the future, I cannot condone and you cannot condone the use of children to these ends."[65] Capturing the sentiments of many northern observers, an editorial letter to the *New York Times* stated: "Granting that justice is often found in the midst of such a struggle against impacted customs and local laws, to make children not yet in their teens actors in it is very questionable procedure indeed."[66] Local leaders, who had been trying to find a way to make King leave Birmingham, feared that the new tactic would undermine their efforts toward quiet negotiations with the new city government.[67] These questions about the rhetorical and moral legitimacy of the movement eventually failed to take hold, however, in light of the symbolic power of the children's demonstrations to challenge the piety of the system they opposed and deliver to the movement its necessary public victory.

The questions raised regarding rhetorical propriety in the children's campaign are not so neatly resolved, however. Much of the success of the strategy resides in how the movement and the media were able either to bury or to quell the contradictory issues of pragmatism and values in the immediate context of the events. The movement never directly addressed the moral issues regarding the use of children as shock troops because it always emphasized the tactical and strategic explanation over the ethical questions. Could a child of six truly understand his or her actions? Would not a jail experience in overcrowded cells damage a young mind? Such questions were quickly brushed aside in favor of explanations such as that offered by King in his account published a year later: "Even though we realized that involving teen-agers and high-school students would bring down upon us a heavy fire of criticism, we felt that we needed this dramatic new dimension."[68] For the news media, the outrage over the violence of the police response to the child demonstrators outweighed the moral questions. In the words of one *New York Times* editorial: "The use of police dogs and high-pressure fire hoses to subdue schoolchildren in Birmingham is a national disgrace. The herding of hundreds of teen-agers and many not yet in their teens into jails and detention homes for demanding their birthright of freedom makes a mockery of legal process."[69] The sheer force of the images and the symbolic drama functioned as a shield for the movement from the thornier issues of ethics regarding the use of children in the face of what they knew to be extraordinarily violent conditions. As *Time* concluded regarding the movement's priorities, "Birmingham's Negroes were certainly not worried about legalities; they were not worried about the niceties of 'timing,' or even about the morality of using children as troops. Instead, theirs was a raging desire to achieve equal human status—now, and by whatever means."[70]

Piety: Exposing Brutality and Challenging Authority

To understand how the movement emerged victorious and avoided questions regarding its legitimacy, the tactic of the 1963 children's demonstrations must be conceptualized as a moment of impiety, a challenge to the moral grounding of the authorities in Birmingham. Robert Cathcart describes how a movement's confrontation with a pious system entails an exposure of its "mystery," the rejection of the code of power that masks its social control mechanisms. Such impiety inevitably produces guilt, a feeling expunged in the recognition of the evil nature of the system.[71] Moreover, as Leland Griffin argues, through rejection of the system, the change seeker undergoes a "purgative act of transformation and transcendence. It affirms the commitment of the converted to the movement."[72] The movement reclaimed the moral ground threatened by questions regarding its impropriety largely on the strength of the rhetorical confrontations enacted by its smallest members.

The dignity of the children and the dramatic depictions of their actions challenged the legitimacy of the Birmingham authorities by accomplishing a rhetorical shift of guilt from the protestors to the system. Where the efforts of the adults had failed to stir public sentiment for the movement, the images of children fully aware of their cause and their commitment rallied a nation. No greater contrast in moral authority can be conceived than the dialectic between a child marching and a police fire hose cutting that same child down. The singing of children cheerfully being loaded into school buses that would transport them to jail effectively drowned out the voices of opposition. The children's demonstrations succeeded in highlighting the evils of the social order by dramatistically altering the relationships of power and control.

The rhetorical impact of the use of the children also can be understood as centrally related to their nature as children and the associated meanings for the movement of their presence in the public spaces of protest. As DeLuca notes, protest strategies that function as "image events" that garner mass media dissemination "revolve around images of bodies—vulnerable bodies, dangerous bodies, taboo bodies, ludicrous bodies, transfigured bodies."[73] In the Birmingham demonstrations, when the movement launched the children, it located the most vulnerable bodies of all in the center of the protest, thereby activating several layers of meaning related to children and democratic struggle. Most provocatively the use of the young demonstrators intersected with what Danielle Allen refers to as the inescapable role of sacrifice in democratic life, such that democracy only is functional when there is mutuality of responsibility. The youngest were sacrificed, arguably, because "sacrifices draw people into networks of mutual obligation,"[74] a cultural truth that Allen argues is intrinsic to African American struggles for rights. Consequently the ultimate success of the children's crusade came from the enactment of this sacrificial drama; the vulnerability of the children evoked a response of mutuality from the larger public that powerfully underscored democracy as an acting together to counteract that which threatens its core principles.

Several accounts from the first day of the children's demonstrations on May 2 exemplify the moral shift engineered by the movement's use of youthful faces to dramatize the conflict and explain the cause. *Time*'s description of the day begins with a series of examples of "unforgettable" scenes, culminating in this account: "And there was the little Negro girl, splendid in a newly starched dress, who marched out of a church, looked toward a massed line of pistol-packing cops, and called to a laggard friend: 'Hurry up, Lucille. If you stay behind, you won't get arrested with our group.'"[75] The *New York Times* reported that "there was no resistance to arrest by the laughing, singing groups of youngsters. . . . Most of the marchers fell to their knees and prayed as the police stopped them."[76] *U.S. News and World Report* provided an example of "the militant attitude growing among Negro youth in the South" in reproducing one child's statement: "We have to demonstrate. It's the only way we can break the wall. If we have to get arrested to do it, then it's worth the price."[77] In his 1964 account of the Birmingham protests, King reported witnessing the following exchange involving a child of eight: "An amused policeman leaned down to her and said with mock gruffness, 'What do you want?' The child looked into his eyes, unafraid, and gave her answer. 'F'eedom,' she said."[78] All of these accounts emphasize the children's clear sense of identification with and commitment to the demonstrations. Far from representing them as helpless pawns of the movement leadership, these descriptions reinforce the willingness of the children to be jail volunteers and their seemingly complete understanding of their actions. Such accounts created an image of piety that starkly contrasted with the flummoxed police forces and the mock superiority of those who presumed to question the children's role in the Birmingham campaign.

The violent reactions of Commissioner of Public Safety Bull Connor and his officers in the ensuing days of the protests—as the columns of young marchers seemed unending—further exposed the dramatic contrast between the morality of the young soldiers in the struggle and the diminishing legitimacy of the Birmingham city authorities. As anticipated, yet also feared, Connor's careful handling of the demonstrations thus far broke down in the presence of the masses of children, as patrol officer Jack Warren recalled: "You could see the tension . . . he was beginning to see that this was so damn big, he wasn't sure what the hell to do."[79] The nation reeled from shock at the now legendary photographs and news footage, images of young children assaulted with high-pressure fire hoses and police dogs, of bodies rolling down the street from the force of the water, of children as young as six being marched off to jail cells. Several statements from Connor, in turn, exemplified the lack of authority wielded by the local officials in light of the children's moral supremacy. According to the *New York Times,* "Mr. Connor, in shirtsleeves with a straw hat cocked over one eye, watched the eager young marchers, some of whom ran to the waiting police wagons. 'Boy, if that's religion, I don't want any,' he said. . . . 'If you'd ask half of them what freedom means, they couldn't tell you.'"[80] After ordering out the police dogs against demonstrators on May 3, Connor stated: "I want to see the dogs work. Look at those niggers run."[81] Rhetorically the children symbolized the transformative power of confrontation to reveal the true face of evil, personified by Connor. As Diane McWhorter concludes, "The K-9 Corps of Birmingham took its mystical place next to the bloodhounds chasing Eliza across the ice floes in *Uncle Tom's Cabin.* Connor had finally acted as the epic anti-hero, and the children had provided the biblical multitudes."[82]

The imagery from the six days of demonstrations provided further rhetorical fuel for the destruction of the moral authority of the Birmingham authorities. In and of itself, the lack of fear of the young demonstrators in the face of police tactics articulated a rejection of the code of control and order that previously held the system in power. Additional, more specific, symbolic enjoinments spoke even more loudly. One of the most powerful images of the dialectical enjoinment enacted by the children in Birmingham came from footage of Connor's armored police vehicle—a white tank—patrolling the fringes of Kelly Ingram Park, where the demonstrators gathered in defiance.[83] Here the visual opposition between white power and black resistance was rendered in undeniably sharp focus. Other prominent images that circulated captured with equal clarity, if not total accuracy, the determination of the children to stand their ground. One of the most famous photographs from the children's demonstrations is that of Walter Gadsden, held by the arm by a Birmingham police officer while the police dog held in the officer's other hand bites Gadsden in the abdomen. The photograph dramatizes "a textbook study in nonviolent acquiescence,"[84] depicting the demonstrator with head bowed and eyes lowered to the police brutality. Though Gadsden himself was not even a demonstrator—he merely had been standing by watching as his classmates left the church—his photo became the quintessential depiction of impiety. *Life* published a different photograph, taken by Charles Moore, to the same effect: beneath an image of firemen thrusting a large hose, cranked up to seven hundred pounds of pressure and aimed at the young demonstrators in the park, the caption read, "They Fight a Fire that Won't Go Out."[85] As Davi Johnson argues, the circulation of these photographs nationally and internationally was key to the movement's success, not only because of the "national wince" elicited but also because of the reflexive knowledge, conveyed by the national press, of the international scrutiny of the events in Birmingham.[86]

The symbolic power of the children to challenge the Birmingham authorities also resided in the sheer force of their numbers and the nature of the treatment such massive numbers necessitated on the part of Connor's forces. Reports of the demonstrations in the national press emphasized the quantities of the demonstrators as well as the quality of their treatment. Successive articles on May 3, May 4, and May 7 in the *New York Times* led with the number of children arrested: "500 Are Arrested," "250 Marchers Seized," and "Birmingham Jails 1,000 More Negroes."[87] The content of such reports further underscored the rhetorical dimensions of the clash between teeming masses of children who were willing to be arrested and the overwhelmed, violent adults they faced down. On the first day, more than 500 children were arrested,[88] on the second, nearly 700,[89] and by the sixth day, an estimated 2,500 youths were in custody.[90] Reports of the conditions under which the children were held reinforced the perception of the brutality of the local city authorities. The juveniles were detained in three jails, local fairground buildings, and the city's boys' home.[91] Distraught parents confronted the movement leaders and Kennedy administration representative Burke Marshall with stories of the incarceration of hundreds of children in an uncovered outside pen, unprotected from a chilly rain,[92] while crowds of relatives attempted to throw blankets and candy bars over the chain-link fence to the drenched young prisoners.[93] These reports symbolically underscored the moral authority of the children as a transcendent force by highlighting their numbers and their poor treatment, thereby rendering the Birmingham authority as inept, brutal, and therefore illegitimate.

The attempts of the white community and the Kennedy administration to raise questions regarding the propriety and morality of the movement's use of children failed to contain the damage inflicted by the children's protests. Inevitably these institutional forces lost their grasp on the mechanisms of social control. The moral ascendancy of the children left no room for the Birmingham or the national authorities to appropriate their actions in the service of their own goals and values; hence they failed to find a way to recast the children's actions to bolster their own legitimacy and reinstate their lost moral ground. The images of the children standing their ground in Birmingham gave the movement an opportunity to confront the system with clarity and force. In response to the criticism of their morality, King and other leaders were able to point to the key contradiction in these caring attitudes; they noted caustically that "this tender solicitude for Negro children had never produced much concern over their consignment to miserable schools or other injuries of segregation."[94] A year later, in his reflections on the children's protest and the criticism of the demonstrations by white observers, King used this contradiction to dramatic rhetorical advantage: "Many deplored our 'using' our children in this fashion. Where had these writers been, we wondered, during the centuries when our segregated social system had been misusing and abusing Negro children? Where had they been with their protective words when, down through the years, Negro infants were born into ghettos, taking their first breath of life in a social atmosphere where the fresh air of freedom was crowded out by the stench of discrimination?"[95]

By sheer force of spirit and numbers, the children succeeded in exposing the secret contradictions that previously held the structures of segregation and moderation alike intact. Their acts of impiety created a moral enjoinment too great for the larger system to absorb. Through the dramatic conflict in Birmingham, the civil rights movement indeed succeeded in elevating its cause from the regional to the international stage by exposing the mystery that had functioned to mask the institution's true impiety.

Conclusion: And a Little Child Shall Lead Them

The 1963 Birmingham children's demonstrations brought the movement the momentum, sympathy from the national press, and moral authority for its negotiations with President Kennedy's administration that it had been lacking. In launching the first waves of children from the Sixteenth Street Baptist Church on May 2, James Bevel successfully moved the civil rights cause forward in unforeseen ways. Due to the pressures put upon the Birmingham city authorities by the "fill the jails" strategy, the media's glare, and the national and international outrage at the harsh treatment of the children by Connor's forces, the city and the Kennedy administration were forced to act quickly to address the situation. On May 9 a settlement was announced that would take steps to desegregate the lunch counters, stores, city parks, and other public facilities in Birmingham, including provisions to hire African Americans in downtown businesses.[96] While these actual gains were small and did little to eradicate the ideology of segregation, the children's demonstrations delivered much more than the local victory for the civil rights cause. An editorial in the *New York Times* captured the transcendent power of the drama of piety enacted in Birmingham: "What was purely an American issue has become a phase in a worldwide struggle.

Aside from the cold war implications, it means something that Negroes should be independent, free and masters of their own destiny in much of Africa, but not in Alabama and Mississippi."[97] Symbolically the children dramatized the fundamental values of the movement and articulated the moral enjoinment at the heart of the struggle, a rhetorical victory that transcended the limits of the specific agreements reached in this one community.

By approaching the 1963 Birmingham events as a complex rhetorical act—with implications for movement image and strategy as well as for the larger issues regarding how movements engage in the rhetorical form of confrontation —this critical analysis of the children's demonstrations illustrates the rewards of considering social movement rhetoric from a perspective that combines insights from both the managerial and the consummatory perspectives. Indeed in the case of the Birmingham conflicts, the questions regarding the propriety of the movement leadership shaded inexorably into issues regarding the morality at the heart of the clash between the civil rights advocates and the national and local authorities. The interaction between the symbolic, dramatistic enactment of the children and the pragmatic motivations of the movement generated the ultimate success in this case for the moral ascendancy of the movement, despite the ethical dilemmas beneath the surface.

The children's protest in Birmingham brings into sharp focus questions about how movement actions translate into assessments of their propriety and legitimacy. Although the use of children in the 1963 Birmingham demonstrations threatened to diminish the moral standing of the SCLC leadership, these questions of ethics were trumped by the efficacy of the strategy and subverted into rhetorical themes of urgency and the greater cause of justice, regardless of the cost. More important, the dramatistic value of the images of the children facing the brutality of the police was inestimable; based on the symbolic power of the demonstrations, the civil rights cause successfully exposed the mystery at the core of the ideologies of both extreme segregationists and white moderates. The impiety of the actions of the children depicted the illegitimacy of those who would deny them rights in a fundamental, moral arena where little hegemonic absorption of the threat was possible. The *New York Times* correctly assessed the transcendent legacy of the children's actions in Birmingham for the cause of civil rights: "Birmingham, after weeks of turmoil in the streets, was quiet as last week drew to a close. Whether it will remain quiet is uncertain. And even if it does there will still be the large questions that the events in Birmingham have brought into focus—the question of where the race struggle in the United States is heading."[98] Tragically the sacrifice of the children who demonstrated was to be answered violently only a few months later, when the Sixteenth Street Baptist Church, the launching site for the children's crusade, was bombed on

September 15, 1963, an attack that claimed the lives of four young girls. The strike against the church underscored the fundamental threat that the impiety of the children posed to the social and political system.

In marching peacefully into police wagons and bravely confronting brute force, certainly, the children had transformed the nature of the dialogue on race relations in America. In this case the impiety of the children transcended the constraints that social change movements face in retaining propriety. As captured in the annals of history, this particular set of events is recalled as a triumph that yielded no lasting repercussions for the movement's leadership, despite the bruises and broken ribs many young demonstrators suffered and the deaths resulting from the church bombing four months later. The children's role in the Birmingham demonstrations still retains echoes of difficult questions regarding the ethics of extreme tactics used in the service of good causes. For the civil rights movement, the 1963 children's crusade proved to be a remarkable strategic move, but what would have been the costs to the movement if Bull Connor had authorized the use of guns and bullets rather than fire hoses and water? As we look at such historical instances, we must be careful not to be too quick to celebrate such acts without placing them in a larger critical and cultural context that sufficiently views the interconnections between interior movement deliberations and the external rhetorical implications. As the events in Birmingham powerfully illustrate, the largest changes in democratic systems often are exacted through the necessary sacrifice of the smallest of heroes.

Notes

1. "Birmingham, U.S.A.," 27.
2. Branch, *Parting the Waters*, 757–802.
3. "Birmingham, U.S.A.," 27.
4. See, e.g., Terry, "Birmingham Protest Had Slow, Reluctant Start" (claiming that black leaders were cognizant of the criticism of the strategy of using children, many untrained); "Robert Kennedy Warns of 'Increasing Turmoil'" (citing the attorney general stating that "an injured, maimed or dead child is a price that none of us can afford to pay"); "Negro Children Held Without Bail" (quoting juvenile Judge Talbot Ellis alleging that adults had "misled these kids"): Eskew, *But for Birmingham*, 261 (regarding business leader A. G. Gaston, who "angrily opposed the marching of schoolchildren").
5. See Branch, *Parting the Waters*; also Garrow, *Bearing the Cross*; and McWhorter, *Carry Me Home*.
6. Lee, "Rhetorical Construction of Time"; Leff, "Rhetoric and Dialectic." See also the issue of *Rhetoric & Public Affairs* (7, no. 1) focusing on King's "Letter from Birmingham Jail." Contributions include Watson, "Issue Is Justice"; Osborn, "Rhetorical Distance in 'Letter from Birmingham Jail'"; Leff and Utley, "Instrumental and Constitutive Rhetoric"; and Patton, "Transforming Response."
7. Johnson, "Martin Luther King's 1963 Birmingham Campaign"; Spratt, "When Police Dogs Attacked."

8. Martin Luther King's reluctance to embrace the strategy of using children is noted in several sources, including Eskew, *But for Birmingham,* 264; Manis, *Fire You Can't Put Out,* 366.

9. DeLuca, "Unruly Arguments," 12.

10. Endres and Senda-Cook, "Location Matters," 261.

11. DeLuca, "Unruly Arguments," 20.

12. The question of the role of children in political change is explored by Allen, *Talking with Strangers,* 25–36; she examines the debate between Hannah Arendt and Ralph Ellison regarding the role of children in democratic politics, in which both analyzed the case of the nine African American youths at the center of the Little Rock High School integration in 1957. Arendt argued that the parents exploited their children to effect no political change but only self-interested social advancement. She concluded that children must be protected in the private realm, which is separate from politics. Ellison alternatively argued that the role of children in democracy is related to ritual and sacrifice and that children are not exempt from the necessary fact of loss and disappointment in democratic politics. He concluded that such sacrifices, including and especially by children, define what citizens must do for each other.

13. The local press in Birmingham gave the movement's activities little coverage, including only short stories buried in back pages. Eskew, *But for Birmingham,* 252, concludes that "as a result of the local newspapers' reportage, Birmingham's residents remained sadly misinformed about the campaign."

14. Halberstam, *Children,* 7.

15. Ibid., 6.

16. See, for example, Simons, "Requirements, Problems, and Strategies"; Smith and Windes, "Innovational Movement"; Stewart, "Functional Approach to the Rhetoric of Social Movements."

17. See, for example, Cathcart, "Movements"; Scott and Smith, "Rhetoric of Confrontation"; Griffin, "Dramatistic Theory of the Rhetoric of Movements."

18. Simons, "Requirements, Problems, and Strategies," 36–37.

19. Stewart, "Functional Approach to the Rhetoric of Social Movements."

20. Cathcart, "Movements," 106.

21. Burke, *Rhetoric of Motives,* 260–67. Specifically he proposes "Order, the Secret, and the Kill. To study the nature of rhetoric, the relation between rhetoric and dialectic, and the application of both to human relations in general, is to circulate about these three motives. . . . We must consider how the fullness of dialectic ('reality') is continually being concealed behind the mists of one or another of these rhetorical overemphases" (265).

22. Burke, *Permanence and Change.* Specifically Burke argues that institutions function through mystification, particularly regarding its principles of order. Such social "mystery" works by creating "depth, persuasiveness, allusiveness, and illusiveness precisely by reason of the fact that it becomes inextricably interwoven with mysteries of these other sorts [death, birth, aging, dreams], quite as these other mysteries must in part be perceived through the fog of social Mystery" (277).

23. Branch, *Pillar of Fire,* xiii.

24. See e.g., Hailey, "4 Negroes Jailed in Birmingham" (noting that the demonstrations were "much less than the 'full scale assault' promised"); Hailey, "Negroes Uniting in Birmingham" (stating that "there still seemed to be resentment against the intrusion" of King into the local situation); Eskew, "Alabama Christian Movement for Human Rights," 81 (focusing on how "the movement struggled along during the two weeks King spent in jail").

25. King, *Why We Can't Wait*, 98.

26. Williams, *Eyes on the Prize*, 187.

27. Garrow, *Bearing the Cross*, 210; "Determined Police Chief" (describing Pritchett as "an outstanding example of the new breed of Southern policeman—tough, dedicated and intelligent"); Torin, "Albany Foresaw Its Role" (describing how Pritchett's program of "non-violent law enforcement has won him respect from both whites and negroes").

28. "Waiting for Miracles," 14. See also Garrow, *Bearing the Cross*, 216 (noting that "many newsmen took the late August halt in Albany's demonstrations as a final sign that the movement had ended in failure"); "Albany, Ga, Hears Negro Pleas" (reporting that "only sporadic protests and no mass demonstrations had occurred").

29. See e.g., Garrow, *Bearing the Cross*, 225; Eskew, "Alabama Christian Movement for Human Rights," 73. However in a later work, *But for Birmingham*, 209–10, Eskew alternatively argues that the evaluation of the Albany campaign at the Dorchester meetings was less focused than as described by Garrow.

30. "Freedom—Now."

31. King, *Why We Can't Wait*, 78.

32. Nunnelly, *Bull Connor*, 186.

33. Garrow, *Bearing the Cross*, 227, notes that neither NAACP nor SNCC in Birmingham was active locally, and therefore the SCLC anticipated "sustained support" for the ongoing protests.

34. Eskew, *But for Birmingham*, 139.

35. Branch, *Parting the Waters*, 689, notes that Walker developed a strategy that included mass marches; Eskew, in *But for Birmingham*, 212, argues that Walker and King devised plans for a "controlled protest" that specifically avoided the "fill the jails" strategy that had been part of the failure in Albany.

36. Eskew, *But for Birmingham*, 214–15. Manis, *Fire You Can't Put Out*, 335, argues that Shuttlesworth was concerned that King might not be fully committed to the local goals in favor of his national aims. Nunnelly, *Bull Connor*, 135, notes that the King and Shuttlesworth agreed to the postponements after urging from A. G. Gaston and other business leaders who feared that March demonstrations would bolster Connor's mayoral candidacy.

37. Abernathy, *And the Walls Came Tumbling Down*, 235.

38. Branch, *Parting the Waters*, 709.

39. "Freedom—Now," 23.

40. "Poorly Timed Protest"; see also "Robert Kennedy Warns of 'Increasing Turmoil.'"

41. Branch, *Parting the Waters*, 709.

42. "Racial Peace in Birmingham?"

43. Eskew, *But for Birmingham*, 225–27; Manis, *Fire You Can't Put Out*, 350–51, notes that Walker was particularly jubilant and "celebrated" the use of the dogs.

44. Manis, *Fire You Can't Put Out*, 354; Eskew, *But for Birmingham*, 237.

45. Branch, *Parting the Waters*, 709–10. See also McWhorter, *Carry Me Home*; Garrow, *Bearing the Cross*; Branch, *Pillar of Fire*.

46. Eskew, "Alabama Christian Movement for Human Rights," 81.

47. Eskew, *But for Birmingham*, 248–50.

48. Ibid., 261.

49. McWhorter, *Carry Me Home*, 363.

50. Branch, *Parting the Waters*, 752.

51. Manis, *Fire You Can't Put Out*, 366.

52. McWhorter, *Carry Me Home*, 363.

53. Branch, *Parting the Waters*, 754–55; Garrow, *Bearing the Cross*, 247–48.

54. Garrow, *Bearing the Cross*, 247; Eskew, "Alabama Christian Movement for Human Rights," 81; Eskew, *But for Birmingham*, 261.

55. Eskew, *But for Birmingham*, 255.

56. "Freedom—Now," 23.

57. Branch, *Parting the Waters*, 754–755; Halberstam, *Children*, 439–40.

58. Manis, *Fire You Can't Put Out*, 368–69.

59. Branch, *Parting the Waters*, 755; Eskew, "Alabama Christian Movement for Human Rights," 82. Alternatively in his autobiography Ralph Abernathy credits himself and King for the decision (Abernathy, *And the Walls Came Tumbling Down*, 262).

60. McWhorter, *Carry Me Home*, 36; Manis, *Fire You Can't Put Out*, 369.

61. "Dogs, Kids, & Clubs."

62. McWhorter, *Carry Me Home*, 368; Eskew, *But for Birmingham*, 265.

63. King, *Why We Can't Wait*, 96.

64. "Dogs, Kids, & Clubs."

65. Hailey, "500 Are Arrested in Negro Protest."

66. Ramsey, "Using Children in Alabama."

67. Branch, *Parting the Waters*, 759.

68. King, *Why We Can't Wait*, 96.

69. "Outrage in Alabama."

70. "Freedom—Now," 25.

71. Cathcart, "Movements," 245.

72. Griffin, "Dramatistic Theory of the Rhetoric of Movements," 465.

73. DeLuca, "Unruly Bodies," 10. See also DeLuca and Peeples, "From Public Sphere to Public Screen."

74. Allen, *Talking with Strangers*, 111.

75. "Freedom—Now."

76. Hailey, "500 Are Arrested in Negro Protest."

77. "Tension Growing Over Race Issue."

78. King, *Why We Can't Wait*, 98.

79. Qtd. in Nunnelly, *Bull Connor*, 147.

80. Sitton, "Birmingham Jails 1,000 More Negroes."

81. "Dogs, Kids, & Clubs."

82. McWhorter, *Carry Me Home*, 375.

83. *Eyes on the Prize* features this image in the segment "No Easy Walk (1961–1963)."

84. McWhorter, *Carry Me Home*, 375. See also Berger, "Fixing Images."

85. "Ominous Spectacle in Birmingham."

86. Johnson, "Martin Luther King, Jr.'s 1963 Birmingham Campaign"; Eskew, *But for Birmingham*, 269, also notes that international condemnation "greatly concerned" the Kennedy administration.

87. Hailey, "500 Are Arrested in Negro Protest"; Hailey, "Dogs and Hoses Repulse Negroes at Birmingham"; Sitton, "Birmingham Jails 1,000 More Negroes."

88. Garrow, *Bearing the Cross*, 252.

89. Hailey, "Dogs and Hoses Repulse Negroes at Birmingham."

90. Branch, *Parting the Waters*, 773; Sitton, "Birmingham Jails 1,000 More Negroes."

91. "Birmingham U.S.A.," 28; Sitton, "Birmingham Jails 1,000 More Negroes."

92. Garrow, *Bearing the Cross*, 252; Eskew, *But for Birmingham*, 276.

93. Branch, *Parting the Waters*, 772.

94. Ibid., 762.

95. King, *Why We Can't Wait,* 97.

96. Sitton, "Birmingham Talks Reach an Accord."

97. "Meaning of Birmingham."

98. "Rights Pact."

THE MUSTARD MAN AND THE STUDENTS' STAND

Analyzing Images from the 1963 Jackson Sit-In

William H. Lawson

On May 29, 1963, under the headline "Negro Is Beaten and Kicked at Lunch Counter in Mississippi's Capital," two images of Memphis Norman appeared on the front page of the *New York Times*.[1] In the first photo, Norman, with another black student from Tougaloo College, sits beside a sign advertising $0.70 roasted turkey dinners and Coca-Cola at the Woolworth lunch counter in downtown Jackson, Mississippi. This image is reminiscent of Norman Rockwell at his best and provides a base of comparison for the image juxtaposed just to the right. In the second image, Norman lies on the ground as retired police officer Benny Oliver kicks him and a group of white men surrounds them to watch. The crowd appears nonplussed; one man is pictured casually smoking a cigarette. The juxtaposition enthymatically allows the viewer to fill in the action between the two images, and thus a story without words begins.

This was not the only photograph taken from the previous day's sit-in. Fred Blackwell, shooting for the *Jackson Daily News*, took what became one of the more iconic photographs of not just the student sit-ins but of the entire civil rights movement. Blackwell's photograph ran the following week in *Newsweek* and endured in the visually mediated consciousness of the movement. This image, along with pictures of dogs and hoses unleashed on Birmingham's protesting youth and Rev. Martin Luther King Jr. marching arm-in-arm with demonstrators in Selma, creates a photographic history of the civil rights movement. The image from the Jackson Woolworth sit-in is the result of a careful, well-executed plan designed to get attention.[2] The photographs capture a moment of transformation. What began as a boycott became a direct-action campaign that continued into the summer and at a critical time helped to maintain much-needed momentum. Mythic criticism reveals that images from the Jackson sit-in function rhetorically in three ways: (1) the photographs link the sit-in to part of a larger American mythos; (2) the sit-in and the protestors in Jackson become mythic figures; and (3) the pictures that Blackwell took provide insight to how images transcend the historic moment they capture to become iconic images. Visual literacy is taking on increasing importance in contemporary society as citizens come into contact with more and more screens. Examining images from the past and understanding their influence, then and now, are essential to democratic societies in need of critically aware citizens.

A State in Tactical Evolution

Since the *Brown v. the Board of Education* U.S. Supreme Court decision, civil rights activity in the Magnolia State had been increasing but yielding few results. Civil rights organizers were, however, aware of the murders of Rev. George Lee, Emmett Till, Herbert Lee, and Louis Allen.[3] Countless other acts of intimidation and violence occurred, but the state and local law enforcement official response went lacking or, in some instances, was the catalyst of violence. For example James Meredith, to integrate the University of Mississippi, had to do so under the protection of three thousand federal troops, causing a riot that left two dead and numerous federal troops injured.[4] Meredith's civil rights victory and the failure of organizations such as the Student Nonviolent Coordinating Committee (SNCC) and the Voter Education Project (VEP) to register blacks in significant numbers only strengthened the segregationists' resolve.[5]

This resolve was evident when the Justice Department was forced to sue the police departments of Winona and Greenwood after they failed to adhere to the 1961 Interstate Commerce Commission mandate that desegregated all bus terminals and buses on the first of the New Year. In late March 1963, thirty miles west of Winona in Greenwood, Mississippi, forty-two black demonstrators started to march home in orderly two-by-two lines when police officers, handling German shepherds, broke up the demonstration. The demonstrators chaotically scattered as dogs nipped at their heels, and white bystanders yelled, "Turn him loose!" and "Sic 'em!"[6]

It makes perfect sense that the Jackson sit-in occurred at the time it happened. Looking over the events above, it is easy to see how almost every other protest tactic had been deployed in Mississippi; even the Freedom Rides came to Jackson just a few years previous to the sit-in. Protestors and activists in Mississippi were not creating new tactics of civil disobedience but were adapting previously used tactics from other parts of the country. Almost every tactic had been attempted in Mississippi: the aforementioned legal challenges, education desegregation, the Freedom Rides, and efforts in voter registration. Boycotts and sit-ins make excellent choices for the next progression of protest activities. All other forms of protest failed up to that point. The media exposure alone, as evidenced by Blackwell's photograph, was a step in the right direction and away from the failures that plagued the movement in Mississippi.

To raise national awareness of the violence against civil rights activists throughout the South, the VEP issued a news release on March 31, 1963, trying to make some of the national Sunday papers.[7] The news release documented sixty-four acts of violence and intimidation against Mississippi blacks attempting to register to vote from January 1961 to March 1963. While the list may not be comprehensive, it still is a solid reflection of the environment leading up to and contemporary with the case and trial. Wiley Branton, director of the project, stated in the report that while the list did not include the riot at Ole Miss or the subsequent harassment of James Meredith,[8] "it does demonstrate conclusively . . . the pattern of discrimination and violence which exists in Mississippi, and makes Constitutional rights virtually inoperative in that state."[9]

Soon after the report was issued, the Voter Education Project pulled its financial support from efforts in Mississippi. The voter registration drives had registered less than four thousand new black voters in almost two years of work, and at the expenditure of more than fifty thousand dollars.[10] Despite the collapse of the Delta campaign sponsored by the VEP, McMillen contends, "the idealistic crusaders for Black suffrage emerged from two years of utter defeat with a healthy sense of realism."[11] McMillen argues that this newfound sense of realism forced leaders to understand that significant and meaningful change would only come from federal intervention and that intervention was only likely to occur with broad, sweeping public support. Voting efforts temporarily stalled in the spring of 1963, and movement members were unsure which direction to go.[12] There was no single leader to look to and no single major organization that could make the decisions.

It is no wonder, given the situation of affairs, that it would be college students who stepped into the void. Moreover it was no secret across the nation that college students in the South were using the sit-in as a form of protest to bring attention to issues of social injustice. Photographs from a sit-in conducted by students from North Carolina A&T brought the nation's attention to Greensboro when the pictures ran in magazines and newspapers three years earlier.[13] Although a direct-action demonstration had never been planned in Mississippi, the starting point for mass demonstrations and direct-action campaigns there seemed to be the lunch counter stools of the downtown Jackson Woolworth store.[14]

Initial Description and Immediate Context

The civil rights movement has its fair share of iconic images, ranging from Emmett Till's open casket to the scene on Edmond Pettis Bridge as state troopers beat participants during the March on Selma, Alabama, but like all iconic images, they did not start out as icons—they became that way. What rhetorical scholars should be aware of is how the historic becomes iconic. It is an important process to understand, because "iconic photographs provide an accessible and centrally positioned set of images for exploring how political action (and inaction) can be constituted and controlled through visual media."[15] At stake is the understanding and meaning of ideologies that shape social reality: "The iconic image's combination of mainstream recognition, wide circulation, and emotional impact is a proven formula for reproducing a society's social order."[16] The Blackwell photo certainly has the emotional impact and continues to expand in the other two factors of circulation and recognition. This is the key to a photograph becoming iconic; it must first have the emotional impact to help initiate circulation and recognition. The classic pathetic appeal is at work in the image, drawing the viewer in for a closer look. This places the Blackwell photograph firmly in the process of becoming one of the iconic images of the civil rights movement. Hariman and Lucaites note "that people don't know a great many circumstantial details regarding any iconic photograph such as its date, specific location, names of the participant, original medium of representation, photographer, and so forth."[17] At this point contextual details are necessary to help understand the environment that the Blackwell photograph captures.

On May 28, 1963, students and professors from historically black Tougaloo College sat in at the Woolworth lunch counter for nearly three hours as a white mob of almost two hundred harassed them. Planning for the sit-in took place for weeks. When the day of the demonstration arrived, everyone involved knew exactly what to do. At 11:00 A.M., Anne Moody, Pearlena Lewis, and Memphis Norman walked into Woolworth through the rear entrance and separated, spreading out through the store.[18] At precisely 11:15, the three black students from Tougaloo met and sat as planned at the lunch counter. Within a few minutes, white customers sitting at the counter left, waitresses abandoned their customers, and reporters and onlookers filled the restaurant. A faux demonstration was held at 10:45 A.M. in front of the J. C. Penney store, proving to be a clever diversion by temporarily confusing the authorities and growing crowd while the protestors moved into position to begin the protest at the lunch counter. From a tactical perspective, an executed feint like this buys some time for the protestors and produces the element of surprise, a key advantage in momentum. The plan for the feint was initiated when organizers informed reporters there would be a demonstration early in the day but withheld the whereabouts so local authorities would not learn the exact location.

Anne Moody recounts that because the beginning of the demonstration was uneventful, reporters left after forty-five minutes.[19] Things changed when high school students arrived at Woolworth for their lunch break. Instantly they began taunting the three demonstrators, chanting derogatory slogans, and made a hangman's noose out of the rope meant to cordon off the area. At this point Norman suggested to the two women that they pray. Moody remembers, "We bowed our heads, and all hell broke loose."[20]

This is when Benny Oliver pulled Norman to the ground and began kicking him savagely in the head. After Oliver had inflicted several kicks, a plainclothes policeman identified himself and arrested both Norman and Oliver.[21] Moody and Lewis had also been pulled to the ground, but they were not beaten, and they returned to their seats after the arrests. The two black women were joined by Joan Trumpauer, a white student from Tougaloo, and Lois Chaffee, the first of two Tougaloo professors to join the demonstration. The four women were covered in ketchup, mustard, salt, pepper, and sugar. John Salter, the second white professor from Tougaloo, sat down and was greeted instantly with a pair of brass knuckles striking him in the back of the head, adding his blood to the mixture of condiments. Finally, when George Raymond, a CORE worker from Jackson State College, sat down, pro-segregationists dumped ashtrays on the demonstrators.

Many details in the above photo are subtle and easy to miss, like the hot coffee and ashtrays that were poured on the protestors. The blood on the back of Salter's head is harder to miss. So too are the looks on the faces of the crowd. Old and young, men and women, look on with a variety of expressions on their faces and range of nonverbal communication coming from the postures of their bodies. Some individuals in the crowd seemed pleased, others nonchalant, and some seem less than entertained. The young man in dark pants on the left side of the frame, arms crossed, glares with such a steady intensity that one would think he was trying to move Salter with telekinetic powers. This crowd recalls similarities with the audiences who gathered at lynchings, witnesses whose presence seemed intended to legitimate the injustice.

Fred Blackwell's photograph can now be found in major works on the civil rights movement and is reprinted in collections of the most important photographs of the twentieth century.[22] From an aesthetic view, the photo has it all; it is well framed and lit, is focused on the dramatic action, and engages the viewer in an active nature.[23] There is depth in the framing due to the row upon row of bodies witnessing and participating. It is an easy picture to look at and engage with because the scene displayed is typical to the American experience and culture of the time—the lunch counter. The photograph shares characteristics with the genre of direct cinema. In this genre the documentarian tries to capture reality and often functions as a fly on the wall, serving in an observational role. The accumulation of documentary-like characteristics creates a sense of ethos for what is being represented; the viewer senses fairness and balance in what the image captures.

This image makes known the conditions in Mississippi; it brings before the eyes a representation of the reality facing black citizens. An all-American scene, the lunch counter, is juxtaposed with un-American actions. The tension of competing ideologies is seen in the bodies of the protestors. Protesting for rights has a long-established precedence in America dating back to at least the Boston Tea Party. It is an American ideal to express oneself and exercise the rights protected by the First Amendment, and that goes for all sides concerning the issue of segregation. Freedom and equality seem to square off; the images represent a parallel struggle between states' rights and the supremacy of the Constitution as the law of the land. Protest can be read as a democratic and patriotic thing, but the reaction of the mob, as evidenced by blood and condiments, indicates that local pro-segregationists viewed the protestors as a challenge to the authority of Jim Crow. The characteristics link the photo, and the protest, to the larger American mythos. Moreover it does not matter which perspective one takes—both protestors and bystanders feel what they are doing is right, justified by their firm beliefs in American values.

What the photograph captures and communicates is of great import: contained within the photograph is a moment that transformed a boycott into a direct-action campaign, which continued into the summer in Jackson and helped maintain the momentum of the civil rights movement in Mississippi.[24] This photograph captures and suspends a link in the legacy of protest in Mississippi, connecting then with the world outside of the state and now with contemporary viewers of the image. This one sit-in led the organizers to take the next step to plan and execute a sustained boycott of downtown Jackson businesses for weeks to follow. Organizers were then able to craft demands to changes in public policy concerning desegregation and start a dialogue with local and state authorities.

Moving from this initial description of Blackwell's photography, this essay now turns to interpret these images from a mythic perspective before evaluating the impact of these images from the Jackson sit-in specifically and the role of photography in social movements more generally. Mythic criticism reveals how images from the Jackson sit-in function rhetorically in three ways: (1) the photographs link the sit-in to part of a larger American mythos; (2) the sit-in itself and the protestors in Jackson become mythic figures; and (3) the pictures that Blackwell took provide insight to how images transcend the historic moment that they capture to become iconic and mythic images. Some attention to myth and the civil rights movement can help to gain insight into the transition from historical event to the realm of the iconic.

Monomyth, not Ghosts, of Mississippi

Put baldly, myths are stories about people doing important things in the past. "In myth there is a story, the story must seem the answer to some compelling question, the dramatis personae must seem larger-than-life, and the story must convey the sense of the sacred in time, place, and symbol."[25] While the presence of myth in human experience is nothing new, the ways myth functions continue to evolve.[26] Michael Osborn states, "The old sense of mythos as narrative structure has been transformed in our time to stories that create social meaning and that can sanction proposals and counter-proposals."[27] Even though the civil rights movement is fairly recent in the historical continuum of America, it has taken up a special place in the continuing narrative of what it means to be American. The movement continues to shape and influence the conceptual understanding of values such as equality and justice. With the passing of time, the moments and figures from the movement are gaining mythic status. The movement is full of dramatis personae who are larger than life, in sacred if not sacrosanct "time, place, and symbol," doing deeds attempting to answer "some compelling question." The images from the Jackson sit-in demonstrate this as a case for the movement more generally.

David Sutton argues that things can be considered mythic when "1) the narrators and audience have elevated the main characters from human status to that of gods or demigods, and 2) when the narrators and audience perceive the narrative's setting to be no longer in the recent historical past but in the remote past, when the world was different."[28] The movement and the individuals associated with it have reached these two conditions. Anne Moody became a key organizer and leader during Freedom Summer in 1964. Moody challenged the state's federal representatives in person at the nation's capital along with Fannie Lou Hamer in 1965 and later wrote one of the finest autobiographies that covered social activism in Mississippi. Joan Trumpauer had already created a name for herself as one of the Freedom Riders that were held at Parchman Farm. She was a planner for the March on Washington, and she too volunteered for Freedom Summer. She is featured in two documentary films, *Freedom Riders* and *An Ordinary Hero: The True Story of Joan Trumpauer Mulholland*. The incident captured in the Blackwell photograph earned John Salter the nickname "The Mustard Man," instantly providing him with clout among his fellow activists. As for the second condition, Blackwell's black and white photograph creates the impression that the world represented is one of a remote past. Susan Sontag suggests that "the images that mobilize conscience are always linked to a given historical situation."[29] The historical situation in this instance is a lunch counter in Mississippi on a day in May more than fifty years ago. The historical situation is moved even further into the past by the fact that the actual Woolworth where the picture was taken is no longer there; the building is gone. Based on Sutton's criteria, the civil rights movement in America appears to be a fertile place for myths and heroines.

There is a particular type of myth unique to the American narrative. These stories focus on race mixing and the supposed dangers to society and culture resulting from black and white reproduction. Interestingly these myths had codified counterparts in the form of Jim Crow legislation throughout many southern states.[30] To maintain these laws and social mores, influential segregationists crafted their rhetorical addendums. Segregationist rhetorical tracts supporting Jim Crow and condemning race mixing, such as Theodore Bilbo's *Take Your Choice: Separation or Mongrelization,* Stuart Omer Landry's *Cult of Equality,* and Judge Tom Brady's *Black Monday,* emerged to justify the practice and reality of segregation along biological, anthropological, and legal lines of reasoning.

"It is true, of course," asserts Janice Hocker Rushing, "that some myths solve problems or overcome contradictions, but others articulate the paradox and seem to leave humanity suspended between the oppositions."[31] In this context Jim Crow laws are a uniquely American myth. The photograph highlights the paradox and tension between Jim Crow and American ideals of equality and justice. While the college-aged, middle-class protestor peacefully sitting at the lunch counter became the archetype of social protestor during the decade of the 1960s, the crowd of predominantly white males who harassed and intimidated the protestors came to represent the archetype of the resister. There were also those who stood by doing nothing, who represent the complacency of American society. What they all share, hero and villain, is the fight. "The creative mythic works of the 'poet' cannot coalesce into a unified tradition to which followers can then adhere; they are models for other individuals—not coercive, but evocative."[32] The models are not just for individuals to emulate; the real power lies in how the models function to provoke, motivate, and stimulate action in those individuals who engage them. These evocative models work like a rhetorical catalyst, inspiring a chain of behavior or thoughts.

According to Rowland, "The key point is that through myth we define the good society and solve problems, not subject to rational solution."[33] The justification and maintenance of segregation in the American South were partly due to the belief in Jim Crow policies and practices as being legitimate. Though it may be the simple logical fallacy of appealing to tradition, Jim Crow played a key role. Despite the crowd being predominantly male, they function much like the Erinyes, or Furies, avenging the violation of Jim Crow sanctity. Because there is no rational justification for treating one group of people as inferior in a democratic society, stories must be invented.

In a civil and democratic society, the photograph serves as evidence, visual proof that violence and intimidation were normal aspects of daily life for blacks in Mississippi. In the top right corner of the photo are a few American flags, not the Confederate Stars and Bars but the flag of the unified nation. The photograph creates cognitive dissonance through the antidemocratic behavior of the mob while the protestors initiate a sacred American right. The flag is a culture type, what Osborn would call "the counterpart to archetypes." He explains that they "are culture-specific symbols that resonate important values."[34] The flag's presence brings with it certain values specific to America (such as freedom, liberty, equality, and justice) that clash with what is happening in the frame. The flag triggers cognitive dissonance not only by evoking American values and ideals but also by anchoring the location. What is seen happening in the frame is happening in America.

This photograph functions synecdochically by representing what daily life is like for blacks and protestors in Mississippi. Showing part of a normal day's activity is *pars pro toto* that blacks face this kind of violence and intimidation every day. The photograph is both building myth and deconstructing myth, all while further strengthening its position in movement public memory.

Protestors Become Mythic

According to Rowland, "There seems to be general agreement that myths are crucial stories that are in some way treated as true by the people who tell them."[35] One of the key components is that "a myth is a story about heroic characters who serve as personal or societal models."[36] The presence of heroines and heroes is of little doubt, but who they are is interesting. Martha Solomon notes, "Certainly, most of us would acknowledge that texts do constrain meanings, but I for one believe that each person's 'meaning' for a text is a product of a complex interaction between that person's perceptual frames, etc. and elements in the text."[37] Depending on the viewers' attitude toward segregation, the archetypes of hero and villain are cast accordingly. Heroes and heroines are engaged in a struggle with an enemy and obstacles that must be overcome. The photograph visualizes a step in the hero's journey.

Joseph Campbell's notion of the monomyth also clarifies the photograph, illuminating characteristics that contribute to the impact of the activists sitting at the counter.[38] Some of the key characteristics of classic heroines and heroes are presented in the photograph, most notably *polutas, arête,* and *metis. Polutas* is the quality of an enduring heart capable of continuing during times of suffering. The three protestors sitting at the lunch counter seem to have this quality as they patiently and calmly endure the crowd's harassment. Just as Odysseus was made to suffer by Poseidon, so too do the nonviolent protestors absorb taunts, physical assault, and intimidation. They also possess *arête,* or excellence. Their purpose of protesting for equality and justice aligns with a sense of virtue and reveals the pursuit of the highest standards of civility and citizenship. *Metis,* or a blending of cleverness, cunning, and wisdom, is demonstrated in the act they are performing. By turning the traditional lunch counter into a place of dissent, they make clear the planning and strategic nature of their actions.

Blackwell's photograph also provides a model for future social movement activity. The photograph depicts protestors in a very specific way. The non-violent nature of their protest activity is civil yet powerful. It is not just the nature of their protest but also the fact that they are doing it in unison that is telling. It would be too easy to read it as "us versus them," a simple black and white rendering, but that misses the chance for the text to unify the viewer not only with the protestors but also with the mob and other people around the country viewing the same image. The protestors are all from Tougaloo, the nearby historically black college, and therefore have an investment in the community, but they come from different locations in the country. The constitutive function here is not one that parcels off particular groups from a larger population or community but rather one of unity through plurality. A black Mississippian, a white southerner, and a Scotch Native American acted in solidarity despite differences in gender, age, race, and ethnic backgrounds. The emotion of shame and guilt arises from comparing the grins and smiles of the onlookers with that of Moody's facial expression. She looks disappointed, let down somehow, by the actions of her fellow Mississippians. She remembers, "After the sit-in, all I could think of was how sick Mississippi whites were. They believed so much in the segregated Southern way of life, they would kill to preserve it."[39] The fact that viewers of the photograph can see Moody's face connects them directly with her and the situation she finds herself in and creates a powerful connection. Through her an emotional connection and response are created, pulling in the viewer and demonstrating one of the key factors that make an image an iconic one.

The Jackson protestors become mythic figures not only in the American story but also connecting to a rhetorical legacy. The protestors used their bodies as a means to visualize what was happening in the Jim Crow American South. Even though most Americans, and admittedly many civil rights scholars, may not know the protestors by name, we are familiar with the mold of protestor that is being shaped and extended. Their sit-in was a deliberately staged protest of *enargia,* an example of what O'Rourke calls "instances of rhetorical somatics, the rhetorical use not of words but of the very bodies of protest."[40] A long procession of bodies has been used as instruments of "rhetorical somatics," stretching from Crispus Attucks to Cesar Chavez, and from Mary Harris Jones to the Guerrilla Girls.

Photos Make It Happen

Myth and legend rarely happen overnight; there is a process of transformation that takes time and rhetorical effect. Blair, Jeppeson, and Pucci argue that "the goal of textual reading is to grasp the multiplicity of any discourse."[41] It is with this goal in mind that this essay uses a mythic orientation to understand how images transcend from the historic moment to the status of iconic, utilizing the Blackwell photography as evidence of this transformative process. Hariman and Lucaites's understanding of what is an iconic image is a useful foundation: "We define photographic journalistic icons as those *photographic images appearing in print, electronic, or digital media that are widely recognized and remembered, are understood to be representations of historically significant events, activate strong emotional identification or response, and are reproduced across a range of media, genres, or topics.*"[42]

Iconic images are recognizable without difficulty, they stir and stimulate viewers pathetically, and they are easily copied. Once an image can achieve all these functions, it reaches iconic status. At that point, because of those functions, the iconic image can maintain and strengthen its position in public discourse.

The criticism that analyzes visual rhetoric considers mythic matters regarding the iconic. Hariman and Lucaites argue that "the iconic photograph is an aesthetically familiar form of civic performance coordinating an array of semiotic transcriptions that project an emotional scenario to manage a basic contradiction or recurrent crisis."[43] The parallels between the iconic axioms and the mythic criteria are striking. The aesthetic familiarity required of the iconic image is reflected in the essential narrative components of myth, like a hero, journey, or obstacle. Representation of civic performance is reproduced in iconic images much as the "moral of the story" in myth. In myth, as with the iconic, the whole process is played out at the symbolic level to guide human behavior in times of crisis. Semiotic transcriptions that aid one in times of contradictions and crisis are not solely confined to the realm of iconic images.

The myth recorded and communicated in Blackwell's photograph is important because of the time and place it captures is no longer with us. The building that housed the Woolworth store has been gone for decades. In its place is an open, green square. On the fiftieth anniversary of the sit-in, a historical marker was placed where the lunch counter once was.[44] A brief description of the protest is on one side, and Blackwell's photograph is on the back. The physical building has been remade by the marker, the photo, and the myth that remains.

One final picture represents the Jackson sit-in. While the previous image is arguably the visual climax of the protest, this photograph provides some resolution. Reverend Edwin King, the chaplain at Tougaloo, pressed through the crowd to check on John Salter, who was thoroughly covered in ketchup, mustard, and his own blood. The condiment assault on Salter earned him the nickname "the mustard man" among his peers, bestowing a type of heroic title as a result of his agency and protest.[45] Heroes in myths earn titles for deeds performed, and while Salter may not be in the upper tier of the civil rights pantheon, he and the students have earned a place of their own in the movement narrative. The women protestors have earned some heroine status as well, as evidenced in the photograph; Moody, with a skunk-like white stripe down the center of her hair, looks at King, and Trumpauer wipes herself off.

Though rarely noted, the man sitting down at the far end of the counter is Tougaloo president Daniel Beittel.[46] Beittel ran in and out of Woolworth for an hour trying to get the ninety or so police officers outside to break up the riot going on in the store.[47] The chief of police refused to enter Woolworth unless the manager of the facility requested it. The frustrated sixty-three-year-old then joined his students and faculty member at the lunch counter. Only after the mob began smashing and breaking things did the manager turn off the lights and shut the store down.[48] In the picture President Beittel is speaking to Ken Toler, a reporter for the *Memphis Commercial Appeal*. Toler, who also covered the mass meetings that followed the sit-in, complimented Salter and his fellow protestors for their tenacity and courage. "Significantly," Salter recounts, "he did this in full view of Mississippi lawmen and Mississippi newsmen."[49] This sit-in ended when protestors were escorted out of the Woolworth store with the protection of the police. Though it ended that day, this sit-in catalyzed the mass demonstrations that were to follow and spread into the summer.[50]

History and public memory should consider the Jackson sit-in a complete success. The best sources of evidence to support this are the actual images themselves and the status that the Blackwell photograph continues to achieve. "As Wittgenstein argued for words, that the meaning *is* the use—so for each photograph," Susan Sontag asserted; it follows that the proof of her extension of Ludwig Wittgenstein is found in the circulation and materiality of the images.[51] The protest garnered not only local and national newspaper headlines, appeared in the issue of *Newsweek* the week after the event, and continues to circulate in published research and materially as a historical marker in downtown Jackson. Even though immediate change did not occur, the protestors generated media attention, learned organizing strategies, and carried out practical tactical acts of protest. The Blackwell photographs are what made it happen then and have continued to shape access and understanding now. Sontag notes that "what is surreal is the distance imposed, and bridged, by the photograph: the social distance and the distance in time."[52] Images such as the ones taken by Blackwell create this push/pull effect on viewers, who become aware of the spatial and temporal distances separating the viewer from the recorded scene but also are afforded an insightful glance into that moment. Examples of such work include James Allen's *Without Sanctuary* and Charles Moore and Michael Durham's *Powerful Days*, the former a collection of lynching photographs and the latter archiving a career of photojournalism covering the civil rights movement.[53]

The images from the Jackson sit-in help aid in mnemonic connection with the moment and help strengthen the mythic status of the protest and the protestors by providing a mass-mediated image to connect with the moment and the movement. Raiford argues, "It is my belief that photography is essential to understanding the civil rights movement and its participants on the ground."[54] The Blackwell images lift the Jackson sit-in off the ground and into a mythic dimension amplifying our memory and understanding of the protest. They connect us to the heroines and villains, to the hero's quest, and with the legacy of protest in America. The Blackwell imagery, like other civil rights photography, "captures moments of embodiment and enactment—moments that are situated within an historical context and transcendent of that context."[55] The rhetorical appeal for Gallagher and Zagacki lies in the immediacy and compelling manner that photography connects viewers with and to historical moments: "Yet it is in its capacity to make things visible that photography functions transformatively, and thereby rhetorically, by mediating between the universal and the particular, enabling viewers to experience epiphanic moments when issues, ideas, habits, and yearnings are crystallized into a single recognizable image."[56] Without the Blackwell photographs, there is no transformative experience for the viewer, and therefore no lifting to mythic status for either the Jackson sit-in itself or for the protestors. The Blackwell photograph visualizes for the viewer the moral imperative that action must be taken, more so than most images from the movement, whereas the dramatic action captured within the frame serves as both evidence and call to action.

Conclusion

The influence of the Jackson sit-in at F. W. Woolworth and Blackwell's photographs are evidenced by the events that followed in Mississippi: mass demonstrations in Jackson, the Freedom Vote campaign in the fall of 1963, the subsequent formation of the Mississippi Freedom Democratic Party (MFDP), and Freedom Summer. The sit-in to a lesser degree may have had an influence on the national level: the MFDP challenge in Atlantic City at the Democratic National Convention, the Freedom Vote of 1964, and possibly the Voting Rights Act of 1965. Organizers at a local level educated, organized, and deployed visual rhetoric. As Raiford notes, the visual rhetoric produced can "provide cues and clues for contemporary viewers to better understand and incorporate the lessons and legacies of the 1960s freedom struggle."[57] Viewing Blackwell's images of the Jackson sit-in from a mythic perspective reveals that the pictures function rhetorically by linking the sit-in to part of a larger American mythos and provides insight to how images transcend the historic moment they capture to become iconic images.

Through these images we learn more about our history and more about ourselves as individuals and as a collective society. This makes the images powerful and meaningful. We must review the images from our collective past, not to get the "correct" interpretation but to see if there is more to see than what was initially glimpsed. Looking at the Blackwell photographs prove that the images from the movement were not a simple matter of photographers luckily being at the right place at the right time. The matter is quite the opposite. What is being witnessed, rather, is what Henri Cartier-Bresson calls a "decisive moment." He argues, "To take photographs means to recognize—both simultaneously and within a fraction of a second—both the fact itself and the rigorous organization of visually perceived forms that give it meaning."[58] The civil rights movement has many more decisive moments to analyze and open up to interpretation the embedded meaning and forms that Cartier-Bresson is referring to.

Rowland reminds us that "myths are our most powerful stories."[59] Americans possess a corpus of myths—Founding Fathers, the American Dream, Jim Crow, and so on—that are uniquely theirs. Examining these myths, and how experiences and events in American history have mythic qualities, gives us insight into who we are. The images of Emmett Till's open casket, Rosa Parks on the bus, a burning bus outside Aniston, the fire hoses and dogs in Birmingham, crowd shots of the March on Washington, and police brutality in Selma all capture moments ripe with heroes and heroines confronting antagonists and performing legendary tasks. While there is no sanctified or official canon of movement photography yet, key images such as those continue to circulate and strengthen their place in our public memories.

Notes

1. "Negro Is Beaten and Kicked at Lunch Counter." The photos are accompanied with a story by Jack Langguth, "3 In Sit-In Beaten at Jackson Store."

2. Carson, *In Struggle.*

3. Dittmer, *Local People,* and Payne, *I've Got the Light of Freedom,* are two excellent sources for coverage of and insight into the struggle for civil rights in Mississippi.

4. Doyle, *American Insurrection.*

5. Fischer and McPherson, *Freedom Riders,* 249.

6. Sitton, "Police Loose a Dog on Negroes' Group."

7. "Press Release," microfilm, CORE Papers, Dave Dennis section, reels 9, 21, and 25.

8. Doyle's *American Insurrection* is an excellent source covering Meredith's integration of the University of Mississippi.

9. "Press Release."

10. McMillen, "Black Enfranchisement in Mississippi," 362.

11. Ibid., 364.

12. Carson, *In Struggle*, 152.

13. This moment has been deemed iconic enough to warrant an exhibit at the Smithsonian National Museum of American History in Washington, D.C.

14. O'Brien, *We Shall Not Be Moved*. This work is an extensive and detailed look at the protest activity in Jackson during the spring and summer of 1963. At the center of O'Brien's work is the Blackwell photograph, which makes the historical narrative immediately and intimately relatable via the visual artifact.

15. Hariman and Lucaites, *No Caption Needed*, 5.

16. Ibid., 9.

17. Ibid., 6.

18. Moody, *Coming of Age in Mississippi*, 286.

19. Ibid., 287.

20. Ibid., 288.

21. Dittmer, *Local People*, 162.

22. Berger, *Seeing through Race*; Branch, *Parting the Waters*; Dittmer, *Local People*; and Kasher, *Civil Rights Movement*, are just a few of the works that reprint the photograph.

23. Blackwell got such a good vantage point because he had asked the management for permission to get on top of the lunch counter. Wagster Pettus, "Civil Rights Sit-In at Woolworth."

24. Branch even uses this argument in his caption of the photograph.

25. Osborn, "In Defense of Broad Mythic Criticism," 121.

26. Salinas, "Ambiguous Trickster Liminality"; Rowland and Frank, "Mythic Rhetoric and Rectification"; Duncan, "Reimagining the Self-Made Man," are examples of the range of texts that rhetorical scholars are applying mythic criticism to.

27. Osborn, "In Defense of Broad Mythic Criticism," 124.

28. Sutton, "On Mythic Criticism," 213.

29. Sontag, *On Photography*, 17.

30. For more see Woodward, *Strange Career of Jim Crow*; Packard, *American Nightmare*; and Higginbotham, *Ghosts of Jim Crow*.

31. Hocker Rushing, "On Saving Mythic Criticism," 140.

32. Ibid.

33. Rowland, "On a Limited Approach to Mythic Criticism," 102.

34. Osborn, "In Defense of Broad Mythic Criticism," 123.

35. Rowland, "On a Limited Approach to Mythic Criticism," 153.

36. Ibid.

37. Solomon, "Responding to Rowland's Myth," 119.

38. Campbell, *Hero with a Thousand Faces*.

39. Moody, *Coming of Age in Mississippi*, 290.

40. O'Rourke, "Circulation and Noncirculation of Photographic Texts," 688.

41. Blair, Jeppeson, and Pucci, "Public Memorializing in Postmodernity," 282.

42. Hariman and Lucaites, *No Caption Needed*, 27, emphasis in original.

43. Ibid., 29.

44. The marker is the twelfth entry in a series of signs sponsored by the state called the Mississippi Freedom Trail.

45. Reverend Edwin King, interview with the author, 2005.

46. During an interview with the author, King recalled having a pocket full of quarters and running back and forth from the Woolworth lunch counter to the nearest pay phone to keep Beittel and others informed.

47. Moody, *Coming of Age in Mississippi*, 290.

48. Dittmer, *Local People*, 162.

49. John Salter, Lair of Hunterbear, blog, http://www.hunterbear.org/.

50. Dittmer, *Local People*; O'Brien, *We Shall Not Be Moved*.

51. Sontag, *On Photography*, 106.

52. Ibid., 58.

53. Allen, *Without Sanctuary*; Moore and Durham, *Powerful Days*.

54. Raiford, "'Come Let Us Build a New World Together,'" 1131.

55. Gallagher and Zagacki, "Epiphanies and Transformations," 116.

56. Ibid., 116–17.

57. Raiford, "'Come Let Us Build a New World Together,'" 1133.

58. Cartier-Bresson, *Aperture Masters of Photography*, 8.

59. Rowland, "On a Limited Approach to Mythic Criticism," 152.

FROM SITTING IN TO SITTING OUT

Gloria Richardson and the 1963 Cambridge Movement

Lindsay Harroff

From March to July 1963, the Cambridge Nonviolent Action Committee (CNAC), under the leadership of Gloria Richardson, organized sit-ins and other demonstrations in Cambridge, Maryland. Demonstrators faced arrest, bayonets, and tear gas to protest racial segregation and inequality. On July 22, 1963, amid the threat of increasing violence, U.S. Attorney General Robert Kennedy brokered a treaty between Richardson and Cambridge officials. City officials agreed to a number of CNAC's demands, including amending the city charter to ban the segregation of public places, in exchange for a moratorium on their demonstrations. The sit-ins, it seemed, were successful in desegregating public places. Thus when a group of white businessmen called the amendment to a referendum, Richardson shocked liberals and moderates, blacks and whites, in Cambridge and nationwide, by urging African Americans to boycott voting on it.

Cambridge residents, black ministers, city and state officials, the local and national media, and national leaders of the mainstream civil rights movement launched vociferous criticisms against Richardson. Richardson's critics reproached her for being too stubborn to compromise or "inconsistent by picketing and demonstrating for civil rights, on the one hand, then refusing to vote for them."[1] Worse, they accused her of betraying the principles of the civil rights movement. A *Time* magazine article titled "A Zealot's Stand" reported, "It all seemed a strange brand of leadership, particularly at a time when in some parts of the U.S., her fellow Negroes were shedding blood in their struggle for the right to vote."[2] Leaders of the National Association for the Advancement of

Colored People (NAACP) and the Southern Christian Leadership Conference (SCLC) attempted to persuade Richardson to change her stance. After being invited to a Frank Sinatra and Lena Horne concert at Carnegie Hall, Richardson found herself seated in a booth with Martin Luther King Jr., only to "receive a lecture on how they were drumming for the vote in the South, and here I was going to boycott a vote."[3] Reverend Theasdar M. Murray, president of Cambridge's chapter of the NAACP, and many of the other black ministers in town closed their churches to CNAC.[4] More personally critics lambasted Richardson for manipulating her followers for personal glory. The mayor of Cambridge, Calvin W. Mowbray, accused her of "sowing her bitter seeds of hatred" to "reap a harvest of violence" and "project herself in the image of a modern-day Joan of Arc." He continued, "Her motive is an obvious one. As long as Public Accommodations are withheld from the Negroes, she will be able to maintain her dictatorial position, her prestige, and her influence both nationally and locally."[5] In a scathing article in the *New Republic,* Murray Kempton wrote, "What deepens her mystery is her entire failure at the conventional commercial civic response. She is one of the few militant integrationists who has deliberately made the poor Negro her resource and this choice peculiar to her nature has given her what power she retains."[6] If the amendment passed, Robert Liston wrote for the *Saturday Evening Post,* Richardson's "days of wine and roses, when power and fame were hers, when she was a household word, an object of widespread admiration, when she was the St. Joan of the civil-rights movement" would be over.[7] Volatile yet stubborn, self-interested yet a modern Joan of Arc—criticisms of Richardson were as contradictory as they claimed her to be.

Stubborn, at least, was accurate. Against these criticisms Richardson refused to change her position and clearly stated her principles. Putting the rights of African Americans to a majority vote, she argued, undermined their status as equal citizens, threatened the concept of inalienable rights, and substituted inclusion in an oppressive democratic process for meaningful social change. Much of what little scholarship exists on the Cambridge movement tends to focus on Richardson's leadership or on how the movement fit within the larger civil rights movement.[8] By focusing on the rhetoric of the Cambridge movement, this essay demonstrates the continuity of the movement's trajectory from sitting in, during the phase of public protests, to sitting out of the referendum vote. Beyond fostering historical reflection on the coherency of Richardson's leadership and the Cambridge movement's strategies and goals, looking beyond the Cambridge movement sit-ins to CNAC's sitting out of the referendum expands understanding of the sit-ins' rhetorical significance and their relationship to public spaces, citizenship, and the formal political process. The criticism Richardson received is evidence of the popular understanding, then as well as now, of the sit-in as a strategy to achieve legislative desegregation. Focusing narrowly on legislative wins or losses as indications of success or failure loses sight of a fundamental symbolic characteristic of the sit-in: it functioned outside the formal democratic process. The Cambridge movement sit-ins, I argue, fulfilled a greater function as enactments of equal rights and citizenship and embodied critiques of the institutionalized oppression African Americans faced within the formal democratic process.

To make this argument, I describe the historical context that influenced the Cambridge movement and the decision to boycott the referendum. Next, through an analysis of the archival materials documenting the Cambridge movement and referendum—including CNAC press statements and official documents, local and national news articles, and an article Richardson published in the African American civil-rights-era journal *Freedomways*—I trace the Cambridge movement's trajectory from sitting in to sitting out. I conclude by discussing the implications of this analysis for our understanding of the civil-rights-era sit-in movement.

Context

The Cambridge movement occurred in a triple liminal space—geographically, chronologically, and ideologically. Geographically Cambridge, Maryland, is located in the region Clarence Lang identifies as the "border South," a region "where both northern and southern political economies, migration and immigration patterns, and modes of black racial control and black politics merged."[9] Chronologically the Cambridge movement occurred toward the end of the 1954–65 classical phase of the civil rights movement and later than most of the sit-ins but prior to the rise of black power.[10] Understanding this context helps explain the ideological commitments undergirding CNAC's strategies and goals and the rhetorical significance of the Cambridge movement sit-ins.

African Americans in Cambridge experienced the contradictory social and political conditions of living in a border state, where there was an "uncertain mixture of North and South in terms of politics and culture."[11] Shannon Harley explains, "Black citizens in Cambridge, Maryland could buy clothes, but not try them on in stores; could buy carry-out food, but not eat in restaurants; and could buy movie theater tickets, but were confined to the balconies of segregated theaters and, later, to the last rows of the segregated balconies. Blacks lived in segregated communities and attended segregated schools."[12] White residents celebrated Cambridge's reputation as a progressive city with model race relations, especially when compared to its southern neighbors. Indeed African Americans had been able to vote and had representatives on the city council and school board since 1881.[13] Yet they still faced significant social, political, and economic discrimination.[14]

Residential segregation was legally enforced until 1957. Almost all African Americans in Cambridge lived in the city's Second Ward, a section of the city divided from the white sections of town by a road aptly named Race Street. After World War II, the decline and eventual collapse of the Phillips Packing Company, an oyster and fruit canning company that sustained much of Cambridge's economy and its political machine, resulted in increased unemployment and poverty, particularly acute among African Americans. At the time of the Cambridge movement, the unemployment rate in Cambridge was three times the national average, with unemployment of African Americans twice as high as the overall rate in Cambridge.[15] With high unemployment came severe poverty and poor, overcrowded housing conditions in the Second Ward. Most residents of the Second Ward lived in small, old houses without hot water or indoor plumbing. The poorest residents lived in "tiny, one story wood and tar-paper constructions" or converted chicken coops. Families of six or more frequently lived in houses of four rooms or fewer.[16] Because black residents were largely restricted to unskilled labor, the sector that had been most affected by the collapse of the Phillips Packing Company, there was little hope of escaping these conditions of poverty. In light of these conditions, the need for broader economic and social equality far outweighed narrower goals of desegregation and legal-political rights, which black experience demonstrated were ineffectual anyway.

In addition to widespread inequality in living, working, and educational opportunities, black residents also experienced significant political oppression, despite possessing formal rights of participation and representation in the democratic process. White conservatives in Cambridge extolled these formal political rights as evidence of Cambridge's racial progressivism and relied heavily on this reputation to attract new industry to the city. According to Richard Levy, "Town officials did not see themselves as bigoted because they knew that blacks in Cambridge enjoyed the vote and representation on the town council and school board."[17] In practice, however, these rights were limited, and Cambridge was less racially progressive than it appeared on the books. The black community had representatives on the city commission and board of education. However, because commissioners were elected by ward and black citizens lived almost exclusively in the Second Ward, they only had one representative in each body, despite comprising a third of Cambridge's population. Further a powerful, white-controlled political machine managed the vote to ensure only black accommodationists won political positions.[18] Both of the Second Ward's representatives followed an accommodationist position and possessed strong interests in appeasing white conservatives and maintaining segregation. Charles Cornish, the city commissioner from the Second Ward, owned the bus company used by the Board of Education to transport black students to segregated schools and was known among the black community as an "Uncle Tom."[19] Helen Waters, the Second Ward's representative on the Board of Education, owned a beauty parlor with an all-white clientele and was openly hostile to CNAC.[20] Thus although African Americans had political representatives, they did not have true political representation and became disillusioned with the political process. CNAC later reported, "They had no other means of expressing their opinion; no officials responsible to them, no needs satisfied other than those deemed necessary by the paternal and occasionally benevolent white power structure. In a very real sense the Negroes were outside of political life."[21]

Conditions for African Americans in Cambridge resulted in a "sense of economic and political powerlessness" and stifled political organization.[22] Although there was a local chapter of the NAACP, Second Ward residents felt it was out of touch with the lower and working classes who suffered the most from discrimination. They believed its demands and action program were too weak.[23] No organized movement or expressions of discontent existed in Cambridge prior to the 1960s, when several national and regional civil rights organizations became more active in the region. The Civic Interest Group of Baltimore (CIG) and the Congress of Racial Equality (CORE) organized Freedom Rides and sit-ins along the Eastern Shore of Maryland from the summer to early winter of 1961, with the goal of achieving a statewide public accommodations measure banning discrimination. In January 1962 two leaders of the Student Nonviolent Coordinating Committee (SNCC) and CIG visited Cambridge and helped organize the first civil rights demonstrations there on January 13, 1962. Approximately one hundred demonstrators marched through the streets of Cambridge, carrying signs protesting segregation and attempting to enter several public places, including the Dorset Theater, the Rescue and Fire Company's Recreation Center, Collins Drugstore, the Dizzyland restaurant, and the Choptank Inn. The demonstrations provoked numerous incidents of violence, particularly at the Choptank Inn, where a white mob beat SNCC organizer William Hansen for entering and physically threw him out the door. Hansen was a veteran of the 1961 Freedom Rides and deeply committed to the philosophy of nonviolence.[24] After peacefully attempting to enter the restaurant two more times, he was arrested for disorderly conduct.[25] During demonstrations the following week, Hansen again attempted to enter the inn's restaurant, and again he was beaten by a white mob, forcibly thrown out, and arrested, this time for trespassing.[26] The violent reactions to the demonstrations destroyed the myth that Cambridge was a peaceful town with model race relations. In the words of several student demonstrators, the reactions to the sit-ins presented Cambridge as a "little Georgia" and "the citadel of race-hate."[27]

Levy explains, "Cambridge became a primary site of the civil rights movement in part by accident and in part due to regional events beyond its control."[28]

Cambridge officials blamed outside forces for stirring trouble in Cambridge and upsetting its otherwise positive race relations.[29] However these outsiders received overwhelming support from Cambridge locals, including some moderate whites, casting "doubt on the claim that the protests were caused (rather than stimulated) by outsiders."[30] The move to direct action within the larger context of the civil rights movement, Herbert Haines argues, was born out of a crisis of faith in the ability of legal change to improve social relations in meaningful ways.[31] Thus the appeal of direct action makes sense in light of black experiences in Cambridge. Cambridge high school students, including Richardson's daughter, Donna, were particularly active in the first demonstrations and later formed a local affiliate of SNCC. Witnessing Donna's and other students' growing disillusionment with the lack of progress in Cambridge, Gloria Richardson assumed leadership of CNAC in the spring of 1962 and established it as one of the only adult-led affiliates of SNCC.[32] Gloria Richardson recounted later for *Ebony* magazine, "Prior to this time . . . individual Negroes had continuously voiced to their friends and in social or religious gatherings, discontent with their life. Although these people were disgruntled, there was no coming together to bring into focus their frustration."[33] Residents of Cambridge were already agitated and eager for change but felt politically ineffectual. Whereas Cambridge's black community felt powerless within the formal democratic process, the national civil rights movement, especially the student-led sit-in movement and Freedom Rides, galvanized Cambridge's black community through collective direct action.

The coordination of protests by regional and national civil rights organizations in concert with the national civil rights movement helped mobilize the black community and laid the foundation for the organization of CNAC and the Cambridge movement. Yet the local political and social conditions in Cambridge, shaped at least in part by its border state location, as well as its later occurrence within the national sit-in movement also molded the local movement. The goals, tactics, and underlying ideologies of the Cambridge movement reflected these local particularities and diverged from the mainstream civil rights movement in meaningful ways. CNAC's ideological commitments wavered between liberal and radical thought and practices. While embracing the sit-in as a tactic, they rejected the philosophical commitment to nonviolence typically associated with it and pursued more radical goals.

From Sitting In to Sitting Out

When, on March 15, 1963, the Dorset Theater sharpened its segregation policies, further confining black audiences from the balcony to its back rows, CNAC representatives made one more attempt to act through traditional political channels and to negotiate with Mayor Mowbray and the city council. When Mowbray and the council "rebuffed the group with vague statements, indignation, and an occasional joke," CNAC vowed "demonstrations would commence immediately."[34] From March to July 1963, participants in the Cambridge movement protested through boycotts, pickets, sit-ins, and mass demonstrations. Although inspired by the national sit-in and Freedom Ride movement, the symbolic function of the Cambridge movement demonstrations were specific to local black experiences in Cambridge. More than protesting against specific segregation policies, demonstrators protested against the entire discriminatory system. The protests disrupted normalized patterns of oppression and discrimination in a way that participating in the formal political process, especially through voting, could not. Moreover through the sit-ins in particular, demonstrators enacted their rights and identities as equal citizens. Tracing CNAC's trajectory from sitting in to sitting out of the referendum supports this interpretation and demonstrates the coherency of CNAC's strategies. Subjecting their rights to a majority vote by participating in the referendum would have undermined their identity as equal citizens and substituted inclusion in an oppressive political system for genuine social and political transformation, negating the symbolic function of the sit-ins. The Cambridge movement sit-ins and sit-out were not about mere inclusion, whether in a public place or in the political process, but about establishing broader conditions of social and political equality.

Sitting In: The Cambridge Movement Demonstrations

Although CNAC adopted the basic tactics of the national sit-in movement—including boycotts and pickets in addition to sit-ins—the goals, philosophical commitments, and, ultimately, the symbolic meaning of the Cambridge movement sit-ins differed in important ways. First, CNAC protested against broader systems of economic, social, and political injustice, of which the segregation of public places was but one symptom. Second, Richardson rejected a commitment to nonviolence, and CNAC demonstrators practiced armed self-defense. Finally, both of these characteristics contributed to the symbolic meaning of the Cambridge movement sit-ins as performances of rights and equal citizenship.

In many ways the Cambridge movement sit-ins functioned similarly to previous sit-ins and direct-action strategies. Whereas electoral politics concealed black oppression under token political rights and representation, sit-ins, boycotts, and marches called attention to specific places of oppression, as well as hateful and prejudicial attitudes. As Gladys Ritchie wrote in 1970, the sit-in's "action carries a powerful rhetoric. It has a special language that writes big on the walls of the Entrenched and the Indifferent. It leaves messages there which the habitually 'blind' and 'deaf' must see and hear."[35]

The first Cambridge movement demonstrations occurred on March 30, 1963. Consistent with the mainstream sit-in movement, demonstrators targeted public recreational places. Seventeen demonstrators, including Richardson, were arrested for attempting to sit in at the Dorset Theater and the local recreation center.[36] In a *Freedomways* article Richardson later wrote about the Cambridge movement, she explains, "Some few years ago when the sit-in movement began, the emphasis was placed on the discrimination inherent in places of public accommodation. This area was the showcase through which the consciousness of the white race would be aroused and through which the apathy of the Negro community could be overcome."[37] CNAC, however, extended its critique beyond "the discrimination inherent in places of public accommodation" to the oppression inherent in and reproduced by political institutions and the democratic process. After this initial demonstration, CNAC broadened its areas of demonstration. Throughout April large groups of demonstrators gathered on Saturdays and picketed segregated businesses but also City Hall, the Employment Security Office, the Board of Education, the Chamber of Commerce, and the office of State Senator Frederick Malkus.[38] By extending the scope of its targets, CNAC called attention to discrimination and oppression, not just in privately owned public places but also in public spaces of government, social services, and political offices.

The particular places CNAC targeted were representative of its broader goals. In relation to many other sit-ins, the Cambridge movement was one of the first campaigns to focus on broader economic and social conditions rather than narrow political rights and desegregation.[39] Students from Swarthmore College conducted a door-to-door survey with almost every resident of the Second Ward in the summer of 1963 and asked respondents to rate CNAC's demands in terms of importance. Forty-two percent responded that employment was most important, 26 percent said housing, 21 percent said education, and only 6 percent said public accommodations.[40] In response CNAC established better housing, full employment, better working conditions, and better education all as more important goals than merely the desegregation of public accommodations. Places of public accommodation were a useful starting point to raise public consciousness about discrimination but with the ultimate goal of achieving broader social and political transformation. According to CNAC's own report on the Cambridge movement and conditions prompting it, "It is significant that although public accommodations has been the major focal point for demonstrations, the Negro community decisively designates employment as the overwhelming need of the hour. Housing and schools, although not as important as jobs, rank high above public accommodations and police brutality."[41]

In addition to being a showcase for consciousness-raising, places of public accommodation were also symbolically important because of their distinctiveness from political institutions. Political rights such as the right to vote, CNAC recognized, were not enough to guarantee broader conditions of equality. CNAC recognized that transforming the entire system that supported discrimination and oppression required working outside the formal political process, which, in their experience, worked only to reinforce the discriminatory system. Reflecting on the city council's rejection of her initial attempt to negotiate a legislative end to segregation, Richardson stated in an interview, "We didn't think they would agree, but we were not asking for anything that was not supposedly guaranteed you as a citizen. Eventually, we did get what we wanted, but only because we took to the street."[42] It is important to note that although CNAC recognized the necessity of working outside the political process, they did not completely reject it. In addition to the meeting in March, Richardson attempted to negotiate with the city council several times. Ultimately, however, she rejected compromises that would not achieve CNAC's goals for broad social and political reform. Rejecting the compromise agreement proposed in June, which required a moratorium on demonstrations, Richardson noted that demonstrations were "the one proven means by which African Americans had effected change."[43] Additionally, prior to the main events of the Cambridge movement, CNAC organized a voter education and registration drive in the summer of 1962, with the goal of unseating the conservative state senator from Cambridge, Frederick Malkus. In addition to failing to achieve this goal, the initiative failed to disrupt patterns of discrimination in Cambridge. While voter registration drives in the South were often met with as much violence as other types of demonstrations, white conservatives in Cambridge heartily endorsed Project Eastern Shore.[44] After all, black citizens had been voting and participating in politics for years, without posing any threat to the white power structure. Furthermore black participation in the election further supported claims that Cambridge was a city with model, progressive race relations.

Unlike in the South, participation in the formal political system through voting was not a subversive act capable of upsetting the system of discrimination and, in actuality, only reinforced it. Only the sit-ins, boycotts, and marches effectively called attention to the discrimination Cambridge's black residents faced by disrupting routinized modes of discrimination and oppression. Describing the effectiveness of direct action, Haines observes, "So long as a state of normalcy could be maintained, reform could be put off; direct action, however, could force issues to center stage."[45] The sit-ins were essential for interrupting the state of normalcy. As early as April 10, however, Cambridge's local newspaper, the *Daily Banner,* remarked that "the sight of youngsters in the picket line is no longer a novelty."[46] When pickets were no longer able to disrupt business as usual, CNAC returned to sit-ins. CNAC staged daily sit-ins from May 11 through May 17. The *Daily Banner* reported on May 16 that "the tempo of the protests has picked up this week after picketing of downtown business places produced few arrests and little public attention. Local civil rights leaders appear to have abandoned the peaceful picketing for sit-ins and a policy of filling the local jail."[47] New demonstrators were arrested daily for attempting to enter or re-fusing to leave segregated businesses and public facilities. Police frequently had to remove and carry protesters physically to their police cars when they refused to move from their positions.[48] While city officials ignored African Americans within the formal political sphere, the highly visible and bodily rhetoric of the sit-ins demanded recognition and a response.

The violence of that response was another distinctive feature of the Cambridge movement. The movement took another turn on June 10, when two youths were arrested and sentenced to indefinite terms in the state reform school.[49] Mass demonstrations replaced sit-ins and picketing with the number of participants increasing from seventy to five hundred. The mass marches incited violent reactions by white counterdemonstrators and resulted in skir-mishes between blacks and whites. Although the national sit-in movement was grounded in the philopspohy of nonviolence, CNAC distinguished between a philosophical commitment to nonviolence and the use of nonviolence as a tac-tic and tolerated armed self-defense. After the first major outbreaks of violence, demonstrators frequently carried weapons for self-defense. The first major out-break of violence occurred on the night of June 14. Several white-owned busi-nesses in the Second Ward burned to the ground, two men were shot, and police found bombs the next day.[50] After Richardson again refused to compromise at an emergency meeting, Gov. J. Millard Tawes declared martial law and called in the National Guard to help preserve order. With images of the National Guard pointing bayonets at black demonstrators in the national newspapers, Cam-bridge's image as a city with model race relations was shattered. Moreover the presence of the National Guard was representative of the violence the system of oppression created and with which it was maintained.

CNAC rejected the philosophy on nonviolence on the principle of refusing to compromise the fundamental right of self-defense in pursuit of desegrega-tion. Levy explains that CNAC's moral position "hinted at a view that would gain adherents in the latter part of the 1960s: that nonviolence as preached by King had the potential to reinforce the inferior status of African Americans because it compelled blacks to adopt a submissive rather than an assertive posture."[51] By allowing armed self-defense, CNAC refused both to passively allow whites to violate their rights against physical harm and to depend on the police force, which it viewed as part of the discriminatory system, for defense. While gaining strength by following the tactics of the national sit-in movement, CNAC rejected a stance that would undermine their identities as equal citizens and their resistance to the oppressive power structure.

This position aligns perfectly with the broader symbolic function of the sit-ins. The sit-ins functioned as a mode of resistance by which demonstrators enacted their rights and identities as equal citizens. As equal citizens under the law—which, as opposed to in the Deep South, was largely true in Cambridge—CNAC and its supporters claimed "they demonstrate to try to exercise the rights they already have."[52] Rather than seeking thin legal protections of their rights from a political system their experiences demonstrated was oppressive, demonstrators constituted their rights performatively by acting outside the system they hoped to transform. The various direct-action techniques transformed rights rhetoric from abstract principles to specific rights violations. Moreover through the sit-ins in particular, demonstrators constituted their identities as equal, rights-bearing citizens. Whereas picketing and mass demonstrations primarily work negatively to oppose some sort of violation or injustice, sit-ins also functioned positively to construct a counter-reality through the insertion of black bodies into previously white spaces.

Throughout the Cambridge movement, Richardson, on behalf of CNAC, refused any political agreements with the city council that required ceasing demonstrations without a guarantee the legal measures would be enacted. When, in late June, the city council proposed a compromise that included the desegregation of places of public accommodation through an amendment to the city charter, Richardson refused and argued for a desegregation ordinance instead, since all amendments to the city charter were subject to approval by referendum. Echoing CNAC's position that they demonstrated "to exercise rights they already have" and foreshadowing arguments she later made to support the boycott, Richardson explained, "We reject this plan because the human rights of any citizen, regardless of race cannot be decided by public vote."[53] Despite Richardson's rejection of the agreement, the council proposed the amendment anyway.

Throughout June and July, Richardson appealed several times to U.S. Attorney General Robert F. Kennedy to intervene. The group met with Kennedy on July 22 and signed the Treaty of Cambridge the next day. The agreement included five provisions: hire an African American at the state employment office, desegregate the remaining segregated grades in schools and enact an open transfer system between schools, establish a biracial Human Relations Commission to address further grievances, work toward establishing a public housing project, and try to avert the filing of a petition to bring the June desegregation amendment to a referendum.[54] In exchange CNAC agreed to suspend demonstrations indefinitely. Although all the parties to the treaty agreed to try to prevent a referendum, a pro-segregation organization of white business interests called the Dorchester Business and Citizens Association (DBCA) submitted a petition on August 9 with 1,700 signatures, 500 more than the necessary 20 percent, to force it to a referendum.[55] Cambridge became the first and only city in the United States to put integration to a direct vote.[56] Although many civil rights leaders and local white moderates and liberals believed the amendment would still pass, Richardson called for African Americans to boycott the referendum vote.[57]

Sitting Out: The Referendum Boycott

Despite the criticism Richardson received for contradicting the goals of the Cambridge movement and, more broadly, the national civil rights movement, Richardson's position on the referendum directly extended from the rhetorical significance of the sit-ins. Richardson argued that black citizens should not subject their inviolable rights to a vote. In CNAC's official statement to the media after the referendum vote, Richardson wrote, "Equal accommodation in public places is a right inherent in citizenship and should not be subject to the wishes and prejudices of any individual or group."[58]

Civil rights are commonly understood as belonging to an individual on the basis of one's membership in a particular community or status as a citizen. CNAC emphasized black citizenship as resulting from participation in and contributions to the community, rather than from formal recognition and legal agreements. Richardson stated for the Associated Press just a few days after she announced the boycott, "We are American citizens. I think it creates a hurt and a disappointment that after 300 years here we are going to have to go to the polls and vote on whether we can go into a place of public accommodations."[59] Although black citizens only gained official legal recognition of their citizenship with the passage of the Fourteenth Amendment in 1868, less than one hundred years earlier, Richardson indicated their inclusion in the community preexisted this formal recognition. CNAC also cited civic actions such as serving in the military and paying taxes as justifications that black citizens should not have to vote on their rights. In the same statement to the Associated Press, Richardson stated, "The people here in the community are telling me they went overseas and fought in a war and came back and now they are expected to vote on this sort of thing. But people can come here from Europe and can go anyplace they wish—people who have not been here for generation after generation and have not fought for America."[60] As opposed to Europeans, black citizens had constituted their membership in the community by fighting in the war. These arguments that citizenship and civil rights must be performatively enacted support the symbolic function of the sit-ins.

Furthermore CNAC challenged the legitimacy of the democratic process, particularly voting, as a mode of ensuring rights. Richardson argued, "Why would we agree to submit to have our civil rights granted by vote when they were ours already, according to the Constitution?"[61] While recognizing the authority of the Constitution, and thus not completely rejecting government, Richardson argued against voting as a means of performing citizenship or protecting civil rights. She also pointed to an inherent irony in the act: the Constitution that granted African Americans the right to vote also already granted them the rights they were being asked to vote for. Commonly understood as the defining element of liberal democracy voting, Robert Asen explains, has traditionally been understood as "the quintessential act of citizenship."[62] Throughout history groups who have been excluded from the protections and rights of citizenship have fought for the right to vote and used the ritual of voting as a means of gaining access to and enacting citizenship. Remarking on the power of voting as "a recognizable ritual of citizenship," Angela Ray describes how disenfranchised women appropriated the ritual to reveal "the profoundly gendered nature of cultural assumptions about who constituted the people." In their attempts to register to vote, these women performed a "participatory, persuasive argument in an ongoing public controversy about the parameters of the U.S. polity."[63] In the context of the civil rights movement, William H. Lawson explains how the campaign for the 1963 Mississippi Freedom Vote, a vote SNCC organized to demonstrate the will of black Mississippians to vote, mobilized "potential constituents into practicing citizens."[64] Many activists in the civil rights movement viewed voting as a defining right and act of citizenship, as well as a means of attaining greater equality. CNAC's referendum boycott challenged this belief and the legitimacy of voting as a means of performing citizenship and protecting the rights supposedly entailed in it.

CNAC's argument that "constitutional rights cannot be given or taken away at the polls" pointed to an oppressive feature of the democratic process—subjecting minority rights to a majority vote—and echoed the sentiment expressed during the sit-ins that seeking rights through legal agreements and the formal political process was insufficient and incapable of transforming the discriminatory system.[65] After observing for years that participating in the traditional democratic process by voting and relying on representatives in government failed to guarantee them the fundamental rights of citizenship, many African Americans in Cambridge and elsewhere viewed the democratic process as an oppressive tool used by the white majority to perpetuate discrimination and inequality. This opinion was evident when Richardson said to the press, "A first-class citizen does not plead to the white power-structure to give him something the whites have no power to give or take away."[66] Richardson explained this position more fully and emphasized the rhetorical significance of the boycott in her *Freedomways* article: "We called for Negroes to boycott the polls in an expression of passive resistance in the face of an illegal hoax being perpetrated against the people. . . . We were being asked to tuck our dignity in our pockets and crawl to the polls to prove in a stacked vote that once again we were going to let the whites in control say what we would be permitted to do in a 'free, democratic country.'"[67] According to CNAC the white majority in Cambridge was asking African Americans to participate in the system that ensured their oppression. Consequently CNAC took the position that African Americans should boycott the referendum on the principle that it "was unconstitutional, illegal and immoral."[68]

CNAC also rejected voting in the referendum for practical reasons, based on their beliefs about the oppressive nature of the democratic system. Just as demonstrators during the Cambridge movement realized they could not achieve meaningful change through formal political negotiations and thin legal agreements, CNAC declared during the boycott that they would not achieve any gain, even if the amendment passed. CNAC stated, "The whites would test [the amendment's] constitutionality in the courts and a decision might not be given for two or three years."[69] Further, although many citizens in Cambridge believed the amendment could pass, CNAC argued that allowing rights to be put up to a majority vote would set a dangerous precedent and threaten the inviolability of rights. Richardson wrote in *Freedomways:* "No one was ready to take a temporary loss and assume responsibility for the thousands of black people across the south who, once we submitted, would be subject to the same tactic although they would not even have the advantage of a swing-vote. They would be forced, in the name of democracy, to submit to the biased whims of a majority, and in the name of the democratic process be bound by it."[70]

For practical and moral reasons, CNAC rejected the mainstream approach of the national civil rights movement and fervently expressed in Cambridge by a coalition of black community groups in an advertisement in the *Daily Banner:* "You can vote! You Must Vote! Your vote is your blow for freedom now!"[71] In response to these appeals for black citizens to exercise their constitutional rights by voting on the amendment, CNAC replied, "Equality is also our constitutional right. Freedom is our constitutional right. It is because these things are our rights that we are asking you not to vote."[72]

Conclusion

By tracing the trajectory of the Cambridge movement from sitting in to sitting out, this essay illuminates a broader symbolic function of the sit-ins than typically understood. Rather than demonstrating for inclusion in public places and legal recognition of their status as equal citizens, CNAC demonstrators asserted their identities as already equal citizens. For CNAC the sit-ins were more than an effective tactic to gain legislative victories. The sit-ins were especially important for CNAC as a mode of demonstration that worked outside the democratic system.

In addition to expanding our understanding of the sit-in as a mode of performing citizenship, CNAC's move from sitting in to sitting out calls attention to the contentious relationship of minority rights and majority rule within a democratic society. Legal scholars refer to this tension as the antimajoritarian nature of rights. Julie Debeljak explains, "Civil and political rights, in particular, attempt to guarantee a voice for the unpopular within the popular; a voice for the minority within the majority."[73] Consequently, however, rights exist in a contentious relationship with a democratic process based on the principle of majority rule.[74] Yet rights and democracy are also assumed to be mutually constitutive. Martin Loughlin states, "Rights provide the basic building blocks of the political structure and give expression to the idea of democracy. Properly understood, rights and democracy do not . . . conflict. Rights and democracy are twin sides of the same coin."[75] For CNAC the sit-ins were an important tactic for both illuminating and countering the antimajoritarian nature of rights while fighting for recognition as equal citizens.

Notes

1. "Gloria Richardson: Lady General of Civil Rights."

2. "Zealot's Stand."

3. Kisseloff, "Gloria Richardson Dandridge," 62. Richardson also recounted this experience in an interview for the Civil Rights History Project. Gloria Richardson, interview by Joseph Mosnier.

4. Levy, *Civil War on Race Street*, 97.

5. "Mayor Charges that Mrs. Richardson Hopes to Defeat Amendment."

6. Kempton, "Gloria, Gloria," 16.

7. Liston, "Who Can We Surrender To?," 80.

8. Levy's *Civil War on Race Street* provides the most comprehensive account of the Cambridge movement as a whole, including Richardson's role but also the historical, social, and political context and a description of CNAC's goals and actions. For scholarship that focuses on Richardson, particularly as a woman leader in the civil rights movement, see Fitzgerald, "Days of Wine and Roses"; Foeman, "Gloria Richardson"; Kisseloff, "Gloria Richardson Dandridge"; Millner, "Recasting Civil Rights Leadership"; Robnett, *How Long? How Long*; Walker, "'Gun-Toting' Gloria Richardson."

9. Lang, "Locating the Civil Rights Movement," 374.

10. Bayard Rustin first used the term *classical* to describe the phase of the civil rights movement bookended by the 1954 *Brown v. Board of Education* decision and the Voting Rights Act of 1965. Rustin, "From Protest to Politics."

11. Lang, "Locating the Civil Rights Movement," 385.

12. Harley, "Chronicle of a Death Foretold," 179. Historian Thomas J. Sugrue describes a similar situation characterizing much of the North at this time. Sugrue, *Sweet Land of Liberty*, xvi.

13. Levy, *Civil War on Race Street*, 7.

14. Thomas Sugrue describes these conditions as common in the North: "Northern blacks lived as second-class citizens, unencumbered by the most blatant of southern-style Jim Crow laws, but still trapped in an economic, political and legal regime that seldom recognized them as equals." Sugrue, *Sweet Land of Liberty*, xv.

15. Cambridge Non-Violent Action Committee (CNAC) Summer Staff, *Negro Ward*.

16. CNAC Summer Staff, *Negro Ward*, 27–28; Kisseloff, "Gloria Richardson Dandridge," 56.

17. Levy, *Civil War on Race Street*, 54.

18. CNAC Summer Staff, *Negro Ward*, 11.

19. Associated Press, "Negro Is Named to Head Council"; Kisseloff, "Gloria Richardson Dandridge"; Levy, "Black Freedom Struggle and White Resistance," 75.

20. Brock, "Gloria Richardson and the Cambridge Movement," 123; CNAC Summer Staff, *Negro Ward*; Kisseloff, "Gloria Richardson Dandridge," 55.

21. CNAC Summer Staff, *Negro Ward*, 11.

22. Harley, "Chronicle of a Death Foretold," 179.

23. CNAC Summer Staff, *Negro Ward*, 46.

24. Levy, *Civil War on Race Street*, 38.

25. CNAC Summer Staff, *Negro Ward*, 46; Levy, *Civil War on Race Street*, 38–40.

26. Levy, *Civil War on Race Street*, 42–43.

27. Qtd. in ibid., 41.

28. Ibid., 36.

29. Ibid., 41.

30. Ibid.

31. Haines, *Black Radicals and the Civil Rights Mainstream*, 47.

32. Levy, *Civil War on Race Street*, 51.

33. "Gloria Richardson: Lady General," 30.

34. CNAC Summer Staff, *Negro Ward*, 46.

35. Ritchie, "Sit-In: A Rhetoric of Human Action," 22.

36. "17 Jailed Saturday."

37. Richardson, "Focus on Cambridge," 34.

38. "44 Are Released from Jail."

39. Brock, "Gloria Richardson and the Cambridge Movement," 124.

40. CNAC Summer Staff, *Negro Ward*, 54.

41. Ibid., 53.

42. Qtd. in Kisseloff, "Gloria Richardson Dandridge," 56.

43. Levy, *Civil War on Race Street*, 83; Millner, "Recasting Civil Rights Leadership," 679; CNAC Summer Staff, *Negro Ward*.

44. Levy, *Civil War on Race Street*, 58.

45. Haines, *Black Radicals*, 47.

46. "11 Pickets Arrested Sunday"; "How to Lose Friends."

47. Rimpo, "Tempo of Protests Steps Up."

48. "Cambridge Jails 14 After Sit-In"; "Sit-Ins May Become Daily Occurrence Here"; Chapman, "9 Students Arrested in Cambridge."

49. CNAC Summer Staff, *Negro Ward*.

50. Levy, *Civil War on Race Street*, 82; Millner, "Recasting Civil Rights Leadership," 677.

51. Levy, *Civil War on Race Street*, 99.

52. "Gloria Richardson: Lady General," 31.

53. Homan, "Negro Leaders Reject City Plan in Cambridge."

54. "Text of the Cambridge, Md., Accord"; Brock, "Gloria Richardson and the Cambridge Movement," 136; CNAC Summer Staff, *Negro Ward*.

55. CNAC Summer Staff, *Negro Ward*.

56. Levy, *Civil War on Race Street*, 3.

57. Brock, "Gloria Richardson and the Cambridge Movement."

58. CNAC, "Press Release," 83; Richardson, "Focus on Cambridge," 32.

59. "Heavy Vote Expected in Tuesday's Referendum."

60. Ibid.

61. Qtd. in Kisseloff, "Gloria Richardson Dandridge," 60.

62. Asen, "Discourse Theory of Citizenship," 205. Asen argues for an expanded notion of what counts as acts of citizenship.

63. Ray, "The Rhetorical Ritual of Citizenship," 2.

64. Lawson, "Citizenship as Salvation," 183.

65. "CNAC Head Back after Resignation."

66. Ibid.

67. Richardson, "Focus on Cambridge," 31.

68. Ibid.

69. Qtd. in "CNAC Head Back."

70. Richardson, "Focus on Cambridge," 31.

71. *Daily Banner*, 1 October 1963.

72. "CNAC Head Back."

73. Debeljak, "Rights and Democracy," 137.

74. According to Burt Neuborne, the tension exists "between a genuine commitment to majority rule and a genuine insistence that areas exist—we call them rights—that are off-limits to the will of the majority, even when that will is expressed with scrupulous fairness"; Neuborne, "Origin of Rights," 187–88. Debeljak describes "the *supposed* tension between a particular expression of popular opinion, known as majoritarian democracy, and the conditions necessary to guarantee the continuing expression of that opinion, known as civil and political rights"; Debeljak, "Rights and Democracy," 137.

75. Loughlin, "Rights, Democracy and the Nature of Legal Order," 44.

WADE IN THE WATER

African American and Local News Accounts of the
1964 Monson Motor Lodge Swim-In

Rebecca Bridges Watts

In the spring and summer of 1964, local and national leaders of the civil rights movement, notably Rev. Dr. Martin Luther King Jr. and the Southern Christian Leadership Conference (SCLC), focused the attention of their nonviolent army on St. Augustine, Florida. During the same months that Freedom Summer brought voter registration and community outreach efforts to Mississippi, leaving James Chaney, Andrew Goodman, and Michael Schwerner missing and murdered, civil rights activists were marching on the Old Slave Market in the nation's oldest city. Just as Nelson Mandela and other anti-apartheid activists were being convicted of treason and sent to Robben Island in South Africa,[1] King was being arrested and jailed for trespassing and conspiracy in St. Augustine. While the Civil Rights Act of 1964 was winding its way through the legislative process in Washington, D.C., civil rights activists were integrating a motel swimming pool in sweltering St. Augustine.

This essay focuses on the June 1964 Monson Motor Lodge "swim-in." Striking photographic images and evocative textual accounts of the swim-in circulated overwhelming evidence of the violent resistance faced when people of color sought to enjoy pursuits such as swimming in a motel pool—a place heretofore segregated by race. Accounts of this image event were featured in print and broadcast news through both local and national media outlets. This rhetorical criticism, however, is focused on the depictions disseminated through six African American news outlets—the Associated Negro Press National News Service, the *Baltimore Afro-American*, the *Atlanta Daily World*, the *Chicago Defender*, the *Philadelphia Tribune*, and the *SCLC Newsletter*—as well as through three local newspapers in northeast Florida, specifically the *St. Augustine*

Evening Record, the *Daytona Beach Morning Journal,* and Jacksonville's *Florida Times-Union.* Focusing this essay on coverage of the swim-in disseminated through these nine news outlets targeted toward citizens with special interest in these events—whether as African Americans or as area residents—allows this rhetorical history to shed light on the ways in which editors and journalists chose to depict the intertwined issues of race, power, and civil rights, specifically through their portrayals of the three principal categories of participants in the Monson Motor Lodge swim-in demonstration: segregationists, integrationists, and law enforcement officers.

The Long Hot Summer

As 1964 began, Dr. Robert Hayling—former president of the St. Augustine chapter of the National Association for the Advancement of Colored People (NAACP)—sent a letter to the Massachusetts Southern Christian Leadership Conference (SCLC) in which he encouraged students to get involved with the Florida Spring Project, with demonstrations scheduled between March 21 and April 4. White and black students, faculty, and chaplains from New England colleges and universities soon arrived, as did reporters and television crews anticipating breaking news of national interest. On March 27 a high-profile protester arrived in the person of Mary Peabody, mother of the Massachusetts governor and wife of an Episcopal bishop. She and around ninety others were arrested the next day for trespass.[2]

On May 18 Dr. King arrived in St. Augustine, calling it "a small Birmingham" and pledging to return with "our non-violent army." On May 25 Dr. King did return, vowing that St. Augustine would have "a long hot summer, but hopefully a long hot non-violent summer." SCLC leaders such as Dorothy Cotton, Fred Shuttlesworth, C. T. Vivian, and Andrew Young conducted training sessions "designed to educate the young people flocking to the cause in the intricate legal and diplomatic art of self-restraint, an absolute necessity for peaceful demonstrations to be successful." Civil rights demonstrations and marches ensued, as did racist counterdemonstrations, leading to state and local officials' enacting curfews and eventually a ban on nighttime demonstrations.[3]

King announced at a June 10 press conference his intention to visit the Monson Motor Lodge the next day, planning an "act of civil disobedience." When he arrived at the motel on June 11, 1964, accompanied by Rev. Ralph Abernathy and others, he attempted to integrate the motel restaurant, a popular downtown meeting place for local white civic groups. (The motel itself provided lodging for many of the out-of-town journalists.) Ultimately King was arrested, with others, on charges of "breach of peace, conspiracy, and trespass with malicious intent" and taken to a Jacksonville jail.[4] One week later, on June 18, five black and two white SCLC activists made a bold, strategic move by attempting to integrate the Monson Motor Lodge's swimming pool, with King observing the event from the safety of a park across the street.

The Monson Motor Lodge Swim-In—June 18, 1964

A week after King was arrested while trying to integrate the motor lodge's restaurant, a rally took place there featuring a contingent of visiting rabbis. Meanwhile some SCLC activists planned to stage an additional protest at the motel that day, June 18, 1964, using the main rally as a distraction to allow them to gain entry to the motel's pool yet knowing that the press would be nearby. As SCLC activist J. T. Johnson recalled in an oral history interview conducted by fellow SCLC veteran Andrew Young, "Well, Hose [Williams] thought that the movement was kind of dying out. He said that we weren't in the news enough and that we needed to do something dramatic to kind of get us back started. So . . . we sat around . . . talking about what could we do and how could we do it. . . . We thought we would ask him [Al Lingo] to check into the hotel and I would be his guest." The next morning, two white integrationists, Rev. Al Lingo and seminary graduate Peter Shiras, registered at the Monson and then invited five African Americans, including Johnson, to go with them into the pool as their guests. As Johnson remembered, "We slipped out of the car and he [Lingo] was already in the pool. They didn't have that brick wall out there, so I came up the curb and over the side and into the swimming pool."

Lingo, a white Methodist minister who had been with the SCLC at the March on Washington, recalled two elements of their strategy in an oral history interview: "I think there was a concern that we stay in the pool as long as we could. We keep this integrated event alive for as long as we could. That was one intent. And then secondly, to be as cool as we could be, because, in a way, I guess, harassment wasn't my biggest fear, but I knew younger people, particularly women, would be in. So we had our eye on them."[5]

The Federal Bureau of Investigation was monitoring the tense situation in St. Augustine, filing regular reports by teletype from their Jacksonville field office on the "racial situation." While some names were later redacted from the FBI reporting, such documents provide a detailed window into the essential facts of the swim-in (and wade-ins) from the perspective of federal agents. According to the FBI field report, the following events occurred at the Monson Motor Lodge that day:

> At about 12:47 PM on June 18, 1964, five Negroes dove into the swimming pool of the Monson Motor Lodge along with two white individuals who were registered at the motel. One of the white men swam to the edge of the pool and told [Brock] "These are our guests. We are registered here, and

want these people to swim with us." [Brock] then ordered the swimmers to leave the swimming pool. After they refused, he ran to his office nearby and returned with two gallons of muriatic acid which he poured into the swimming pool after shouting "I am cleaning the pool right now." Deputy Sheriff [name redacted] ordered the swimmers to leave the swimming pool and after they refused to, he called for dogs to assist in getting them out of the pool. However, before the dogs arrived, [Henry Billitz] a regular St. Augustine, Florida Policeman who was off duty and dressed in old clothes, volunteered to jump into the pool and effect the arrests of the swimmers. He grappled with the white demonstrators both of whom resisted arrest but they were finally "dragged" from the pool. The Negroes then followed offering no resistence [*sic*]. It took about 19 minutes before the demonstrators were removed from the pool.

A few hours after the pool integrationists were taken to jail, the FBI noted that "three Negroes" made an attempt to integrate the Monson pool but were arrested before they could enter the water.[6]

News Coverage of the Swim-In

The graphic reports of African Americans (and like-minded whites) being met with violent resistance for simply trying to swim in a refreshing pool on a hot summer day gave people around the world, as President Lyndon Johnson complained, a vivid picture of the race issue: "Our whole foreign policy will go to hell over this. Yesterday in the swimming pool in St. Augustine they jumped in, and police jumped in with their clothes on, and started pouring acid in the pool." As historian Derek Gilliard notes, "Countries all over the world, the Communist countries, used this. It was propaganda. Well, this is America, the land of the free and the home of the just, and look what they're doing to black people."[7] These images and stories also served as additional, undeniable evidence to Congress, charged that summer with deliberating as to whether or not to extend integration into more quarters of U.S. public life. In their reporting on this event, news outlets devoted significant column inches to characterizing the key groups of players involved: the segregationists, the integrationists, and the police.

African American Coverage of the Monson Motor Lodge Swim-In: The Segregationists

Reporting on the segregationist element at the Monson Motor Lodge focused on James Brock, the manager of the motel who poured muriatic acid into the pool. Faced with five blacks swimming in his pool with two whites, Brock was described in multiple African American accounts as having "retaliated" against the unwelcome swimmers. Regarding pouring the acid into the pool, the Associated Negro Press reported that Brock, "frustrated in attempts to keep his place 'uncontaminated,' . . . hustled around and got what looked to be a couple of pounds of muriatic acid and dumped it into the pool." In the *SCLC Newsletter*'s special St. Augustine issue, a photographic essay included Horace Cort's iconic photo of Brock pouring the acid into the pool, accompanied by a caption reporting that "when a group of white and Negro integrationists entered a segregated motel pool, manager James Brock poured acid into it, shouting, 'I'm cleaning the pool.'" As the Associated Negro Press observed, Brock "descended to a new low in racial attacks when he sadistically threw quantities of muriatic acid in the pool in an attempt to cause physical harm to the swimmers."[8]

What becomes clear through this reporting is the idea that Brock's choice of pouring acid into the pool was not simply a matter of expediency in the eyes of the black press. The *Chicago Defender* declared, in the headline accompanying the acid-pouring photograph of Brock, that the incident should be seen as "the acid test of human dignity," emphasizing in the accompanying caption that "muriatic acid is another term for hydrochloric acid, which is excessively corrosive." Throughout the coverage of the swim-in by the African American press, Brock represented segregationists and their view that whites and their spaces must be kept purified from contamination by integration—the presence of blacks in previously all-white spaces. Further the Monson swim-in was also used in African American reporting to illustrate dramatically the level of physical threat to African Americans in the racially charged crucible of St. Augustine.[9]

In addition to reporting on Brock's violent reaction to the attempted integration of his motel's pool, the African American media also included reporting on his volatile yet vulnerable emotional state. In his interview with white swim-in participant Peter Shiras, Baker Morten reported that during the swim-in, "all the while Brock was screaming irrationally." Reporting on Brock's emotions in the aftermath of the swim-in, an article published in the *Chicago Defender* described how, "after the excitement was over, Brock lost control of his emotions for the first time and broke out into tears. 'I can't take much more of this,' Brock said. 'I'm going to get mean and when I get mean I get real mean.'" However this does beg the question as to whether this report was implying that Brock had not yet lost emotional control when he was "screaming irrationally" and dumping muriatic acid into the pool.[10]

Al Kuettner wrote an article profiling Brock headlined, "Motel Manager 'Shaken' after Protest Hits," which was published in the *Atlanta Daily World* on June 21, just three days after the swim-in. In the article readers were given a glimpse into the manager's private life and his emotional state:

Motel manager James Brock sat at a small table in his restaurant, a tall glass of ice tea before him. Listlessly, he squeezed in a slice of lemon and stirred. Across the table sat a friend who finally broke the silence by saying, 'Jimmy, we are going to take care of you. Your friends are going to protect you.' Brock ceased stirring, buried his head in his hands and for the first time in the tense weeks of racial demonstrations that have swirled across his place of business he broke into sobs that shook his body. 'I can't stand it. I can't stand it,' he cried. . . . Other acquaintances came by, slapped Brock on the shoulder and consoled the man who had just gone through the frightening experience of being invaded by Dr. Martin Luther King's "non-violent" integration army.

The inclusion of this reporting on Brock's seeming emotional devastation after not only the swim-in but also repeated attempts by activists to integrate his motel's restaurant—notably the attempt by King that sent the SCLC leader and fellow activists to jail—served somewhat to humanize the impact of the civil rights campaign on businessmen such as Brock. Of course such coverage may also have encouraged readers to consider how much deeper were the impacts, emotional and otherwise, long felt by African Americans. However the previous reporting on Brock's choice to run a Confederate flag "up the pole where the Stars and Stripes fluttered above it" likely would have mitigated the impact of this human-interest profile.[11]

Local Coverage of the Monson Motor Lodge Swim-In: The Segregationists

Meanwhile among the three local newspapers, coverage of the Monson Motor Lodge swim-in varied, especially in their depictions of the segregationists involved. The June 18 evening edition of the *St. Augustine Record* included reporting on the swim-in within the front-page article "More Arrests Made as Demonstrations Continue." However the emphasis of the article, as reflected by its headline, was more on the arrested activists and the roles of various law enforcement agencies with officers on the scene than on any segregationist involvement. The *Record*'s depiction of Brock's reaction to the swim-in was brief yet imbued with sympathy: "Monson Manager James Brock threw a chemical described as a cleaning agent and not harmful into the pool in an effort to clear the demonstrators out." Here the potential shock value of Brock's throwing acid into the pool was minimized by emphasizing the harmlessness of the substance. At the same time, his deed was justified as the reasonable action of a business-person who wanted to disperse unwanted people from his property. Especially noteworthy is the fact that the newspaper of the city in which the swim-in took place chose not to publish any photographs of Brock throwing the acid into the pool (or of anyone else involved, for that matter). Editors of newspapers in nearby Jacksonville and Daytona Beach did choose to publish these photographs, however, alongside more comprehensive articles about St. Augustine's continued racial unrest.[12]

Jacksonville's *Florida Times-Union* published an article headlined "Wild Incidents Precede St. Johns Jury Report Urging 30-Day Armistice." The extended, thirty-six-paragraph article led with a brief description of the swim-in in paragraph 3. However not until midway in the article, in paragraphs 15 and 16, did readers learn about Brock's role in the incident: "During the swimming pool incident, Brock poured a large quantity of an acid cleaner into the pool and announced it was being closed indefinitely. Brock's place of business has been a prime target for demonstrators, presumably because most of the news cameramen are staying there." Staff writer Hank Drane included substantial details about the incident overall and about Brock in particular. It should be noted, though, that editors chose to publish this story far within the edition's interior, on page 26, alongside other local and state news—though this was in keeping with the newspaper's practice of reserving the front page for national and international news. Within the context of the local news section, however, the article on St. Augustine's "wild incidents" was given prime placement.[13]

The more liberal-progressive *Daytona Beach Morning Journal* featured the events in St. Augustine as the lead, page-one news story, "Jury Wants Truce in Racial Crisis," in its June 19 edition. Positioned prominently above the fold on the front page, the Associated Press wire photograph of Brock pouring acid into the pool—captioned "DISCOURAGING BATHERS . . . James Brock pours acid into his swimming pool"—was situated immediately beneath the headline, alongside the subhead "Proposed Biracial Body after Month; King Says He Won't Go Along." Juxtaposed beside this headline and subhead, the photograph of Brock (as well as one police officer, Henry Billitz, jumping into the pool) served as visual explanation for why the grand jury hoped a truce would be possible, as well as why King did not want to go along with a truce, given the intensity of the reaction against seven activists staging a peaceful swim-in in a motel pool. As reported in the accompanying Associated Press article, "Cries of, 'Arrest them! Get the dogs!' came from a watching crowd of 100 Whites," reinforcing the impression of St. Augustine's populace as one with a substantial and vocal segregationist element. In the second half of the article, Brock's actions and attitude in response to the demonstration in the front of his motel as well as to the swim-in were described in some detail. In response to the preceding rabbis' rally, he "went to the steps of the motel restaurant to meet the group," but "soon, Brock was angrily pushing and shoving the demonstrators. He joined police in grabbing several rabbis . . . and pushing them into police trucks." Brock's emotional state—already agitated through this first altercation—was primed for further hotheadedness, so that "later, when five Negro and two White demonstrators appeared wearing swim suits, Brock ran into the driveway and shouted: 'Get off! This is private property!'" Once the activists were in the water, "Brock rushed to the poolside with two gallons of muriatic acid, a water purifier, and slushed it at the demonstrators. Some of the liquid spilled on his arm, burning it, and he washed the acid off in the water. None of the demonstrators was burned." Including these additional details made it clear that Brock had to be aware of the potential harm of muriatic acid, seeing as he felt its burn on his own skin and immediately knew to rinse it off.[14]

Just as two of the African American newspapers offered insight into Brock as a person impacted emotionally by the racial turbulence, so too did the *Florida Times-Union* feature a more in-depth profile of him in the days following the swim-in. Three days after the swim-in, an article by Hank Drane acquainted readers with the "genial Ancient City businessman caught in middle of race issue" (as the headline described him). In the feature Brock was portrayed as a reluctant participant in the St. Augustine racial unrest "who never dreamed he was destined to play a major role in the drama." Brock described himself as "just an average fellow," while Drane asserted that the Monson Motor Lodge "has become a target not because he is an arch-segregationist (he considers himself a moderate on the racial issue) but because it is near the heart of the downtown area and is headquarters for a majority of the newsmen here." Drane portrayed Brock as having "pleaded" with integrationists to leave his property willingly so as to avoid arrest, and as previously being "rarely provoked to anger." However after his mother-in-law, who lived on the property, suffered a heart attack on the night of a three-hundred-person prayer vigil at the lodge, followed soon after by the rabbis' rally and swim-in, "mild-mannered Brock suddenly became an angry, shouting man." Looking back on the events of June 18, he said, "I regret it happened but there is a limit to what anyone can endure." Addressing his throwing the acid into the pool, Drane reported that Brock "said the muriatic acid is a cleaning agent for the pool and wouldn't have hurt the swimmers. 'I did it as a bluff,' he said, 'to get them out.'" Later in the profile, Drane described how "the change in Brock's mood toward the integrationists is reflected in a Confederate flag which he raised yesterday and a Latin motto over the entrance to his restaurant which reads: 'Illegimati Non Carborundrum.' Translated it means, 'Don't let the illegitimates grind you down.'" An image of Brock standing beneath this motto, arms crossed with a stern look on his face, is the only photograph to accompany the profile, undercutting visually Drane's overwhelmingly "genial" depiction of the manager throughout most of the profile.[15]

African American News Coverage of the Monson
Motor Lodge Swim-In: The Integrationists

In their coverage of the swim-in, African American media also spent significant space depicting the integrationists—focusing mainly on the seven swimmers but also more broadly on the SCLC and all those participating in the civil rights activism that summer in St. Augustine. The swimmers themselves were portrayed as organized and bold yet victimized, while those behind the movement in St. Augustine overall were characterized as disciplined, persistent, and media savvy.

Reporting in the African American press made clear that the pool integration was not merely a spur-of-the-moment act of heedless young activists but rather the result of some planning and coordination on their part. Multiple articles noted that elsewhere on the property, Brock and law enforcement officers were preoccupied with a protest by rabbis and other activists. For instance the *Chicago Defender* reported that "while this was going on the seven young Negroes and whites burst out of an automobile and headed for the pool." The same article described "the 'jumpers,' who appeared clad in bathing suits and made a bee line for the pool." The Associated Negro Press wire service offered more details, describing how "five Negro youths dressed in bathing suits jumped out of an auto and into the pool. They were joined by two white demonstrators who had earlier registered as guests of the motel." In an article published in the *Atlanta Daily World,* the swimmers were described as "seven taunting demonstrators" who, when faced with police demands that they exit the pool, shouted, "Come in and get us." Even in the midst of the acid-throwing, "the acid apparently had no effect on the swimmers and they refused to get out."[16]

Not only were the seven swimmers depicted as having acted with deliberation, but they were also situated as part of a larger movement characterized as disciplined, intentional, and media savvy in its tactics. The *Chicago Defender* explained that "the so-called non-violent army led by men like Dr. Martin Luther King, Jr. no longer is a rag-tag band of singers and marchers. Today the group is well organized, well-financed, and wel[l]-publicized. The campaigners keep up with what is written about them better than their white opponents. Their moves are made in step with maximum national publicity advantages. In St. Augustine, Fla. King's Southern Christian Leadership Conference currently is running a campaign to integrate the nation's oldest city. Here's the way it works . . ." Further the *Defender* described how "Negro demonstrators in St. Augustine have proved to be far better disciplined than white marchers. It requires only a strong command from one of their marshals who walk beside the parade line to produce complete and instant silence." Regarding how the swim-in fit in with the SCLC's overall strategy, when asked by the *Baltimore Afro-American* "if he approved of the jump-in tactics used by the demonstrators at the pool, Dr. King said, 'Yes. We haven't done this before, but I think it is an effective way to dramatize the struggle.'"[17]

The photography of and reporting about the Monson swim-in disseminated by the African American media served to "dramatize the struggle" for civil rights in St. Augustine and beyond by emphasizing the physical and even emotional turmoil to which the swimmers were subjected. Though the muriatic acid did not end up having the physical impact seemingly desired by Brock, his action did cause emotional turmoil, as white activist Peter Shiras recounted in his interview with the *Afro-American:* "The girls (two in all) were alarmed when Brock dumped acid into the pool." While the photograph of Brock throwing the acid into the pool was published alongside some of the reports, more time was spent in many of the articles on the violence exacted by the police, especially Billitz, the off-duty officer who jumped into the pool in his civilian clothes—not to assist the swimmers' escape from the acid but rather to intimidate them by physical force into exiting the pool. The swimmers were portrayed as passive recipients of Billitz's aggressive force, as reported in the *Atlanta Daily World:* "He advanced on the group, swinging both fists. They retreated. One was grabbed by an officer on the pool's edge and had his arm twisted. The other[s] crawled out and were put into a police truck and hauled away." This passage illustrates the passive nonviolence attributed to the swimmers in this and other African American coverage of the incident. As reported the following week in the *Afro-American*, "Bruised on their backs, arms, and shoulders, the demonstrators emerged from the pool to be arrested." However such suffering on behalf of the civil rights cause was portrayed as being a mark of status within the movement, especially being arrested: "Jail is getting to be more and more a status symbol of these young demonstrators—much like battle stars on the tunic of a soldier."[18]

Local News Coverage of the Monson Motor Lodge Swim-In: The Integrationists

Not surprisingly local coverage of the integrationists who staged the swim-in as well as of the civil rights leaders overseeing the movement in St. Augustine varied substantially among the three area newspapers, given their distinctive editorial stances on civil rights. The *St. Augustine Record,* with its more conservative leaning, depicted the seven swimmers as reckless activists and King as the detached yet power-hungry leader of the movement. Their article covering the incident described how "seven demonstrators, including two white youths, drove up in an automobile and jumped into the Monson's private swimming pool." This account emphasizes the purposefulness of the activists as well as the point of view that the motel swimming pool was private property being invaded rather than a public space that they could rightfully occupy. In the article's lead, the integrationists were portrayed as having "staged a so-called 'jump in' at a private motel swimming pool. They were hauled away to jail and charged with trespassing, disorderly conduct and conspiracy to violate state laws." Here the choice of the word *staged* denotes the perspective that the act was a performance designed to gain attention, while qualifying the jump-in as "so-called" communicates disrespect for their activism. The emphasis on "more arrests made" in the headline, accompanied by the listing of the crimes with which the activists were charged in the opening lines of the article, frames the article as primarily reporting on crimes committed rather than on nonviolent civil disobedience.[19]

The swim-in also occasioned commentary on the role of the SCLC's leader, King. The *Record*'s reporting on the scene of the swim-in mentioned how "the Rev. Martin Luther King, who has been directing the demonstrations here, stood across the street from the motel and watched." Phrased in this way, this observation gives the impression of a detached King, who allowed others to be arrested while he chose not to intervene. Several days later the *Record* published on its editorial page a reprint of an editorial that appeared first in the *Tampa Tribune* titled "King—The Firewalker." The editorial depicts King as concerned primarily with gaining an audience: "The Rev. Martin Luther King is a professional firewalker, who dances bare-footed over the glowing coals of racial passion. If the fire dies out, so does the act. That would leave the Rev. Mr. King with no audience—a dreary prospect, indeed. . . . Thus, when the red-hot conflict at St. Augustine appeared to be at the point of cooling, the King forces applied themselves to the bellows. Demonstrators leaped into the pool of a segregated motel, sending the manager into a foolish frenzy and bringing the police on the run to strike wildly at the trespassers in the water."

Within the context of this editorial, the swim-in was presented as an act calculated to stoke the fires of racial conflict rather than allowing the embers of conflict to cool. The impression this communicated of King and the civil rights activists in St. Augustine was one of people motivated by self-interest seeking to enflame further the racial conflict—rather than of people motivated by selflessness and seeking peace.[20]

Florida Times-Union reporter Hank Drane took a more neutral-to-positive perspective on the pool integrationists, describing how "four [actually five] Negroes and two white integrationists leaped into the large swimming pool while officers were arresting other integrationists staging a 'kneel-in' at the lodge." As with the African American press coverage, Drane directed readers' attention to the strategic nature of the swim-in, emphasizing that the activists chose to leap into the pool when police were distracted by the kneel-in taking place elsewhere on the property. Drane further reported that "the two white men who jumped into the pool were registered at the motel and the Negroes were their guests." Explaining that two of the activists (Lingo and Shiras) were registered lodgers who had invited the African Americans into the pool as their guests communicated the point that these integrationists had not entered the property illegally but rather had gone through the proper channels of registering for a room before entering the pool with their chosen swimming companions.[21]

The Associated Press account published by the *Daytona Beach Morning Journal* took a similar neutral-to-positive stance in its reporting on what ensued when the "seven Negroes and Whites attempted to desegregate the swimming pool of a motel." Surrounded by a "crowd of 100 Whites as police ringed the pool," the black integrationists were reported to be the victims of violence as police "rained blows on heads, back and shoulders of five Negro men and women in the water." After enduring this physical abuse, "finally, the bruised Negroes, along with two white companions, climbed out and went to jail." King, again identified as having "witnessed the near-riot at the pool from across the street," attested to the violent turn of events when he telegrammed Attorney General Robert Kennedy: "I implore you to investigate this blatant police brutality immediately." Including King's account as an onlooker could have enhanced, for readers who respected him, the wire report's claims regarding the violence inflicted on the activists. Given the consistently liberal-progressive stance the *Morning Journal* took regarding the civil rights conflict, many readers of this newspaper were likely to be interested in and sympathetic with King's perspective on how the swim-in unfolded.[22]

In contrast the next day the *Times-Union* published a brief newswire item from Washington under the headline "Pool Jumps Likened to RFK Antics." In the article U.S. Senator Spressard Holland, a Florida Democrat, commented on the "sorry spectacle of Dr. Martin Luther King and his platoon of Negroes and misguided preachers and Rabbis insisting upon violating the law of Florida— and it is still our law—by forcing their presence into a segregated motel property and even into the segregated motel swimming pool." The senator said he "could not help wondering if the eager Negro youths who had trespassed into the water" had been inspired by Kennedy's reported dunking of guests in his family's pool at their Virginia residence. Reporting these views from Senator Holland, whom the article described as "an opponent of the civil rights bill," communicated a more openly disrespectful view of the integrationists as an "eager" and "misguided" "platoon" of King followers, who disregarded Florida law through "forcing their presence" as they "trespassed into the water." However this negative view of the integrationists was marked clearly as the perspective of Holland, whom the article emphasized was opposed to the civil rights legislation.[23]

African American Coverage of the Monson
Motor Lodge Swim-In: The Police

Law enforcement officers were the third set of players who figured prominently in African American coverage of the Monson swim-in. The main characteristics attributed to the police in reporting on this incident were that they were the ones on the offensive and that their actions toward the swimmers constituted police brutality. Reporting on the police involvement featured many aggressive verbs. An example of this appeared in the *Atlanta Daily World* report that described Henry Billitz as having "jumped into the swimming pool to pummel the seven taunting demonstrators." The same article reported that "police surrounded the pool and commanded the youths to leave. . . . He [Billitz] advanced on the group." Reporting on the violent police tactics, the *Philadelphia Tribune* described "club-swinging police" who "hauled the demonstrators off to jail." The *Chicago Defender* reported how the "off-duty policeman plunged into the swimming pool and mauled the five young Negroes and two whites until they crawled out and were hustled away to jail." The Associated Negro Press noted that even once Brock and the police were successful in getting the activists out of the pool, the violence continued: "That was when Brock, the off-duty cop and the city and county police got their sadistic kicks out of beating the swimmers and 'goosing' them with the cattle prods." The *Baltimore Afro-American* depicted the overall brutality of the tactics used by police in St. Augustine when they reported how "police in this 400-year-old tourist city have armed themselves with electric cattle prods and brought out dogs to deal with an unexpected new round of demonstrations." Likewise the Associated Negro Press wire reported that King said of the police response, "Raw police brutality, that's what it was," characterizing this incident as but "the latest brutality of southern law officials against non-violent protestors."[24]

Local Coverage of the Monson Motor
Lodge Swim-In: The Police

No photographs of the swim-in and its aftermath were published in the *St. Augustine Record.* Thus readers of that newspaper did not see Horace Cort's photograph for the Associated Press of Billitz diving into the pool fully clothed to force the integrationists from the pool. However Jacksonville's *Florida Times-Union* published the Associated Press photograph with the caption "Policeman Henry Billitz Dives into Pool to Clear Out Negroes" at the top of the local news page. Meanwhile in the *Daytona Beach Morning Journal*, the photograph of Billitz was situated just beneath the front-page masthead alongside the dominant, stacked headline announcing, "Jury Wants Truce in Racial Crisis." Placing the AP wire photograph of Billitz's pool jump—captioned "AMPHIBIOUS POLICE-MAN . . . dives after demonstrators"—immediately to the right of the headline resulted in the photograph functioning as an extension of the headline. These three local newspapers' varying decisions about whether and where to publish Cort's striking photograph capturing the off-duty police officer in midair as he dove into the pool provide insight into each newspaper's stance in reporting on law enforcement's role in this event.

Throughout its coverage of the swim-in and the beach wade-ins, the *St. Augustine Record* tended to portray the city police and St. Johns County sheriff and deputies with great admiration, but they took a more disrespectful tone in its reporting on the role of Florida Highway Patrol troopers and other state law enforcement sent to keep the peace in their city. For instance in reporting on the swim-in, the article contrasted Billitz's action with the perceived inaction of state troopers: "While state policemen, sent here by Gov. Farris Bryant to maintain law and order, stood around, City Police Patrolman Henry Billitz, off duty and in plain clothes, jumped into the pool and forced the bathing-suit clad demonstrators to get out." The article also reported that "state Troopers at the scene were quickly surrounded by at least 30 angry white businessmen who demanded to know . . . why officers were so long in making arrests today. They threatened to call Florida Attorney General John Kynes and lodge a formal complaint about the patrol's activities." Not only did the *Record* include this anti-trooper bias in its reporting, but it even went so far as to publish an editorial on the front page of its June 18 edition (just beneath the article reporting on the swim-in), in which the newspaper's editors complained that "the state police force apparently has assumed powers here which border on making the city a 'police' state." In the wake of a large prayer vigil troopers allowed to take place outside the Monson Motor Lodge the previous night, the editors argued, "surely they had the authority to have kept the demonstrators marching instead of invading private property at this late hour of the night." In contrast to complaining about the ineffectiveness of the state troopers, an editorial published that same day on the inside editorial page advocated that, in addition to "heap[ing] praises and numerous forms of thanks to local police and sheriff's deputies for their untiring efforts in recent weeks, . . . a financial bonus should be in the offering [*sic*] for their fine service 'above and beyond the call of duty.'" Throughout the *Record*'s coverage of the swim-in and later wade-ins, its editors and writers communicated overt resentment toward the outside law enforcement presence, seeing not only civil rights activists as interlopers, but so too the state troopers sent in to protect them.[25]

In response to their rival newspaper's editorial, the *Florida Times-Union* published an article headlined "St. Augustine Paper Charges Patrol Is Abridging

Rights of White Citizens," highlighting how the Florida Highway Patrol "came under fire from the *St. Augustine Record*." When one newspaper chooses to report on another's content, the differences in editorial perspective become all the more apparent. The *Times-Union* article afforded representatives of the Florida Highway Patrol the opportunity to explain their actions. While "the Patrol would not release an official statement on the criticism, . . . one officer admitted to the *Times-Union* that errors in judgment have been made under extremely tense and often trying conditions." Regarding the swim-in specifically, "the officer said the Patrol made no attempt to arrest the swimmers because local officers were there and arrests during sit-in demonstrations have been handled by local officers."[26]

Meanwhile the *Daytona Beach Morning Journal*, in stark contrast to the *St. Augustine Record*, emphasized police brutality in their coverage of law enforcement's response to the swim-in. In the Associated Press article selected to run as the most prominent front-page article, not only could readers see Billitz seeming to jump right off the headline and into the pool, but they also read of how on-duty police "ringed the pool" and "rained blows on heads, back and shoulders" of the five black activists in the Monson pool that day. They also read of how rabbis were grabbed and shoved into police vehicles after the preceding rally, and of how King witnessed the scene himself and called on U.S. Attorney General Robert Kennedy to do something about "this blatant police brutality" that, if left unchecked, would lead to "a new breakdown of law and order." In choosing to publish this version of events from the Associated Press wire, the Daytona Beach editors aligned their coverage closely with that published in the African American press. When we consider the long history of African American influence in Daytona Beach—home to such respected African Americans as Howard Thurman and Mary McLeod Bethune (and her institution Bethune Cookman College), combined with the liberal-progressive sensibilities of the Davidson family who published the *Morning Journal* for many decades—it makes sense that the Daytona Beach newspaper would take this pro–civil rights stance in its coverage of the police response to the swim-in, kneel-in, and the civil rights movement in St. Augustine overall.[27]

Offering Their Very Bodies for Freedom by Wading in the Water

Photographs of motel co-owner and manager James Brock pouring acid into the pool and of off-duty patrolman Henry Billitz jumping into the water were transmitted by the wire services and published in newspapers throughout Florida and the nation—if not in the *St. Augustine Record*. Visualizing whites and blacks in the water together carried great significance. For one thing the image of blacks in the chemically purified water of the pristine pool flew in the face of the same white stereotypes about sanitation that led to separate water fountains and restrooms for whites and blacks; blacks were perceived to be unclean and therefore must be kept separate in order to keep whites clean and protected. Further these images were powerful in that they showed white men swimming with black women; not only that, but the women of color were holding onto the white men for dear life, their relatively scantily clad bodies pressed against one another for all of the world to see. Though fear of miscegenation in the South focused mainly on sexual contact between black men and white women, photographs of white men with black women were still sure to evoke angst and disgust on the parts of those who were against any such racial mixing. In addition the image of blacks enjoying leisure activities such as swimming in the motel pool rather than being at work in the service of whites (as motel housekeepers, dishwashers, or pool boys) gave further evidence of a new era in which leisure was no longer reserved for whites only.

Finally, and perhaps most important, the images and descriptions of the Monson Motor Lodge swim-in painted a stunning picture of what racism looks like. Racist segregation looked like a man frantically pouring acid into a pool of passive, peaceful swimmers who just happened to have a variety of skin tones. Racist segregation looked like a policeman who so urgently wanted to rid his community of this threat to racial purity that he dived in fully clothed to expunge it. Racist segregation looked like a motel owner draining his pool of perceived impurities and hoisting the Confederate flag in an act of rebellion. Racist segregation looked like a redneck, rabble-rousing moonshiner rounding up alligators to sic on the next person who dared to race-mix in the local pool. Such vivid pictures—visual and verbal—of racism made it difficult to think that U.S. citizens would continue to make excuses for Jim Crow laws. These images and articles likely gave African Americans a reason to hope that perhaps their fellow citizens and their elected leaders and representatives would begin to take their demands for equal rights under the law seriously.

The swim-in in St. Augustine in 1964 came at a crucial time in the trajectory of the civil rights movement. The movement had successfully put the issue of equal rights and opportunities for all citizens on the national agenda, both in the legislative and executive chambers as well as in the pages of the nation's newspapers and on the television sets of America's living rooms. In the long, hot summer of 1964, it was imperative for integrationists to bring before the eyes of the nation and the world a vivid picture of why they could wait no longer for civil rights. When Dr. King preached in St. Augustine's "stifling hot churches where they gathered to sing the old slave songs, mournful and sweet, and the new civil rights songs, spirited and challenging. . . . He told them to purify themselves, to 'prepare to offer your very bodies for freedom and be ready to be clubbed and kicked without retaliating.'" One of the freedom songs they likely sang was "Wade in the Water," which had been used originally in the days of the Underground Railroad to give "explicit instructions to fugitive slaves on how to avoid capture and the route to make their way to freedom successfully. Leaving dry land and taking to the water was a common strategy to throw pursuing bloodhounds off one's trail." Just as Moses led the Israelites through the Red Sea to freedom from slavery in Egypt, so too did integrationists see a way to freedom in the hope that "God's gonna trouble the water."[28]

In St. Augustine in 1964, when civil rights activists waded in the water, they, too, were taking to the water as a way to get their freedom. As Davi Johnson has asserted, "For King, the best means of making racism visible was by exposing its action on black bodies." King and the civil rights movement sought "literally to *make visible* the oppression of black Americans, to rout out the abuses that occurred on a regular basis and display them before the eyes of the nation and the world."[29] The Monson swim-in on June 18, 1964, allowed journalists—be they from the African American, local, or national press—to bring before the eyes of a watching world the violent, racist resistance faced by African Americans seeking to partake in life's simple pleasures, such as seeking solace from the sweltering heat of summer by taking a swim in a refreshing pool or by wading in the waters of the Atlantic. When the images and stories of placid integrationists wading in their swimsuits and swim trunks being peppered with pool chemicals and bludgeoned with sticks by frenzied segregationists made front-page news, it became even more strikingly clear why they couldn't wait.

Notes

1. Branch, *Pillar of Fire*, 356.
2. Warren, *If It Takes All Summer*, 65–66; Mitchell, "Racial and Civil Disorders in St. Augustine," 213.
3. Mitchell, "Racial and Civil Disorders in St. Augustine," 217; Warren, *If It Takes All Summer*, 78, 80–81.
4. Garrow, *St. Augustine, Florida, 1963–1964*, 218; Warren, *If It Takes All Summer*, 90; Branch, *Pillar of Fire*, 339; Mitchell, "Racial and Civil Disorders," 218; Branch, *Pillar of Fire*, 339; Warren, *If It Takes All Summer*, 118; Branch, *Pillar of Fire*, 355.
5. Johnson, Young interview; Lingo, interview.
6. Many names redacted by the FBI were included in the press accounts, so the identities of those involved are well known and are placed in brackets in the cited passages. U.S. Department of Justice, Federal Bureau of Investigation, Racial Situation, St. Johns County, Florida.
7. *Dare Not Walk Alone*.
8. References to retaliation found in UPI, "15 Rabbis among New Fla. Arrests"; "St. Augustine Motel Is Scene of Wild Fracas"; UPI, "Rabbis Join Negroes in Fla. Freedom Battle"; "Muriatic Acid, Police Brutality"; "Photos Tell Violent Story of St. Augustine."
9. UPI, "Acid Test of Human Dignity."
10. Morten, "Man from St. Aug."; UPI, "Rabbis Join Negros in Fla. Freedom Battle."
11. Kuettner, "Motel Manager 'Shaken'"; Roswig, "Grand Jury Rejects 'Good Faith' Bid."

12. "More Arrests Made."

13. Drane, "Wild Incidents Precede St. Johns Jury Report."

14. Associated Press, "Jury Wants Truce in Racial Crisis."

15. Drane, "Genial Ancient City Businessman."

16. UPI, "Rabbis Join Negros in Fla. Freedom Battle"; "Muriatic Acid, Police Brutality"; UPI, "15 Rabbis among New Fla. Arrests." As revealed in oral history interviews with both Al Lingo and J. T. they were aware that the muriatic acid would have no significant impact on them, awareness informed especially by Johnson's lifeguarding experience.

17. UPI, "'Agitators' Ready for a 'Long, Hot Summer'"; "'Long, Hot Summer' Already Under Way."

18. Morten, "Man from St. Aug."; UPI, "15 Rabbis among New Fla. Arrests"; "'Long, Hot Summer' Already Under Way"; UPI, "'Agitators' Ready for a 'Long, Hot Summer.'"

19. "More Arrests Made."

20. Ibid.; "King—The Firewalker."

21. Drane, "Wild Incidents Precede St. Johns Jury Report."

22. Associated Press, "Jury Wants Truce in Racial Crisis."

23. Associated Press, "Pool Jumps Likened to RFK Antics."

24. UPI, "15 Rabbis among New Fla. Arrests"; "St. Augustine Motel Is Scene of Wild Fracas"; UPI, "Rabbis Join Negroes in Fla. Freedom Battle"; "Muriatic Acid, Police Brutality"; "'Long, Hot Summer' Already Under Way."

25. "More Arrests Made as Demonstrations Continue"; "Two Sides to the Coin"; "City Police and Sheriff's Deputies Rate a Bonus."

26. "St. Augustine Paper Charges Patrol."

27. AP, "Jury Wants Truce in Racial Crisis."

28. Loh, "St. Augustine Still Torn by Racial Strife"; "African American Spirituals"; Underground Railroad Freedom Singers, "Wade in the Water."

29. Johnson, "Birmingham Campaign," 20.

3

EMBERS

The Legacies of the Sit-Ins

The sit-ins of 1963–64 were by no means the last in the civil rights era. However with its landmark 1963 decision, *Peterson v. Greenville*,[1] the U.S. Supreme Court settled the question of whether the Fourteenth Amendment's Equal Protection Clause and state action requirement reached beyond purely public accommodations, such as public libraries and courthouses, to quasi-public buildings and facilities, including lunch counters. Congress, with the Civil Rights Act of 1964, used its Commerce Clause power to guarantee "full and equal" access to and enjoyment of "any place of public accommodation . . . without discrimination or segregation on the ground of race, color, religion, or national origin."[2] The act swept away the last feeble attempts to justify segregation in public accommodations on a private-property theory and opened a new era of legal protection for citizens who, only four years before, had been routinely denied service in, and sometimes even access to, most stores, inns, libraries, restaurants, beaches, skating rinks, and countless other places.

We have learned, however, that such hard-won gains are all too often followed by reaction, backlash, and retrenchment. In the wake of the civil rights movement's early successes came the well-publicized murders of James Chaney, Andrew Goodman, and Mickey Schwerner at the start of Mississippi Freedom Summer in 1964,[3] the assassinations of Malcolm X and Martin Luther King Jr. in 1965 and 1968,[4] massive white flight in the late 1960s and 1970s,[5] and the long resistance to busing and affirmative action in the 1970s and 1980s.[6] While these events were disjointed, uncoordinated, and of course not directly responsive to the sit-in protests, they were quite clearly opposed to the underlying principles —integration, racial equality, and equal accommodation—of the movement. They have been followed by repeated attempts to undercut both the Civil Rights Act of 1964 and the Voting Rights Act of 1965,[7] undermine and roll back important legal and constitutional advances made under the Warren Court— including a slow erosion of *Brown v. Board of Education*[8]—and move the nation steadily away from the rapid and progressive change of the early 1960s. And the pattern of advance-and-reaction on matters of race is as present now as it has ever been. Talk of a "post-racial America" with the election of President Barack Obama in 2008 proved most premature and has been followed by battles over neo-Confederate monuments, rebel battle flags, police violence against people of color, Black Lives Matter, voter ID laws and intimidation, and a surge of race-based backlash that supported the candidacy and unlikely presidency of Donald Trump.[9]

We must look closely, therefore, at the various legacies of the civil-rights-era sit-ins. In this section six scholars consider the ways in which the sit-ins were and continue to be depicted in movements, media, museums, memorials, and, oddly, outside an important Memphis motel. The story they tell is one of contrasting words and images, contested public memories, fragmented but enduring lessons, and an ongoing effort to find justice. The civil-rights-era sit-ins, these essays suggest, are still present but in far more complicated ways than we may have imagined.

Notes

1. *Peterson v. Greenville*, 373 U.S. 244 (1963).

2. Civil Rights Act of 1964, tit. II, §§ 201–7 (1964) (current version at 42 U.S.C. § 2000a (2017)).

3. See, e.g., Huie, *Three Lives for Mississippi*; Ball, *Murder in Mississippi*; Cagin and Dray, *We Are Not Afraid*; Watson, *Freedom Summer: The Savage Season of 1964*; McAdam, *Freedom Summer*.

4. For a good sense of what these two assassinations meant, and continue to mean, for America, see Cone, *Martin and Malcolm and America*.

5. For an interesting study of white flight in one southern city, see Kruse, *White Flight*.

6. Two important studies include Delmont, *Why Busing Failed*, and Formisano, *Boston against Busing*.

7. On attempts to gut the Civil Rights Act, see the rather sweeping discussion at the Gates Public Service Law Program titled "The Rollback of Civil Rights Era in America," https://www.law.washington.edu/multimedia/2008/rollback/transcript.pdf. For the Voting Rights Act, see Rutenberg, "Dream Undone."

8. See *Parents Involved in Community Schools v. Seattle School District No. I*, 551 U.S. 701 (2007). But see also Wilkinson, "Seattle and Louisville School Cases" (arguing that the Court decided the cases correctly).

9. This claim no longer seems debatable. See McElwee and McDaniel, "Economic Anxiety Didn't Make People Vote Trump, Racism Did"; Tesler, "Views about Race Mattered More in Electing Trump than in Electing Obama."

TELEVISUALITY AND THE PERFORMANCE OF CITIZENSHIP ON NBC'S "SIT-IN"

Marilyn DeLaure

The Nashville, Tennessee, sit-ins were not the first to launch in 1960, but they were arguably the most carefully planned and executed, and they won the earliest victory: on May 10 Nashville became the first major city in the South to desegregate its department store lunch counters. From the Nashville campaign emerged a cadre of new young leaders, who became core members of the Student Nonviolent Coordinating Committee (SNCC) and played a central role in the Freedom Rides the following year.[1] Another important part of Nashville's legacy was an hour-long documentary film about the protests that aired nationally on television during prime time on December 20, 1960. This episode of NBC's series *White Paper,* titled "Sit-In," was in many respects a remarkable piece for the period. Narrated by *NBC Nightly News* coanchor Chet Huntley, the show included dramatic footage of the sit-ins that had appeared in news reports the previous spring and also provided additional contextualization for the sit-in actions, allowing the story to be told almost entirely by the principals involved. *New York Times* television critic Jack Gould proclaimed that NBC's "Sit-In" was "one of the network's superior accomplishments, a vivid and exciting social document that contained well-organized factual data and enjoyed brilliant pictorial composition."[2] Following its initial broadcast, recordings of "Sit-In" circulated among civil rights organizations and were used for recruiting and training purposes.[3]

NBC's "Sit-In" provided a platform for a wide range of views: it features interviews with the student demonstrators, black and white community leaders, and a diverse group of local residents, some of whom vehemently opposed integration. While Huntley's authoritative narration stopped short of rendering judgment on the sit-ins, the show's visual rhetoric implicitly favored the demonstrators and celebrated their acts as exemplary models of thoughtful, principled citizenship. The student activists appeared disciplined, earnest, courageous, and deeply committed to democratic ideals. This *White Paper* episode also invited viewers backstage, giving a rich and intimate picture of the black community in Nashville, which was quite a contrast to the typical representations of blacks on television at the time.[4] The show featured scenes where black adults praised and lent support to the sit-ins, thus revealing the campaign to be a collective effort on the part of an entire community. By contrast segregationist whites spoke in isolation, often shot in unflattering close-up.[5] The most extreme figure interviewed is a slurring, buck-toothed young hoodlum behind bars who described his assaults on blacks and white sympathizers with smug self-satisfaction. Other whites appeared more genteel, articulating their resistance to integration as grounded in a desire to maintain southern tradition. Their rationalizations, though, are ultimately undone by the imagery and narrative sequences of the show. Furthermore the norms of civility and decorum so cherished by many southern conservatives are visibly violated not by the student demonstrators but by the jeering white onlookers who taunted and attacked them. Through its narrative structure, strategic editing, careful use of point-of-view shots, and juxtaposition of images with verbal claims, NBC's "Sit-In" performed a refutation of the segregationists' arguments and invited viewers not only to sympathize but also to identify with the student protestors.

Televising Civil Rights

Television in the mid-twentieth century was a powerful site for the negotiation of social, cultural, and political values.[6] Over the course of the 1950s, the television set had grown from a novel invention into a common household fixture.[7] Amid anxieties about television's deleterious effects on the public—best captured in FCC chairman Newton Minow's 1961 "vast wasteland" speech—television journalism sought to establish itself as a serious institution positioned to address a national audience. For this aim civil rights provided the ideal subject matter, and it became the first major social movement to unfold in front of the television camera.[8] Civil rights leaders were quite savvy about staging visually dramatic protests and using the news media to their advantage; southern police and segregationists also quickly learned the power of the camera. As Thomas Leonard explains, "Segregationist mobs were smashers of the instruments that threatened the widest distribution of their activities: cameras and broadcasting gear. Cameras and all types of electronic equipment such as lights and tape recorders were invitations to mayhem in the South. . . . Blinding the press was the first priority of a southern mob."[9]

The visibility of civil rights demonstrations on national news offered a striking contrast to the limited, stereotypical, and overwhelmingly negative representations of African Americans on television. Blacks were largely absent from 1950s television screens, and when they did appear, it was usually in the form of exaggerated caricatures: the comic buffoon, the placating and subservient Uncle Tom, the domestic mammy, the smiling entertainer.[10] Furthermore, as Herman Gray explains, "In the televisual world of the early 1950s, the social and cultural rules of race relations between blacks and whites were explicit: black otherness was required for white subjectivity; blacks and whites occupied separate and unequal worlds; black labor was always in the service of white domesticity . . . black humor was necessary for the amusement of whites. Culturally, because blackness served whiteness in this way, the reigning perspective of this world was always staged from a white subject position."[11] News coverage of the civil rights movement, at least to some extent, challenged these dominant depictions of race on television; NBC's "Sit-In" specifically worked to destabilize the hegemonic white point of view.

In her book *Black, White, and in Color: Television and Black Civil Rights,* Sasha Torres argues that TV news coverage of civil rights from 1955 to 1965 effectively established "an emergent black political agency."[12] She states, "The capacity [for protestors] to see themselves—both figuratively and literally—as political actors was something long denied black activists in the South, where local papers generally refused to cover black protest."[13] In this respect television played an important rhetorical function through broadcasting images of African Americans performing as citizens, as agents of social change. Molefi Kete Asante elaborates upon the fundamentally democratic reach of television news broadcasts: "With the rise of street demonstrations, boycotts, praying, sit-ins, bombings, political murders, and violent rebellions, television clearly put to the public the question 'Where do you stand?' To amplify, television, like radio, is a non-discriminatory mass instrument. In print journalism, the audiences must know how to read; in radio, audiences must be able to imagine; but in television, audiences do not have to be able to read or to imagine to understand its message and in this respect its politicization potential is greatly increased."[14] Here Asante highlights the interrogative power of television to hail viewers politically, positioning them vis-à-vis the protests being reported. Television coverage of the sit-ins, in particular, made visible to a national audience the contradictions between southern norms of civility and propriety and the democratic values of freedom and equality.

"Bad Manners" and Modes of Citizenship

The struggle to redefine citizenship lay at the heart of the civil rights movement. As the nation's highest court refined and expanded the meaning of "equal protection under the law" and courageous individuals sought to enact their rights—risking bodily harm to register to vote or attend school—many old and deeply embedded practices of citizenship were called into question.[15] Particularly in the South, entrenched norms of civility had governed interactions between whites and blacks since Emancipation.[16] As Danielle Allen explains, "white Southern citizens had been accustomed to maintaining key public spaces as their exclusive possession; for the sake of preserving life and stability black Southern citizens had been accustomed to acquiescing to such norms and to the acts of violence that enforced them. Each set of customs, exclusionary on the one hand and on the other acquiescent, constituted the practical rules of democratic citizenship for a set of citizens."[17] The civil rights movement contested those norms, treating citizenship not as a static position or fixed set of relationships but as a mode of enactment open to creative revision. The question was not merely who formally counted as a citizen but also what citizenship itself entailed and how it could be performed. While the movement did endeavor to secure equal access to the existing institutions of citizenship, such as the franchise, it also struggled more broadly to eradicate the exclusionary and acquiescent customs governing public life. Something as ordinary as ordering a cup of coffee at a Woolworth lunch counter, then, became a significant political act.[18]

Here I draw on Robert Asen's discourse theory of citizenship, which frames "citizenship as a *mode of public engagement*" and "recognizes the fluid, multimodal, and quotidian enactments of citizenship in a multiple public sphere."[19] Asen conceptualizes citizenship as a mode, process, and performance rather than a possession or station; his model, like Danielle Allen's, highlights risk and engagement with strangers. Importantly, Asen's understanding of citizenship also valorizes unruly acts and indecorous speech: "Modes may unsettle as they proceed," he states, "potentially calling into question the taken-for-granted and discounting notions of propriety."[20] Whereas propriety and decorum have conventionally been understood as rhetorical norms governing actions of citizens and safeguarding civil order, they also serve to perpetuate the status quo and mask the preservation of injustice.[21]

The sit-ins openly and directly confronted conventional southern norms of decorum: hence they were deemed inappropriate and indecorous. The *Nashville Banner* declared that the sit-ins were an "incitation to anarchy," while the *Greensboro Daily News* suggested that they were ill-conceived because civility and order should take precedence over civil rights.[22] A decade later rhetorical critic Gladys Ritchie opened her essay with this remark: "Even if we consider the technique of the sit-in despicable and its manners bad, we are forced to agree that the sit-in is effective." Her framing of sit-ins as "despicable" and exhibiting "bad manners" reveals the hegemonic power of decorum in defining the proper limits of citizenship. Because the sit-ins violated the southern rules of etiquette that dictated proper behavior between the races, thousands of sit-in demonstrators were arrested and carted off to jail, charged with "disorderly conduct."

And yet, as viewers could clearly see on NBC's "Sit-In" and other news coverage of the protests, the lunch counter demonstrations were the epitome of orderly decorum: in their dress and comportment, the student protestors exemplified middle-class respectability. The contrast between the poised, polite, and studious demonstrators and the white ruffians who assaulted them was undeniable. Even conservative white southerner James Kilpatrick, who was editor of the *Richmond News-Leader,* wrote the following in an op-ed piece on February 22, 1960: "Here were the colored students, in coats, white shirts, ties, and one of them was reading Goethe and one was taking notes from a biology text. And here, on the sidewalk outside, was a gang of white boys come to heckle, a ragtail rabble, slack-jawed, black-jacketed, grinning fit to kill, and some of them, God save the mark, were waving the proud and honored flag of the Southern States in the last war fought by gentlemen. Eheu! It gives one pause."[23] The sit-ins effectively turned traditional pieties on their head.[24] By calmly occupying seats at whites-only lunch counters and remaining stoically poised as they were attacked and arrested, the students precipitated a kind of perspective by incongruity.[25] The demonstrators effectively broke down outmoded notions of propriety and reconstituted new ones, through embodying and enacting new modes of citizenship. And television brought those performances into living rooms across the nation.

Watching NBC's "Sit-In"

Broadcast news in the 1950s and early 1960s was governed by the FCC's Fairness Doctrine, which required networks to "be fair, balanced, and equitable" in their treatment of controversial public matters. Television documentaries about civil right struggles thus typically featured both pro- and anti-integration perspectives. NBC hosted a series of debates on its public affairs program, *The Nation's Future,* where opposing speakers would spar on contentious topics. In fact less than a month before "Sit-In" aired, the network broadcast a debate between Dr. Martin Luther King Jr. and James Kilpatrick on the question "Are the sit-in strikes justified?"[26]

That same question is implicitly raised by "Sit-In." The *White Paper* episode is bookended by Chet Huntley's authoritative introductory and concluding remarks; his deep, commanding voice-over also comments periodically throughout the film.[27] The show features many solo interviews, interspersed with shots of Nashville, news footage of the sit-ins, scenes depicting violent confrontations at the lunch counters and elsewhere, and images of demonstrators being arrested and jailed. There are also several extended segments that provided a window into black community life in Nashville. These scenes were surely re-creations, staged for the *White Paper* camera crew, but they feature what appear to be natural, candid conversations. Early on three young black men sit on a riverbank discussing their parents' resistance to the sit-ins after one student reads aloud from an anxious letter from his mother. Later in the episode viewers join a gathering of black students in a gymnasium where they joke, sing, and share stories about sitting in and being arrested. Other scenes feature African American adults: four ladies playing bridge in someone's home and men conversing in a barbershop.

Since the *White Paper* episode recounts protests that had occurred—and succeeded—months before its broadcast, the film relies heavily on flashbacks: there are several sequences that intersperse footage of the winter and early spring events with reflective commentary by the participants.[28] As Sasha Torres notes, "'Sit-In' purports to show not what is happening, but what has already happened. In the process, it makes the Nashville movement's victories seem all but inevitable."[29] Torres also remarks that "Sit-In" was made before the generic conventions of the civil rights documentary were established, and so it "is a strikingly open text in its discursive strategies and address."[30] The film's discursive strategies operate rhetorically toward three specific ends: first, "Sit-In" invites viewers to identify with the protestors by foregrounding the perspective of the students; second, the episode powerfully dramatizes how the sit-ins subverted southern norms of decorum and civility; and third, the documentary performs important work in redefining citizenship and community.

Perspective: Seeing and Being Seen

Being seen was a primary tactic of the sit-ins. As John Lewis, a student leader of the Nashville sit-ins, explains in his memoir: "We wanted them to see us. . . . We wanted white people, everyday citizens, everyday customers to be exposed to us, to see us as we were, not as something in their minds, in their imaginations. We wanted them to watch how we responded to the people who refused to serve us. And we wanted them to watch those people as well."[31] Lewis and thousands of other demonstrators performed the action that they demanded, arguing for integration of social spaces by physically, visibly integrating them. "While boycotters or strikers made their point through concerted absences," states Rebekah Kowal, "sit-inners exerted pressure by insistent presence, occupying spaces from which they were usually prohibited. Sit-inners put themselves center stage instead of removing themselves from the scene."[32] That visible presence of the students' bodies in public spaces made for a powerful, performative argument.

"Sit-In" takes visibility a step further: in addition to showing the students sitting peacefully at the lunch counters and reactions by various onlookers (where the televisual viewer is positioned as a neutral, detached observer), the documentary also puts viewers into the point of view of the protestors and elicits fluid perspective-shifting throughout. [33] The first segment of "Sit-In" —preceding the title sequence and Huntley's introduction—performs subtle but important work in establishing perspective. The opening shot is of Lewis's solemn face in profile as he walks along a downtown street. Then the camera switches to his point of view as he walks up to and then opens a store door, enters, and approaches the lunch counter. Lewis states in voice-over: "It was on February 13, and we had the very first sit-in in Nashville. And I took my seat at the counter, and I asked the waitress for a hamburger and a Coke." The camera pans vertically from the countertop, up a stout, apron-clad torso, to arrive at the dour face of a middle-aged woman wearing horn-rimmed glasses, who says, "I'm sorry, our management does not allow us to serve Nigras in here." This short opening sequence puts viewers in Lewis's shoes, giving them some vicarious sense of being refused service. Later shots do similar work: the camera peers into a paddy wagon, as though its holder is about to climb in; a large metal door swings open before viewers, putting them face to face with an imposing jailer.[34]

In addition to these filmic techniques, the interviews with student demonstrators are deeply introspective, highlighting their inner thoughts and deliberations, their emotional and philosophical struggles. Early in the documentary, Angeline Butler recounts her participation in the nonviolent training workshops led by James Lawson starting in the fall of 1959. "They were having some role-playing," Butler explains as people are shown acting out a sit-in scenario, "and in some of the scenes, you almost cried, because they would have someone play the part of . . ." Butler trails off, and the viewer sees workshop participants, both black and white, viciously shout, "Nigger!" and chant "Eeny, meeny, miny moe. Catch a nigger by the toe!" as they drop ashes on a demonstrator's hair, extinguish a cigarette on his eyeglasses, and then pull him backward off his stool. All the while Butler stands perfectly still next to the man being attacked. The film then cuts to a static shot of Butler looking with steady determination directly into the camera, as her voice-over soberly states, "These kinds of comments, they touch to your soul. And it makes you realize that it's all the more important that you do something about it." In a similar vein, early in the film Bernard Lafayette carefully walks viewers, step by step, through the experience of sitting in: "You go to the counter, and you do not request that the person sitting next to you get up and leave. You merely come in and sit down beside him, as any human being would do. You cause no violence; you have no angry words. You're friendly, and it sort of helps to project the idea that 'here sits beside me another human being." Lafayette's use of the second-person *you* compels viewers to imagine themselves taking similar action.[35]

A lengthy sequence later in the film dramatizes another instance of perspective shifting. Wilson Yates, a young white divinity student, dressed in coat and tie, tells his story of being beaten for marching in solidarity with the black students. On his way to put a nickel in a parking meter, Yates saw a demonstration in a nearby park where black students with placards were being jeered at by whites. He recalls, "I walked over and asked the Negroes if it would help or harm if I carried the poster. They said it would help." Yates was then approached and threatened by white boys with derogatory posters. As a tense scene builds to a confrontation, the camera zooms in on a buck-toothed kid in a hat and then cuts to a close-up image of that same young man in a jail cell. Yates testifies, "Here I was holding a sign saying 'Equal Rights for All,' and the crowd was shouting 'get rid of the nigger-lover!' . . . The boy came towards me, he cursed me out." Then the young man in the cell continues the story: "As I recall, he was white, takin' up with the niggers. That—really got me, two white boys carryin' signs for the niggers." Then Yates continues, "And then the momentum began to build from the crowd, and they said, 'Hit the nigger lover! Hit the nigger lover!' And then there's that strange, long lonely feeling where you're waiting for something to happen . . . and he walked up behind me." Jump cut to the man in jail: "I grabbed that Yankee boy, to see how hard I could hit 'im." Yates says, "He hit me in the back of the neck. I lurched forward, but I didn't fall. I regained my balance, and then in the midst of it, with the shouting and the jeering, and the crowd of people, I suddenly felt this, this tremendous humiliation. Suddenly I had crossed into another race, I'd moved into a different world, I was a Negro feeling all of the rejection and humiliation he must have to go through every time he's rejected." In this scene Yates's point of view is clearly the preferred one: the young man in jail comes off as a backward and self-centered troublemaker, whereas Yates exhibits poise and maturity. Yates narrates his profound, if brief and incomplete, moment of empathic recognition of the pain of being black in a segregated, racist society.

"Sit-In" further destabilizes the dominant white southern perspective through the tactic of juxtaposition.[36] Shortly after Huntley's introductory remarks, viewers meet Nashville's smiling mayor, who states proudly: "I am Ben West, and this is my city." West explains that while the ways of Nashville are "small-townish," its people are "not country yokels" but rather "well-educated cosmopolites." Several landmarks and historic buildings appear, including the Parthenon, the only replica of the one on the Acropolis in Greece. Nashville, West reports, "has been called the Athens of the South," and "we think we have earned this fine title with our rich background of culture." West's honorific assessment, however, is followed immediately by the deliberate baritone voice of

Rev. Kelly Miller Smith, who avers, "Nashville is considered to be the Athens of the South, and I suppose this is true in several ways. The old Athens, the ancient Athens, was a place of both shame and glory—and I think this is true of our Athens of the South here." Smith mentions Nashville's educational institutions and praises the fact that African Americans serve on some levels in city government. "But it's to the shame of Nashville," he continues, "that when you go down to the city hall, not only do you see segregation signs on the restrooms, but you see the signs of segregation in many other places. Stores where you can come in as a customer, but if you come in as an employee, it is only in a very menial capacity. . . . There are virtually no places downtown where a Negro citizen could get a cup of coffee, or a hamburger, or a meal." Smith's pointed critique here undermines the glowing claims made by Mayor West.

Later, in an extended sequence near the end of the film, West's reflections are juxtaposed and intercut with those of student leader Diane Nash, as both recount the events of April 19, when more than four thousand people marched on city hall demanding to speak with the mayor. The house of Alexander Looby, a black lawyer and respected community leader, had been bombed early that morning. West explains how he sympathized with the students' perspective: "Here was a group of youngsters," West recalls, "who were outraged because their leader had been dynamited. And I felt outraged right along with them. And to that extent, we had a community of feeling between us, which made me have a feeling that really, we were after the same thing. . . . The great majority of thinking white people were outraged by such a thing." As the scene continues, there is an interesting moment of reciprocity and recognition articulated by Nash. She maintains, "This was the very first time that I personally had ever felt the mayor's presence as a human being. Because up until this moment, he had always been a name on a sign that I had seen. But now, I felt a real concern for him. I could sympathize with his situation, because he was really on a spot: here were five thousand people who were really angry with him, in a sense. Because we felt that he should have done something that he hadn't done, and we were telling him so. I'm sure he must have felt rather alone at that moment." Just as Yates experienced a flash of identification with blacks when he was jeered and attacked, Nash came to recognize the humanity of Mayor West at this moment. "Sit-In" thus powerfully dramatizes several instances of perspective shifting across the racial divide and invites audience members to see the Jim Crow South and struggles to win integration from the demonstrators' point of view.

Subverting Decorum and Reconstituting Propriety

In addition to performing these perspective-shifting moves, the visual rhetoric of NBC's "Sit-In" dramatizes the ways that the sit-in protests subverted traditional norms of decorum and reconstituted a new version of propriety. While there is no explicit taking of sides by the documentary—Huntley's concluding remarks give off the aura of objective neutrality—a close analysis of "Sit-In" reveals that the visual evidence presented undermines verbal arguments by segregationist whites. The voices of those who oppose the sit-in actions are discredited by images more than by explicitly stated claims.

Take, for instance, the segment documenting the first day that major violence broke out against the protestors, February 27. Angeline Butler narrates, explaining that the authorities had entreated the students not to come downtown that day, due to threats of violence. The students decided to go ahead with the sit-ins, despite the risks; one of them was Paul LaPrad, a white student from Fisk University. Viewers see footage of LaPrad sitting calmly next to a young black woman, with white male onlookers pacing behind the demonstrators. Butler explains, "They always pick on the white students, because they hate to see white sympathizers." Then the audio track cuts abruptly to a young man's voice saying, "And I saw a bunch of coloreds sittin' on the stools, they looked like a bunch of idiots up there, waitin' for people to throw 'em off; they just looked like they were tryin' to egg on a fight." As he speaks there is a static shot of three black students, two women and one man, sitting calmly at the counter. Then Butler again: "None of us looked back, but we could see everything that was going on through the long mirror." Next viewers see white hecklers pulling LaPrad off his stool, beating and kicking him as he curls into a ball on the floor, the crowd shouting, "That's right! Get 'em, man!" In this scene the segregationist's claims and the visual footage are incongruous: it is clear that the students at the counter were neither looking like idiots nor egging on violence. Quite the contrary—the demonstrators are the picture of civility, and the white aggressors are the indecorous, uncivilized parties warranting condemnation.[37]

A second example of traditional piety being undermined involves commentary by an older white man, presumably a Nashville resident, whose interview is split such that he speaks both early and late in the documentary. About fourteen minutes into the film, he states: "Breaking bread is essentially a family custom, almost a sacrament. Now when you claim that you have been denied equal rights in participating in something that is regarded as a family custom or sacrament, and *insist* on being recognized, you're getting into dangerous ground. . . . The people in the South have always fed people who came and knocked at the back door and asked for something to eat. But they have always reserved the right to eat only with invited guests." Here the man blurs the line between private and public, familial and social—suggesting, apparently, that a department store lunch counter is a semiprivate, quasi-familial space rightfully governed by whites. The rules of etiquette there demand formal invitation for admission and acceptance.

Near the end of the film, the same man declares, "If I were called in to advise the Negro race . . . I would say consolidate your gains in the field of education and become the type of people who would be invited to dinner, rather than breaking down the door to eat a piece of pie on a stool next to a white person." Between these two interview segments, however, the documentary has shown that the student demonstrators *are in fact already* precisely this type of people: principled, studious, pious, gracious, and magnanimous.[38] Viewers have also seen clearly that the white toughs are the only people doing anything even remotely akin to breaking down doors, and it is only members of that "rougher element" who need to focus more on education and improving their manners. The documentary thus participates in the sit-ins' subversion of traditional decorum: the pieties of southern civility are shown to be myopic, outmoded, and incompatible with the new modes of citizenship performed by the students.

Other segregationist whites interviewed in "Sit-In" similarly cling to the traditional norms of civility to resist the confrontational tactics of the sit-ins. A man standing in front of shelves full of law books also offers his "advice" to the demonstrators: "I would say that they should examine the white person very closely first to see whether or not they're going about it in the right way. Now, if I'm a business man, and people who I do not want in my business insist on either coming in or boycotting, which is their perfect right to do, then certainly it's not going to make me love them." This man faults the sit-in demonstrators for failing to empathize adequately with his point of view. Along similar lines a segregationist woman states, "I think that people who strive to gain social acceptance through—although they're called nonviolent, or passive resistance, they're the most violent, uh . . . I also think, uh, that it is in violation to my civil rights, if someone can say, 'You MUST serve me.' If a man owns an eating establishment, and he can't choose whom he pleases to serve, or not to serve, that can affect me, and you, and anyone else." This woman's feeble assertion that the sit-in participants are violent has been disproved by footage of the protests, and the way she attempts to claim a civil rights defense for the store owners presumes that the addressee—the NBC interviewer or camera operator, and the television viewing public—is white and sympathizes with her position.

These two Nashvillians' claims are grounded in the assumption that stores are private, not public spaces, and that southern whites are the only, or most significant, audience for the sit-ins. If *their* code of etiquette, *their* sense of decorum is offended, then the sit-ins must be condemned as bad manners. However, thanks to television news coverage, the sit-in protests reached a much broader and more diverse audience, including many viewers who would see the students as performing virtuous citizenship and applaud their disciplined actions.[39] In fact Torres asserts that "Sit-In" directly addressed black viewers at several points, mobilizing "black idiom in ways that may have been scarcely legible to whites, and that may have allowed black audiences to feel singularly addressed by the program."[40] "Sit-In" renders visible the contradictions between southern conventions of civility and the egalitarian practices of democratic citizenship. While on the surface the NBC episode maintains "balance" by letting both demonstrators and members of the white establishment have their say, the carefully edited documentary visually argues to a national audience that the segregationist position is untenable.

Citizenship and Community

Finally "Sit-In" did important work redefining notions of citizenship and community, especially when taken in the context of post–World War II consumer culture—what historian Lizabeth Cohen calls "the Consumers' Republic." Cohen explains that in postwar America, mass consumption was understood not as "a personal indulgence, but rather a civic responsibility designed to provide 'full employment and improved living standards for the rest of the nation.'"[41] Television, of course, was a key site for the construction and promotion of this consumers' republic, and the plethora of advertisements and corporate-sponsored programs throughout the 1950s helped fuel the decade's "hyperactive consumer culture."[42]

Through its scenes depicting the broader African American community in Nashville, "Sit-In" offered both an affirmation of growing Negro economic power and, perhaps surprisingly, a fairly explicit critique of the dominant ideal of 1950s citizenship that emphasized individualism and patriotic consumption. At first glance it might seem as though the sit-ins are fully complicit with consumer capitalism: after all the ostensible goal was simply to be allowed to purchase and eat food at a dime-store lunch counter.[43] However, as Ella Baker so aptly explained in April 1960, the sit-ins were "concerned with something much bigger than a hamburger or even a giant-sized coke."[44] Reporting on the gathering at Shaw University that brought together 126 students from twelve states,[45] Baker emphasized that the scope, aims, and ultimate significance of the lunch counter sit-ins was much greater than obtaining the simple right to make a consumer purchase. The students, she noted, had a "feeling that they have a destined date with freedom, [which] was not limited to a drive for personal freedom, or even freedom for the Negro in the South." Baker characterized the historical moment thus: "Here is an opportunity for adult and youth to work together and provide genuine leadership—the development of the individual to his highest potential for the benefit of the group."[46] NBC's "Sit-In" reflects Baker's argument by showing youth and adults working together, not for individual gain but with a focus on the greater good of the community.

A key part of the sit-in protests in Nashville and elsewhere was a broad, concerted boycott of the offending stores.[47] "Sit-In" features an interview with a black economist who explains that since World War II, there had been a tremendous change in the income levels of African Americans. Images are presented of finely dressed women wearing hats and formal coats and carrying big shopping bags, together with shots of a white salesman showing appliances, televisions, and automobiles to black shoppers. The economist reports that "Negroes spend $10 million a year in downtown Nashville," but they "were not aware of their economic power at the local level. It took the sit-ins to bring that awareness."

A few moments later, the scene transitions to four black women playing bridge; Huntley's voice-over recounts the popular myth that the massive economic boycott of Nashville stores started over a game of cards. The ladies talk about how they have changed their shopping habits as a result of the sit-ins. One woman declares that she has decided to wear pantyhose with runs in them, rather than buy new; another proudly reports that she found the "best coat" for her growing child at Goodwill—and it was just two dollars. To help expand participation in the boycott, the women decided to call names randomly selected from the phone book, to ask people to forego shopping at the stores where the sit-ins were taking place. Sometimes they would ring up white women and engage them in conversation. One bridge player remarks, "There were many whites who actually didn't know what we had been going through all these years. They hadn't given it a thought! And for me, the sit-ins did nothing else than to focus the attention on it. And I'm saying frankly, from here on out, every means that's fighting for democracy—I'm for it. I'm going to work with it. All of us should really be ashamed of ourselves. We just spend too much time playing bridge." In this conversation the ladies reflexively critique their own consumer habits and lack of political engagement.

Immediately following is a scene shot in a black barbershop where the patrons discuss the sit-ins. One man states, "Well, this sort of thing can be an effective weapon in the future, for Negroes obtaining their rights." Another replies, "It's always effective as long as we stand together. That's something we haven't felt before, you know, we always feel that we're alone in this thing: any time anything happens, it happens to me alone. But once we get the feeling it happens to all of us, and all of us at the same time, it'd be a different thing." Here the men credit the sit-ins with creating a felt sense of community. Moments later another man claims, "We think of our students as being the very best that we have to offer. In fact, it is our future, our students are. And when our students are treated as the very worst elements of our society, then it makes all of us become more aware of the moral implications of it, the economic implications of it. . . . When the whole community rallies behind something, as they rallied behind the students, then it made a tremendous impact." Here the man frames the unjust treatment of the students—"our future" and "the best we have to offer" —as the catalyst for solidarity.

Embedded in both of these adult scenes is a rare and refreshing critique of consumer culture. One of the female bridge players asserts: "We have a lot of wants that are manufactured by advertising." Another says, "You know, I've lost interest in dressing. My closet is full, and things don't wear out." A man getting his hair cut remarks, "We always buy a bunch of new clothes for Easter, you know, you just got to have this and you just got to have that. But seems like we took a great pride in not buying things for Easter." Another man replies, "Well, I never had it so good, pocketbook-wise! We didn't go downtown at all. We paid out all our bills, every account. And during that time, we bought NOTHING. And personally, I wouldn't mind it happening again." These remarks go against the grain of the consumers' republic by celebrating the satisfactions of not spending money on consumer goods. Citizenship here shifts from patriotic consumption to principled political action. Community solidarity trumps individual achievements and the materialistic pursuit of "the good life."

Conclusion

As the *White Paper* "Sit-In" episode draws to a close, Huntley offers closing remarks that, taken at face value, maintain an air of journalistic neutrality. He declares: "One may disagree with the sit-in tactic to achieve the human aspirations of the Negro, and some may disagree with the aspirations themselves. But perhaps the most important thing is to realize not only that they exist, but that the Negro leaders of the immediate future are demanding they be satisfied and are impatient with the slow pace of change. What we are witnessing is a new kind of militancy, and with it, a new kind of soldier." As he utters the final words, the film cuts back to the gymnasium scene, where students sing and play the ukulele. Are they truly soldiers? Have viewers really witnessed in the last hour something warranting the term *militancy?* Surely not. Or, at the very least, the juxtaposition of Huntley's sober assessment with footage of the convivial community of students creates dissonance, prompting viewers to question the appropriateness of the term *militant.*

I have argued here that the visual rhetoric of NBC's "Sit-In" invites audience identification with the demonstrators, who are depicted as exemplary citizens. This hour-long *White Paper* episode powerfully documents how the sit-in demonstrators embodied and performed virtuous citizenship, confronting and ultimately breaking down antiquated norms of decorum. The students appear firmly committed and courageous, and the only bellicose words and aggressive acts witnessed in this documentary come from segregationist whites.

In taking viewers backstage, "Sit-In" also gave a richly layered portrait of the black community in Nashville. The African American adults performed progressive modes of citizenship through critiquing the individualistic habits of the consumers' republic and promoting community solidarity and valuing the collective good over private consumption. By contrast southern whites who opposed integration appear either as lone individual talking heads (whose claims are debunked by the images in the film) or as part of a rowdy and threatening mob—the "ragtail rabble" that gave even staunch conservative James Kilpatrick pause.

Using visual rhetorical tactics, "Sit-In" effectively impugns the segregationist position, but without Huntley making an explicit verbal statement to that effect. Given that this *White Paper* episode aired in December 1960—when national television coverage of civil rights was still in its infancy and public opinion about the propriety of the sit-in tactic was far from unified or settled—this strongly favorable depiction of the Nashville campaign was significant. In his memoir Andrew Young recalls watching "Sit-In" in his Queens, New York, living room: "I have rarely been so moved by a television program," he states. "As my family watched, we could literally feel God calling us back to the South."[48] Surely this hour-long show had varying impacts on different viewers, with perhaps few experiences as powerful as Young's. Still "Sit-In" did important rhetorical work in crafting new ways of seeing and fostering recognition across racial lines and in documenting the performances of citizenship that profoundly challenged norms of decorum across the South.

Notes

1. Clayborne Carson (*In Struggle*, 16) states that "it was these Nashville activists, rather than the four Greensboro students, who had an enduring impact on the subsequent development of the southern movement." SNCC historian Wesley C. Hogan (*Many Minds, One Heart,* 31) concurs, claiming that it was the "quality of reflection, conversation, and commitment to intellectual and moral examination in the ongoing workshops that differentiated the Nashville movement from the thousands of other protest sites across the nation."

2. Gould, "TV: Study of Sit-Ins."

3. See Torres, *Black, White, and in Color,* chap. 2; Young, *Way Out of No Way.*

4. See Lewis (*Walking with the Wind,* 68), who said of the documentary: "It was a powerful piece of television, broadcast nationally in prime time, something rare in those days for a program featuring black people doing anything besides singing or dancing." See also Gray, *Watching Race,* and essays in Dates and Barlow, *Split Image.*

5. Torres (*Black, White, and in Color,* 41) notes that "Sit-In" "shoots most [segregationist] interview subjects in unforgivingly tight close-ups, their faces filling the frame, luridly, suggesting a lack of perspective, an over-proximity both to the camera and to their own self-serving desires."

6. McCarthy (*Citizen Machine,* 87), states, "Television occupied a small but privileged place in these postwar visions of discussion as a tool for the making of citizens. It could

present arguments, promote grassroots reform, and meet people's needs for personal development on a mass scale, and it provided a battery of expressive forms—reenactment or role play, documentary film, the authoritative speech of experts—from which reformers might draw techniques for civic education."

7. In 1950 only 9 percent of American homes had a television; by 1960 that figure had grown to 87 percent. See Bodroghkozy, *Equal Time,* and "Television History: The First 75 Years."

8. Ackerman and DuVall (*Force More Powerful,* 332) assert that "the media's presence created new strategic possibilities in waging nonviolent campaigns, especially the opportunity to involve third parties who do not have a direct stake in a conflict but who have the means to tip the balance toward one side or the other." See also Sumner, "Nashville, Nonviolence, and the Newspapers."

9. Leonard, "Antislavery, Civil Rights, and Incendiary Material," 125.

10. See Miller and Nowak, *Fifties;* Gray, *Watching Race;* Dates and Barlow, *Split Image.* Miller and Nowak (192) explain that in the 1950s TV networks aired "the prefifties movies with their full complements of servile blacks, jungle savages, and brutal Indians. New series programs were scarcely more innocent."

11. Gray, *Watching Race,* 158.

12. Torres, *Black, White, and in Color,* 13.

13. Ibid., 27.

14. Asante, "Television and Black Consciousness," 61.

15. See, for instance, the careful reading of the 1957 Little Rock photographs by Allen, *Talking with Strangers.*

16. Doyle's *Etiquette of Race Relations in the South,* originally published in 1937, lays out in painstaking detail the social rituals and manners commonly observed by whites and blacks, including proper modes of gesture and address (e.g., "sir" for whites, "boy" for blacks of any age). Doyle explicitly articulates the ideology of white paternalism, assuring readers that "the Negro is quite all right in his place" (xxvii).

17. Allen, *Talking with Strangers,* 4.

18. As Allen (*Talking with Strangers,* 12) puts it, "ordinary habits *are* the stuff of citizenship."

19. Asen, "Discourse Theory of Citizenship," 191 (emphasis in original).

20. Ibid., 195.

21. See Scott and Smith, "Rhetoric of Confrontation"; Deem, "Decorum"; Lozano-Reich and Cloud, "Uncivil Tongue"; Cmiel, "Politics of Civility."

22. See Cmiel, "Politics of Civility," 267.

23. Kilpatrick as quoted in Zinn, *SNCC,* 27.

24. As Ackerman and DuVall (*Force More Powerful,* 327) explain, "the sit-ins had been designed to disarm the superficial imagery of blacks that racists cherished: The students were polite, well dressed, and resolutely nonviolent—practically the picture, apart from darker skin color, of how Nashville's white establishment liked to view its own sons and daughters. The sight of them being bullied and hauled away in paddy wagons had been disquieting."

25. Rosteck and Leff, "Piety, Propriety, and Perspective," describe this process in their essay on Kenneth Burke's notions of piety, propriety, and perspective by incongruity. They argue that propriety "is not limited to main-stream political discourse" (338) but also functions in radical rhetoric through the creation of perspective by incongruity—"a linguistic impiety, an upsetting of normal patterns of association . . . the wedge that pries apart established linkages" (330).

26. According to Brodroghkozy (*Equal Time*, 64–65), Kilpatrick more than held his own against King, and many civil rights activists were disappointed with King's performance in the debate.

27. Huntley's authority as a neutral, "objective" narrator was surely colored by his controversial editorial remarks closing a February 1959 show about school integration in Georgia. Bodroghkozy (*Equal Time*, 68) explains that Huntley's "provocative tailpiece" described the NAACP as "militant negro leadership." White southerners flooded the station with letters of support, praising Huntley's report as unbiased, whereas pro-integration viewers lambasted the network. One viewer from Jamaica, New York, wrote, "I have heard many stupid things on TV but yours was the most asinine and illogical suggestion yet to emanate from a single network. . . . It is evident that you have been wined and dined and brainwashed in the homes and country clubs of the white Southerner until you have become a better advocate for them than they could be for themselves" (qtd. in Bodroghkozy, *Equal Time*, 69).

28. For more on witness commentary via flashback, see Griffin, "Movement as Memory."

29. Torres, *Black, White, and in Color*, 39.

30. Ibid., 47.

31. Lewis, *Walking with the Wind*, 105.

32. Kowal, "Staging the Greensboro Sit-Ins," 136.

33. Historian Howard Zinn (*SNCC*, 6) asserts that the sit-ins on the whole worked to achieve this effect. He states that the United States, "now forced by the young Negro to see itself through his eyes (an ironic reversal, for the Negro was always compelled to see himself through the eyes of the white man), is coming closer to a realistic appraisal of its national personality."

34. One more example: near the end of the film, the first image of attorney Alexander Looby's bombed-out home was shot from within, as if from Looby's point of view, looking out through the debris where the front window would have been, onto a crowd of journalists and police officers surveying the damage.

35. My *Liminalities* essay explores how a similar dynamic of performative enactment functions at the Greensboro International Civil Rights Center and Museum. See DeLaure, "Remembering the Sit-Ins."

36. For more on the rhetorical function of juxtaposition, see Schwarze, "Juxtaposition in Environmental Health Rhetoric." Schwarze argues that juxtaposition "creates the appearance of an incongruity between symbolic characterizations of reality, and it encourages audiences to take sides and make judgments in order to resolve the incongruity" (319).

37. Hariman ("Decorum, Power, and the Courtly Style," 155) notes that Cicero presents decorum "as a grammar of self-control, including control of the body in public and control of the body's disruption of our mental life." The students sitting at the lunch counter exhibited incredible bodily control and discipline; their attackers did not.

38. Indeed even when viewers see footage of the black students in jail, they are sitting calmly, or singing, or reading books: at the film's midway point, there is a poignant shot of many pairs of black hands sticking out from jail cell bars, holding books to catch light from the hallway better.

39. As Bodroghkozy (*Equal Time*, 3) explains, "For many Americans, television became a key site on which they grappled with the changes fomented by the civil rights movement. Television brought the nonviolent campaigns of the Jim Crow South to viewers in all parts of the country. Television challenged viewers on ideals of color-blindness. Television brought black people, imaginatively at least, into white people's living rooms."

40. Torres, *Black, White, and in Color,* 44. For example, just after the opening sequence shot from Lewis's point of view, a series of shots are presented of demonstrators marching and being arrested in downtown Nashville. The sound accompanying these images is the voice of a man who appears to be older, black, and southern. He half-sings, half-preaches: "My brothers, I'm glad. I'm glad to have the opportunity to tell people today that they're sleeping in a dangerous time. Riii-se, rise, rise, rise . . . Mens and womens, that hasn't made a start, to go before, to put up and do something for your race: wake up, wake up, and go and make a start and see if God will take a hold of ya."

41. Cohen, *Consumers' Republic,* 113.

42. McCarthy, *Citizen Machine,* 243.

43. As Cohen (*Consumers' Republic,* 189) states, "Articulating black discontent in the language of a liberal struggle to pursue individual rights in a free capitalist marketplace and then successfully securing those rights, moreover, only reinforced the legitimacy of the capitalist order as a way of organizing economic life."

44. Baker, "Bigger than a Hamburger," 4.

45. Zinn, *SNCC,* 33.

46. Baker, "Bigger than a Hamburger," 4.

47. Cohen (*Consumers' Republic,* 370–71) states, "At the height of civil rights activism, mobilizing consumers through sit-ins, picketing, selective buying, and boycotting provided a strategy for punishing discriminatory merchants—whether small-town southern store-keepers, northern restaurant owners, or national chains like Kress and Woolworth—and more basically, for linking equal economic participation to equal political participation."

48. Young, *Way Out of No Way,* 49.

FORGETTING THE 1960 BILOXI, MISSISSIPPI, WADE-INS

Collective Memory, Forgetting, and the
Politics of Remembering Protest

Casey Malone Maugh Funderburk & Wendy Atkins-Sayre

Mississippi has never been associated with a fondness for change, and the civil rights movement in the state was slow to take root. Even after events such as the *Brown v. Board of Education* decision and the horrific 1955 Emmett Till murder created an opening for social change, the state movement developed slowly. As Dittmer states, "By the end of 1955 the black freedom movement in Mississippi was in disarray. With the school desegregation drive stopped in its tracks and voter registration campaigns crumbling in the face of intimidation and violence, activists were left without a viable program."[1] National civil rights organizations such as the National Association for the Advancement of Colored People (NAACP) and the Southern Christian Leadership Conference (SCLC) deemed the state too entrenched in segregation and violence to make any progress, and pro-civil-rights Mississippians found movement organizing to be nearly impossible. It seemed the civil rights movement would bypass the state entirely.

Additionally the Mississippi State Sovereignty Commission, enacted in 1956 to preserve segregation in the state, provided an institutionalized reinforcement of the segregationist efforts in a state known for its violence and intimidation against African Americans.[2] The commission's powers included the charge of performing any and all acts necessary to protect the sovereignty of Mississippi from the federal government; thus, as Dittmer noted, "simply belonging to the NAACP in Mississippi was risky business."[3]

Despite the Sovereignty Commission's efforts to slow civil rights actions in Mississippi, the Biloxi wade-ins signaled a change in the state. Much of the credit for the wade-ins goes to the organizational skills of Gilbert Mason, a Mississippi physician who moved to Biloxi after studying and practicing medicine outside of the state.[4] Moving back to Mississippi, Mason knew that it would be difficult to tolerate segregation laws. As he described it, "As an idealistic young physician, I had no intention of living my life or seeing my son live his life within the narrow confines laid out by racist segregation laws."[5] Mason viewed Biloxi's segregated public beaches as a prime location for testing the laws. Claiming that the beach belonged to private property owners, the city enforced segregation laws on the beach and in the water.[6] "For a man who loved swimming," Mason wrote, "and who had gloried in the free use of the parks in Chicago and Washington, D.C., the idea that a marvelous oak-lined public beach was forbidden territory was just too much to abide."[7] The first protest to integrate Biloxi's beaches took place on May 14, 1959. Primarily designed to test the police response to the action, the protest included only a few participants, all of whom were arrested.[8] Mason alone attempted a second protest on April 17, 1960.

A week later, more than one hundred black protestors conducted a wade-in demonstration, completing "the first indigenous, nonviolent, direct action protest in Mississippi during the civil rights era."[9] The action successfully brought attention to the segregation policies of the city but was also met with an explosion of violence. Having prepared for an attack, in one location "forty white men assaulted the swimmers with iron pipes, chains, and baseball bats."[10] The immediate violent reactions on the beaches quickly became known as "Bloody Sunday."[11] As Mason described it, "Our folks were like lambs being led to the slaughter. I thought, 'Lord, what have I gotten these people into.' Some of the forty or fifty blacks at the foot of Gill were already in the water with at least four or five hundred whites surrounding them and beating whomever they could lay hands on."[12] Moreover the violent reactions on the beach carried over into neighborhoods, creating the worst racial riot in Mississippi, in which "at least fifteen African Americans sustained serious injuries inflicted by the white mobs who patrolled the area into the next morning."[13]

As a result of this protest, Biloxi's black citizens began to organize more formally as the national civil rights movement recognized the significance of the organized activities and made plans to bring the Biloxi wade-in model to other parts of the segregated South.[14] Given the effect the wade-ins had on the Mississippi movement, those actions have not received the recognition they deserve. As Matthew Pitt observes, "Though the wade-ins were sandwiched by the Greensboro lunch counter sit-ins and the famed Freedom Riders, the protests have gone largely unheralded, even though they served as a litmus test for future segregation challenges."[15] The wade-ins challenged the segregationist mandates of Mississippi, calling into question the rights of African Americans in the state. Great resistance from local and state officials to the integration of the beaches led to a federal lawsuit in the late 1960s that eventually opened the beaches to public use, demonstrating the power of the wade-ins to enact change in Mississippi. This powerful yet gradual change in Biloxi's integration policies made way for the integration of the Biloxi public schools in 1964. This essay analyzes public discourse surrounding the 1960s wade-in attempts, specifically focusing on the way public officials minimized the violence of the wade-ins, blamed outside agitators for organizing the events, and actively worked to create laws aimed at penalizing peaceful protest. The public narrative served to preserve an active agenda of forgetting and distorting public memory of the wade-in events.

As the rhetoric surrounding the wade-in events resulted in a dominant narrative of minimizing the power of the attempts at racial integration, so too did the commemoration events emphasize a narrative of erasure. Fifty years later, the anniversary remembrance celebrations in Biloxi served to commemorate the wade-ins as a significant turn in the civil rights movement. While serving to remember the wade-ins, the ceremony and historical marker placement also muted some of the memory of the past. While the rhetorical image of the protests energized the civil rights movement in the1960s, the fiftieth-anniversary efforts minimized the significance of the wade-ins as an integral part of civil rights history. By analyzing the public discourse of the 1960s wade-ins and two specific anniversary events, this essay advances general understanding of how the rhetoric of forgetting permanently alters remembrance and suggests wade-ins as an alternative to the sit-in model of protest.

Remembering to Forget

The Biloxi wade-ins came at a time in the American South when laws and local authorities routinely subdued protest. The rhetorical framing of the protests matters to the study of rhetoric because it demonstrates how culture and language have political implications on race. While a relationship of *memoria* existed between the wade-ins and their commemoration, public forgetting was required for the commemoration's success and for healing to occur in a state known for its resistance to integration in all forms. Layered within these discourses of memory and forgetting are the complexities of race.

To understand how forgetting and memory are interwoven, we turn to memory scholars who view memory as the opposite of and antithetical to the act of remembrance. Some acts of forgetting occur when attempting to remember historical events productively. Andreas Huyssen suggests that, "inevitably, every act of memory carries with it a dimension of betrayal, forgetting, and absence."[16] Likewise Maurice Halbwachs argues that in the process of remembering, societies tend to restructure the acts of remembrance in ways that are invariably not the same as the original event. As societies make efforts to commemorate, they must selectively choose that which they will remember.

Halbwachs argues this process is a part of our social memory, in which "the various groups that compose society are capable at every moment of reconstructing their past. However, as we have seen, they most frequently distort the past in the act of reconstructing it."[17] Halbwachs further argues that to achieve equilibrium societies tend toward erasing memories that might divide groups: "It is then reason or intelligence that chooses among the store of recollections, eliminates some of them, and arranges the others according to an order conforming with our ideas of the moment."[18] For the wade-ins forgetting emerges as an inevitable act to find peace within remembered pasts, made more complex because race is at the center of the events.

To undertake an effective rhetorical analysis of the Biloxi wade-ins and their fiftieth-anniversary remembrance, race must be considered as an integral factor in the construct of memory. Derek H. Alderman calls the struggle over which parts of memory get preserved the "politics of memory"[19] and frames this concept within the painful remembrance of slavery: "This recovery process requires finding a suitable commemorative surrogate for representing the often traumatic experiences of the enslaved, which invariably involves a struggle to find the 'right' words to describe the nature of slavery."[20] The politics of memory surrounding the wade-ins' commemoration are complicated by the tension between remembering hurtful pasts and the desire to commemorate such a significant historical event. Victoria Gallagher, writing of the Birmingham Civil Rights Institute, argues that issues surrounding race emerge within the public memory: "The consequences of materiality include issues of partisanship, particularly institutionalization of memory and, thereby, value. As a result, the highly contested nature of race relations and civil rights in the United States means that related memorials enact a dialectical tension between reconciliation and amnesia, conflicts resolved and conflicts simply reconfigured."[21] Embedded within the rhetoric of the wade-ins and their remembrance are the cross-sections of race, memory, and culture, making those intersections potential sites for forgetting.

To read the wade-ins rhetorically, we turn to archived documents of the 1960s and the memorializing features from the fiftieth-anniversary commemoration. Three sites of rhetorical analysis emerge. First, this study analyzes the way the wade-ins and opposition to those wade-in attempts were rhetorically constructed during the 1960s. Second, we analyze the documents surrounding the publicizing of the commemoration within the historical context of the original wade-in events. Finally, we critically analyze the commemoration by deconstructing the rhetoric of the historical marker as a reaffirmation of both active and inevitable forgetfulness, including the site of the marker as an important feature of the rhetorical landscape. While the 1960s narrative emphasized forgetting as a means of minimizing a rhetoric of protest and inevitable change for Mississippians, the commemorative events likewise deploy rhetorics of forgetting in order to commemorate. Each of these analysis sections deconstructs acts of remembering, forgetting, and the implications of race and discrimination, concluding with the implications of this text on the politics of memory as well as our understanding of sit-in protests and memory.

The Wade-Ins—Past and Present

Documents housed within the Mississippi State Sovereignty Commission archives as well as local news coverage of the fiftieth anniversary events give insight into the ways that discourse surrounding the wade-ins functioned to frame the events in a particular way. Rhetorical analysis of those documents covers the existent representation of wade-in history shaping the memory of the event. First, an analysis of the historical events of the 1960s wade-ins helps to construct a rhetorical timeline for this project and demonstrates that from the initial wade-ins until to the present day, public officials constructed intentional forgetting as a means to restructure public memory.

1960s Resistance and the Construction of Forgetting

As the first act of resistance against the segregationist policies in Mississippi, the Biloxi beach wade-ins signaled the beginning of organized civil rights actions in the state. Official discourse and public response utilized tactics of minimization, intimidation, and distraction, serving to incite public forgetting and alter permanently the discourse of the wade-ins. This section serves to frame three rhetorical themes as a way of capturing the politics of memory that allowed public forgetting to become an active part of the unfolding wade-in discourse from 1959 to 1963. First, local officials minimized and mischaracterized the wade-in efforts. Second, public officials blamed "outside agitators" for protests and violence related to the wade-in. Finally legal efforts to ban protesting and narratives related to African American misuse of public spaces helped frame resistance to the integration in Biloxi.

The first in a series of integration attempts at Biloxi's beach occurred in 1959. However local police officers and town officials made great efforts to keep the wade-in demonstrations out of the media by downplaying each integration attempt. News articles from the *Jackson Clarion Ledger* and *Memphis Commercial Appeal* labeled Mason's solo April 17 wade-in attempt as the "first specific passive demonstration against segregation practices in strictly-segregated Mississippi in the current wave of such protests in the South."[22] News outlets, using reports from local officials, helped to reinforce the narrative of forgetting through inaccurate reporting of wade-in attempts.

After the April 17 wade-in, local officials tried to undermine the attention that the actions received. Mayor Laz Quave, for example, said, "They're trying to make a national issue out of it, but we're trying to handle it locally." Police Chief Herbert McDonald, meanwhile, avoided the press and their requests for arrest records, claiming that "it would take too much time to look it up."[23] Minimizing the importance of the integration efforts continued even after the Bloody Sunday riot, when a desk sergeant from the police station reported that he was not aware of any white persons arrested. "Maybe some Negroes were arrested," he stated; "I understand they were fighting among themselves."[24] Although media outlets reported incidents of injury and several nonfatal shooting victims on Bloody Sunday, local officials and police continually hid arrest numbers and records.

In an attempt to contain the story, local authorities turned their attention toward outside agitators as the true instigators of the protest and riot. The Associated Press reported Mayor Quave's estimation that the entire protest was a "cold calculation" and that "most of the Negroes who started the agitation were from out of state or upstate."[25] This was an accusation frequently used to downplay the significance of collective civil action. As Bruce D'Arcus explains, "This is the essence of the outside agitator argument: that individual inciters enter localities from elsewhere, spark unrest that otherwise would not occur and then disappear, leaving local communities to deal with the aftermath."[26] In the case of the wade-ins, officials claimed that the outsiders included foreign nationals, black residents of surrounding states, and members of the NAACP. In the April 24 *Clarion Ledger,* the general manager of the Biloxi Chamber of Commerce blamed the NAACP for the event and claimed that it was funded "with overseas money from enemies of the United States."[27] Locally accusations of the NAACP's involvement in the wade-ins served to vilify the organization, even though the organization denied organizing the wade-ins and resulting riots.

According to D'Arcus riots challenge local authority and order as well as what it means to enact citizenship.[28] In the case of the Biloxi wade-ins, particularly Bloody Sunday, the resulting riots acted as threats to the social order and segregationist politics of Mississippi as enforced by the Mississippi State Sovereignty Commission. Mayor Quave said he was afraid that this was just the beginning of the racial riots in Biloxi, stating, "We've got Negroes here from Alabama, Louisiana, all parts of Mississippi and everywhere else."[29] Mason denied that external groups organized the wade-in efforts on Bloody Sunday and insisted that mobs of local whites incited the subsequent violence, chasing African Americans back into their neighborhood and tormenting them through the night.[30]

Eventually a federal court case filed against Biloxi officials claimed that Quave and local police officers "aided and abetted" the white mob. In August 1960 the *Commercial Appeal* reported that "the federal government charged . . . that Gulf Coast law enforcement authorities permitted a white mob to attack a group of Negroes when they tried to integrate the beach." Furthermore evidence revealed that a local physician alerted the sheriff of Gulfport that the wade-in would happen on April 24.[31] Despite national recognition of city culpability, the strategic labeling of the protestors as outsiders served to undermine the significance of the event to the national integration efforts.

The final rhetorical strategy used during the wade-ins relied on public discourse that attempted to intimidate the African American community through legal means and a misinformation campaign. Bloody Sunday was the most dramatic of the wade-in attempts. In the days after the brutal attacks on beach demonstrators, Mississippi governor Ross Barnett signed a bill that allowed "prison terms up to 10 years for anyone inciting a riot in which a person is killed or injured."[32] Gulfport, Mississippi, district attorney Boyce Holleman told the *Jackson Daily News* that the bill "provides that persons who gather in a crowd in a public place with intent to create a breach of the peace and refuse an officer's request to disperse may be charged with disorderly conduct. This simply means that even the peaceful exercise of a constitutional right can, at certain times and under certain circumstances interfere with public safety and must yield in the interests of public safety."[33] The *Jackson State Times* reported that Mason was responsible for the violence.[34] In the days following the rioting, local city and county officials publicly discussed separatist beach areas for African Americans. The public deliberation framed this as an effort to deter any planned wade-in or riot attempts. The *Times Picayune* reported that "further race riots were apparently staved off here Saturday after city and county officials met. . . . In this view, Negro leaders said their people would refrain from demonstrations Saturday and Sunday, risking clashes with whites."[35] The rhetorical tactic served to delay further integration efforts, but Mason rejected segregationist compromises, stating, "We merely wish to have the right to use any part of the beach we choose."[36]

As local government worked to mitigate future wade-in attempts, sheriffs began to regulate weapons sales. Local sheriffs in the three coastal Mississippi counties demanded that all firearms be registered. The sheriff in Jackson County denied a connection to the wade-in violence, insisting that "merchants must keep a record of all sales of firearms and amunition [*sic*], including make, caliber and name of purchaser."[37] Statewide media reported that all three Biloxi hardware stores sold out of ammunition, rifles, and shotguns in the days following Bloody Sunday.[38] The registry of firearms along with citywide curfews and a heightened police presence in Biloxi demonstrated the fear that another protest would prove far more violent than Bloody Sunday.

State segregationists also worked to discredit Mason's reputation in several newspapers. On the editorial page of the *Jackson Daily News,* in an article questioning Mason's commitment to his patients, the author cited an uptick in

African American use of the Harrison County Health Department since the riots. In an effort to discredit Mason, the editor claimed that while he "moved himself to the publicity limelight, no new medical business is coming Dr. Mason's way."[39] The editorial argued that the African American community was turning to the public services provided by the state of Mississippi and away from Mason because of his involvement in the wade-ins.

The final form of intimidation came in the form of a disinformation campaign in the national news that skewed the relationship between the African American community and the beaches. Granted for black use in the 1950s, a section of Gulfport's beach (a city adjoining Biloxi) was revoked because "they littrede [sic] the beach and used it for a love-making ground" and were unsanitary, causing residents to insist on closing the beach. One resident said, "That the Negroes once had use of the beach is general knowledge around here, but the reason for closing it will never get into a newspaper north of the Mason-Dixon line."[40] Local government employed multiple tactics to discredit and disrupt the wade-in efforts and future integration advances. Eventually, Mason relied upon the federal case to mandate public access to the beaches. Though local officials made efforts to minimize the significance of the wade-in, accused outside agitators of instigating the integration movements, and blamed African Americans for the segregation needs, Mason held out hope that the federal suit would force integration and overturn strong segregationist efforts in Mississippi.

In June 1963 Mason again organized a wade-in, alerting Biloxi mayor Daniel Guice of the integration plans some five weeks in advance. Police officials gathered to watch the protest and fended off more than two thousand white spectators who, after less than an hour, began to slash tires of the protestors and act unruly. A group of sixty-eight African Americans and three whites were arrested for protesting. After this event no other organized wade-ins occurred. The federal suit (*United States v. Harrison County*) mandated beach integration in 1968 but was followed by several years of appeals to overturn beach integration. Finally the limitation on appeals lapsed, opening Harrison County beaches to all citizens on July 31, 1972.[41]

The rhetorical themes emerging from the original protests illustrate purposeful attempts at minimizing the desegregation efforts, leading to an altered memory of the integration efforts of the civil rights era in Mississippi. The active work by local officials to diminish publicly the impact of the wade-ins and the violence of Bloody Sunday further reinforced the relationship between racial politics and the public forgetting. Public memory for the segregationist was best served through active efforts toward forgetting and erasure of the wade-ins by public officials. In the fiftieth-anniversary remembrances, similar efforts at forgetting emerge in the preservation of progress; selective memory prevails.

Fiftieth-Anniversary Remembrance

Though a modest marker and ceremony commemorated the fiftieth anniversary of the wade-ins, it was the public conversation, awareness raising, and recollection of memories that proved significant for rhetorical analysis. James Young suggests that "it may even be the activity of remembering together that becomes the shared memory; once ritualized, remembering together becomes an event in itself that is to be shared and remembered."[42]

Prior to 2009 members of the Biloxi community began organizing a set of commemorative events. For example a local resident's Facebook page called for regular meetings near the historical marker to raise awareness, and the page served as a place for announcing meetings on the beach to gather in remembrance. The *Smithsonian Magazine* completed a retrospective story about the anniversary, bringing the event to a larger audience. Most interesting, however, was the limited exposure the actual remembrance events heralded. Though the wade-ins were the first demonstration of Mississippi's civil rights efforts, the dedication and remembrance ceremonies received little public attention. Initial press accounts remembering the wade-in started in 2009 with a story announcing the planned ceremony by a local television reporter on her blog.[43] Gilbert Mason's son coordinated the planning of a three-day ceremony along with local community members, university and college faculty members, and the NAACP. The program included panels on the wade-ins, conversations about race, and the dedication of the historical marker, all held at the Jefferson Davis branch of Mississippi Gulf Coast Community College. In June 2010 a much smaller ceremony held under a tent near the beach unveiled the historical marker at its current site. The state's public broadcasting station publicized a remembrance of the final wade-in on June 24, 2013.[44] The 2009 commemoration is of particular interest, however, as it included a significant keynote address by former governor William Winter. Winter's speech, in particular, highlights the ways racial politics encourage public forgetting.

Winter, Mississippi's Democratic governor from 1980 to 1984, was part of the "New Mississippi" movement, referring to the efforts to bring Mississippi into the civil rights era and leave segregationist politics behind. Winter's passion for education and healing the racial divide earned distinction nationally.[45] In his keynote address at the 2009 wade-in commemoration, he lamented, "You didn't see this white face on the beach with Mason because white people, like me and many others, were intimidated by the massive forces of racial segregation. I have to admit I could not stand up to the pressure for being in public life in Mississippi and come out four-square for the elimination of segregation and for that I apologize today."[46] Even with, or perhaps because of, his reputation for aiding in the creation of New Mississippi, Winter administered an apologia in his address, recognizing that he did not do enough to aid Mason in his fight for civil rights during the wade-ins. Winter's remarks, rather than emphasizing the great changes in the state or his fight against discrimination during that tumultuous time, focused on what was left undone, leading to violence. A reporter at the commemoration noted that the other speakers at the anniversary weekend, most of them African American, thought the former governor had little for which he needed to apologize.[47] However a critical reading of Winter's remarks reveals that upon reflection, some fifty years later, he recognized that his relationship to the civil rights work did not truly help to accomplish change. Charles Bolton, Winter's biographer, argues that the speakers at the commemoration "understood that he had done what he had to do in order to remain politically viable, a strategy that allowed him to retain enough power to fight successfully for educational improvement and racial healing in the years ahead."[48] With political aspirations in his future, Winter did not participate in such battles during the height of the Civil Rights era. Witnesses at the event emphasized strong opposition to hearing Winter's apology, asserting that his record of service to the state erased his need to apologize. Given this tension between speaker and audience, Winter's act of apology has far greater implications for the understanding of memory and forgetting than speakers at the commemoration realized.

Winter continued his remarks after the apology for his unwillingness to stand beside African Americans, speaking about racial progress and ending segregation. He said, "There has also been much tangible progress on race in this country, including the election of Barack Obama, as the first black president."[49] Winter's reference to electing a black president has been a much-used trope in political speech in recent years. While the election of a black president is progressive in many ways, as Winter suggests, it certainly does not demonstrate healing from the wade-in era, nor even progress in Mississippi, given President Obama's lack of support in the state.[50] Michael Newsom reported Winter's perspective on race, writing, "the efforts of Mason and others helped to end a system that was contradictory to what [Winter] thinks the U.S. is about. [Winter] said whites also benefited from the end of segregation as people of all races were prisoners of the system. [Mason] helped free us too."[51] Winter's address deemed Mason a hero and a leader of civil rights in the state. Undoubtedly these accolades were true; however Winter's remarks focused on the heroism of Mason without reference to the violence of the wade-ins. He praised Mason as the man who freed all people from oppression, when in the case of the wade-ins, white officials and citizens were the perpetrators of brutal violence against peaceful black wade-in demonstrators. Winter's revision of the wade-ins serves to cull memories, forgetting the violence and brutality of the white citizenry. Winter preserved Mason as a hero while being careful not to vilify Mayor Quave, Police

Chief McDonnell, the State Sovereignty Commission, or any other guilty parties. Rather he deferred to an apology where he accepted blame for not helping while being careful not to blame others.

Though Winter did not become governor until twenty years after the wade-ins, he was an active political figure in Mississippi during the civil rights era. His address at the anniversary highlights how the discrimination politics during the Biloxi wade-ins have been impacted by time. James Young argues that "the reasons for memory and the forms memory takes are always socially mandated, part of the socializing system whereby fellow citizens gain common history through the vicarious memory of their forbears' experiences."[52] Winter's apology, as a former governor and state leader, frames the wade-ins through his ideological lens, further reinforcing the politics of memory where race is concerned. Winter's keynote address at the commemoration served to empower the public toward holding memory as a perspective in time rather than actively remembering the events in order to heal. This type of rhetorical response encourages listeners to forget the brutality of Bloody Sunday and the civil rights era through apology and blame. Winter, however well-intentioned as a representative of the state, allowed his apology to take the place of true remembrance during the anniversary efforts.

In 1999 Biloxi announced plans to create a monument to the wade-in struggle; however by 2010 a single historical marker stood as the only public commemoration of the wade-ins, acting as the monument in the lack of a more robust commemorative form. The final act of the fiftieth-anniversary commemoration ceremony was the dedication of the marker. Combining analysis of the rhetoric of the commemoration ceremony and a close reading of the historical marker affords a more robust reading of public forgetting.

Historical Marking

A historical marker can be viewed as an act of pure remembrance. A sign becomes a monument, especially without obvious physical markers of events, such as memorials, buildings, or other historical objects. In the absence of other forms of remembering, the historical marker is granted the authority to stand in for all memories. Additionally this historical marker becomes the place of memory, the site from which memory springs. Young asserts that "traditionally, the monument has been defined as that which by its seemingly land-anchored permanence could also guarantee the permanence of a particular idea of memory attached to it."[53] Although the problem of segregated beaches existed across the Gulf Coast, the integration efforts primarily occurred in Biloxi, led by Mason. Today the commemorative marker preserves, selectively displays, and contains the memory of the wade-ins through forgetting.

This example of a marker "containing" the memory is full of potential in that it provides an opening for public dialogue about the historical event but is also constraining in that it makes the event smaller and less significant in some ways. If the marker acts as a container—a marker of physical space—then the violent acts are remembered as happening in only one location, and the symbolism of the event is also located and contained within one small space, the physical marker itself. As Victoria Gallagher argues, "Memorials serve multiple rhetorical functions and in the case of civil rights memorials, communities attempting to reclaim moral high ground . . . may use memorials to perform a kind of public apologia or therapeutic cleansing."[54] In this case the historical marker appears to be a significant recognition and remembering of the event, thus making an argument that the community has reached a point where it can come together and reflect on the meaning of the protest and the reaction to it. At the same time, the physical location of the marker erases many other spaces where integration efforts and bloody counterprotests took place. Thus without yet accounting for the words that are placed on the historical marker, the physical presence of the marker alone serves as a rhetorical example of both remembering and forgetting.

The beachfront location of the historical marker also defines and confines the location of the space in meaningful ways. In the space that now separates the beach from the privately owned historic homes of such controversy sits the historical marker near the newly constructed visitor's center and the lighthouse, all public spaces. The tall, white lighthouse serves as a constant reminder of Biloxi's location and a beacon of light in the darkness. That the original wade-in protests occurred near the lighthouse calls forth the metaphor of moving from darkness into light. Given that the wade-ins were a symbolic action, the addition of the light/dark symbolism brings another layer of meaning to the act, emphasizing the morality of the protest. Moreover today the sandy beach and gulf waters are the backdrops of the marker, further signifying a rhetorical cleansing. The marker itself is an act of cleansing sins, as it serves to commemorate while at the same time containing memory in a single artifact, thus permitting the act of forgetting. The rhetorical washing-away of the wade-in events on the same soil bloodied fifty years prior also gives the community permission to heal. Simultaneously the marker forgets and forgives, all the while sacrificing true remembrance.

In addition to the symbolism of the marker, the discourse on the marker is the next indicator of the rhetorical strategy at work in this act of remembering and forgetting. The language of a historical marker is not without careful consideration. The term *historical marker* proves challenging on its own, as it portends to tell a neutral version of a past event. Historical markers such as the one describing the Biloxi wade-ins include language about the event, however, and this selection is inherently rhetorical. As Alderman asserts, "commemorative narratives, although having the appearance of being objective and value-free, are deeply implicated in the social construction and contestation of history."[55]

The marker's account of the historical event acknowledges the earlier wade-ins, unlike the scarce media attention and accounts from the Mississippi State Sovereignty Commission. Listing three separate occasions in the opening paragraph, including the original 1959 action, the marker acknowledges the broader extent of the organizing efforts. The passive nature of the opening sentence is noteworthy, however. Readers are told that "the Biloxi beach front was the site of planned civil rights wade-ins demanding equal access to the public beach." In this case there are no actors to applaud or blame, although the wording indicates that it was "planned," alluding to actors. As others have argued, the use of the passive voice can have the effect of taking the emphasis off of the actor (speaker or, in this case, protestor or reactionary) and placing it onto the occasion.[56] Thus in this case the sentence highlights the beach—not the actors—and leaves only physical space to commemorate.

The next sentence, though, clarifies who was involved in the action: "On April 24, 1960, several citizens, both black and white, were injured and arrested, including the leader of the wade-ins, physician Dr. Gilbert R. Mason, Sr." The selection of the word *citizens* is noteworthy here, because earlier attempts to mark protestors as outsiders are erased with this discursive indication of belonging. Of course the marker does not necessarily label them as Biloxi or Mississippi citizens, but the assumption is that the protestors and those who opposed them all belonged there—they were citizens. More significantly the choice to emphasize that both black and white citizens were injured and arrested muddles understanding of the events and, because it too is in the passive voice, begs the question of who did the injuring. It is not clear based on this description who was protesting or reacting, whether there were both black and white protestors and violent responders, nor who was primarily injured and arrested Thus, this sentence brings noteworthy attention to the event but, at the same time, seems to leave out significant details. It is also noteworthy that the marker notes the leader of the Biloxi wade-ins, Gilbert Mason, in this sentence. The recognition of Mason as the leader who brought about significant changes in the Biloxi area, however, is not necessarily clear. On the marker he is recognized as the leader of protests, but viewers have to make a connection on their own that he can be credited for the positive change, as well. Of course the limited space on historical markers can always be blamed for brevity, but the rhetorical message that this brief description sends is powerfully distorting.

The final sentence on the marker indicates the significance of the events: "This series of protests gave birth to the Biloxi branch of the NAACP, major voter registration drives in 1960, and a 1968 federal court ruling opening the beach to all citizens." Since the previous sentence makes clear that both black and white citizens were involved in the event, reading this next sentence against that message indicates that all of those involved in the protest were part of the actions that brought forth the positive outcomes. That is, of course, true in many ways. As Davi Johnson explains, the Birmingham civil rights campaigns needed both the villains and the martyrs to portray visually the severity of racial violence in the South.[57] In reality, though, the violent white reaction to the Biloxi wade-ins mainly delayed progress in this area, given the lack of media coverage (and thus the same rhetorical cachet that the Birmingham images yielded for the movement). It is also noteworthy that the outcomes that are highlighted on the marker are all systemic changes—organizations being formed, voting rights advocated for, and a court decision ending segregation. Potentially more powerful results were the cultural shifts that might have been stimulated by these actions. Although structural change is easier to recognize, cultural change is more likely to bring about fundamental improvements in the lives of African Americans. Moreover in this case the empowerment of the African American protestors—seeing that it was possible to organize protest action in Mississippi—was far more meaningful to the long-term success of the state movement.

Thus the historical marker both commemorates—remembers—an important event in Biloxi and Mississippi history but also forgets much of the story. As Bradford Vivian points out, "Intentional or unintentional episodes of distortion, excision, or loss in regard to the past understandably signify not only commemorative but ethical failings when imperatives to archive, document, and preserve hold the moral high ground."[58] The brevity of the historical description may account for some of the forgetting, but because this is the only commemorative marker of the Biloxi wade-ins, the historical omissions, passive voice, and vague wordings are particularly significant. At the same time, regardless of intentions, public forgetting may serve, in some cases, an important rhetorical function of allowing communities to move forward. As Vivian notes, "In their pragmatic outcomes, public appeals to forget neither solicit immediate and complete amnesia nor insert yet another selective interpretation of the past alongside myriad partial recollections that comprise the ordinary fabric of collective memory. Rather, such appeals function rhetorically by calling on the public to question whether communal affairs would be improved by radically altering the normative form and content of collective memories that have hitherto defined its past, and hence its current identity."[59] Thus the act of remembering is important because it concentrates memories on one location or event, erasing other places and events and making it easier to forget painful memories. The easing of painful remembrance is a way of sanitizing the bloody history of the wade-ins, truly complicating remembrance.

Implications of the Commemoration

Pierre Nora notes that "modern memory is, above all, archival. . . . The less memory is experienced from the inside the more it exists only through its exterior scaffolding and outward signs."[60] In the 1960s Biloxi's public officials actively worked to deny the grassroots initiatives that led to the wade-in demonstrations. From the moment of the first civil rights protest in Mississippi, memory was denied, omitted, and forgotten. Today the only physical monument to the Biloxi wade-ins is a historical marker, which serves as the sole physical representation of the first civil rights demonstration in the state of Mississippi. In the case of the wade-ins, acts of forgetting in the face of remembrance ceremonies are in some ways inevitable and simultaneously purposeful. An analysis of the remembrance surrounding the Biloxi wade-ins leads to important conclusions about the way that the event is remembered, as well as broader conclusions about the rhetorical act of remembering and forgetting.

Analysis of wade-in rhetoric shows that responses to the protests changed over time. During the height of the civil rights movement, public officials actively sought to omit and obscure details regarding the wade-ins. The mayor and police officers intentionally placed blame on outside agitators and sought to minimize the impact of the wade-ins on the community and the larger civil rights efforts. Media outlets reported these inaccuracies, further skewing the public's perception of the wade-ins and motivating violence. Important details of the wade-ins were routinely omitted and underreported, making it likely that local citizens were not aware of the demonstrations or, if they were, were encouraged to dismiss the events as insignificant.

The active encouragement of forgetting in the 1960s influenced the ways that the wade-ins are remembered and commemorated today. Some of the modern-day forgetting appears to be motivated by the belief that forgetting a painful past removes barriers to healing. However the historical relationship between forgetting and remembrance emphasizes the danger of forgetting.

In every case the divisive details are removed from memory, affording the community an opportunity to reconcile. However to reconcile requires that the conversation is halted, the haunting details omitted, and memory sanitized. Works of memory such as these acknowledge wrongdoing but do so by containing and placing boundaries around the pain and violence of the wade-ins. Remembrance, no matter how painful, may be necessary to unmask the evils of the past truly. However motivations to forget seem far more likely given the constraints of race associated with the Biloxi wade-ins.

To ignore the glaring boundaries of race on Biloxi's remembrance efforts is not possible. For Mississippi racism and its shameful past are central to any memory work. Forgetting may be inevitable; however this is tempered by the need never to forget the racist oppression and history of violence of the Jim Crow South. Although Mississippi was slow to join the civil rights movement, the wade-ins forced the state to confront inequities for blacks, resulting in violence and pain over the integration of its beaches. Given the early efforts to obscure the facts, the recent remembrance efforts were already destined toward forgetting. The Biloxi wade-ins and fiftieth-anniversary events reveal the power of memory and the politics of forgetting. Memory's inevitable foe has historically been viewed as forgetting. The danger of forgetting is the real possibility that it will be done unconsciously or surreptitiously. In some instances forgetting may be necessary for healing, but only when it is taken seriously and done thoughtfully, not out of passive defensiveness but as an active response.

In addition to conclusions about forgetting, this example also sheds light on the role that the sit-in (or in this case, wade-in) protest model plays in the forgetting process. The wade-ins find their strength in the same way as their weakness. Sit-ins are an appealing rhetorical strategy because they are easier to form and organize than other protest events. That apparent simplicity is partially because the sit-in is a temporary commitment on the part of the protestor. Moreover that brief commitment means that a movement is not dependent on known actors in the movement. All of these characteristics mean that sit-ins are quick to form and quick to dissipate. Thus movements can use sit-ins to draw attention and to send a message with less of an investment (in all senses—money, time, and political/networking efforts) than other actions might take. This also means that sit-ins are potentially problematic regarding their rhetorical strength. In this case the wade-ins were certainly successful in drawing additional people into the civil rights movement, forcing negative action on the part of the segregationists, and providing a legal challenge for the movement. However because the actors and actions were so fleeting, they were easy to forget. For example the immediate forgetting was made easier because few names could be associated with the event. Additionally because this was not a slowly brewing action that could easily be filmed, photographed, or reported on, many of the details were lost (intentionally or not). Thus the Biloxi wade-in memorial may seem somewhat disingenuous when accolades are given to many unnamed actors. That is both a failure of the marker discourse and also potentially a weakness regarding the sit-in protest model and its role in remembering a movement.

Is Mississippi ready to move forward? Throughout the state memorials and historical markers note a few of the events of the civil rights movement in the state. Historical markers have been erected in recent years as part of a new state-sponsored Freedom Trail project in order to denote the lunch counter sit-ins at an F. W. Woolworth store in Jackson, James Meredith's admission to Ole Miss,

Bryant's Grocery Store where Emmitt Till was accused of whistling at a white woman, and the Greyhound Bus station where the Freedom Riders peacefully entered Mississippi, to name a few. Those markers demonstrate a desire simultaneously to remember the civil rights struggle and to forget the years of inactivity and resistance.[61] More recently the Mississippi Civil Rights Museum opened in Jackson on December 9, 2017. A significant step for the state, the museum is the largest effort for reconciliation and remembrance in the history of Mississippi. Of course the dual challenge of remembering and forgetting exists within the design, creation, and display of artifacts at the museum.

The Biloxi wade-ins, public commemoration, and dedication of a historical marker each remind us of the challenges of memory, especially with the existence of a strong desire to forget. We take away from this study a better understanding of the complexities of forgetting and its relationship to issues of race. The wade-ins and their commemorations serve as touchstone examples for moving forward in a state known for its past resistance to racial healing. These lessons about memory and forgetting in the face of racism will be important as Mississippi negotiates future racial healing.

Notes

1. Dittmer, *Local People,* 70.
2. During the 1950s several prominent African American leaders were murdered in the state of Mississippi. The year 1955 marked the slaying of NAACP leader Rev. George Wesley Lee, political activist Lamar Smith, and fourteen-year-old Emmett Till. By the 1959 wade-in and subsequent integration efforts, intimidation through violence and the threat of death was well understood as not just possible but, in some parts of Mississippi, expected. For more on these events and others, see John Dittmer, *Local People,* 29.
3. Dittmer, *Local People,* 29.
4. Pitt, "Civil Rights Watershed."
5. Mason and Smith, *Beaches, Blood, and Ballots,* 49.
6. Pitt, "Civil Rights Watershed."
7. Mason and Smith, *Beaches, Blood, and Ballots,* 50.
8. Pitt, "Civil Rights Watershed."
9. Ibid.
10. Dittmer, *Local People,* 86.
11. Pitt, "Civil Rights Watershed."
12. Mason and Smith, *Beaches, Blood, and Ballots,* 68.
13. Butler, "Mississippi State Sovereignty Commission," 107.
14. Ibid.; Mason and Smith, *Beaches, Blood, and Ballots*, 68.
15. Pitt, "Civil Rights Watershed."
16. Huyssen, *Present Pasts,* 4.
17. Halbwachs, *On Collective Memory,* 182.
18. Ibid., 183.
19. Alderman, "Surrogation and the Politics of Remembering Slavery," 90.
20. Ibid., 93.
21. Gallagher, "Memory and Reconciliation," 304.

22. United Press International, "Negro Doctor Breaks Color Line."

23. Ibid.

24. United Press International, "Racial Battle Enlivens Beach."

25. Associated Press, "Biloxi Patrolled by Armed Cops."

26. D'Arcus, "Dissent, Public Space and the Politics of Citizenship," 363.

27. United Press International, "All Biloxi Police Called to Duty in Race Crisis."

28. D'Arcus, "Dissent, Public Space and the Politics of Citizenship."

29. United Press International, "Negroes Fined in Biloxi Rioting."

30. Mason and Smith, *Beaches, Blood, and Ballots;* United Press International, "Racial Battle Enlivens Beach."

31. United Press International, "Police Accused of Aiding Mob."

32. "Aims to Forestall New Coast Clash."

33. Ibid.

34. "Tension Simmers in Biloxi."

35. Ferguson, "Separate Beach Facilities on Coast Are Discussed."

36. Ibid.

37. United Press International, "Racial Meeting Held at Capitol."

38. United Press International, "All Biloxi Police Called to Duty."

39. Sullens, "Dr. Mason and His Patients."

40. "Biloxi Beach Quiet Sunday."

41. Butler, "Mississippi State Sovereignty Commission," 142–43.

42. Young, *Texture of Memory,* 7.

43. Roberts, "Remembering the Biloxi Wade-Ins."

44. Burnett, "Final Biloxi Wade-in Anniversary Remembered."

45. Bolton, *William F. Winter and the New Mississippi,* 269.

46. Ibid.

47. Ibid.; Newsom, "Marker Honors Struggle of Many."

48. Bolton, *William F. Winter,* 269.

49. Newsom, "Marker Honors Struggle of Many."

50. Blow, "Election Data Dive."

51. Newsom, "Marker Honors Struggle of Many."

52. Young, *Texture of Memory,* 6.

53. Ibid., 3.

54. Gallagher, "Memory and Reconciliation," 317.

55. Alderman, "Surrogation and the Politics of Remembering Slavery," 94.

56. Leff, "Dimensions of Temporality in Lincoln's Second Inaugural."

57. Johnson, "Martin Luther King Jr.'s 1963 Birmingham Campaign."

58. Vivian, *Public Forgetting,* 6.

59. Ibid., 47–48.

60. Nora, "Between Memory and History," 13.

61. The state of Mississippi's Freedom Trail website announces the historical markers and lists them, stating that the trail was created "in commemoration of the state's pivotal role in the American Civil Rights Movement." Mississippi Development Authority, "Mississippi Freedom Trail." Although the wording of the website calls for its own rhetorical analysis, the website does indicate a desire to recognize the significance of these historical sites. To date twenty-five markers have been put in place, and four are planned in the future. Mississippi Development Authority, "MDA Tourism Announces Mississippi Freedom Trail."

VISUALIZING A CIVIL RIGHTS ARCHIVE

Images of the Sit-in at the Counter and Other Objects

Diana I. Bowen

Traditionally objects of memory in museums are represented as tangible, authentic, and whole. Even when parts are physically missing, the pieces' materiality manifests its relationship with a particular history. The F. W. Woolworth Company store in Greensboro, North Carolina, is an example of just that—a place in civil rights history that serves as a historical marker of sit-ins during the 1960s. The location itself is no longer in business. However it forges a relationship to a significant moment in history when four African American students did something transgressive—they sat at a lunch counter when segregation norms would have them leave without service. As acts of transgression, the sit-ins, along with their corresponding images and objects, advanced the civil rights movement.

A countertop and barstools from the Woolworth store in Greensboro—separated in different physical and virtual places—remain powerful icons of civil rights sit-ins. While each piece is significant, the journey of the artifact provides meaningful layers, albeit sometimes competing, of memory. Although conventional understandings of archives suggest that they include valuable objects of history, rhetorical methods examining artifacts' paths across archival collections add to the historicity of an event through its objects. A discussion of the fragmentation of archives, the various governing bodies they represent, and their emergence as icons contributes to the memory of the civil rights movement and methodologies for examining artifacts across archival homes.

Fragmented Archives and Varying Physical Locations

Where and how objects of history are preserved bear theoretical and practical significance. From a rhetorical perspective, Greg Dickinson, Carol Blair, and Brian L. Ott note that spaces and places are significant markers of the past.[1] Dickinson, Blair, and Ott state that places are concrete and spaces are open and define one another; the underlying narrative assumes a unified or well-defined location and how that site might use the undifferentiated space.[2] What happens, then, when the artifact is prodded, taken apart, and separated from its counterparts for archival purposes? Such is the case, for example, when sets of paintings and collections are sold and dispersed. Images, objects, and their corresponding narratives rhetorically glue together pieces of the past. The journey of the countertop and barstools starts in one location and history and, through their separation, the items take on features of their own. The countertop and barstools originated at a Woolworth flagship store in North Carolina; however portions of the artifact moved to different geographic locations as part of various efforts to preserve civil rights history. The International Civil Rights Center and Museum (ICRCM) located in Greensboro, North Carolina, and the National Museum of American History, a member of the Smithsonian Institution in Washington, D.C., each owns a piece of the artifact.

Providing the research community with an account of the countertop and barstools results from and is aided by the archive. More specifically rhetorical archival research enables a move away from a singular account and opens the site to a more layered understanding of the pieces and the history they represent. "The archive," rhetorical scholar Barbara Biesecker explains, is "a scene of a doubled invention rather than . . . the site of a singular discovery."[3] In other words the critic participates in the history of archival material through analysis and rhetorically connects the dots of discourse. Analysis corresponds to the number of meanings available in a single location. Rhetorical links across archives and bodies of ownership expose deeper layers of meaning. To help explain the level of connections across archives, consider the example of a modern city with a well-documented history—that is until the discovery of ruins below the city suddenly creates a multiplicity of connections between old and new, above and below, past and present, and everything in between.

Research about archival collections reveals a multiplicity of meanings in single locations, and further separating the artifact to different places adds layers of context to the countertop and barstools. The result includes parts of an artifact housed in two separate archival locations that share meaning in some aspects, contradict each other in important ways, and together add layers to the civil rights movement. To understand the meanings of historical artifacts in museums, literature about museums expands this notion of the archive. Bernard J. Armada explains, "to ignore the museum's bodily placements and displacements is to overlook a central dimension of how memory is executed."[4] Those placements, although rhetorically united, may be physically and geographically separate. Biesecker explains that the archive is "neither simply absent nor present, but both."[5] In this case the artifact is present in each location, but a part of it is missing at all times.

As objects representative of deep divisions within society, the lunch counter and barstools, too, are physically separated yet connected in meaningful ways. As a result an examination of the split archive and its history of institutionalization parallels the problematic history that it represents. Beyond the physical space between the countertop and stools, their locations perpetuate competing memories of civil rights history. While both sites tell a history of the civil rights movement, their focus varies. The Greensboro site contributes an account of transgression, and federal forms of remembrance of the Smithsonian focus more on nostalgia. Each place also offers the objects' specific journey to their corresponding archives that interestingly parallels transgression and nostalgia respectively. For example both websites provide a chronology of events of the civil rights movement. The ICRCM confronts the viewer with images of the civil rights movement, including photographs of the Woolworth building. The audience immediately confronts the history of the movement via the sit-ins. At the top of the center's website, a passage reads: "The International Civil Rights Center & Museum is an archival center, collecting museum and teaching facility devoted to the international struggle for civil and human rights. The Museum celebrates the nonviolent protests of the 1960 Greensboro sit-ins that served as a catalyst in the civil rights movement."[6] This caption is telling; it reveals the purpose of the ICRCM and its direct connection with a history of struggle.

Another player in the place's history of struggle is the fact that it was going to be torn down. The Woolworth in North Carolina housed the countertop and barstools, and it was vacant after the store's closing. In fact it was the thought of having this location completely lost that jump-started the process of preservation. As part of the museum's history, the founders explain that this flagship store was going to be torn down; this fact was the impetus for creating the ICRCM in Greensboro.[7] Guildford County Commissioner chair Melvin "Skip" Alston and North Carolina State Representative Earl Jones created Sit-In Movement, Inc., which would "purchase and renovate the Woolworth building to preserve its history in the civil rights movement."[8]

The National Museum of American History maintains a similar origin story. William Yeingst, a curator at the Smithsonian Institute in Washington, D.C., saw a television report of the stores' closing, and his feelings of nostalgia inspired a journey to remember the objects from this perspective.[9] Yeingst explained: "This was, after all, the common lunch counter at the local five-and-dime that for African Americans across the South symbolized something terribly wrong in American life—the inhumanity of racism. This same lunch counter later came to symbolize Americans' ability to reform their political system through largely peaceful means."[10] In his statement Yeingst emphasizes the multiplicity of meanings surrounding the countertop and stools including a history of racism, reform, and struggle. However, in line with the broader scope of the National Museum of American History, he recalled the reasoning for requesting these historical artifacts: "We cast our interest in broad terms: the symbolic power of the lunch counter would help the museum interpret not only the history of the civil rights movement, but also aspects of recent Southern history, Woolworth's role in American business history, and the process of urbanization of the South. We also stressed the museum's ability to provide long term care and preservation of the objects."[11]

The broader scope of the request made by the National Museum of American History is apparent when visiting its website; the home page features many facets of the nation's past. To find the countertop and barstools, one has to click several times or search within the site. The placement of the artifact was also one of compromise. As Lonnie Bunch relates, the museum discussed its decision of whether to "keep the lunch counter in storage indefinitely, or exhibit it in a very modest manner that would allow only a limited discussion of historical context."[12] While the choice reflects the importance of the artifacts— "these artifacts deserved immediate exposure, even in a temporary and limited setting"[13]—it also highlights the constraints once the objects enter their new home. Similarly finding a space for the exhibit proved difficult: "The only available site in the museum large enough for the lunch counter was the building's main hallway, which connected displays of the Star Spangled Banner and a monumental sculpture of George Washington—two of the museum's most prominent icons."[14] Bunch continues that perhaps that hallway was a better space for smaller pieces that did not "requir[e] extensive historical context," but it was a worthwhile compromise to create the exhibit.[15] The exhibition includes posters, buttons, and newspaper articles from the civil rights movement along with a portion of the Woolworth lunch counter.[16] Therefore the ICRCM and the National Museum of American History are united rhetorically because they each own the artifact, but they advance their corresponding narratives. The ICRCM focuses on a history of struggle. The National Museum of American History focuses on the exhibition in the context of a broader history, which includes conflict but also nostalgia and even patriotism.

There are times in which the experiences associated with an archive fail to intersect with institutional functions of the objects in the collection.

The fragmentation of the archive also points to the ways history itself (and the historical moments that are discussed) are separate and varied. Although discussions of the countertop and barstools often presuppose a "whole" artifact, this is only done to represent the moments in history in which they appeared in physical proximity from one another. The notion of a cohesive whole is intriguing but does not exist. With this in mind, the parsed archive represents the fragmentation of the moment it embodies. For example each location includes information and pictures that serve as representations of when the set was in one place, and the narrative behind each location boasts of a whole object. However as locations that are physically separate, each exhibit gains a story of its own, a story that explains each item's journey leading to its corresponding place. While together the artifact symbolizes a moment in history—the sit-ins—on their own they gain a history independent of one another. To explain this phenomenon, consider the following comparison to a couple who shares custody of their offspring. The children claim a unified origin; but, say, for tax purposes, the parents may split their family into separate dependents. For this reason the kids are both parts of and separate from their parents' union.

Discourse produced over these visual artifacts—the lunch counter and barstools—represents an invisible, yet apparent and observable, barrier between blacks and whites. Although blacks were physically allowed to purchase items in the Woolworth store, they were not to be served food at the lunch counter. The act of sitting despite being denied service performed a crossing of a border marked by the countertop and barstools. It is one thing to discuss the divisions of society; it is another thing to have a visual of the boundary between blacks and whites marked by lunch counter and barstools.

Although the stakeholders in Greensboro let go of a portion of the artifact to the Smithsonian Institution, the caption located at the ICRCM and on its website is telling. It exemplifies claims to the authenticity of the museum through its location and the fact that the images pictured in newspapers of the four original students taking part in the sit-ins authenticate the space. On the other hand, the online narrative advanced by the National Museum of American History is not concerned so much with authenticity but with nostalgia and patriotism. The curators of this museum include information about the exhibit and discuss how it arrived at the Smithsonian.[17] They describe in detail the condition of the barstools and lunch counter and the registrar's documentation. In essence this section of the museum's website focuses on why the objects are an important part of history.

Included on the collection web page are four short audio recordings with transcripts. They are labeled as "four oral histories [that] deal with the planning and execution of the sit-in at the Greensboro Woolworth's Lunch Counter on February 1, 1960."[18] When compared to the extensive information about each object and nostalgic description of Woolworth, the interviews are much shorter and do not include images.

These objects become part of an archive that captures this important part of history. Jacques Derrida explains, "A science of the archive must include the theory of this institutionalization, that is to say, the theory both of the law which begins by inscribing itself there and of the right which authorizes it. This right imposes or supposes a bundle of limits which have a history, a deconstructable history."[19] In other words the archive must be examined in a context along with the body of discourse that brought it into being. The different components of the archive can also be taken apart to derive pieces of meaning that make up the whole. Institutions, laws, and experiences might seem external to the archive when in fact they help define it. Such is the case with the creation of the museum, which then expanded to include the Smithsonian.

The lunch counter and barstools became part of the ICRCM in Greensboro and served an institutionalizing function on a local level (as a state institution). The separation of the object into two locations also adds to its history of institutionalization. Part of the artifact inhabits its original site, and the other part moved to Washington D.C. On the face this action would appear to increase possible audiences for the objects. Both spaces perform an institutionalization of the object. By keeping the barstools at the original location, they maintain their original home. Also placing the artifact at the National Museum of American History institutionalized the object on a second level—becoming part of an official and a federal account of history. Both museums perform this institutional function; however one occurs in the state and the other at the national level of discourse.

Federal and State Distinctions

The countertop and stools exemplify a federal and state divide that functions similarly to the relationship between remembering and forgetting. Two key bodies of literature help explain this federal/state distinction as a function of competing narratives: memory studies and cultural studies. Public memory scholar Bradford Vivian explains, "We remember because we forget, and we forget in order to remember," and each of these distinct forms of culture work expands knowledge on commemoration and historiography.[20] Both memory and forgetting constitute an active agenda that deserves attention, and the countertop and stools display both functions based on whether they are located in a federal or state institution. In *Picture Theory* cultural theorist W. J. T. Mitchell discusses the duality of the image, which in this case is also applied to objects of history: "Rather than talk of what we 'know' . . . then, we must talk of what we are prevented from knowing, what we can never know, and how it is figured for us in the partial access we do have."[21] Walter Benjamin, also a cultural theorist, adds a concept of authenticity, a work of art's "presence in time and space, its unique existence at the place where it happens to be," a concept that is also helpful in explaining the uniqueness and relevance of original objects and their journey. Benjamin continues, "This unique existence of the work of art determined the history to which it was subject throughout the time of its existence. This includes the changes which it may have suffered in physical condition over the years as well as the various changes in its ownership."[22] Although a distinction may exist between works of art and historical objects, they are both celebrated as valuable relics of the past. Notably both players are using the same artifact in their corresponding stories. To explore this dichotomy, issues of federal and state distinctions follow. Federal players focus on a broader memory, and state institutions depict a more local focus. Similarly federal players emphasize a memory that advances an interest of broadly preserving U.S. history, while local stakeholders emphasize the specificity of their location and its contributions. Neither narrative is more or less valuable; however they represent competing interests.

On a federal level, two curators for the Smithsonian Institute, William Yeingst and Lonnie Bunch, met with the vice president for corporate relations of Woolworth in New York in the early 1990s, stressing the significance of the Greensboro objects to both the sit-in movement and the history of industrialization of the South.[23] At the same time, Sit-In Movement Inc., a local nonprofit comprising African American residents, wanted to make the Greensboro Woolworth store into a national museum of civil rights.[24] The exact nature of these deliberations is not readily available. However both parties expressed an interest in preservation at the federal level. In what seems like a compromise, the Smithsonian curators provided their expertise to members of Sit-In Movement Inc., the Greensboro community, and city council and, in return, gained a portion of the lunch counter from the Woolworth store.[25] As Karen Plunkett-Powell states: "They were interested in acquiring four stools, a section of the lunch counter, mirrors, the soda fountain, and a section of cornice. A satisfactory agreement was reached with all parties. The F. W. Woolworth Company, along with the Greensboro Sit-In Movement, would receive national recognition for their donation to the Smithsonian; the members of the Sit-In Movement Inc. would also continue with their own local museum plans."[26] In some ways the Smithsonian Institution helped preserve this important point in history by "enabling the museum's six million yearly visitors to view, and remember, that critical era."[27] On their website the Sit-In Movement Inc. states that it is unknown whether the barstools in the ICRCM are original since the store underwent remodeling and reupholstered the stools.[28] However rhetorical claims to authenticity made by the Greensboro institution entice visitors and virtual audiences to make the connection between the exhibit and its place in history. The authentic aspect of the International Civil Rights Center and Museum in Greensboro is that it is the same location in which the sit-ins took place. Even though audiences may never know the veracity of which stools were specifically used, for example, the fact that they are located in the ICRCM authenticates the space.

Moreover divisions over the artifact reveal divisions in society, such as more historical divisions over segregation and voting rights; one can look at the characteristics of its owners. For example the federal players have the know-how to preserve historical materials. The local players are more concerned with the preservation of a specific history of struggle. Several local and federal players make ideological moves that contribute to the evolution of the object, from its origin to its subsequent split, which at times limit and expand the artifact's accessibility to multiple audiences. Just as laws vary from federal to states, the lunch counter and barstools take on new identities as both are separate and always about one another.

The Smithsonian Institution's intervention affected the ICRCM in other ways as well. As objects at the ICRCM, the lunch counter and barstools face accessibility issues, closing off their relationship to building business for Woolworth. On the one hand, the entire artifact was available to people who live in Greensboro and may have close ties with civil rights history. On the contrary the placement of these objects in an institution with an admission fee offered restricted access to those who could go to the ICRCM and learn about the subject matter. Although technically available to the masses, calling the Woolworth lunch counter and barstools a museum changes the nature of the space. This transformation adds admission requirements and surveillance necessities, inevitably changing the dynamics of the place. The objects also underwent another change, from politicized objects of history to less politicized objects in an exhibition space As such, the countertop and barstools lose their ability to host events such as sit-ins and instead stand for this moment in history. They maintain a sense of authenticity because they remain in one of the places that marked the beginning of the sit-in movement.

As historical artifacts, negotiation over meaning continues even though sit-ins no longer take place on these objects. For example separating the objects exemplifies the tension of staying in their original location or separating them and placing each in a different part of the country. The objects transmit the original story, but separating and moving the artifact create new meanings. As distinct objects the barstools and lunch counter perform a dual function—they keep their authenticity in the original location in Greensboro and simultaneously join other official objects in a central location of history in the Smithsonian. An online observer can also view each separately on the institutions' corresponding websites.

The ICRCM may have been prevented from forging their ties to both federal and state audiences through their donation to the Smithsonian. By giving the artifact to a government institution, the ICRCM foregoes its stake as the national organization despite its title and claim as an international museum. Moreover as continuing representations of the legacy of the civil rights movement, the space in Greensboro faces other conflicts. One of the difficulties in maintaining the memory of the relevant historical events that authenticate the place is the continuing operational issues for the site. As recently as 2014, the museum was running a monthly deficit, and the city considered taking over operations.[29]

This state/federal distinction parallels the divide between local and national differences during the civil rights era and beyond. Local communities participated in the sit-in movement, and state institutions responded through an enforcement of the law via arrests. The federal government lingered in taking action and remained quiet on the issue. President Kennedy failed to act for political reasons, namely wanting to keep the southern Democrats on his side. For this reason the sit-ins started off as a grassroots movement; then the state governments got involved, and finally public pressure forced the federal government to become a part of the issue. Similarly the countertop and barstools were deemed a significant object of history first on a local level, then state, and finally national.

Iconic Representations of Objects and Beyond

Objects preserved from historical events become iconic images of particular moments in history, and examining how they become icons is also an important part of mapping their journey. Visual rhetoric scholars Robert Hariman and John Louis Lucaites developed theories on icons, specifically the way they haunt public culture. Images are re-created, parodied, and built from established cultural meanings linked to the original to advance new understandings and agendas.[30] This phenomenon is evident in reiterations of the object, shifts in media, and integration in popular culture. Accordingly through their preservation the countertop and barstools have gone from unique historical moments to iconic representations. Kendall R. Phillips and G. Mitchell Reyes' work on memoryscapes helps account for the federal/local split of the objects through a theory of the intersection of memory and the nation-state in a globalized society. They state that glocality, or "the movement of ideas or people or technologies is always a matter of the introduction of new objects into a local environment, and locals operating in specific localities will always perform the subsequent adoption of resistance."[31] Because the countertop and barstools achieve iconic status, they can stand in multiple places at the same time and even advance competing narratives.

The countertop and barstools inhabited one place—the Woolworth store in Greensboro, North Carolina. The images of the four students sitting on the objects during the sit-ins became an iconic representation of the struggle because the photographs were seen in newspapers nationwide. Although many other images of sit-ins became available through the advancement and growth of the struggle for civil rights, the countertop and barstools maintained their role as catalysts. These reiterations of images across media reached iconic status, and the objects became signifiers of this historical period.

Multiple state and federal players maintain established meanings of the objects and add new agendas. By keeping the original countertop and barstool where the four students sat, the location maintains particular meanings. The museum celebrates its founders for their contributions to civil rights history by recovering the place and objects of the movement. The site in North Carolina represents a glocality. Since the space was vacant, reintroducing the Woolworth store and its objects to the community enables the space to maintain relevance as a signifier of the movement. It also serves as a reminder and a memory of segregation, racism, and violence inflicted on black bodies. The space retained its relevance over time: "In 1993, two of the original four . . . learned of plans to raze the building for a parking lot. Realizing that a part of civil rights history would be lost, they bought it and began plans to create the museum, of which the lunch counter is a part."[32]

On the other hand, glocality was established on a national level when a portion of the countertop and barstools joined the Smithsonian National Museum of American History. A short video on the Smithsonian's website discusses the relationship of the objects to U.S. history: most department stores, drugstores, and five-and-dimes had a lunch counter, soda machine, and a row of stools where patrons could get a hamburger, a slice of pie, and a cup of coffee. They were public places and important as sites of not just of legal segregation but of racial bigotry itself. They were sometimes segregated by custom and sometimes by law.[33]

Although the speaker refers to racism and bigotry, an element of nostalgia is evident. What made racism so awful, according to the video, was an inability to take part in such banal experiences of the time. The narrator acknowledges the location and objects and the people who became visible through interaction with the objects. The ambiance is inviting; people can purchase a cup of coffee and buy time in the store—the amount of time is determined by how quickly one finishes the cup of coffee. The remaining artifacts represent the racial injustice experienced by those involved in sit-ins.

As cultural critic Terry Eagleton notes, the aesthetic object may be considered a "double-edged concept."[34] On the one hand, it is important to include these markers of African American history. On the contrary, in doing so their institutionalization also creates a greater distance between the object and the masses. While its location on the National Mall is a place of splendor, the artifacts within the Smithsonian are located far from where the sit-ins occurred and available only to people with the ability to travel to Washington, D.C. With a much larger collection and multiple buildings, this marker of history has more competition to bear than Greensboro's dedicated civil rights museum. People who live in the Washington, D.C., area, who may not have considered traveling to North Carolina, now have access to this history. Even if the pieces transform into two separate installations, none was previously available to the citizens and tourists when the counter and stools stood in a vacant Woolworth store.

The final stage in the artifact's history introduces a new form of remembrance; it occurs when the countertop and barstools join the digital revolution. The information listed on the websites and images form part of the virtual tour. Dickinson, Blair, and Ott agree: "Technologies of communication and preservation do not so much replace each other in most cases as they supplement and reanimate one another."[35] Visitors who are physically present at the destinations or connected online gain access to the collections. Some might claim that touring an archive via the Internet takes away from its authenticity. Technological attempts to make the exhibits more accessible expand audiences who can make claims about the artifact. This move, however, is not without ideological factors at play.

The inclusion of images and interviews about the Woolworth lunch counter and barstools in virtual tours resonates with a goal of increased access to the masses. The interviews with the curators of the National Museum of American History and images of the barstools and lunch counters—not just in Greensboro but across the nation—expand the public's understanding and awareness of these valuable pieces. In some ways more people have access to these virtual objects. Issues of access remain, however, even with the expansion of the objects into new media.

The history of the countertop and barstools, as seen above, is an ideological one. The pieces of the artifact are now accounted for by both state and federal institutions, both of which have not escaped the demands of the technological age. Each historical shift in the objects' existence marks changes in relationships between the audience and artifact. These changes do not communicate a decreased relevance of the installations; instead they mark its historical significance by what multiple locations want to "own" this moment in history. Each recurrence of the countertop and barstools takes on new ideological turns, marks its significance, and shifts the dynamics of the artifact.

Conclusion

As a lunch counter and barstools located at the Greensboro Woolworth store, the objects compose a vernacular memory. Nestled somewhere between Rosa Parks, Dr. Martin Luther King Jr., and Malcolm X, the sit-ins do not enjoy as much academic and institutional attention. Therefore a lack of attention exists for works that cover sit-ins in their own right. The process of moving and separating the object takes a step toward institutionalization. A tug of war exists between the way objects are archived at the museum and the way they are talked about, with institutional memory winning out in both locations.

Archival research, memory, and visual rhetoric studies have taken steps toward exploring the role of visual artifacts' contributions to history. The fragmentation of archives serves as a call for future work on historical objects that transcend one particular rare book collection toward an understanding of the complexities across archival collections. Examining objects for both memories and the erasures they evoke plays a vital role in underlying ideological issues. Finally the examination of how an artifact becomes iconic serves to explain further its visual role in history. Hariman and Lucaites, for example, have contributed to considering how photographs of Dorothea Lange's 1936 "Migrant Mother" and Nick Ut's 1972 "Accidental Napalm" furthered cultural understandings of icons in contemporary culture. As part of their approach, they examined the history and context of these images and what they reveal and simultaneously conceal. Using archives, memory studies, and visual culture, the countertop and barstools prove to be more than simply props in a picture. Rather they are objects full of meaning, expressive of ideology, and layered narratives. The lunch counter and barstools are not empty signifiers; they join other archival materials, such as newspapers, correspondence, and books, deemed as relevant for preservation. The visual artifact becomes a part of a cultural memory—an artifact that is not immune to technological shifts and effects of globalization. The visual archive is rich with meaning and affect and rooted in deeply contentious rhetorical moments. Meanings of the visual artifacts and their subsequent (dis)placements exemplify shifts in meanings of their relationship to history and, perhaps more important, changes in how the events and people represented are remembered.

Notes

1. Dickinson, Blair, and Ott, *Places of Public Memory*, 23.
2. Ibid.
3. Biesecker, "Of Historicity, Rhetoric," 124.
4. Armada, "Memory's Execution," 217
5. Biesecker, "Of Historicity, Rhetoric," 126.

6. International Civil Rights Center and Museum website, http://www.sitinmovement.org/ (accessed 16 October 2019).

7. Dillon Tyler, Museum Interpretive Staff and Tour Coordinator, phone conversation, October 16, 2019.

8. Ibid.

9. Plunkett-Powell, *Remembering Woolworth's,* 164.

10. Yeingst, "Sitting for Justice."

11. Ibid.

12. Bunch, "Exhibiting a New Icon."

13. Ibid.

14. Ibid.

15. Ibid.

16. Ibid.

17. "Origins of the Sit-In: A Sibling Remembers."

18. Ibid.

19. Derrida, *Archive Fever,* 4.

20. Vivian, *Public Forgetting,* 12.

21. Mitchell, *Picture Theory,* 190.

22. Benjamin, "Work of Art in the Age of Mechanical Reproduction," 220.

23. Plunkett-Powell, *Remembering Woolworth's,* 164.

24. Ibid.

25. Ibid., 164–65.

26. Ibid.

27. Ibid., 164.

28. Schlosser, "Greensboro's Civil Rights Landmark."

29. "Greensboro Seeks to Take Over Civil Rights Museum."

30. Hariman and Lucaites, *No Caption Needed.*

31. Phillips and Reyes, *Global Memoryscapes,* 11.

32. "Saving a Lunch Counter."

33. "Lunch Counter: Overview."

34. Eagleton, *Ideology of the Aesthetic,* 28.

35. Dickinson, Blair, and Ott, *Places of Public Memory,* 21.

DIRECT ACTION, THEN AND NOW

Comparing the Sit-Ins and Occupy Wall Street

Jason Del Gandio

This essay approaches direct action as a form of embodied rhetoric and compares and contrasts the 1960s civil rights sit-ins to the 2011 Occupy Wall Street movement. The specifics of each movement were different—the civil rights sit-ins were polite, orderly, and rational, while Occupy was indignant, disorderly, and chaotic. However the general purpose was the same—to rupture the public consciousness in the hopes of creating social change. This latter issue "sits at" and "occupies" the heart of direct action as embodied rhetoric. Such an insight often evades public understanding, thus leading to confusion, dismissal, and backlash. Such responses and misunderstandings stem, in part, from the public's unfamiliarity with direct action: while listening to and deciphering speeches and political debates (verbal rhetoric) is commonplace, the same is not necessarily true for direct action and civil disobedience (embodied rhetoric). This essay seeks to mend this gap by looking at the rhetoric of direct action in general and the direct action of the civil rights sit-ins and Occupy Wall Street movement in particular.

Occupy Wall Street: An Overview

The Occupy Wall Street movement (OWS) officially began on September 17, 2011, in Zuccotti Park located in New York City's financial district.[1] Organizers circulated a call in June asking people to "occupy Wall Street." Initially September 17 did not produce a large turnout. The occupation grew moderately larger within the following days and weeks. Then on October 1 approximately seven hundred protesters were arrested on the Brooklyn Bridge while march-ing without a permit. The media covered the story, and occupations suddenly erupted in every major U.S. city, with many satellite occupations occurring in other countries. Occupy Wall Street became a national and even international phenomenon.

The Occupy Wall Street movement was driven by two primary issues: eco-nomic inequality and a lack of political accountability. The basic idea is that the United States suffers from an obscene gap between the rich and the poor and, consequently, that the overall American system is run by and for the wealthiest while the wants and needs of average citizens are ignored. It should be noted, though, that Occupy addressed a plethora of issues—everything from global warming and the two-party system to healthcare, education, student debt, home foreclosures, workers' rights, immigration, mass incarceration, genetically modified foods, war, and the military-industrial complex. Economic inequality and political accountability drive these interrelated issues. If the country is run by the rich for the rich, then all of the subsystems will be oriented to producing a profit to benefit the private wealth of a small percentage of individuals—hence the slogan "We are the 99%." Occupy NY drafted and circulated a declaration stating that "all of our grievances are connected," which succinctly summarizes the intersectional network of issues and problems addressed by OWS.[2]

Every social movement is motivated by numerous precipitating factors. With Occupy two of the more iconic factors included (1) the $700 billion bank bailouts of 2008 and (2) the 2010 Supreme Court case *Citizens United v. Federal Election Commission.* The bailouts gave taxpayer money to the world's richest institutions. Individual citizens experiencing economic woes are often forced to declare bankruptcy and, for the most part, fend for themselves. However billion-dollar banks are bailed out with taxpayer money. Many eventual occupi-ers, feeling betrayed, believed they were witnessing "communism for the rich and capitalism for the poor." Regarding *Citizens United,* the Supreme Court argued that the First Amendment (free speech) prohibits the government from restricting the political spending of corporations. In this case that means the government cannot inhibit corporations from donating money to influence elections, candidates, campaigns, and so forth. The logic can be summarized like this: corporations have been deemed "natural persons" by the Supreme Court; natural persons have freedom of speech; freedom of speech includes political spending; corporations are thus allowed to contribute to political campaigns like other citizens. The only problem is that corporations are not like other citizens. Corporations, by nature, are collections of people dedicated to the accumulation of private wealth. Considering that we live in a capital-ist society, wealth equals power. If money equals speech, which is what the Supreme Court essentially argued, then the large majority of actual people are systematically excluded from expressing their political speech; only the wealthiest can "speak." Both the bailouts and the *Citizens United* case point to the previously mentioned issues of economic inequality and political accountability.

Occupy Wall Street was based on horizontal rather than vertical structures: it rejected the notion of top-down leaders and presumed that everyone could and should contribute to and participate in the movement. Occupy thus adopted a "working group" model: that is, each occupation—whether it be in New York City, Denver, Oakland, or wherever—was composed of small working groups responsible for particular tasks. Working groups commonly assumed such assignments as sanitation, food, library, security, entertainment, outreach, public relations, daycare, art, education, interfaith, media, finances, and legal. Working groups met independently to work on their respective tasks and then designated one person from the group to report back to the General Assembly Committee or provide a public report during the General Assembly (GA). The GA was the main gathering open to the public that would discuss, debate, and make collective decisions. The GA would occur on a regular schedule. For some locales that meant each day at a certain time; for others it might be every other day or as little as once per week. Regardless of the schedule, the GA was open to all those who wanted to attend, and everyone was invited to participate. Models of consensus decision-making were used to facilitate the GA. In many ways consensus—as a form of direct rather than representative democracy—was Occupy's cornerstone.[3]

Occupy's rhetoric was unique in that it relied on "network rhetoric" and "body rhetoric." Network rhetoric, as used herein, refers to a complex intersection of diverse and even competing ideas (think of all the issues addressed above). Body rhetoric refers to the use of one's body to make an argument or political point. For instance, what does it mean to occupy Wall Street literally? What does that action itself say or argue? What political messages are generated by a broad network of embodied rhetors spanning the nation or globally? What type of rhetorical effects and challenges are produced by this form of social movement?

Occupy Wall Street failed to provide a coherent political platform capable of pressuring elected representatives to create concrete policy changes. However that was not necessarily Occupy's goal. Instead Occupy was more of a sudden insurrection; an outpouring of resistance; a public rejection of the status quo; a moment of hope in which millions of people believed that the American system could be altered to benefit a majority of citizens. Occupy produced no immediate, concrete policy changes, but it did place the issue of economic inequality at the center of national discussion, and it created a context in which other groups, organizations, issues, and causes could come to the surface. In other words it created a context in which more social movements could be created.[4]

Understanding Direct Action

Uri Gordon, a contemporary anarchist theorist, defines direct action as "action without intermediaries, whereby an individual or a group uses their own power and resources to change reality, according to their own desires."[5] A similar but slightly longer definition comes from the French activist group Sans Titres:

> In brief, direct action implies one's acting for one's self, in a fashion in which one may weigh directly the problem with which you are confronted, and without needing the mediation of politicians or bureaucrats. In the same way, if you see some bulldozers about to wreck your house, you engage in direct action to directly intervene to try to stop them.
>
> Direct action places moral conscience up against the official law. Direct action implies not caring about the rules and procedures that the economists and politicians apply, and deciding for yourself that which is just and that which one should resist.[6]

Gene Sharp, a world-renowned scholar of nonviolent direct action and a three-time Nobel Peace Prize nominee, defines direct action like this: "When people refuse their cooperation, withhold their help, and persist in their disobedience and defiance, they are denying their opponent the basic human assistance and cooperation which any governance or hierarchical system requires. If they do this in sufficient numbers for long enough, that government or hierarchical system will no longer have power. This is the basic political assumption of nonviolent action."[7]

Activist and anthropologist David Graeber distinguishes direct action from civil disobedience. As he argues,

> When one burns a draft card, one is withdrawing one's consent or cooperation from a structure of authority one deems illegitimate, but doing so is still a form of protest, a public act addressed at least partly to the authorities themselves. Typically, one practicing civil disobedience is also willing to accept the legal consequences of his actions. Direct action takes matters a step further. The direct actionist does not just refuse to pay taxes to support a militarized school system, she combines with others to try to create a new school system that operates on different principles. She proceeds as she would if the state did not exist and leaves it to the state's representatives to decide whether to try to send armed men to stop her.[8]

Uri Gordon makes a similar case when he states that civil disobedience is "any conscious collective defiance of the law, either for moral reasons or in an attempt to mount pressure on the authorities to respond to one's demands."[9]

Meanwhile direct action is a "dual strategy of confrontation to delegitimize the system and [a] grassroots alternative-building from below."[10]

Within this framework civil disobedience is more symbolic, while direct action is more militant and directly interventionist; civil disobedience is an act of protest, while direct action is the prefiguration of a different system, a system in which people are directly empowered and self-determined. I believe that such distinctions are valuable but too rigid. All direct action is symbolic to some degree (if for no other reason, because humans are symbol-using creatures), and all civil disobedience involves some level of militancy and intervention (the intensities of which are defined, in part, by the context and the perceptions of the actors and witnesses).

For example civil rights activists directly interfered with the laws and practices of segregation by strategically placing their bodies in public locations that were legally zoned for "whites only." These activists refused to leave until they were served or until they were physically (and often violently) removed. The activists might not be perceived as militant given their commitment to "nonviolent civil disobedience." However militancy is defined by combativeness rather than violence or nonviolence. The civil rights activists were directly and publicly combating racist segregationist practices. A large part of that combativeness was the symbolism of their rhetorical performance. They were not reciting speeches while standing atop lunch counters. Instead they used their bodies as rhetorical tools for indicating segregation and arguing for antiracist legislation.

In Occupy's case activists approached Wall Street as both the literal and symbolic epicenter of the corporate world. That corporate world has vast influence over American life, affecting not just the prices of the stock market but also, and more ubiquitously, elections, legislation, mass media, and cultural practice (art, music, fashion, sports, etc.). Occupying Wall Street thus infers a taking back and democratizing of the corporate world—a redistribution of its power and influence. Such an action closes the gap between symbolic gesture and militant action. The occupation was simultaneously the action and the argument. Here appropriating the words of Marshall McLuhan can help explain the nature of Occupy: the movement *is* the message.

In light of these definitions and debates, I believe that direct action can be understood as the conscious disruption of social operations for the intended purpose of political change. This definition seems to cover most if not all of the various sit-ins discussed in this present volume. For instance there are many differences in the composition, execution, and intent of Eleanor Roosevelt's 1938 sit-between[11] and the 1964 St. Augustine swim-ins and wade-ins.[12] However these actions (along with the many others outlined in this volume) consciously disrupt social operations to bring about some form of political change. That change can vary from temporarily altering consciousness to pressuring elected representatives to pass particular legislation. These actions are politically direct regarding the participants' taking matters into their own hands. It must be noted, too, that these actions are consciously conducted with political intent and purpose. Accidentally falling in front of the U.S. Capitol building is not an example of direct action. Although security guards and passersby may stop to help and, perchance, ponder the operations of our congressional representatives, there is no conscious intent to stop business as usual. However the situation changes once political intent is introduced. Perhaps security guards are unusually cruel and rough with the fallen victim—perhaps even beating and unjustly arresting the victim. Shocked onlookers then rush over, lock arms, surround the security guards, and directly interfere with the arrest. The guards are eventually forced to free the victim. This now becomes an example of direct action.

Traditionally direct action involves the use of one's body—some physical intervention in which the body is the main source, site, and tool of disruption. This is not always the case nowadays with such tactics as "hacktivism" and "virtual sit-ins" and the rise of Anonymous, a virtual activist group.[13] However for the most part, direct action usually relies upon the body as a form of intervention and disruption. For instance a group of protesters might block the entrance to a corporation whose business practices are harming the public. In doing so the protesters are temporarily disrupting the operations of that corporation: people are unable to enter or leave the building, which affects everything from delivery services to scheduled meetings; security guards attend to the protesters and devise a strategy of dispersal; the public relations department drafts a media response; the CEO is notified and consulted; and company employees are distracted for some portion of their workday, resulting in lost revenue. In brief the company's energies are focused on the protesters rather than working toward profit.

Most likely the protesters contacted local media beforehand, thus turning this specific action into a local, regional, or even national story. The story then brings public attention to the corporation's business practices. Perhaps the protesters anticipated the coverage and organized their action into an "image event"—that is, a cluster of visual signifiers that purposefully challenges and disrupts audiences' taken-for-granted assumptions about the world.[14] The direct actionists have rhetorically crafted their image event by adorning business suits covered in red-painted one-dollar bills while wearing oversized, clown-like sneakers with the corporation's logo prominently displayed. They also wear face and hand makeup that makes them look old, tired, and fatigued—droopy eyes, deeply ingrained wrinkles, and beat-up, swollen hands and fingers. A large, colorful sign attached to the doorframe above their heads reads "Cheap Labor = Abuse. Stop Sweatshop Labor Now!" This cluster of signifiers exposes the exploitative practices of the corporation and suggests a moral imperative for ending such practices.

Such an action is conducted for at least three purposes: (1) to intervene directly into social affairs on behalf of one's own beliefs and values; (2) to argue for or against something; and (3) to implicate audiences. Given the nature of mass society, citizens are often forced to rely on others to effect social change— for example, mass media, elected representatives, lawyers, lobbyists, and professional advocates. People are forced to seek mediation rather than acting on their own, thus prohibiting their rhetorical agency. Direct action violates that prohibition and circumvents the mediating process, thus enabling people to act for themselves. A direct action is thus a form of rhetorical empowerment. That empowerment implicates audiences in at least two ways. First direct actions often target specific audiences—corporations, politicians, the government, the military, school administrators, and so forth. And second the public nature of direct action often implicates onlookers and passersby. Individuals are called to conscience and invited to reflect upon the message of the action. As Gladys Ritchie argues, direct action is "effective because its action carries a powerful rhetoric. It has a special language that writes big on the walls of the Entrenched and the Indifferent. It leaves messages there which the 'blind' and 'deaf' must see and hear."[15]

Direct actions normally occur within broader, multipronged public campaigns that involve a plethora of tactics and foci: letter-writing campaigns, door-to-door canvassing, radio and television interviews, letters to newspaper editors, social media strategies (websites, email listservs, Facebook, Twitter, etc.), lobbying elected representatives, organizing rallies and marches, posting flyers around town, and so forth. Each effort works toward the single goal of effecting one's desired social change, and direct action is often part of that package. This is particularly true for social movements. Nonprofit organizations, for instance, might or might not incorporate direct action. However just about every social movement that has ever existed has used some form of direct action. Such actions have included, but are not limited to, the following: labor strikes, tax strikes, hunger strikes, boycotts, buycotts, road blockades, school walkouts, divestment campaigns, sabotage of machinery, destroying property (like smashing a Nike storefront window), lock-ins, lock-outs, kiss-ins, pray-ins, die-ins, sit-ins, sit-downs, building and park occupations, and encampments.

Direct action is sometimes construed as "violent," particularly with more disruptive practices such as road blockades, building occupations, and property destruction. However notions of violence and nonviolence are socially conditioned. The Boston Tea Party, for instance, involved American colonists deliberately damaging British property. Such defiance is framed as a necessary step for American independence and thus celebrated in children's history books. However contemporary activists who destroy property are commonly labeled as criminals or even as terrorists. These kinds of issues are widely debated within social movements. Many activists argue that violence can only be committed against sentient creatures—that is, humans, nonhuman animals, and perhaps the natural environment. In this case breaking windows and overturning dumpsters are not acts of violence. While this is debatable, the overall issue highlights the rhetorical complexities of direct actionist practices.[16]

Differences between the Sit-Ins and Occupy

General Appearance

For the most part, the young sit-in participants were well dressed and well groomed, with attention to how they might appeal to America's traditional middle-class core values. Activists developed this rhetorical strategy during direct-action workshops, where they were taught "how to behave in the face of a hundred possible emergencies, how to avoid violating the loitering laws, how to move to and from the lunch counters in orderly shifts, how to fill the seats of students who needed to go to the bathroom, even how to dress: stockings and heels for the women, coats and ties for the fellows."[17] The sitters used their overall appearance as a way to position themselves as insiders rather than outsiders, thus making it easier for Americans to accept the notion of racial equality. As Gladys Ritchie argues:

> The dress of the young students was a rhetorical act which spoke of order, dignity, and non-violence. Its contrast to the black jackets [worn by white vigilantes], long a symbol of violence and disregard for civil and moral law in this country, spoke of what these young people stood for. The Bibles they carried, symbols of brotherhood and love, were silent rhetorical challenges to the Confederate flag, a symbol of division and hate. There was a special rhetoric in the calculus book, the volume of Goethe and the biology text, which showed by contrast the animal ignorance and behavior of the taunters and spectators.[18]

By contrast the occupiers were much more diverse in their appearance and, for the most part, were indifferent to how they might appeal (or not appeal) to traditional sensibilities. One might say that, on average, occupiers were scruffy, messy, unkempt, and even dirty. This was obviously not true of all occupiers, and such stereotyping carries a trace of classism in which one is simultaneously deemed dirty, poor, and lazy. Such a perception makes it more difficult to accept occupiers' political claims. It should be acknowledged, too, that camping outside for an extended period inevitably produces an unkempt appearance.

Regardless of the reasons, occupiers' general appearance contrasts with that of the sitters: occupiers sat *outside* of, and thus challenged, corporate opulence and corruption; sitters assumed a normative middle-class appearance in the hopes of being accepted *into* the American system.

Emotional Comportment

Like appearance, the overall emotional comportment of the young sit-in demonstrators was polite, respectful, quiet, reserved, and deferring. This is true even in light of the disruptions they caused. It was the white racists who were upset and outraged, not the sitters. The sitters' overall emotional style reflects the practices of passive resistance and nonviolence, with the rhetorical intent of transforming the moral and political conscience of the oppressor. By contrast Wall Street occupiers were rowdy, angry, scrappy, disrespectful, and obnoxious. Sitters sat quietly, while occupiers occupied loudly. Sitters spoke with respect and reverence, while occupiers yelled and shouted. Sitters exhibited inner calmness, while occupiers flaunted outward indignation. In brief the rhetoric of each group embodied and provoked different forms of emotional experience.

However sitters' and occupiers' contrasting emotional styles did not necessarily translate into contrasting audience responses. Both movements were met with sympathy and anger. In fact the polite and respectful sitters experienced a far greater degree of repression and violence. It becomes obvious, then, that publicly protesting predominate ideologies provokes the possibility of negative backlash, regardless of one's emotional comportment. Challenging people's beliefs (about American exceptionalism, white supremacy, and capitalism) and socially conditioned behaviors (of segregation, social compliance, and consumerism) provokes defensiveness. This occurs even when audiences stand to benefit from the protesters' demands: whites could eliminate their emotional turmoil by accepting sitters' calls for racial equality, and America as a whole can become more economically democratic by accepting Occupy's call for politico-economic reform. In brief audiences blame the protesters—rather than the wider social structures—for their emotional dissonance. Such emotional reactivity then blinds people to the rational benefits of the proscribed social change.

Racial Composition

While both groups were multiracial, the sitters were overwhelmingly African American, and the occupiers were overwhelmingly Caucasian. The first is easy to understand given the fact that African Americans were targets of racial oppression and fought for their basic rights. However Occupy's inability to attract greater racial diversity posed a rhetorical problem—for example, Occupy's claims about fighting for the 99 percent were called into question.[19] In brief, where were the people of color?[20] This question and its answers are complex. Most official reports do indicate that Occupy was overwhelmingly white. However the methods of data collection were commonly conducted online and focused on Occupy NY. Particular questions thus arise: Do the poorest of the poor participate in online surveys? Does Occupy NY properly represent all Occupy locales? Is direct physical participation the same as support, interest, and investment?

It should also be acknowledged that racial composition is socially constructed; in other words it is an amalgamation of discourses repeatedly enacted over time resulting in a recognizable, though perpetually changing, style of racial identity. Race is obviously an important signifier of diversity given America's history of racial oppression, but race is not the sole indicator of diversity. Age, bodily ability, sexual orientation, gender, economic class, and political ideology are also important. It is thus possible to perceive occupiers as more diverse than the sitters since the latter consciously chose to present themselves in a normative manner: young, able-bodied African American students publicly performing traditional gender and heteronormative characteristics.[21] As Rebekah J. Kowal observes:

> By dressing, speaking, and acting as they did, the protesters performed their right to be served "as if" they were white, thereby "integrating" their black bodies into formerly white public space. By adopting characteristics of costume, speech, and manner that, in their particular social context, were marked as "white"—read "civility"—they performed the similarity of their bodies to the (symbolic and to a large degree fictional) white body. Read in this way, the protesters seem to have accommodated the racist assumption that black people had to prove that they could be "as if white" before being granted equal rights.[22]

However historical perspective is needed. The sit-ins were a precursor to Black Power and occurred years before gay liberation, second and third wave feminism, and the rise of identity politics. In many ways, then, Occupy reflects a contemporary emphasis on what we might refer to as the "diversities of diversity" —that is, understanding diversity in a diversity of ways. It is that same issue that motivates the question about people of color participating in the Occupy movement. As Angela Davis argues:

> Today, many of us speak effortlessly about intersectionality, thanks primarily to the work of women of color feminism. We can conceptualize these

issues not as discrete, disconnected issues whose relationship we have to me-
chanically orchestrate but, rather, as issues that are already in crosshatched,
overlaid, intersectional patterns. Class, race, gender, sexuality, ability, and
other social relations are not simplistically separate. They can never remain
uncontaminated by each other. So, when the OWS movement appeals to the
99%, which is constructed in relation to economic criteria, we ought to be
already aware that the class hierarchies that produce this differentiation between the super rich and the rest of us are already shot through with gender
and race and sexual hierarchies. . . .

How, then, do we produce a more complicated unity of the 99%, a unity
that does not erase the important internal differences? Difference can be
at the very heart of that unity rather than serving as an obstacle to unity.
Difference can serve as that which binds us all together. It was Audre Lorde
who insisted that it is not our differences that divide us. It is our inability to
recognize, accept, and celebrate those differences.[23]

Diversity of Self-Presentation

The emphasis on diversities of diversity leads to issues of self-presentation and
self-expression. For instance the sitters strategically decided to present themselves in a reserved and civil manner. In doing so the importance of individual
style was downplayed. Rhetorically this reads like an effort for collective gain
rather than an opportunity for individual expression. This allowed the sitters to
be perceived as a united front—one people, one movement, one goal. As Kowal
explains, the "protest organizers conventionalized/ritualized their behavior to
enhance the communicative aspects of the performance as well as to limit the
ambiguity of message"; the organizers wanted to "ensure the efficacy of communication through the repetition of patterns of speech and action."[24] Everyone
enacts the same rhetorical performance to delimit misinterpretation of the action. This is their strategic, agreed-upon rhetorical choice.

The Occupy Wall Street movement assumed no such strategy. One might
even guess that such a strategy would be contested if not outright rejected.
Consequently there was a much greater diversity of self-presentation among
occupiers—everything from hard hats and union patches to dreadlocks, khakis,
hoodies, dress shirts, baseball caps, nose rings, Converse Chucks, and steel-toe
work boots. The "ninety-nine percent" was visually presented as an assemblage
of difference rather than a unified mass. This had at least two implications. First
it helped account for the visual tension in the composition of occupiers: a diversity of subjectivities in light of a mostly white population. And second it helped

account for why Occupy was not perceived as a unified group with a unified message. The look of individual difference was read as a political incongruity.

Goals

The young sit-in activists fought for racial justice, while occupiers fought for economic justice. One can easily argue that these forms of justice are interrelated and that each group would fight for both forms of justice. This is particularly true as the civil rights movement became more radical and anti-capitalist in the mid- to late-1960s. Stokely Carmichael, who participated in the sit-ins and eventually became chairperson of the Student Nonviolent Coordinating Committee, once said some years later, "We want to economically destroy capitalism because capitalism goes hand-in-hand with racism and exploitation. Wherever capitalism has gone, those two characteristics are sure to follow, racism and exploitation."[25] Many occupiers made similar claims. For example Slavoj Žižek, an ardent supporter of Occupy, states: "Following a kind of Hegelian triad, the Western left has come full circle: after abandoning so-called 'class-struggle essentialism' for the plurality of anti-racist, feminist, and other struggles, 'capitalism' is now clearly re-emerging as the name of *the* problem. The first lesson to be learned is not to blame individuals and their attitudes. The problem is not individual corruption or greed, but the system that encourages you to be corrupt. The solution is not 'Main Street, not Wall Street,' but to change the system in which Main Street is dependent on Wall Street."[26]

Anti-capitalist sentiment constitutes a unique connection among sitters and occupiers. On the one hand, the rhetorical parameters of each movement were defined by differing goals: the sit-ins targeted legal segregation (racism), while Occupy targeted Wall Street (economic injustice). Nevertheless the movements share a common "collective economic identity." Occupiers rejected gross economic inequity and believed that alternative economic structures could benefit the majority rather than a minority. Likewise the sit-in movement began by targeting Woolworth—a profit-making enterprise. Black people could shop there but could not sit at the lunch counter. Sitters used their collective economic power to desegregate the store. As Stephen Schneider explains, "the collective identity found in sit-in protests was aligned with a collective economic identity that might have been less easily recognized. Nonetheless as boycotts continued and stores elected to shut rather than integrate their restaurants, this collective economic force became more and more apparent."[27] Racial equality was thus achieved, at least in part, by the fear of lost revenue. Ironically the Occupy Wall Street movement could not muster the same type of pressure point. This was largely due to Occupy's brief lifespan. Three months—September to

December—is not long enough to impact economic interest. However many occupiers argued that the fear of lost revenue motivated the sudden rash of camp evictions that began in mid-November. City mayors, fearing that occupiers would keep away holiday shoppers, coordinated their efforts to clear the occupations, making it safe to buy, spend, and consume.[28]

Long-Term Legislative Strategy

The young sit-in activists sought to change the public policy of legal segregation. Occupiers never advocated for a unified policy change. In many ways the act of occupying was the prefiguration of direct democracy and the (re)distribution of decision-making power. "People didn't come to pay homage to a celebrity as they would at a music festival, or to hear a speaker as they would at a political rally or church. They didn't come to witness a performance, they came to *be* the performance, and what they were enacting was a kind of unscripted political theater in which argument, polemics, complaint, proposals, and insights were experimentally exchanged."[29]

Similar things can be said for the civil rights activists: sitting in was the prefiguration of a racially desegregated society. However the difference between the two is this: the sit-ins were a strategy tethered to a larger legislative goal and plan; Occupy had no larger goal or plan—the occupation *was* the goal/plan. This helps explain, once again, the insider/outsider distinction embodied by and cast upon the sitters and occupiers respectively. The first sought acceptance into the system, while the second rejected the system; seeking acceptance can be aided by legislative efforts, while promoting rejection fundamentally excludes such a possibility.

Verbal Arguments

The early sit-ins, as well as the civil rights movement as a whole, focused on the contradiction between the "American creed and the American deed."[30] The founding documents of the United States argue that "all men are created equal." If America was to live up to its name, then it must outlaw segregation and recognize African Americans as full citizens entitled to equal rights. In brief sitters used the notion of American exceptionalism as an argument against legalized segregation. By contrast occupiers rejected American exceptionalism. Occupy intensified the negative and downplayed the positive of American society. In the eyes of occupiers, economic inequality and political corruption—as well as war, poverty, student debt, a broken healthcare system, an inflated prison system, and the like—are unexceptional and underachieving. Occupiers thus argued for wholesale change rather than specific policy reforms. At the surface the sitters' rhetorical challenge seems much easier to accomplish: America can live up to its name by making only one, albeit a major, change. This is much different from indicting the entire system. However, at the same time, racial tension sits at the center of American identity: slavery, the abolitionist movement, the Civil War, Reconstruction and post-Reconstruction, Constitutional amendments, Jim Crow laws, the Ku Klux Klan, Woodrow Wilson's White House screening of *The Birth of a Nation,* segregation of soldiers in two world wars, and finally, the civil rights movement.[31] When viewed in this light, the sitters' call for racial equality was as daunting as occupiers' call for economic structural reformation. In both cases the very inner workings of American society must undergo profound, fundamental change.

Sociohistorical Context

Many of these contrasts can be attributed to the sociohistorical context of each group.[32] The sit-ins began in the aftermath of World War II during a time of economic prosperity. America had fought off Nazism and became one of two world superpowers. The nation situated itself as the beacon of democracy in contrast to the communism of the Soviet Union. A cultural ethos of family, work, and patriotism permeated the American landscape. The overall rhetoric of the sit-ins —from appearance to argument—parallels the era's mind-set. That rhetoric changed later in the decade with the rise of Black Power, which coexisted with the hippie countercultural movement, the anti–Vietnam War movement, and women's liberation and gay liberation. The times, and thus the rhetoric of movements, were more radical. In many ways Occupy's rhetoric reflects that of the late 1960s rather than that of the sit-ins. This results, at least in part, from the events leading up to Occupy: the Iraq war in which no weapons of mass destruction were found; the long, drawn-out war in Afghanistan; overzealous antiterrorist rhetoric; the tragedy of Hurricane Katrina in Louisiana, during which fellow Americans drowned while the federal government and corporate America responded with nonchalance; an ongoing battle over same-sex marriage in which nonheterosexual citizens are still not fully equal; an economic recession; bank bailouts; the *Citizens United* case; rising economic inequality; overwhelming student debt; a lack of jobs; home foreclosures; a deflated hope in President Obama's progressive rhetoric; and a generation of youth raised in a networked society of instantaneous social media. It is no surprise, then, that the Occupy Wall Street's rhetoric was more messy than orderly, more scattered than linear, more insurrectional than strategic, more spontaneous than planned, and more indignant than inviting.

Similarities between the Sit-Ins and Occupy

Occupation of Public Space

The occupation of public space was central to both the Woolworth store sit-ins and Occupy Wall Street. This type of public act implicates others who are not even in that physical space. Writing letters to newspaper editors, lobbying officials, and delivering speeches all involve some form of public discourse that implicates a wider audience. However such acts can be construed as addressing particular recipients. Audiences outside of those recipients can psychologically distance themselves from the message. This is true even if the message is addressed to all Americans. However the contours of occupying public space are much more ambiguous, because no single recipient is addressed. Who is the intended audience? Whom is the message addressed to? Is there just one audience, such as Woolworth lunch-counter wait staff or Wall Street bankers? If that were the case, then why not speak to those people privately? Such rhetorical ambiguity establishes a condition for the possibility of self-reflection—one is called to conscience and invited to experience the message emanating from the occupation psychologically. How might *I* respond to those young African Americans who are asking for service? How might I respond if I were sitting there next to them? How might I respond as the store owner or the arresting police officer? One's beliefs, values, and practices are suddenly called into question. This is true even though one is not *specifically* addressed by the sit-in.

Occupy Wall Street was even more ambiguous, since it framed itself as an open forum—anyone could attend and participate, even Wall Street bankers. If this is true, then notions of us versus them begin to break down. On the one hand, such distinctions as the 1 percent versus 99 percent are rooted in brute facts of economic inequality. In 2009, for instance, the salary for an American CEO was 263 times that of the average American worker. That number was lower than normal due to the economic recession. In 2007 a CEO was earning 364 times more than the average worker. The ratio peaked in 2000 when it was 500 to 1. By contrast the pay ratio in 1980 was only 40 to 1, and in the mid-1970s it was 30 to 1.[33] On the other hand, the 1 percent versus 99 percent distinction was a discursive construction communicated through the corporeal rhetoric of a public occupation. In that context the distinction becomes metonymic for the failings of an entire system. In what world does a supposedly democratic system founded on the right to life, liberty, and the pursuit of happiness enable so few to have so much and so many to have so little? Such inequality is more representative of an exploitative plutocracy than a thriving democracy. This insight, which was the cornerstone of the Occupy Wall Street movement, implicates everyone, even the occupiers. That helps explain why people decided to occupy Wall Street—they were subtracting themselves from the current system to prefigure an alternative society. Occupy's rhetoric through subtraction exerts an ideological hailing, and people are called to recognize their compliance with a system of economic oppression. People then begin questioning themselves: Why am I not occupying? Do I support the material realities of economic inequality? Am I part of the problem or part of the solution? Why am I not fighting against this economic oppression that directly impacts my life?[34]

Multiple Locales

Occupy Wall Street is known as a decentered, networked phenomenon composed of multiple interlocking locales. The Woolworth store sit-ins were composed in similar ways fifty years earlier. This is most evident with the "movement centers" that existed throughout the South before the 1960 Greensboro sit-in. Those centers revolved around the black church and included official organizations such as the NAACP, CORE, and SCLC. These centers were rhetorically activated in the wake of the Greensboro sit-ins and acted as communication hubs that disseminated news, devised movement strategies, and trained activists in direct-action tactics.[35] The communicative activities of the centers enabled the sit-ins to spread to sixty-nine locales in the first two months and to nearly eighty locales within another four months.[36] Such rapid spread is even more astonishing given the early controversy over the sit-in tactic. Not everyone agreed, and the debate was often divided along generational lines. "The novel, extralegal sit-in method was mainly attracting puzzled frowns and widespread suspicion. Even the major Negro newspapers were reporting the sit-ins cautiously. They registered as a newfangled teenage rumble with a partially redeeming purpose. They were not controlled or approved by the adult civil rights organizations, and for that reason alone the NAACP Legal Defense Fund refrained from defending the first students arrested."[37]

Unlike the movement centers of the sit-ins, Occupy's rapid rise primarily relied on social media, which might account for its short lifespan. As Malcolm Gladwell argues, the "strong personal ties" produced by the face-to-face interaction of, say, movement centers, is much more sustainable and productive than the "weak mediated ties" produced by social media.[38] Either way the spread of the Occupy movement was unprecedented. One report listed 462 locations of Occupy-related activities,[39] and the "Day of Rage," which was organized approximately one month after the start of Occupy, involved eighty countries worldwide.[40] This rapid spread is perhaps best summarized by a Cairo protester whose sign read, "FROM TAHRIR TO OCCUPY OAKLAND AND THE USA, ONE GOAL: SOCIAL JUSTICE FOR ALL."[41]

Such rapid spread, whether it be manifested through Occupy or the sit-ins, constitutes a roving multiplicity—that is, a social force exerting an affective allure of attraction. That attraction is a form of corporeal rhetoric in which bodies beget bodies. People are not sitting home silently agreeing with the movement; instead they are moving into the streets and occupying locales. What begins as an occurrence of loosely connected events soon becomes a coherent phenomenon with a multiplicity of moving parts.

George Katsiaficas's notion of the "eros effect" is a helpful heuristic for explaining this phenomenon. "Such spontaneous leaps may be, in part, a product of long-term social processes in which organized groups and conscious individuals prepare the groundwork, but when political struggle comes to involve millions of people, it is possible to glimpse a rare historical occurrence: the emergence of the *eros* effect, the massive awakening of the instinctual human need for justice and freedom. When the *eros* effect occurs, it becomes clear that the fabric of the *status quo* has been torn, and the forms of social control have been ruptured."[42] Katsiaficas acknowledges that the conditions of industrialization and the global communications of radio, television, newspaper—and nowadays social media— are contributing factors. However he contends that these conditions cannot fully explain the alluring effect of spontaneous mass political awakening. Katsiaficas argues that a deeper, innate human phenomenon—*eros*—motivates these rapidly spreading mobilizations. If this is true, then one can argue that the eros effect is communicated through embodied rhetoric—bodies collectively acting in public attract other bodies into the fold of action, resulting in a groundswell of sudden activity.[43]

Direct Democracy and Suspicion of Hierarchies

The Occupy Wall Street movement was largely defined by its use of direct democracy and its rejection of hierarchies. The sit-ins followed similar values and practices, though not nearly as rigidly or dramatically. Iwan Morgan, commenting on the formation of the Student Nonviolent Coordinating Committee (SNCC), accentuates the point: "In many respects the new group was born as an anti-hierarchal organization that upheld the sovereignty of local activists to determine their own agendas to challenge Jim Crow in the communities. Giving expression to this outlook, veteran civil rights campaigner Ella Baker . . . perceived SNCC in an 'inclination towards *group-centered* leadership, rather than toward a *leader-centered pattern of group organization.*'"[44]

Embodying such directly democratic practice threatens the assumed naturalness of two American cornerstones: representative democracy and the interlocking hierarchies of boss-worker, teacher-student, politician-citizen, police-civilian, lawyer-client, and so forth. It is no wonder, then, that both the sit-ins and Occupy sent shockwaves throughout the American landscape. Many Americans, whether conscious of it or not, felt threatened not just by the politics but also, and more dramatically, by the practices of both movements. Intellectually grappling with ideas and arguments is not the same as actually seeing people practice alternative ideologies. Such viewing alters one's perception of not just the protesters but also the locations in which the actions are performed.[45] Woolworth was no longer a site of racial segregation but became a battleground for racial equality. Wall Street was no longer the epicenter of corporate dominance but became a springboard for insurrection. The changing perceptions of these locations then extend to America as a whole—it becomes difficult for Americans to see themselves and their country in the same way. To borrow from the Burkean terminology, large-scale terministic screens begin shifting, unsettling the overall cultural landscape.[46]

Goals

The goals of racial and economic justice were specific to sit-ins and to Occupy respectively. However the key focus was the same: to create a more socially just society. It is no coincidence that the sit-ins and SNCC contributed to the eventual rise of Black Power and that Black Power was based, in part, on the notion of intercommunalism—that is, the belief that each community should be self-determining while also sharing a sense of affiliation for all other self-determining communities. As the Black Panthers said, "All power to all the people." That slogan's ideological force prefigured Occupy's decentered network model. In other words there is a lineage of directly democratic practice running throughout radical-leftist-libertarian social movements. That lineage includes both the sit-ins and Occupy and relies heavily on the self-empowerment and rhetorical agency of direct actionist practice—one enacts something different in the here and now, thus inviting others to do the same.

Disruption and Production

The sit-ins sought to disrupt the practice of legalized segregation, while Occupy sought to disrupt the operations of economic inequality and political corruption. However disruption is also a form of (rhetorical) production.[47] Disrupting business as usual produces new experiences, social relations, subjectivities, and epistemologies, all of which produce the conditions for the possibility of a new society.[48] As sociologist AK Thompson argues, "Direct action is more than an effective and courageous means of resistance; it can be a potentially effective research practice and pedagogy."[49] In other words people learn by *doing* social change and political resistance. That learning is not only private and personal but also public and social. Audiences are affected by, and gain insights from, the disruption caused by the direct action. Audiences may not always understand the politics or philosophies of that action, but their experience of disruption calls attention to their taken-for-granted assumptions about the world. Such disruption may not constitute grand social change, but it does produce a crack in the tiny capillaries of the social body.[50] Judith Butler suggests such an insight when addressing Occupy Wall Street:

> I came here to lend my support to you today, to offer my solidarity for this unprecedented display of democracy and popular will. The people have asked, so what are the demands? What are the demands all these people are making? Either they say, there are no demands, and that leaves your critics confused, or they say that the demands for social equality and economic justice are impossible demands. And the possible demands, they say, are just not practical. If hope is an impossible demand, then we demand the impossible. If the right to shelter, food, and employment are impossible demands, then we demand the impossible. If it is impossible to demand that those who profit from the recession redistribute their wealth and cease their greed, then yes, we demand the impossible. But it is true that there are no demands that you can submit to arbitration here, because we're not just demanding economic justice and social equality; we are assembling in public, we are coming together as bodies in alliance; in the street and in the square, we're standing here together making democracy [and] enacting the phrase "We the People."[51]

Butler is arguing that doing the impossible makes the impossible possible. It is not surprising, then, that a general panic spreads throughout society, since people do not have a framework for understanding this new possibility. This relates back to the ambiguity of embodied rhetoric and the call to conscience. How do people make sense of something that is not yet sensible? In brief they make sense of it by doing it: they embody it and stumble, fall, and fumble along the way; the understanding comes after the doing. This process of embodying the uncertainty of one's politico-visionary rhetoric was followed by the Woolworth store sit-ins, which challenged the stranglehold of racial inequality, and by Occupy Wall Street, which challenged not just economic inequality but also the overall hegemonic discourse of Wall Street that says greed is good.

Conclusion

The differences between the Woolworth store sit-ins in Greensboro and Occupy Wall Street are numerous. However it is the similarities and overlaps that are more helpful for understanding the nature and function of both movements.

Those similarities can be classified into three unifying themes: empowerment, equality, and prefiguration. Sitters and occupiers sought to empower themselves and others. People taking matters into their own hands and choosing to occupy public space shifts the politico-rhetorical landscape, enabling those people to speak and act on their behalf. Such empowerment produces a particular type of equality that precedes and exceeds the specific goals of racial and economic justice. It is an equality in which power is equally distributed among all participants. As feminist activist/author Starhawk explains, this is a *power-with* rather than a *power-over.*[52] People work together to challenge and overcome an oppressive opposition, but they do so in a way that does not reinscribe wider social oppression. It is not about replacing one oppression with another but about removing the conditions that make oppression possible. This is no easy task, and there is a great debate within the direct-action tradition about the merits and pitfalls of such goals. However the basic purpose is to prefigure a different kind of society—as Butler claims, to make the impossible possible. These insights precede and exceed the parameters of the sit-ins and Occupy, and that is because of direct action—and the conjoining issues of empowerment, equality, and prefiguration—are a part of most if not all social movements. From labor strikes to courthouse kiss-ins, the underlying purpose is to materialize alternative realities in the name of social justice. Understanding the relationship between activism and the reality-creating process helps facilitate a general "social movement literacy."[53] Given the widespread confusion and emotional reactivity surrounding activism and direct action, this seems like a worthwhile project.

Notes

1. I should note that I was an active participant with OWS, specifically Occupy Philly. Much of this overview is derived from my intimate knowledge of the movement. However some helpful sources include the following: *Time,* ed., *What Is Occupy?*; Taylor and Gessen, *Occupy!*; and Byrne, *Occupy Handbook.*

2. Declaration of the Occupation of New York City; and Myerson, "How Do You Illustrate Corruption?"

3. For an excellent overview of Occupy's consensus decision-making process, see the video "Consensus (Direct Democracy @ Occupy Wall Street)."

4. In the wake of Occupy, there has been, for instance, growing movements for relieving student debt, resisting home foreclosure, and increasing fast food worker pay. Also, at the time of this writing, the Democratic Party has begun to discuss the possibility of increasing the national minimum wage. A one-to-one causal relationship cannot be drawn between Occupy and these movements and issues. But it is safe to assume that Occupy has had an influential effect.

5. Gordon, "Dark Tidings," 254.

6. A-Infos News Service, "What Is Direct Action?"

7. Sharp, *Politics of Nonviolent Action,* 64.

8. Graeber, *Direct Action,* 203.

9. Gordon, *Anarchy Alive!,* 17.

10. Ibid., 18.

11. Lehn, "Liminal Protest," in this collection.

12. Watts, "Wade in the Water," in this collection.

13. A quick online search will produce numerous sources for understanding Anonymous and virtual direct action.

14. DeLuca, "Unruly Arguments"; DeLuca, *Image Politics*.

15. Ritchie, "Sit-In," 22.

16. See the following sources for examples of how the media discussed the violence of OWS: "'Occupy Wall Street' Protests Turn Violent"; "Occupy Oakland." For scholarly discussion on these and related issues, see Scott and Smith, "Rhetoric of Confrontation"; DeLuca and Peeples, "From Public Sphere to Public Screen"; Best and Nocella, *Terrorists or Freedom Fighters?*

17. Branch, *Parting the Waters*, 274.

18. Ritchie, "Sit-In," 23.

19. See these sources as examples: Cordero-Guzman, "Mainstream Support for a Mainstream Movement"; Sen, "Race and Occupy Wall Street"; Patton, "Why African Americans Aren't Embracing Occupy Wall Street"; Sciullo, "Social Justice in Turbulent Times"; Berman, "Occupy Wall Street Actually Not at All Representative."

20. This very question was raised more than a decade ago in a landmark essay among social movement participants. Martinez, "Where Was the Color in Seattle?"

21. It should be noted that nonheternormative identities were involved, at least with the wider civil rights movement. Some of the more famous examples include Bayard Rustin, James Baldwin, Pauli Murray, and Lorraine Hansberry. See "Role of Gay Men and Lesbians in the Civil Rights Movement."

22. Kowal, "Staging the Greensboro Sit-Ins," 149.

23. Davis, "Critical Refusals and Occupy," 436–37.

24. Kowal, "Staging the Greensboro Sit-Ins," 140.

25. Senate Committee on the Judiciary, Testimony of Stokely Carmichael.

26. Žižek, "Occupy Wall Street," 77–78.

27. For more, see Stephen Schneider's essay, "Nothing New for Easter," in this collection.

28. Cherkis, "Occupy Wall Street Monitored."

29. Greenberg, "On the Meaning of Occupation," 265–66.

30. Riches, Civil rights Movement, 13–14

31. For a concise overview of this history, see Riches, introduction.

32. This relates, at least in part, to the notion of the "rhetorical situation." See Bitzer, "Rhetorical Situation."

33. Anderson et al., "Executive Excess 2010."

34. For the notion of ideological hailing, see Althusser, "Ideology and Ideological State Apparatuses."

35. Morris, "Black Southern Student Sit-In Movement," 753.

36. Ibid., 756; Morgan, "New Movement," 5.

37. Branch, *Parting the Waters*, 276.

38. Gladwell, "Small Change."

39. Mother Jones News Team, "Map: Occupy Wall Street."

40. Sherter, "Days of Rage."

41. Tharoor, "Hands across the World," 26.

42. Katsiaficas, *Imagination of the New Left*, 10.

43. Del Gandio, "Extending the Eros Effect."

44. Morgan, "New Movement," 8.

45. For a similar argument about the rhetoric of action and location, see Endres and Sendra-Cook, "Location Matters."

46. Burke, *Language as Symbolic Action.*

47. For notions of rhetorical/communicative production, see Greene, "Rhetoric and Capitalism"; Greene, "Communist Orator"; Del Gandio, "Rethinking Immaterial Labor"; May, *Soapbox Rebellion.*

48. For an interesting approach to this insight, see Medina, *Epistemology of Resistance.*

49. Thompson, *Black Bloc, White Riot,* 60.

50. For similar arguments see Del Gandio, "Performing Nonhuman Liberation"; Perucci, "What the Fuck Is That?"

51. "Judith Butler at Occupy Wall Street."

52. Starhawk, *Truth or Dare.*

53. "Social movement literacy" is a concept that I am currently developing. It follows in the tradition of civic literacy, critical literacy, and media literacy. The basic goal is to facilitate the public's ability to read properly, understand, think about, and discuss accurately the nature and function of social movements

THE LONGEST SIT-IN

David Worthington

On April 4, 1968, Rev. Dr. Martin Luther King Jr. was assassinated as he stood on the balcony of the Lorraine Motel in Memphis, Tennessee. Almost twenty years later, on March 2, 1988, after she resisted eviction for nearly three months, police physically removed the last resident of the Lorraine Motel, Jacqueline Smith.[1] Smith fought the eviction, claiming that plans to turn the Lorraine into an $8.8 million museum would "force poor people out of the neighborhood." Before sheriff's deputies arrived to carry out the eviction, Smith told reporters: "My family is here and I have a home, but that's not what I want. . . . If I can't live at The Lorraine, I'll camp out on the sidewalk out front."[2] And camp out on the sidewalk she did: as of June 2012, a sign at Smith's protest site claimed that she had been there for twenty-four years and ninety days.[3] In what began as a protest against eviction from her home, and fearing the worst from the new museum, Smith has undertaken the longest, and most likely the last, sit-in of the civil rights era.

This essay explores Smith's protest as a counter-memory to the official King/civil rights narrative that is embodied by the existence of the National Civil Rights Museum and the narratives contained within it. Taking rhetoric in a general sense as a process that leads auditors toward judgment about how to remember the past, this case specifically represents a contest over how to think about and recall the civil rights era as well as King. The essay begins with a discussion of how memory and counter-memory can lead to a more complex consideration of the past. Second I discuss the Lorraine Motel and the arguments that Smith makes about the museum as a means of constructing somewhat divergent narratives of King. Finally I examine how the protest acts as a material counter-memory to the official narrative told in the museum.

Memory and Counter-memory/Counter-monuments

Memory

As sites that demonstrate, exhibit, and propagate national memories, museums and their environs are rich rhetorical texts that scholars have only recently begun to examine in regard to the important relationship they have in constructing contemporary memory and accompanying notions of reality, truth, and knowledge.[4] Roy Rozenzweig and David Thelen underscore the significance of museums and memorials as sites for understanding and cultivating national identity when they assert that "Americans put more trust in history museums and historic sites than in any other site for exploring the past."[5] Museums, when studied as rhetorical texts, draw together scholarly work from a variety of academic disciplines that implicate the power of collective memory.

For all the intellectual scholarship dedicated to "memory studies," however, the notion of collective memory remains slippery. Collective memory is part of the burgeoning interdisciplinary movement broadly encapsulated under the rubric of memory studies. The study of memory falls into different linguistic classifications; thus public, collective, cultural, mass, historical, community, and national all reference the phenomenon of memory outside the individual. Each term also provides varying, and sometimes subtle, emphasis on understanding memory. These valences are important because they shape the boundaries of how memory is publicly understood. For example Marita Sturken defines "cultural memory" as grounded in the intersection and interplay between material objects and the past; for Bruce Gronbeck, collective memory is "socialized memory" and the product of widely understood and accepted cultural myths; and John Bodnar distinguishes between "national" memory (pertaining to "official" state memories) and "vernacular" memory (located and negotiated in local and regional communities).[6]

Museums are important sites for producing and reproducing national narratives and ideologies. They are the consequence of culling history from artifacts that are subsequently deployed to create narratives about the past that inform the discourse about how the present is understood. In a sense museums are the face of the public archive; as such they often stand for the official history of a community, region, or nation. Increasingly museums have become sites of struggle over the ideological formation of the past. For example the Smithsonian's Air and Space Museum in Washington, D.C., was wracked with controversy when the Smithsonian made plans to display the Enola Gay in the context of artifacts and narratives from both the American and the Japanese perspectives on the dropping of the atomic bomb on Hiroshima.[7]

Significantly, museums are often sites where the past is solidified in public consciousness. Museums incorporate ideas and reflections about the past that later come to serve as the foundations for public understanding of history. These foundations are important to understanding the past and how it interacts with the present, because they tend to solidify public discourse into entrenched narratives. Thus Elaine Heumann Gurian argues that museums are culture-bound, in that visitors must share cultural history to comprehend the narrative presented, and they are where visitors confront a "one-time indelible impression to which all subsequent exposures will be referenced."[8] Museums are also a locus of cultural myths that animate and narrate public consciousness. These national myths, Nina Tumarkin argues, are especially significant in nations (like the United States) whose origin is in revolution, because myth acts to justify the creation story and "bolster the legitimacy" of the state itself.[9]

It is important to remember that while museums are often contested in the planning stages, once these structures are complete, so too, in a sense, is their concretization of the past. Put another way, museums close history; a museum's very existence posits that this history is at an end. The act of preserving the Lorraine Motel "as it was" on April 4, 1968, suggests that this day was the endpoint of the civil rights movement. Using the "old" signs and the "old"—but not historically relevant—automobiles and preserving rooms as they were on the day of King's assassination is a punctuation point to the end of the movement.[10]

Counter-memory/Counter-memorials

In one sense counter-memory is a misleading way to discuss Jacqueline Smith's sit-in. For Michel Foucault counter-memory is not simply a different way to remember; rather it is a complete transformation of the way we remember the past.[11] And yet by Foucault's logic the poor, homeless, and illiterate will almost certainly remain outside the discursive space where remembering may be most pertinent and necessary. Whether the story of an Afghani villager or a homeless woman on the street in Memphis, the economic and cultural power to create a transformative site of counter-memory is unlikely. However the capacity to engage in a vernacular construction, one that does not transform but suggests alternatives to the "settled" historical narrative, not only is within the grasp of the disempowered, but the fractured counter-memory may also well be the only way for them to resist and retell their version of history. Thus when James Young argues that counter-memory (in the form of a "counter-monument") "refers not only to its own physical impermanence, but also to the contingency of all meaning and memory—especially that embodied in a form that insists on its eternal fixity," space is carved out to account for vernacular counter-memory.[12]

Counter-memorials, located at memory sites such as the National Civil Rights Museum, challenge visitors to find ways to reconcile what they learn (or perhaps just see)—inside the museum from official sources—with what they see outside from vernacular sites.[13] Cecily Harris argues that counter-memorials "are the antitheses of conventional monuments—not permanent, didactic, grandiose or celebratory. Rather, they turn on its head the hierarchical relationship between artist and viewer, forcing the spectator to be an active participant in the formation and transmission of memory."[14] Indeed if museums are, as they often claim, sites that seek to teach and instigate contemplation about the past, then the synthesis of competing narratives should not trouble them; it should propel more considered thinking to find reconciliation.

The Lorraine, the Museum, and the Protest

Located behind the facade of the original Lorraine Motel, the National Civil Rights Museum (NCRM) is located on Mulberry Street in what was at the time of Dr. King's assassination, and for many years both before and since that event, a largely African American section of Memphis, Tennessee. The Lorraine was important in Memphis because in the Jim Crow South it was one of the few places that would lodge African Americans. The motel was popular among musicians who visited Memphis and hosted luminaries such as Louis Armstrong, Sarah Vaughan, and Nat King Cole.[15]

According to D'Army Bailey, the founder of the NCRM, after the King assassination the Lorraine "continued to operate, although, frankly, the clientele were prostitutes mostly and just sort of transient trade. They had maybe eight or ten weekly tenants here. It was on hard times."[16] The motel went into bankruptcy and was bought by Bailey's group in 1988. He notes that while the motel deteriorated in the years after the assassination, the motel's previous owner, Walter Bailey (no relation), had maintained King's room as a "shrine."[17]

Completed and opened in 1991, the NCRM's original cost was $9 million.[18] Additionally in 1999 the museum purchased the former Canipe's Amusement store and the rooming house across the street from the museum, from where James Earl Ray fired the fatal shot.[19] Titled "Exploring the Legacy," an annex was opened in this space as part of the museum complex—at the cost of $11 million—in 2002. The museum completed a $27 million renovation to make it "more interactive" as of its reopening on March 1, 2014.[20] Money to support the museum and develop its exhibits has come largely from the state, deep pockets, and corporate sources. The *Memphis Commercial Appeal* reports on funding that "about $23 million of those costs have been raised so far through major contributions, including $5 million from the Hyde Family Foundations, $4.95 million from the state, $2.25 million from FedEx and $1 million each from the Ford Motor Company Fund, Links Inc., the City of Memphis, Southeastern Asset Management Inc. and the Longleaf Partners Fund."[21]

The NCRM exhibits are laid out temporally in a series of rooms that start with a history of slavery, race relations, and oppression in North America. This exhibit is followed by a series of displays on the struggles and triumphs of the civil rights era. The museum includes Jim Crow literature, "colored only" signs, and a Ku Klux Klan hood. The museum narrative inexorably leads to April 4, 1968, via a series of exhibits that delve into major civil rights actions such as the Montgomery Bus Boycott, lunch counter sit-ins, Freedom Rides, and finally the Memphis sanitation worker's strike.[22] The crescendo of the museum is when visitors stand behind glass next to room 306, where King was staying on April 4, looking out at the spot on the balcony where he fell.[23] The museum narrative is both triumphalist and tragic: struggle, death, oppression, and success all lead toward the inexorable victory of the civil rights movement in its fight against discrimination and toward equality but just as inexorably toward the death of the movement's most important figurehead.

As noted above, Smith's protest began when the Lorraine was evacuated to begin the massive renovation that transformed the motel into the museum. The exact site of her sit-in has changed over the years. Initially moved to the sidewalk outside the Lorraine, she was later—again by sheriff's deputies—moved across Mulberry Street near what is now the entrance to the "Exploring the Legacy" annex.[24] Bernard J. Armada explains the importance of this location, noting that Smith had placed herself "at the precise temporal point of the museum's emotional climax—the balcony and King shrine—where visitors were confronted with two competing rhetorical visions: the museum's lamentation of King's death on the one hand, and Smith's indictment of the museum's economic exploitation of King's death site on the other."[25] However in 2002, when the annex construction began and the city ceded the section of Mulberry Street between the Lorraine and the annex to the museum, Smith was again forced to move from the front of the motel/museum, this time to the southwest corner of Mulberry and Butler Streets, where her protest site is currently located.[26]

Though visitors and critics may be impressed by Smith's protest—and many are—her quest is quixotic. With the National Civil Rights Museum renovations completed in 2014, almost $50 million has been committed to the complex. There is little doubt that Smith is sincere in her desire to close the museum and use the complex as a community center or housing for the poor; however the likelihood of the museum acceding to Smith's protest is nil. Consequently if closing the museum is an impossible goal, the question for a rhetorical understanding of the sit-in becomes, toward what judgments does Smith's protest direct visitors?

Smith's critique focuses on several objections to the National Civil Rights Museum: (1) that King would object to the amount of money spent on a memorial, Money that could otherwise assist the poor; (2) that the museum is a catalyst for gentrification and has resulted in the displacement of poor blacks as upscale condominiums take the place of affordable housing for the poor; (3) that the NCRM is used as a location for parties and celebrations, which Smith claims is analogous to dancing and drinking at atrocity sites such as Auschwitz or "Ground Zero" in New York City; and (4) that the "tone" of the museum encourages division rather than calling for unity.[27] Specifically she argues that by displaying the darkest elements of Jim Crow, the museum teaches impressionable young people the mechanisms of subjugation rather than uplifting and unifying them.

The central claim against the museum is that the cost of acquiring, renovating, and operating the site would be better spent, and more consistent with King's philosophy, if it were used to house the homeless and help the poor.[28] It is clear that Smith is well schooled in King's philosophy; indeed her website offers an extensive timeline of King's life from birth to death and several pages of quotations from his speeches.[29]

The juxtaposition of King's ideal of economic justice with Smith's protest against the museum argues that visitors should reconsider the wisdom of accepting the official museum narrative. As a site that enacts the vision of a counter-memorial, this would be much more powerful if it did more than present a counter-narrative. Smith's desire to see foundational change is enacted only in the claim that there should be a change that serves the poor. Nowhere does the protest site imagine how an alternative Lorraine would look or whether the museum could act as a fulcrum to leverage a more active response to the needs of the poor. Indeed the crux of Smith's protest is an indictment of the status quo. However, unlike other sit-ins that called for workable changes (i.e., the integration of lunch counters), Smith's goals remain unreachable. Her protest calls for others to enact the change that she craves much as a powerful other decided what to make of the Lorraine in the first place; her calls for change come not from a movement that she leads—or is a member of—but rather for some unnamed force to take charge. In this she obviates the central thematic of the civil rights movement to ensure rights so individuals can make their own decisions and work to build collectively.

Another element of the protest site is location/style. As noted Smith's site has moved since she first began protesting in 1988. Currently at the corner of Mulberry and Butler Streets, she is engaged by visitors, generally, from one of two points. Since the museum is located south of the main downtown area of

Memphis, museumgoers either travel south on Mulberry Street from the corner at Huling Avenue or after walking through Founders Park, which is directly across Mulberry Street from the National Civil Rights Museum. The second way that visitors tend to encounter Smith's protest site is from the NCRM parking lot, which is just south of the museum via the Butler Avenue entrance.

What visitors see when they encounter the site looks like a homeless encampment.[30] At various times Smith has had a sofa, a large desk, a table with literature, and a large umbrella as a sunshade and cover from inclement weather. John Branston of the *Memphis Flyer* explains that since 1988 she has "encamped, more or less continuously, on the sidewalk with her blue tarps, desk, posters, worldly possessions, and well-worn books."[31] It is clear from watching people who go to the museum that there are several responses to Smith's protest by those aware of her site. Some avoid her site and move circuitously to avoid it. Some look at what the signage says but display an unwillingness to approach. Others walk up and look at the signs without speaking. Others ask questions and listen as Smith speaks or wait to take photos with or of Smith. Smith takes this opportunity to explain to people why they should boycott the NCRM and often suggests they view her website for further explanation.

Smith's appearance underscores her argument that the museum has contributed to gentrification that, she claims, has displaced poor blacks from the area.[32] The museum, as an anchor for economic development that includes an arts district, "new" restaurants, and, most important, condominium development that caters to upper middle class, often white, buyers, has displaced those who lived in the area.[33] Thus the area where King was able to find haven in the 1960s has now priced his base constituency out of the market. Indeed her concerns seem to be coming to fruition. In 2011–12 the City of Memphis moved forward with a program tentatively titled "Triangle Noir," which will develop a twenty-block section of the city that includes the NCRM into a "super-tourist district."[34] Despite the social invisibility that confronts many homeless people, Smith does, in fact, draw audiences who are invited to recognize her as the embodiment of her principal argument: the NCRM, as a tribute to King, is more concerned with its edification than it is with helping those King was most concerned with at the time of his death, the poor.

This is the point where Smith's protest could have been most consequential. In the temporal gap between closing the Lorraine in 1988 and the mid-2000s gentrification of the area near the museum, the neighborhoods were ripe for development. Early reports about the museum complained that walking the several blocks to it from the uptown area was considered a dangerous journey. Rather than assuming the continuation of a permanent underclass of poor for the area, this would have been the moment to use King's legacy to push for gentrification that favored the historic residents of the area—an effort that might make real King's efforts to empower the poor.

The most volatile claim that Smith makes is that the NCRM, which she views as sacred ground, is used to host parties and receptions, which she likens to celebrating at Ground Zero in New York City or at Auschwitz.[35] Smith cites at least one such party on her website: in 2008 the Memphis River Arts Festival used the NCRM as a performance venue for jazz, gospel, Motown, and Lindy Hop music.[36] Also Nike hosted a reception at the site in 1998.[37] The imagery she uses is an Auschwitz atrocity photograph and a Ground Zero picture of the ruins of the World Trade Center. Her efforts to identify the King assassination locale with other atrocity sites call to mind the promises that echo through both the Shoah and the post-9/11 United States: "Never Again" and "Never Forget." This is entirely consistent with Smith's central argument that the museum violates King's ideals and aspirations. However the juxtaposition of hundreds of thousands deadat Auschwitzor thousands deadas a result of the September 11, 2001, attacksto the singular death at the Lorraine, no matter how significant King was, is jarring. In many ways it denies the vitality and energy of the civil rights movement, which was animated by song. Music, whether the spirituals of the early movement or the more commercially oriented songs of the later years, invigorated, motivated, and bonded civil rights workers whether they were singing or listening.[38] John Lewis recalls "some of the deepest, most delicious moments of my life were getting out of jail . . . and let[ting] that music wash over me, just wash right through me. I don't know if I've ever felt anything as sweet."[39] The irony of Smith's complaint is that using the NCRM to stage festivals where there is no segregation or overt racism illustrates the success of the movement. The idea that Americans can—at this of all sites—transcend the tragedy committed on these grounds is suggestive of what is possible in terms of wrenching the museum out of the maudlin ethos that is so often associated with sites of public death.[40]

The final argument that Smith advances is that the tone of the museum teaches the wrong message to impressionable youth. Smith is at a distinct disadvantage as she advances this argument, because she has never been inside the museum. The boycott that she urges on visitors is grounded in her refusal to enter the site. Thus her condemnation of the museum exhibits and narrative, which her website claims is a story of violence and aggression, depends on what is, in legal language, hearsay evidence.[41] Despite her lack of direct observation, she argues that the museum contains exhibits that are inappropriate for impressionable youths, who may take the wrong message from the museum: learning the mechanisms to oppress rather than a lesson more consistent with King's central message of peace and tolerance. She asks, "Do we really want our children to gaze upon exhibits from the Ku Klux Klan, do we need our children to experience mock verbal abuse as they enter a replica bus depicting the Montgomery bus boycott"?[42] Put in Burkean terms, Smith's argument is about identification; and in her pessimistic view, children are more likely to identify with the KKK than with the various groups that protested and overcame the hatred of the Klan. This argument belies a contemporary culture where young people are exposed to many more threatening ideas and images in their day-to-day lives and across multiple media outlets.[43]

The fact that she has never been inside is also problematic because her critique is specific to the exhibits inside and is, at least to some extent, wrong. For example there is no "exhibit from the Ku Klux Klan," though there is a Klan hood and anti-integration/pro-segregation materials displayed on the walls of the "background" exhibit.[44] On her website Smith's antipathy toward those who go into the museum is illustrated in stark terms. She tells the story of persuading former president Jimmy Carter to avoid the museum, only to have him return two and a half years later to accept a "Freedom Award" from the NCRM. When he returned to visit Smith's site, she "could not shake his hand on principle and . . . she was ashamed of him."[45]

Taken as a whole, Smith's arguments about excesses and problems with the NCRM are coherent and commonsense. It is easy and satisfying to imagine that King would have preferred that money spent on this museum go to the poor. Gentrification and economic inequality is a serious problem across the United States; it does seem unseemly to "celebrate" at the location of national tragedy; and nobody wants children to learn the wrong lessons from any museum, let alone this one. Yet as much as the arguments hold together, there is the nagging idea that despite their cogency, they are not worth spending a lifetime fighting against.

Material Counter-memory at the Lorraine Sit-ins take multiple forms, most commonly as an act of civil disobedience, such as lunch-counter sit-ins to protest segregation and Jim Crow laws, campus sit-ins to oppose conscription or war, and efforts to undermine university militarization or complicity with political issues such as apartheid. Direct-action sit-ins draw attention not only to particular issues but also to the material space that often embodies the problem. Thus when protestors occupied "whites only" lunch counter seating at department stores in Nashville or Greensboro, the rhetoric—writ broadly in word, image, and song—captured the argument against segregation as well as pointing directly to the corporate and civic bodies that enabled and enacted Jim Crow.[46] It was the physicality of those protests that most vividly animate historical memory. Jacqueline Smith's protest seems to follow this tradition as she attempts to influence visitors to boycott the NCRM. Indeed it is the materiality of her presence at the protest site—day after inexorable day—that most powerfully conforms to the public memory of and tactics deployed by "authentic" civil rights protestors and activists.

The body, particularly the black body, is central to the imaginary of United States memory of the civil rights movement. I think it important to heed the caution of Christine Harold and Kevin Michael DeLuca against romanticizing the black body, when they note that "lynchings served as a kind of racial terrorism, anchoring white supremacy in a mutilated black body."[47] Likewise romanticizing the violence committed against protesters similarly belies the real pain and suffering that protests often entailed. However with this caution in mind, it is still fundamental to civil rights memory that we imagine the body in trauma as the material object that most forcefully carried forth the argument for change. Protestors used their bodies—and those of racial victims—as the central fulcrum for affecting public opinion about race, Jim Crow laws, civil rights issues, and social justice. Images of the battered body of Emmett Till, the stoicism of James Meredith and the "Little Rock Nine" among hate-filled white faces, the fractured humanity of those set upon by police dogs and fire hoses, and fingers pointing toward the sniper's nest as King's already lifeless body lay splayed across the balcony of the Lorraine Motel are among the events that illustrate the collective imagination of Americans who remain mired in the problem of race in the United States. Moreover the sacrifice and exhibition of the violated body had material consequences; Sasha Torres explains that "there is wide consensus that Birmingham and Selma contributed considerably to the passage of the Civil Rights Act and the Voting Rights act. . . . These televisual moments are linked not just by the power of their impact, but also by a specific element of their content: the intersection of African American bodies and the violent tactics of southern police."[48]

Jacqueline Smith's protest is interesting if we consider her arguments. However it is enticing to place her materially into the argument; in some ways Smith interpellates the bodies of protestors that visitors have seen (or will see in the museum) in documentaries, photographs, and other media. While she was not in Greensboro sitting in at the lunch counter, she has surrounded herself and enacted the topoi of civil rights protests: signs that demand change, a stern countenance that stays focused on change, and a counter-narrative that tells a distinctly different story than that of the establishment. The most forceful evidence of Smith's link to the glory days of the civil rights movement is that she has been sitting in for so long. The determination exemplified by Smith's presence at the museum during construction, expansion, and renovation is a formidable signifier of the commitment of this one person. On the one hand, when coupled with the relentless count-up clock that documents the length of the protest, Smith is framed as the embodiment of King's politics. On the other hand, her continued protest becomes an indictment of those who view the civil rights movement as a moment of history. Her continued sit-in is a demonstration (in both senses of the word) that what John Paul Jones III calls "street politics" can continue to urge memorial spaces—or at least those who visit memorial spaces—to think reflexively about the flexibility and subtlety of the stories they tell.[49]

There remains a nagging suspicion that Smith's protest is appealing because it is an indictment of a scattered and weak contemporary civil rights movement. In a world where her protest seems to echo the 1960s, there remain battles to be fought. The National Civil Rights Museum cannot end with the assassination, because racial injustice did not end with King's death. Republicans across the United States are advancing and in some cases enacting voter rights restrictions.[50] Stop and frisk policies remain in effect, and "driving while black" episodes remain endemic.[51]

Smith also acts as a reminder of the visibility and public voice that once characterized the civil rights movement. Masses of people protesting segregation, Jim Crow laws, and violations of human dignity once captured the attention of the nation and made prospects for the future seem hopeful. While many prominent members of the civil rights era moved on to party and organizational politics within the governmental structure they once protested, Smith's presence is itself an exhibit of the form and content that animated the movement. For some who visit her, this alone is a valuable purpose behind her protest.[52] Indeed as many leaders of the civil rights movement shifted their politics into other outlets, memory of the movement began to stultify into a grand modernist narrative of events starting with the *Brown v. Board of Education* decision and ending with King's assassination. In this interpellation Smith is an echo of those earlier civil rights workers. While they dedicated their efforts and blood toward real change, Smith tilts at her windmill with inflexible determination. In that sense she is unlike King, who when faced with long odds of success in Albany, Georgia, in 1961–62 withdrew and adopted new goals and tactics, saying, "You don't win against a political power-structure where you don't have the votes."[53] He went on to note that "our protest was so vague that we got nothing, and the people were left very depressed and in despair."[54] Thus in her rigidity against insurmountable odds, Smith's determination seems to ring hollow.

Smith's protest magnifies the nostalgic tension. Specifically her call for an ongoing civil rights movement that attends to the concerns of the poor, addresses gentrification in the neighborhood, and encourages more active consideration of ongoing civil rights issues obliterates the simple narrative of having overcome in the past. Present and past, official and vernacular, and most forcefully ownership of memory all compete for authority and authenticity, particularly about what visitors take away from the museum site. There is little evidence that the Smith sit-in has had any real effect either at the museum or on the public's perception of ongoing civil rights issues. As noted earlier effective counter-memorials incorporate those who are displaced, unrepresented, and yet have a stake in how and to whom history is told. While Smith assumes the posture of the displaced, it is difficult to see her as more than a self-appointed stand-in for the underrepresented. She has no clear constituency who respond to her calls for change; indeed there is little evidence that the protest she engages in is about anybody else. Her website and her protest site are both regular stops for media that find a reason to write about the museum, but the few lines dedicated to Smith rehearse the same arguments she has made for more than twenty-five years without any progress toward fundamental change with or without the museum.

Public memory of the civil rights sit-ins is animated in the popular imagination as the brave acts of selfless students using their bodies to right a dramatic and clear wrong perpetrated against African Americans. Indeed one of the features of the sit-in movement that was clear and compelling was the resolution sought by the protestors: equality of access, service, and opportunity. It was clear what was being denied—and what the solution was—when merchants accepted cash for goods from black shoppers yet denied them concurrent access to food and drink service. In Jacqueline Smith's protest, it is hard to discern what outcome she envisions. While she calls for shuttering the Lorraine as a museum and reimagining it as a site for community action, unlike previous sit-ins there are no clear and reachable objectives; indeed one argument might posit that Smith's protest is more about Smith than it is about making substantive change.

It is worth briefly contemplating why Smith has been unsuccessful with her sit-in in light of the productivity of early sit-ins during the civil rights era. In Greensboro, North Carolina, and Nashville, Tennessee, and then across the South, protestors focused on several strategies that ultimately allowed for and motivated change. In a rhetorical sense, the Greensboro and Nashville sit-ins both took advantage of temporal opportunities: the kairotic moment when the nation was ready to be pushed to confront endemic discrimination and intimidation across the United States. Following on significant events—both strategic successes and widespread publicity of tragedy—the *Brown* decision; the murder of Emmett Till, with the subsequent publicity that surrounded the trial, acquittal, and confession of the killers; and the Montgomery Bus Boycott all created a national atmosphere that made resistance plausible. When combined with careful and targeted organizing that prepared protestors for the resistance they would meet, alerted the press to media events, and provided political support for the protestors, the age was ripe for political and cultural change.

In Memphis, Smith's protest remains a determined act without demonstrable metrics for success. Without significant public support, with scattered and rare attention from the press, and lacking dramatic demonstration of tortious action by the museum or the City of Memphis, she remains, largely alone, on the sidewalk looking for small successes. Unlike the sit-ins of 1960 that realized material and philosophical change for the people of Greensboro and Nashville —and in a larger sense for the nation—in Memphis the museum continues to grow, expand, and redevelop without significant public concern over the realization, or failure to realize, King's vision for racial and economic justice.

Jacqueline Smith's body has become the counter-memorial to the National Civil Rights Museum. In her presence, physicality, and discourse, she embodies her protest, an epideictic engagement of a rhetoric of blame. Condemnation of what is designed to be the definitive commemorative site of the civil rights era engages visitors who attend the protest site in an alternative vision of what the resources behind the museum could do and calls into question the post-Vietnam American impulse to commemorate in static rather than dynamic forms.

Conclusion

Edwin Black envisions the hermeneutic function of rhetoric in the metaphor of the translator. For Black the translator is linked to the hierarchical formation of epistemological dissemination. As a minister presents an exegesis of a holy text, authority figures across cultures select and interpret history as a means of constructing and disseminating myths and memories that shape public perception of the state. Black puts it this way: "Remembering and forgetting are linked to disclosure and certainty. . . . They are the *enthymematic premises* on which arguments may be constructed" (emphasis added).[55]

The consequence, of course, is that the past then becomes a distillate; the richness and complexity of memory are boiled down to leave only the parts of the past that lack controversy and serve the state in its self-aggrandizement but not in its function to act as a buffer against dangerous tendencies. Thus, Black argues, "historic myths that intoxicate the popular imagination are composed of salient, representative characters and events distilled in a process that purifies their motives and moral qualities, and exchanges complexity for dimension and depth for definition. . . . We fabricate our history, true enough, but not entirely of synthetic yarns. We make our collective past, even as Blanche DuBois made her personal past, through selection and interpretation, a phylogenesis in which some few events are brought to great prominence and many other events are suppressed."[56]

One important consequence of any cultural artifact, and this is especially true in the case of museums, is that the past often calcifies into immutable facts. Narratives, once enshrined in museums, take on the status of officially sanctioned truth. However museums can best serve the public and democratic processes when they remain supple and open to question and criticism. Actively calling into question our moral certainty that echoes out of a deeply cut inscription of memory, counter-narratives create, and remind us of, counter-memories that complicate truth claims about the past. Bringing contrary stories to the discussion will broaden the way we understand links between past and present. Hence the probity of Black's claim about the creation of enthymematic premises can better prepare the public to grapple with complex issues in the present.

The National Civil Rights Museum claims that its mission is to chronicle "the culture and lessons from the American Civil Rights Movement and explore how this significant era continues to shape equality and freedom globally"—in other words to stimulate people to take action.[57] It is ironic that a woman who has never visited the museum, yet lives her life in constant tension with its existence, takes the most vigorous "action."

In the end Smith's counter-memorial does not tell us much that is different about King. Both the National Civil Rights Museum and Smith extoll King as a mythic figure for righteousness and erase the mundane parts of the movement. Ted Dreier puts it well when he explains that "King, the human being, is eclipsed by the hero, the great man, the martyr bleeding on the balcony."[58] The NCRM is a place where, in Dreier's words, "There is no place in the liturgy for the mundane complexities of King's earthly life . . . no room, in other words, for the challenges and vulnerabilities that reveal his humanity and call us, despite our own shortcomings, to act in his spirit."[59] Both the NCRM and Smith articulate similar visions about the good that King accomplished and both lament the terrible loss that the nation suffered when he was assassinated. If there is a struggle here, it is a squabble over how to commemorate King; Smith seeks concrete action not only in the now but also specifically in the here of the Lorraine site. Other locations for the outreach to the poor and disenfranchised are unacceptable due to the sacred space that she—and many others—assign to the Lorraine/NCRM site. Smith has spent years decrying the museum as a place where King's dream is lost because the museum does not embrace an agenda of action—including job training, feeding the hungry, and fighting poverty —that she would approve. The past is important and can teach us much about ourselves and instruct us in how to approach and avoid important issues. However, for it to do so, we must wrench ourselves away from viewing museums, memorials, and counter-memorials as epideictic sites of praise and blame and redirect our energies toward building a future out of prior accomplishment. After twenty-five-plus years of protesting, there is little doubt that Jacqueline Smith is a determined woman who will challenge anybody who crosses her in her effort to fight the museum. It is at least tempting, then, to imagine what she might have accomplished if she had turned her energies to helping the poor, establishing shelters, and feeding the hungry.

Notes

1. "Eviction Empties Motel Where Dr. King Died," *New York Times* March 3, 1988, accessed March 10, 2013, http://www.nytimes.com/1988/03/03/us/eviction-empties-motel -where-dr-king-died.html?emc=eta1

2. Ibid.

3. David Worthington, Field Notes, July 2012.

4. See for example: Tamar Katriel, "Our Future is Where Our Past Is: Studying Heritage Museums as Ideological and Performative Arenas," *Communication Monographs* 60: 69–75. Tamar Katriel, "Sites of Memory: Discourses of the Past in Israeli Pioneering Settlement Museums" *Quarterly Journal of Speech* 80(1): 1–20.

5. Roy Rozensweig and David Thelen, *The Presence of the Past: Popular Uses of History in American Life*, (New York: Columbia University Press, 1998): 105.

6. Marita Sturken, *Tangled Memories: The Vietnam War, the AIDS Epidemic, and the Politics of Remembering* (Berkeley: University of California Press, 1997): 42–3; Bruce Gronbeck, "The Rhetorics of the Past: Argument and Collective Memory" *Doing Rhetorical History: Concepts and Cases,* ed. Kathleen J. Turner (Tuscaloosa: University of Alabama Press, 1998): 47–60; John Bodnar, *Remaking America: Public Memory, Commemoration and Patriotism in the Twentieth Century* (Princeton, NJ: Princeton University Press, 1992): 13–20.

7. Edward T. Linenthal and Tom Engelhardt, *History Wars: The Enola Gay and Other Battles for the American Past,* (New York: Metropolitan Books; Henry Holt, 1996): 140–70. Museums are also sites where the past is represented for contemporary use. See, for example: Ivan Karp and Steven Lavine, *Exhibiting Cultures: The Poetics and Politics of Museum Display,* (Washington, D.C.: Smithsonian Institution Press, 1991); Richard Handler and Eric Gabler, *The New History in an Old Museum: Creating the Past at Colonial Williamsburg,* (Durham, NC: Duke University Press, 1997); Bryan Hubbard and Marouf Hassian, "Atomic Memories of the *Enola Gay*: Strategies of Remembrance at the National Air and Space Museum," *Rhetoric and Public Affairs* 1(3): 363–85; Barbara Kirshenblatt-Gimblett, *Destination Culture: Tourism, Museums and Heritage,* (Berkeley: University of California Press, 1998).
   Controversy, of course, is not limited to the "Enola Gay" exhibit. As Homer Neal, Vice-President for Research at the University of Michigan put it: "A far from complete list of examples might include the 'West As America' exhibit in the National Museum of American Art; the 'Science of American Life' exhibit in the National Museum of American History; the recreation of a slave auction at Colonial Williamsburg; and various controversies surrounding aspects of the Columbus quincentenary." Homer Neal, "Presenting History Museums in a Democratic Society," *The University Record* (Ann Arbor: University of Michigan, 1995), [Online] http://www.umich.edu/~urecord/9495/April17_95/perspect.htm.

8. Elaine Heumann Gurian, "Noodling Around with Exhibition Opportunities," *Exhibiting Cultures: The Poetics and Politics of Museum Display* eds. Ivan Karp and Steven Lavine (Washington, D.C.: Smithsonian Institution Press, 1991), 181.

9. Nina Tumarkin, *The Living and the Dead: The Rise & Fall of the Cult of World War II in Russia* (New York: Basic Books, 1994), 8.

10. I refer here to the presence of the Lorraine Motel sign that stands outside the museum; preserved to look as it did in 1968 as does the room King was staying in when he was assassinated. In addition, the museum has parked 1960s era automobiles in the Lorraine parking lot to better create the "atmosphere" of late 1960s Memphis.

11. Michel Foucault, *Society Must Be Defended: Lectures at the College de France,*

1975–6, eds. Mauro Bertani and Alessandro Fontana, trans. David Macey, (New York: Picador, 2003), 8–9.

12. James E. Young, *The Texture of Memory: Holocaust Memorials and Meaning* (New Haven, CT: Yale University Press, 1993), 48.

13. Readers might be familiar with other vernacular sites; an example of such is the "Rolling Thunder" site near the Vietnam Veterans Memorial.

14. Cecily Harris, "German Memory of the Holocaust: The Emergence of Counter-Memorials," *Penn History Review* 17 (2010): 1–26.

15. "The Story of the Lorraine Motel in Memphis," *Yahoo Contributor Network*, accessed October 7, 2013, http://voices.yahoo.com/the-story-lorraine-motel-memphis-14303 .html

16. Ibid. However, this is an assertion that Jacqueline Smith rejects. She claims that the Lorraine was a place that housed the poor and that it was not in deep disrepair.

17. Amy Goodman, "National Civil Rights Museum: The Motel Where Dr. King was Shot Today a Museum that Preserves his Legacy," *Democracy Now!*, accessed March 3, 2013, http://www.democracynow.org/2007/1/15/national_civil_rights_museum_the_motel

18. Michael Sheffield, "Fighting For Civil Rights Tourism," *Memphis Business Journal*, May 2, 2012, accessed Oct. 18, 2012, http://www.bizjournals.com/memphis/print-edition/2012/03/02/fighting-for-civil-rights-tourism.html.

19. Ibid.

20. Ibid.

21. Michael Loller, "National Civil Rights Museum in Memphis Will Have Presence During One-year Hiatus," *Commercial Appeal*, November 1, 2012: http://www .commercialappeal.com/news/2012/nov/01/national-civil-rights-museum-in-memphis-will -one/?print=1

22. Worthington, Field notes, July 2012.

23. The museum removed room 307 so visitors can see into the King room as well as look out at the place where Dr. King was shot.

24. "Protester Is Removed From King Motel Site," *New York Times*, July 17, 1990, accessed March 10, 2013, http://www.nytimes.com/1990/07/17/us/protester-is-removed-from -king-motel-site.html?emc=eta1

25. Bernard J. Armada, "Memory's Execution: (Dis)placing the Dissident Body," in *Places of Public Memory: The Rhetoric of Museums and Memorials* ed. Greg Dickinson, Carole Blair, and Brian L. Ott (Tuscaloosa: University of Alabama Press, 2010), 221.

26. Ibid. Also see Armada for excellent analysis of the importance of the position of the protest site.

27. To view the claims, readers can both visit the site or look at Smith's website, http:// www.fulfillthedream.net/pages/mlk.boycott1.html.

28. The first element of the permanent exhibit at the museum is the film, "The Witness: From the Balcony of Room 306" which discusses the 24 hours leading up to the assassination including discussion of Dr. King's "I've Been to the Mountaintop" speech delivered the evening of April 3rd. In that speech, King emphasizes that the sanitation worker's strike is important precisely because of economic justice issues. See: Adam Pertofsky, "The Witness from the Balcony of Room 306," (2008); For Dr. King's speech see: http://www.american rhetoric.com/speeches/mlkivebeentothemountaintop.htm

29. These quotations are not attributed on Smith's website. Searches reveal that they come from varied speeches including Dr. King's 1964 Nobel acceptance speech and his 1959 "Speech Before the Youth March for Integrated Schools." The one excerpt that is attributed is from the "I've Been to the Mountaintop" speech.

30. The details are at best fuzzy, but Smith for years lived at the site although today she often sleeps off-site with friends. Armada notes that Smith draws a distinction between herself and the homeless since she chose to live on the sidewalk (222). John Branston, "The Longest Occupier," *The Memphis Flyer,* November 2, 2011, accessed March 10, 2013, http://www.memphisflyer.com/CityBeat/archives/2011/11/02/the-longest-occupier.

31. Branston, "The Longest Occupier."

32. This is not to suggest that Jacqueline Smith is untidy, unkempt or dirty. To the contrary, she carries none of the stereotypical visage of the homeless. Like many in the Civil Rights Movement, looking good is important to Smith.

33. John Paul Jones, III, "The Street Politics of Jackie Smith," in *The Blackwell Companion to the City,* ed. Gary Bridge and Sophie Watson, (Oxford: Blackwell, 2000), 453.

34. "Coffee Break: Memphis Wants Suggestions for Project," The Commercial Appeal, March 16, 2012, accessed March 13, 2013, http://www.commercialappeal.com/news/2012/mar/16/coffee-break-city-wants-suggestions-for-project/

35. fulfillthedream.net; http://www.fulfillthedream.net/pages/mlk.boycott1.html.

36. See: http://www.memphissound.com/events/river-arts-fest/2008-Entertainment-ALL.html.

37. "Nike Board Hosts Reception at National Civil Rights Museum in Memphis," accessed, March 13, 2013, http://www.thefreelibrary.com/Nike+Board+Hosts+Reception+at+National+Civil+Rights+Museum+in+Memphis.-a053022523

38. Lewis, John with Michael D'Orso. *Walking With the Wind: A Memoir of the Movement.* (Harvest Books, 1999), 268–69.

39. Ibid., 169.

40. I am thinking here of both Ford's Theater in Washington, D.C. and the Fourth Floor Museum at the former Texas School Book Depository in Dallas, Texas. Both of these sites seem to move well beyond the tragedy that occurred there and engage in various elements of the carnival.

41. National Civil Rights Museum, [Online] http://www.civilrightsmuseum.org/Visitor-FAQs.aspx?pid=5&spid=59#sthash.1JDZl6Xa.dpbs

42. fulfillthedream.net; http://www.fulfillthedream.net/pages/mlk.boycott1.html.

43. Kenneth Burke, *A Rhetoric of Motives* (Berkeley: University of California Press, 1969), 21.

44. Worthington, *Field Notes,* April 2013.

45. http://fulfillthedream.net/pages/mlk.protest3.html.

46. Lunch counter integration in Nashville was not solely the product of sit-ins. As John Lewis makes clear in his memoir of the movement, it was a mass march following the dynamiting of civil rights lawyer Alexander Looby's home that led to the end of whites-only seating. Lewis, *Walking With the Wind,* 109–111.

47. Christine Harold and Kevin Michael DeLuca, "Behold the Corpse: Violent Images and the Case of Emmett Till," *Rhetoric and Public Affairs,* 8 (2005): 23.

48. Sasha Torres, *Black, White and In Color: Television and Black Civil Rights,* (Princeton, NJ: Princeton University Press, 2003), 8.

49. Jones, "The Street Politics of Jackie Smith."

50. The Brennan Center for Justice reports that in 2013 laws requiring voter identification, restricting early voting, limits on third party registration, ending election day registration, limiting the restoration of voting rights, and making it more difficult for students to vote have been enacted and introduced in various states. Jerry Goldfeder and Myrna Perez, Brennan Center for Justice at the New York University School of Law, "After 'Shelby County' Ruling, Are Voting Rights Endangered?," See http://www.brennancenter

.org/analysis/election-2013-voting-laws-roundup and also: http://www.brennancenter.org/analysis/after-shelby-county-ruling-are-voting-rights-endangered.

51. Ongoing policy for "Stop and Frisk" can be found [Online] http://www.cnn.com/2013/10/31/justice/new-york-stop-frisk/; a good overview of "Driving While Black" police stops can be found [Online] http://www.washingtonmonthly.com/magazine/january_february_2014/ten_miles_square/driving_while_black048283.php?page=all.

52. See: https://iggyz.com/?p=1603.

53. *Autobiography of Martin Luther King, Jr.,* The Martin Luther King, Jr Research and Education Institute at Stanford University, http://mlk-kpp01.stanford.edu/index.php/kingpapers/article/chapter_16_the_albany_movement/.

54. Ibid.

55. Edwin Black, "Secrecy and Disclosure as Rhetorical Forms," *Quarterly Journal of Speech,* 74 (1988): 139.

56. Aristotle argues that the purpose of rhetoric is directed to those "listeners as are not able to see many things all together or to reason from a distant starting point" so that audiences might more easily follow complicated arguments. However, I am suggesting here, and throughout this project, that the enthymemes should be considered, at best, too simple. See *Aristotle On Rhetoric: A Theory of Civic Discourse,* trans. George A. Kennedy, (New York, Oxford University Press, 1991) 1357a—12.

57. NCRM website: http://www.civilrightsmuseum.org/Mission-Facts.aspx?pid=9&spid=20#sthash.j4WdhpFn.dpbs.

58. Ted Dreier, "Remembering the Movement: A Question for the National Civil Rights Museum," *Truthout,* July 8, 2013, accessed October 6, 2013, http://www.truth-out.org/speakout/item/17439-remembering-the-movement-a-question-for-the-national-civil-rights-museum.

59. Ibid.

AFTERWORD

Chiseling at a Fossilized Memory—Connections, Questions, and Implications

Keith D. Miller

Challenging and reinvigorating our understanding of the civil rights movement, scholars in this collection reclaim and interpret often overlooked (or underestimated) protests that contributed to a groundswell of dissent that eventually precipitated historic civil rights laws. In order to grasp these writers' contributions, it might prove helpful to consider four ways people have access to events and accounts of events from civil rights movements: (1) directly exploring the plethora of demonstrations for racial equality staged before and soon after the middle of the twentieth century; (2) investigating the dramatization of (some of) these campaigns by the national news media; (3) grasping the enshrinement or erasure in popular memory; and (4) understanding historians' accounts. Partly overlapping and partly diverging from the others, each of these instantiations of the civil rights movements merits examination.

The gap between the first and second approaches is notable. Numerous African American newspapers—including the excellent, nationally distributed *Chicago Defender* and the *Pittsburgh Courier*—covered race relations extensively from the 1920s onward.[1] However apart from showering attention on Eleanor Roosevelt and Jackie Robinson during the 1940s, mainstream news outlets remained largely inattentive to race before the U.S. Supreme Court issued its watershed *Brown v. Board of Education* decision in 1954. One huge reason for this neglect was the widespread failure of major white newspapers and television networks to hire African American reporters, including very capable, veteran journalists who wrote for the *Defender,* the *Courier,* and other black periodicals.[2]

The *Brown* ruling, the murder of Emmett Till, and the Montgomery Bus Boycott awoke the slumbering mainline media. Then, beginning with the lunch counter sit-ins in Greensboro and Nashville in 1960, white reporters covered more or less continual protests throughout the next eight years. During that span, while pressed by deadlines, journalists coped with racial flashpoints that rapidly shifted from one city to another. Then there were the beatings. While assaulting peaceful demonstrators, white supremacists sometimes tried to prevent exposure of their crimes by assailing journalists and photographers as well.[3] Confronting highly fluid and dangerous situations, many reporters and photographers cogently—and sometimes brilliantly—conveyed to the nation the stout, largely nonviolent African American resistance to the daily belittlement and grotesquerie of Southern segregation.[4]

At the same time, the press corps seriously filtered and dramatically oversimplified the racial struggle. Operating in a largely patriarchal culture, the almost entirely male journalists gravitated to male leaders, such as Medgar Evers and (especially) Dr. Martin Luther King Jr. While doing so, reporters frequently downplayed or outright erased the pioneering leadership of such women as Ella Baker, Dorothy Height, Pauli Murray, Fannie Lou Hamer, Daisy Bates, Lola Hendricks, Casey Hayden, and Diane Nash.[5]

Today the national memory of the civil rights movement largely enshrines a King-centered narrative. Consider the many schools, community centers, boulevards, and freeways named after King; an annual national holiday celebrating his birthday; and the larger-than-life marble statue of him that stands beside the National Mall in Washington, D.C.[6] History textbooks frequently—at times almost exclusively—invoke him as a synecdoche for the movement. Of the thousands of primary texts produced during the African American awakening of the twentieth century—including literally hundreds of scintillating speeches and scores of trenchant memoirs and autobiographies—many students listen only to his "I Have a Dream" speech and read only his "Letter from Birmingham Jail." And they often ignore his crucial sources—Frederick Douglass, Ida B. Wells, Archibald Carey, Harry Emerson Fosdick, Vernon Johns, C. L. Franklin, and Benjamin Mays—whose texts he mirrored and adapted in "I Have a Dream" and many other orations. Nor do they consider his extended effort to reconceptualize the poetry of Langston Hughes.[7]

Hated by many during his lifetime, the now-lionized King obviously proved significant. But unfortunately the nation's generally laser-like focus on him ignores a whole series of protests—including many in New York City and one led by his father in Atlanta—during the 1930s, 1940s, and 1950s that were seldom relayed by national news outlets but that prepared African Americans to stage the extremely well-publicized demonstrations of the 1950s and 1960s. The King-centered national memory also obscures numerous racial campaigns between 1955 and 1964—the Little Rock Nine, lunch counter sit-ins, Freedom Rides, Ole

Miss, and Freedom Summer—in which white segregationist violence dominated newspaper headlines in the United States and across the globe. Each of these efforts assaulted the conscience of the nation and occurred either largely or entirely without King. The now-normalized King-centric narrative also omits other important protests at the time, including a campaign that Gloria Richardson sparked in Maryland to pressure Attorney General Robert Kennedy, a campaign that Lindsay Harroff explains in this volume. Further, even King's greatest triumphs—in Montgomery, Birmingham, and Selma—were initially spurred by largely unsung leaders, including (but not limited to) JoAnn Robinson and E. D. Nixon in Montgomery; Fred Shuttlesworth, N. H. Smith, Charles Billups, and Lola Hendricks in Birmingham; and Bernard Lafayette and Amelia Boynton in Selma.

By concentrating so heavily on one person, the national memory further screens and further skews the already screened and already skewed version of the civil rights movement that the male-oriented, often beleaguered news media rushed to the public during the late 1950s and the 1960s. What David Worthington, in this volume, calls the "official," King-centered memory produces what Casey Malone Maugh Funderburk and Wendy Atkins-Sayre here aptly term the "forgetting process." Contributors to this volume replace the process of forgetting with a process of inquiry. While reviving largely forgotten instigators of a mass movement, they also join Jacqueline Dowd Hall in challenging its reified, historical periodization into a "civil rights era" that allegedly lasted between 1955 and 1968. Sadly such a periodization appears to imply counterfactually that African Americans remained silent between the almost ninety years that separate President Lincoln's assassination from the *Brown* decision. Those who blithely reiterate this periodization often even neglect the achievements of Mary McLeod Bethune and Eleanor Roosevelt, the feats of the Tuskegee Airmen, and Jackie Robinson's ballyhooed integration of Major League Baseball.

The rigidity of this reified periodization means that numerous salient, scholarly accounts—such as Stephen Schneider's examination of the Highlander Folk School in Tennessee—enrich and surprise those fortunate enough to read them. Activists' memoirs also overturn the standard narrative. To encounter Pauli Murray's *Song in a Weary Throat* and scholarly treatments of her life is to learn that she lobbied Eleanor Roosevelt during the 1940s and undertook ceaseless trailblazing for racial and gender equality throughout the 1960s and 1970s before becoming an Episcopal priest in the 1980s.[8] To read Dorothy Height's *Open Wide the Freedom Gates* is to discover her astonishingly lengthy push for human rights from the 1930s into the years of Barack Obama's presidency. To open *Hands on the Freedom Plow*, a collection of memoirs by women of the Student Nonviolent Coordinating Committee (SNCC), is to meet many who pressed for racial and gender equality during the 1960s and continued their dissent—often widening it to include protests against poverty and war and in favor of Chicano/a rights and gay rights—unimpeded over the decades after King's death. Like Murray and Height, these women—and many other activists as well—never for a moment thought that the movement only occurred when television cameras showed up. Many who created the civil rights movement did so long before the "civil rights era" began in 1955 and believed—and today still believe—that it never ended at all. Refusing to relinquish agitation, today some veteran activists are vigorously protesting restrictions of voting rights and recent acts of police violence against African Americans.

By agitating not only against injustice but also against the calcified periodization of their movement, nonviolent veterans from the 1960s raise several questions: Is that movement defined by those who generated it? Or by the mainline media, which largely ignored events before *Brown* before spotlighting race between 1955 and 1968? What grants reporters and textbook authors the authority to wrest a movement away from its creators to define, periodize, and freeze it? Other questions also arise: Given the nature of group dynamics, how could any one person—no matter how captivating—adequately encapsulate or symbolize a mass movement? Don't many people and much rhetoric combine to propel a national struggle? Moreover if people misunderstand this signature movement, how will they learn to generate grassroots efforts to end climate change, overcome poverty, end mass incarceration, embrace refugees, and mothball nuclear weapons?

The sit-in chapter of the familiar narrative focuses on four young African American men at an F. W. Woolworth lunch counter in Greensboro, North Carolina. As Diana I. Bowen explains here, the iconic stools and lunch counter at Greensboro are now so coveted that they have been separated into two sets of artifacts—one enshrined at the International Civil Rights Center and Museum in Greensboro and the other showcased at the National Museum of American History in Washington, D.C. Related by Judith Hoover in this volume, another often noted sit-in episode occurred in Nashville almost simultaneously with the one in Greensboro. Marilyn DeLaure explores an *NBC White Paper* about Nashville that was broadcast coast to coast. Nashville reverberated mightily when, as Roseann M. Mandziuk notes here, one of its well-trained young participants, James Bevel, later spurred children in Birmingham to undermine the "piety" and "propriety" that buttressed the intolerable status quo. Also, in contrast to the standardized narrative, some scholars here relate sit-ins before Greensboro and Nashville that served as harbingers for later dissent in Greensboro, Nashville, and elsewhere. David Molina recalls a "Double Victory" sit-in that Murray led in Washington, D.C. in 1943. Victoria J. Gallagher, Kenneth S. Zagacki, and Jeffrey C. Swift analyze a sit-in staged in Durham, North Carolina, in 1957. Joshua Phillips adds his examination of sit-ins organized in St. Louis between 1948 and 1954. Stephen Schneider concentrates on unrest that began in Louisville in 1959, and Sean Patrick O'Rourke explores what he terms a "dynamic, multifaceted rhetorical trajectory" of activism that began in Greenville, South Carolina, in 1959.

Greensboro and Nashville did appear to spark the almost immediate instantiation of parallel demonstrations throughout much of the South. The sit-ins *did* spread—to use the phrase of Lesli K. Pace and Sean Patrick O'Rourke— "like wildfire." However by ignoring much earlier, parallel racial dissent, the grand, official narrative does not begin to explain how that could have happened.

Richard Gregg claims that nonviolent tactics enable activists to reverse an opponent's powerful, physical aggression, thereby neutralizing that opponent. In his words, "nonviolent resistance acts as a sort of moral jiu-jitsu . . . causing the attacker to lose . . . moral balance."[9] As Melody Lehn astutely explains in this volume, Eleanor Roosevelt performed an ingenious act of jiu-jitsu in Birmingham when, refusing to sit in a "whites-only" section of a large room, she instead placed her chair in an aisle that divided the segregated assembly. By silently rejecting the racist seating arrangement, Roosevelt confounded and neutralized Commissioner of Public Safety Bull Connor, a hate-filled segregationist. Despite his hair-trigger temper, not even Connor would arrest the president's wife. In line with Gregg, Gene Sharp explains the process that he terms "political jiu-jitsu": "Nonviolent discipline combined with persistence against violent repression causes the adversaries' repression to be exposed in the worst possible light. This, in turn, may lead to shifts in opinion and then to shifts in power relationships favorable to the nonviolent group."[10]

Following Eleanor Roosevelt, subsequent sit-in dissidents used the physical force of bigoted police and out-of-control hooligans to create public sympathy for their cause. In various cities protestors' thoughtful, disciplined jiu-jitsu also created what Gallagher, Zagacki, and Swift (following Leland Griffin) call an "emerging rhetorical trajectory." In St. Louis jiu-jitsu fostered what Phillips describes as an "emerging counterpublic"; in Louisville jiu-jitsu sprang from what Schneider calls "micro-mobilizational" work. However, why didn't nonviolent jiu-jitsu work everywhere?

Both Molina and Schneider emphasize what Schneider terms "the kairos of the public accommodations battle," that swelled with each successive protest before cresting at the end of the lengthy congressional battle over what became the Civil Rights Act of 1964. Pivotal in creating the emerging rhetorical trajectory was what Schneider terms "bodily rhetoric." Whereas martial arts are physical arts, moral jiu-jitsu involves both verbal and physical performance. Protestors used language—to orate, write, conduct press conferences, pray, and sing—and their bodies to sit in, march, and picket. Also they performed nonviolent jiu-jitsu through the bodily rhetoric of absorbing jailings and beatings—a rhetoric conveyed nationally through newspaper articles, photos, and television images. As William Lawson explains here, Anne Moody and other polite, well-dressed activists in Mississippi appealed through their willingness to suffer humiliation from mustard-throwing white hooligans while remaining at their lunch counter and refusing to retaliate. Lawson analyzes the impact of Fred Blackwell's photographs of the scene to provide a "transformative experience for the viewer" while bestowing "mythic status" on the protest by communicating the dissenters' bodily rhetoric.

In another essay included here, Rebecca Bridges Watts explains how, in 1964, Hosea Williams and others tested a less familiar version of bodily rhetoric by conducting a "swim-in" at a segregated motor lodge in St. Augustine, Florida—a protest that the lodge operator countered by dropping acid into the swimming pool. As Watts remarks, Williams's creative version of bodily rhetoric gained far more publicity than did King's by-then familiar—and, therefore less newsworthy —gesture of being arrested for integrating the restaurant of the lodge.

I suggest further investigations, including a rhetorical examination of the Alabama Christian Movement for Human Rights (ACMHR). Founded in 1956, it choreographed the Birmingham campaign of 1963. For four long years before the *New York Times* broke the national silence about racist cruelties in Birmingham and seven years before the children's marches of 1963, the ACMHR held sizable, exuberant, weekly rallies for civil rights orchestrated by an extremely devoted core group of ministers and laypeople. Although middle-class African Americans shunned these rallies, Fred Shuttlesworth, N. H. Smith, Charles Billups, Lola Hendricks, and other trailblazers managed to attract large numbers of janitors, maids, and other working-class blacks to alternating churches every Monday night. Unnoticed by whites outside Birmingham, several years of these energetic Monday-night rallies—not Shuttlesworth by himself, as is sometimes claimed—enticed King to launch a campaign in Birmingham. Amazingly, despite being tortured by the Ku Klux Klan and ceaselessly arrested, Billups continued his participation. Equally amazingly, despite a string of unsolved church and house bombings also conducted by the Klan, crowds continued to rally joyously at the weekly gatherings. The undimmed enthusiasm there created a rhetorical trajectory that culminated during the critical months of April and May 1963. Then, as the nation recoiled in horror, Bull Connor accosted black children with sharp-toothed police dogs and powerful sprays from water cannons. A key question is: How could African American organizers sustain weekly rallies from 1956 through 1960 with no indication whatsoever that the dozing national press would *ever* pay attention to Birmingham?

Second, I propose diachronic rhetorical investigations. Here Jason Del Gaudio analyzes diachronically by juxtaposing lunch counter sit-ins of 1960 against Occupy Wall Street of 2011 and 2012. Another diachronic exploration could tie James Baldwin's heated eloquence during the 1960s to that of Ta-Nehisi Coates in 2015. An additional diachronic perspective might emphasize sit-in activists' well-dressed bodies and utterly dignified manner about the respectability of anti-lynching crusader Ida B. Wells, who wore prim Victorian dresses that flowed from neck to ankle. Another diachronic rhetorical analysis could relate the protests of the well-attired Frederick Douglass against segregated northern trains during the 1850s to the protests of well-attired Freedom Riders against segregated southern buses in 1961. Further studies could also reveal significant rhetorical threads that connect abolitionism to twentieth- and twenty-first-century racial struggles.[11]

Third, I suggest explorations of Michael Klarman's argument that, in civil rights cases, the U.S. Supreme Court weighed not only constitutional theories and legal precedents but also evolving public opinion.[12] Fourth, I applaud Heather Ann Thompson's recent, exhaustively researched account of the Attica prison riot of 1971. I also salute Lisa Corrigan's new study of the relationship between the prison experience and the new black radicalism of the late 1960s and the 1970s. The connection between prison experiences and many manifestations of African American protest rhetoric certainly warrants further scholarly attention. Fifth, I echo Pace and O'Rourke's call, in their introduction to this volume, for additional scrutiny of the national memory of African American protests. Sixth, I encourage researchers to notice that, in her contribution to this volume, Mandziuk is implicitly pointing toward further use of rhetorical theories grounded in the study of religion, such as Kenneth Burke's guilt-redemption cycle, to understand bodily rhetoric. Such theories might also prove useful in interpreting the rhetorical process of transforming murder victims (e.g., Medgar Evers, Malcolm X, Viola Liuzzo, and King) into martyrs and some of them into icons.

Seventh, I urge rhetorical scholars to join the superb political scientists Erica Chenoweth and Maria Stephan in investigating the victories and failures of many nonviolent movements around the globe during the last roughly ninety years. Fortunately Chenoweth and Stephan break sharply with the conventional wisdom among many political scientists who continue to reiterate Thucydides and Machiavelli decade after decade to justify the cynical assumption that tyrannical governments are inevitable and absurd wars unstoppable. Along with their predecessor Gene Sharp, Chenoweth and Stephan have only begun the comparative analysis of worldwide nonviolent movements, an analysis that is essential to grasp how and why nonviolent campaigns sometimes triumph and sometimes languish. Further, like Sharp, they employ a secular framework for understanding nonviolence. This entire body of analysis provides a valuable alternative to the insistently religious explanations of nonviolence offered by Mahatma Gandhi, Cesar Chavez, Desmond Tutu, King, and Fannie Lou Hamer.

Encouraged by the outstanding scholars in this book, by Maegan Parker Brooks (who examines Hamer), Dave Tell (who analyzes the memory of Emmett Till), by Chenoweth and Stephan, and by activists around the globe, other researchers who study persuasion, identification, counter-identification, African American feminism, and Critical Race Theory can contribute to this evolving, intellectually invigorating discussion of nonviolent movements and social change. As an older researcher, I am thrilled that so many more members of the rhetorical community are now choosing to probe African Americans' centuries-old efforts to shove the principle of racial equality into American life. Will more join the discussion? Is it possible that experts in political science, history, religious studies, and other disciplines—and even members of the public—will listen? Like those who, despite persecution, exulted during the Birmingham mass meetings, we can always hope.

Notes

1. Michaeli, *Defender.*

2. Roberts and Klibanoff, *Race Beat,* address both the paucity and the vapidity of white newspapers' accounts of African American life and suffering before (and sometimes after) 1954. One of the few African American reporters who did write for a white newspaper was the superb Ted Poston of the *New York Post.* For a collection of his astute reporting on race relations, see Poston and Hauk, *First Draft of History;* for an account of his life, see Hauke, *Ted Poston.*

3. Roberts and Klibanoff, *Race Beat,* depict the beatings of reporters by white mobs in Little Rock, Arkansas, in 1957 and throughout much of the 1960s.

4. For a compilation of the best journalism about the movement, see the two volumes of *Reporting Civil Rights.*

5. For important statements by the female pioneers, see Height, *To Open Wide the Freedom Gates;* Murray, *Song in a Weary Throat;* Bates, *Long Shadow of Little Rock;* Mary King, *Freedom Song;* and Holsaert et al., *Hands on the Freedom Plow.* For outstanding scholarship on female trailblazers, see Bell-Scott, *Firebrand and the First Lady,* and Gilmore, *Defying Dixie* (on Murray); Ransby, *Ella Baker and the Black Freedom Movement;* Brooks, *Voice That Could Stir an Army* (for Hamer); and Olson, *Freedom's Daughters* (for an overview).

6. For a fascinating, new account of the effort to establish a King Holiday in Arizona, see Stewart, *Victory Together.*

7. See K. Miller, *Voice of Deliverance;* K. Miller, *Martin Luther King's Biblical Epic;* Vander Lei and Miller, "Martin Luther King's 'I Have a Dream' in Context"; For King's oratorical relationship to Hughes, see W. Miller, *Origins of the Dream.* For an intriguing interpretation of King's mental health, see Ghaemi, *First-Rate Madness,* 99–113.

8. See Gilmore, *Defying Dixie;* Bell-Scott, *Firebrand and the First Lady;* and Rosenberg, "Conjunction of Race and Gender."

9. Gregg, *Power of Nonviolence,* 44.

10. Sharp, *How Nonviolent Struggle Works,* 112.

11. For example, many abolitionists (including Frederick Douglass and Wendell Phillips) and many civil rights orators (including Dr. King and Fannie Lou Hamer) brandished the same verse of scripture for literally three hundred years for the same purpose—to argue for racial equality. See K. Miller, "All Nations, One Blood, Three Hundred Years."

12. For the court's response, see Klarman, *From Jim Crow to Civil Rights.* For the interaction of the court, the White House, and Congress, see Ackerman, *We the People.*

Selected Bibliography

"1939 Library Sit-In Anniversary." Alexandria Library. https://alexlibraryva.org/1939-sit-in.

Abernathy, Ralph David. *And the Walls Came Tumbling Down.* New York: Harper & Row, 1989.

Ackerman, Bruce. *We the People,* vol. 3, *The Civil Rights Revolution.* Cambridge, Mass.: Harvard University Press, 2014.

Ackerman, Peter, and Jack DuVall. *A Force More Powerful: A Century of Nonviolent Conflict.* New York: St. Martin's, 2000.

"African American Spirituals." *Authentic History.* http://www.authentichistory.com/1600–1859/3-spirituals/index.html.

"Aims to Forestall New Coast Clash." *Jackson (Miss.) Daily News,* 26 April 1960.

A-Infos News Service. "What Is Direct Action?" *Sans Titres,* 22 November 1999, http://www.ainfos.ca/99/nov/ainfos00282.html.

"Airport 'March' Peaceful." *Greenville (S.C.) Piedmont,* 2 January 1960.

"Airport Protest is Held." *Greenville (S.C.) Piedmont,* 1 January 1960.

"Albany, Ga, Hears Negro Pleas But Refuses to Take Action." *New York Times,* 6 August 1962.

Alderman, Derek H. "Surrogation and the Politics of Remembering Slavery in Savannah, Georgia (USA)." *Journal of Historical Geography* 36 (2010): 90–101.

"Aldermen 'Kill' Human Relations Bill." *Louisville (Ken.) Defender,* 28 April 1960.

"All About CORE, 1963 CORE Papers." in *Documentary History of the Modern Civil Rights Movement,* edited by Peter B. Levy, 83. New York: Greenwood, 1992.

Allen, Danielle. *Talking to Strangers: Articles of Citizenship since* Brown v. Board of Education. Chicago: University of Chicago Press, 2004.

Allen, James, ed. *Without Sanctuary: Lynching Photography in America.* New York: Twin Palms, 2000.

Althusser, Louis. "Ideology and Ideological State Apparatuses." In *Lenin and Philosophy and Other Essays,* 127–86. Trans. by Ben Brewster. New York: Monthly Review Press, 1971.

Anatomy of a Demonstration. Documentary narrated by Douglas Edwards, CBS, 1960. Available in Civil Rights Room, Nashville Public Library.

Anderson, Karrin Vasby. "The First Lady: A Site of 'American Womanhood.'" In *Inventing a Voice: The Rhetoric of American First Ladies of the Twentieth Century,* edited by Molly Meijer Wertheimer, 17–30. Lanham, Md.: Rowman & Littlefield, 2004.

Anderson, Sarah, Chuck Collins, Sam Pizzigati, and Kevin Shih. "Executive Excess 2010: CEO Pay and the Great Recession." Institute for Policy Studies, 2010. www.ips-dc.org/reports/executive_excess_2010.

Andrews, James. "Confrontation at Columbia: A Case Study in Coercive Rhetoric." *Quarterly Journal of Speech* 55 (1969): 9–16.

Archibald, Robert. "Life in the City, St. Louis: Vibrant Downtown of 50 Years Ago Is Gone: Can its Enchantments Be Re-created?" *St. Louis Post-Dispatch*, 16 February 1997.

Armada, Bernard J. "Memory's Execution: (Dis)placing the Dissident Body." In *Places of Public Memory: The Rhetoric of Museums and Memorials*, edited by Carole Blair, Greg Dickinson, and Brian L. Ott, 216–37. Tuscaloosa: University of Alabama Press, 2010.

Asante, Molefi Kete. "Television and Black Consciousness." In *Channeling Blackness: Studies on Television and Race in America*, edited by Darnell M. Hunt, 60–73. New York: Oxford University Press, 2005.

Asen, Robert. "A Discourse Theory of Citizenship." *Quarterly Journal of Speech* 90, no. 2 (2004): 189–211.

Asen, Robert, and Daniel C. Brower. "Introduction: Reconfigurations of the Public Sphere." In *Counterpublics and the State*, edited by Robert Asen and Daniel C. Brower, 1–32. Albany: State University of New York Press, 2001.

Associated Press. "Biloxi Patrolled by Armed Cops; Tension High." *New Orleans States and Item*, 25 April 1960.

———. "Jury Wants Truce in Racial Crisis." *Daytona Beach Morning Journal*, 19 June 1964.

———. "Negro is Named to Head Council." *Lake Charles (La.) American-Press*, 22 July 1964.

———. "Pool Jumps Likened to RFK Antics." *Florida Times-Union*, 20 June 1964.

Aubespin, Mervin. Interview by Betsy Brinson. Kentucky Civil Rights Oral History Project, Kentucky Historical Society, 22 October 1999.

Austin, J. L. *How to Do Things with Words*. Oxford: Oxford University Press, 1975.

Azaransky, Sarah. *The Dream Is Freedom: Pauli Murray and American Democratic Faith*. Oxford: Oxford University Press, 2011.

———. "Jane Crow: Pauli Murray's Intersections and Antidescrimination Law." *Journal of Feminist Studies in Religion* 29, no. 1 (2013): 155–60.

Bainbridge, Judith. "Integrating Greenville's Library in 1960." *Greenville (S.C.) News*, 14 July 2016, https://www.greenvilleonline.com/story/life/2016/07/14/integrating-greenvilles -library/87084922/.

Baker, Ella. "Bigger than a Hamburger." *Southern Patriot*, June 1960.

Ball, Howard. *Murder in Mississippi*: United States v. Price *and the Struggle for Civil Rights*. Lawrence: University Press of Kansas, 2004.

Ballenger, William L. "City Library Calm During 'Sitdown.'" *Greenville (S.C.) Piedmont*, 17 March 1960.

———. "Negroes Stage Sit-Ins at City Lunch Counters." *Greenville (S.C.) Piedmont*, 18 July 1960.

———. "Violence Flares on Main Street: Officers Break Up Incident." *Greenville (S.C.) Piedmont*, 21 July 1960.

"Baptists Against Negro Protests." *Charlotte Observer*, 27 February 1960.

Barbour, Chuck. "Judge Won't Drop Store Trespass, Nearing Jury Now as It Is Labeled 'Test Case.'" *Durham (N.C.) Sun*, 17 July 1957.

Bates, Daisy. *The Long Shadow of Little Rock*. 1962. Fayetteville: University of Arkansas Press, 2007.

Battles, David M. *The History of Public Library Access for African Americans in the South: Or, Leaving Behind the Plow*. Lanham, Md.: Scarecrow Press, 2009.

Bayor, Ronald H. "Atlanta, Georgia, 1960–1961: Sit-Ins and Student Activism." *Georgia Historical Quarterly* 75 (1991): 557–65.

Beasley, Maurine H. *Eleanor Roosevelt: Transformative First Lady*. Lawrence: University of Kansas Press, 2010.

"Behind the Scenes with the Curators of the National Museum of American History." The Object of History, http://objectofhistory.org/objects/brieftour/lunchcounter/ (accessed February 16, 2015).

Bell, Derrick. *Silent Covenants:* Brown v. Board of Education *and the Unfulfilled Hopes for Racial Reform.* New York: Oxford University Press, 2006.

Bell-Scott, Patricia. *The Firebrand and the First Lady: Portrait of a Friendship: Pauli Murray, Eleanor Roosevelt, and the Struggle for Social Justice.* New York: Knopf, 2016.

Benford, Robert. "An Insider's Critique of the Social Movement Framing Perspective." *Sociological Inquiry* 67 (1997): 409–30.

Benford, Robert, and David Snow. "Framing Processes and Social Movements: An Overview and Assessment." *Annual Review of Sociology* 26 (2000): 611–39.

Benjamin, Walter. "The Work of Art in the Age of Mechanical Reproduction." In *Illuminations: Essays and Reflections,* edited by Hannah Arendt, 217–52. Translated by Harry Zohn. New York: Schocken Books, 1968.

Berger, Martin A. "Fixing Images: Civil Rights Photography and the Struggle over Representation." *RIHI Journal* 10 (2010), http://www.riha-journal.org/articles/2010/berger-fixing-images.

———. *Seeing through Race: A Reinterpretation of Civil Rights Photography.* Berkeley: University of California Press, 2011.

Berman, Jillian. "Occupy Wall Street Actually Not at All Representative of the 99 Percent, Report Finds." *Huffington Post,* 29 January 2013, http://www.huffingtonpost.com/2013/01/29/occupy-wall-street-report_n_2574788.html.

Berrey, Stephen A. *The Jim Crow Routine: Everyday Performances of Race, Civil Rights, and Segregation in Mississippi.* Chapel Hill: University of North Carolina Press, 2015.

Best, Steven, and Anthony J. Nocella II, eds. *Terrorists or Freedom Fighters? Reflections on the Liberation of Animals.* New York: Lantern Books, 2004.

"A Better Strategy." *Louisville Defender,* 28 January 1960.

Biesecker, Barbara. "Of Historicity, Rhetoric: The Archive as Scene of Invention." *Rhetoric and Public Affairs* 9, no. 1 (2006): 124–31.

Bilbo, Theodore B. *Take Your Choice: Separation or Mongrelization.* Poplarville, MS: Dream House Publishing, 1947.

Biles, Roger. *The South and the New Deal.* Lexington: University Press of Kentucky, 1994.

"Biloxi Beach Quiet Sunday." *Jackson (Miss.) Advocate,* 7 April 1960.

"Birmingham, U.S.A.: Look at Them Run." *Newsweek,* 13 May 1963, 27.

Bitzer, Lloyd F. "The Rhetorical Situation." *Philosophy and Rhetoric* 1 (1968): 1–14.

Black, Allida M. *Casting Her Own Shadow: Eleanor Roosevelt and the Shaping of Postwar Liberalism.* New York: Columbia University Press, 1999.

———. "Championing a Champion: Eleanor Roosevelt and the Marian Anderson 'Freedom Concert.'" *Presidential Studies Quarterly* 20, no. 4 (1990): 719–36.

———. "Civil Rights." In *The Eleanor Roosevelt Encyclopedia,* edited by Maurine H. Beasley, Holly C. Shulman, and Henry R. Beasley, 89–96. Westport, Conn.: Greenwood, 2001.

———, ed. *Courage in a Dangerous World: The Political Writings of Eleanor Roosevelt.* New York: Columbia University Press, 1999.

———. "A Reluctant but Persistent Warrior: Eleanor Roosevelt and the Early Civil Rights Movement." In *Women in the Civil Rights Movement: Trailblazers and Torchbearers, 1941–1965,* edited by Vicki L. Crawford, Jacqueline Anne Rouse, and Barbara Woods, 233–49. Bloomington: Indiana University Press, 1990.

Black, Edwin. "Gettysburg and Silence." *Quarterly Journal of Speech* 80 (1994): 21–36.

———. "Secrecy and Disclosure as Rhetorical Forms." *Quarterly Journal of Speech* 74 (1988): 133–50.

Black Public Sphere Collective, eds. *The Black Public Sphere.* Chicago: University of Chicago Press, 1995.

Blair, Carole. "Contemporary U.S. Memorial Sites as Exemplars of Rhetoric's Materiality." In *Rhetorical Bodies,* edited by Jack Selzer and Sharon Crowley, 16–57. Madison: University of Wisconsin Press, 1999.

Blair, Carole, Martha S. Jeppeson, and Enrico Pucci Jr. "Public Memorializing in Postmodernity: The Vietnam Veterans Memorial as Prototype." *Quarterly Journal of Speech* 77 (1991): 263–88.

Blair, Carole, and Neil Michel. "Reproducing Civil Rights Tactics: The Rhetorical Performances of the Civil Rights Memorial." *Rhetoric Society Quarterly* 30, no. 2 (2000): 31–55.

Blair, Diane Marie. "'I Want You To Write Me': Eleanor Roosevelt's Use of Personal Letters as a Rhetorical Resource." *Western Journal of Communication* 72, no. 4 (2008): 415–33.

Bloom, Jack M. *Class, Race, The Civil Rights Movement.* Bloomington: Indiana University Press, 1987.

Blow, Charles M. "Election Data Dive." *New York Times,* 9 November 2012.

Bodnar, John. *Remaking America: Public Memory, Commemoration and Patriotism in the Twentieth Century.* Princeton, N.J.: Princeton University Press, 1992.

Bodroghkozy, Aniko. *Equal Time: Television and the Civil Rights Movement.* Urbana: University of Illinois Press, 2012.

Bolton, Charles C. *William F. Winter and the New Mississippi: A Biography.* Jackson: University Press of Mississippi, 2013.

Bowen, Harry W. "Does Non-Violence Persuade?" *Today's Speech* 11 (1963): 10–31.

"Bowling Segregation Is Cause of Disagreement." *Louisville Defender,* 6 October 1960.

Brady, Tom P. *Black Monday.* Winona, Miss.: Association of Citizens' Councils, 1955.

Branch, Taylor. *Parting the Waters: America in the King Years, 1954–1963.* New York: Simon & Schuster, 1988.

———. *Pillar of Fire: America in the King Years, 1963–65.* New York: Simon & Schuster, 1998.

Branston, John. "The Longest Occupier." *Memphis Flyer,* 2 November 2011, http://www.memphisflyer.com/CityBeat/archives/2011/11/02/the-longest-occupier.

Brock, Annette K. "Gloria Richardson and the Cambridge Movement." In *Women in the Civil Rights Movement: Trailblazers and Torchbearers, 1941–1946,* edited by Vicki L. Crawford, Jacqueline Anne Rouse, and Barbara Woods, 121–68. Bloomington: Indiana University Press, 1990.

Brooks, Megan Parker. *A Voice that Could Stir an Army: Fannie Lou Hamer and the Rhetoric of the Black Freedom Movement.* Jackson: University Press of Mississippi, 2016.

Brown, Flora Bryant. "NAACP Sponsored Sit-ins by Howard University Students in Washington, DC, 1943–1944." *Journal of Negro History* 85, no. 4 (2000): 275–86.

"Brown Theater Protest Points Up Bias Problem." *Louisville Defender,* 14 January 1960.

Brummett, Barry. "How to Propose A Discourse—A Reply to Rowland." *Communication Studies* 41 (1990): 128–35.

Bryant, Donald C. *Rhetorical Dimensions in Criticism.* Baton Rouge, La.: Louisiana State University Press, 1973.

Bunch, Lonnie. "Exhibiting a New Icon." National Museum of American History, http://amhistory.si.edu/docs/Bunch_Yeingst_Exhibiting_New_Icon_1997.pdf (accessed 15 July 2015).

Burge, Daniel. "Senator Graves's Speech: Dixie Bibb Graves and the Changing Conception of 'The Southern First Lady.'" *Alabama Review* 66, no. 4 (2013): 253–77.

Burke, Kenneth. *Language as Symbolic Action: Essays of Life, Literature, and Method.* Berkeley: University of California Press, 1966.

———. *Permanence and Change: An Anatomy of Purpose.* 3rd ed. Berkeley: University of California Press, 1984.

———. *A Rhetoric of Motives.* Berkeley: University of California Press, 1969.

Burnett, Evelina. "Final Biloxi Wade-in Anniversary Remembered." Mississippi Public Broadcasting, 24 June 2013, http://mpbonline.org/News/article/final_biloxi_wade_in _anniversary_remembered.

Butler, J. Michael. "The Mississippi State Sovereignty Commission and Beach Integration, 1959–1963: A Cotton-Patch Gestapo?" *Journal of Southern History* 68 (2002): 107–48.

Butler, Judith. *Bodies that Matter: On the Discursive Limits of "Sex."* New York: Routledge, 1993.

———. *Excitable Speech: A Politics of the Performative.* New York: Routledge, 1997.

———. *Gender Trouble: Feminism and the Subversion of Identity.* New York: Routledge, 1990.

———. "Judith Butler at Occupy Wall Street." Filmed and posted, 23 October 2011, 3:40. http://www.youtube.com/watch?v=JVpoOdz1AKQ.

———. "Public Assembly and Plural Action," Filmed 11 February 2014. Posted 23 May 2017. https://www.youtube.com/watch?v=8hBh6vrnrhU.

Bynum, Thomas L. *NAACP Youth and the Fight for Black Freedom, 1936–1965.* Knoxville: University of Tennessee Press, 2013.

Byrne, Janet, ed. *The Occupy Handbook.* New York: Back Bay Books, 2012.

Cagin, Seth, and Philip Dray. *We Are Not Afraid: The Story of Goodman, Schwerner, and the Civil Rights Campaign for Mississippi.* New York: Macmillan, 1988.

Calhoun, Craig, ed. *Habermas and the Public Sphere: Studies in Contemporary German Thought.* Cambridge, Mass.: MIT Press, 1997.

"Cambridge Jails 14 After Sit-In." *Washington Post,* 14 May 1963.

Cambridge Non-Violent Action Committee. Press Release. Box 32, Folder: "Demonstrations, General, 1973 September – December and Undated." John F. Kennedy Presidential Library. Available at: https://www.jfklibrary.org/asset-viewer/archives/BMPP/032/ BMPP-032-001

Cambridge Non-Violent Action Committee Summer Staff. *The Negro Ward of Cambridge, Maryland: A Study in Social Change.* Cambridge, Md., September 1963.

Campbell, Colton C., and Sean E. McCluskie. "Policy Experts: Congressional Testimony and Influence of First Ladies." In *Presidential Companion: Readings on the First Ladies,* edited by Robert P. Watson and Anthony J. Eksterowicz, 169–91. Columbia: University of South Carolina Press, 2003.

Campbell, Karlyn Kohrs, and Kathleen Hall Jamieson. "Form and Genre in Rhetorical Criticism: An Introduction." In *Form and Genre: Shaping Rhetorical Action,* edited by Karlyn Kohrs Campbell and Kathleen Hall Jamieson, 9–32. Falls Church, Va.: Speech Communication Association, 1978.

Campbell, Joseph. *The Hero with a Thousand Faces.* New York: New World Library, 2008.

"Can't Eat—Don't Buy." *Louisville Defender,* 2 June 1960.

Capeci, Dominic J. Jr., and Martha Wilkerson. "The Detroit Rioters of 1943: A Reinterpretation." *Michigan Historical Review* 16, no. 1 (1990): 49–72.

Carl, Earl Lawrence. "Reflections on the 'Sit-Ins.'" *Cornell Law Quarterly* 46 (1960–61): 447–57.

Carson, Clayborne. *In Struggle: SNCC and the Black Awakening of the 1960's.* Cambridge, Mass.: Harvard University Press, 1981.

Carter, Michael. "Stasis and Kairos: Principles of Social Construction in Classical Rhetoric." *Rhetoric Review* 7, no. 1 (1988): 97–112.

Cartier-Bresson, Henri. *Aperture Masters of Photography.* Hong Kong: Aperture, 1997.

Cartwright, Samuel. "Report on the Diseases and Physical Peculiarities of the Negro Race." Originally in the *New Orleans Medical and Surgical Journal* (1851) and *DeBow's Review* (1851). Available at https://www.pbs.org/wgbh/aia/part4/4h3106t.html.

Cassie, Ron. "And Service for All: Sixty Years Ago, Morgan State College Students Staged the First Successful Lunch-Counter Sit-Ins." *Baltimore Magazine,* January 2015, http://www.baltimoremagazine.com/2015/1/19/morgan-students-staged-reads-drugstore-sit-in-60-years-ago.

Cathcart, Robert. "Movements: Confrontation as Rhetorical Form." *Southern Speech Communication Journal* 43 (1978): 233–47.

"Celebrating Civil Rights in Greensboro." *Springfield (Mo.) News-Leader,* 20 January 2016, https://www.news-leader.com/story/news/local/good-morning-show/2016/01/20/celebrating-civil-rights-greensboro/79048756/.

Certeau, Michel de. *The Practice of Everyday Life.* Trans. by Steven Rendall. Berkeley: University of California Press, 1982.

Chafe, William H. *Civilities and Civil Rights: Greensboro, North Carolina, and the Black Struggle for Freedom.* New York: Oxford University Press, 1980.

Chapman, William. "9 Students Arrested in Cambridge." *Washington Post,* 16 May 1963.

Cherkis, Jason. "Occupy Wall Street Monitored By U.S. Conference Of Mayors, Emails Show." *HuffPost,* 25 January 2012, https://www.huffpost.com/entry/occupy-wall-street-us-conference-of-mayors_n_1232080?guccounter=1.

Chenoweth, Erica, and Maria Stephan. *Why Civil Resistance Works: The Strategic Logic of Nonviolent Conflict.* New York: Columbia University Press, 2011.

"CIO Delegates 'Sit In' at Columbia Hotel as Waitresses Refuse to Serve Negroes." *New York Times,* 17 March 1947.

"CIO Group Stages Coffee Shop 'Sit-in' As Racial Protest." *Washington Post,* 18 March 1947.

"Citizens Rally to Hear Core Leader." *Louisville Defender,* 28 April 1960.

"Citizens Repudiate Non-violence Program: Feel Gandhi's Way Is Not Comparable to U.S. Situation." *Pittsburgh Courier,* 24 April 1943.

"City Police and Sheriff's Deputies Rate a Bonus." *St. Augustine Record,* 18 June 1964.

Clark, Andrew. "Falling through the Cracks: Queer Theory, Same-Sex Marriage, *Lawrence v. Texas,* and Liminal Bodies." *disClosure: A Journal of Social Theory* 20, no. 1 (2011): 25–43.

Clark, Gregory. *Rhetorical Landscapes in America: Variations on a Theme by Kenneth Burke.* Columbia: University of South Carolina Press, 2004.

"Close Counter Rather Than Serve Negroes: Miami CORE Heads Fight on Race Bias." *Chicago Defender,* 26 September 1959.

Cmiel, Kenneth. "The Politics of Civility." In *The Sixties: From Memory to History,* edited by David Farber, 263–90. Chapel Hill: University of North Carolina Press, 1994.

"CNAC Head Back After Resignation: Business Association Drive Gets Assist from CNAC Boycott." *Cambridge (Md.) Daily Banner,* 26 September 1963.

"Coffee Break: Memphis Wants Suggestions for Project." *Memphis Commercial Appeal,* 16 March 2012, http://www.commercialappeal.com/news/2012/mar/16/coffee-break-city-wants-suggestions-for-project/.

Cohen, Lizabeth. *A Consumers' Republic: The Politics of Mass Consumption in Postwar America.* New York: Knopf, 2003.

Coman, Mihai. "Liminality in Media Studies: From Everyday Life to Media Events." In *Victor Turner and Contemporary Cultural Performance*, edited by Graham St. John, 94–108. New York: Berghahn Books, 2008.

Cone, James H. *Martin and Malcolm and America*. Maryknoll, NY: Orbis Books, 1990.

Conley, Thomas M. *Rhetoric in the European Tradition*. Chicago: University of Chicago Press, 1994.

"Consensus (Direct Democracy @ Occupy Wall Street)." Youtube.com, 13 October 2011, 8:25. http://www.youtube.com/watch?v=6dtD8RnGaRQ.

Cook, Blanche Wiesen. *Eleanor Roosevelt: Volume 2, 1933–1938*. New York: Viking, 1999.

Cooper, Brittney. "A'n't I a Lady? Race Women, Michelle Obama, and the Ever-Expanding Democratic Imagination." *MELUS* 35, no. 4 (2010): 39–57.

Cooper, Melissa. "Reframing Eleanor Roosevelt's Influence in the 1930s Anti-Lynching Movement around a 'New Philosophy of Government.'" *European Journal of American Studies* 12, no. 1 (2017): 1–15.

Corbett, Katharine T. *In Her Place*. St. Louis: Missouri Historical Society Press, 1999.

Cordero-Guzman, Hector R. "Mainstream Support for a Mainstream Movement." School of Public Affairs, Baruch College, 19 October 2011, http://occupywallst.org/media/pdf/OWS-profile1-10-18-11-sent-v2-HRCG.pdf.

Corrigan, Lisa. *Prison Power: How Prison Influenced the Movement for Black Liberation*. Jackson: University of Mississippi Press, 2016.

Couch, W. T. "Southerners Inspect the South." *New Republic*, 14 December 1938, 168–69.

"Counters to Remain Closed: Decision Made By 2 Stores." *Greensboro Daily News*, 8 February 1960, http://sitins.com/clipping_020860b.shtml.

"The *Courier*'s Double "V" for a Double Victory Campaign Gets Country-Wide Support." *Pittsburgh Courier*, 14 February 1942.

"A Creative Protest." In *The Papers of Martin Luther King, Jr.*, vol. 5, edited by Clayborne Carson et al., 367–70. Berkeley: University of California Press, 2005.

Crenshaw, Carrie. "Resisting Whiteness' Rhetorical Silence." *Western Journal of Communication* 61, no. 3 (1997): 253–78.

"A Crisis of Conscience." *Louisville Defender*, 16 March 1961.

Crocker, James W. "Judge Dismisses Library Suit Here." *Greenville (S.C.) News*, 15 September 1960.

"Curfew Keeps City Quiet; Officials Say No Plans to Lift It." *Greenville (S.C.) News*, 29 July 1960.

Danielson, Leilah C. "'In My Extremity I Turned to Gandhi': American Pacifists, Christianity, and Gandhian Nonviolence, 1915–1941." *Church History* 72, no. 2 (2003): 361–88.

D'Arcus, Bruce. "Dissent, Public Space and the Politics of Citizenship: Riots and the 'Outside Agitator.'" *Space and Polity* 8 (2004): 355–70.

Dare Not Walk Alone. Directed by Jeremy Dean. Indican Pictures, 2008. DVD.

Dates, Jannette L., and William Barlow, eds. *Split Image: African Americans in the Mass Media*. Washington, D.C.: Howard University Press, 1990.

Davidson, Osha Gray. "Martin Luther King, Jr., and the Day the World Changed—50 Years Ago Today." Trueslant.com, 17 February 2010, http://trueslant.com/oshagray davidson/2010/02/17/martin-luther-king-jr-the-day-the-world-changed-50-years-ago-today/.

Davis, Angela. "Critical Refusals and Occupy." *Radical Philosophy Review* 16 (2013): 425–39.

Davis, Virginia. "Meet Disappoints Citizens' Leaders." *Rock Hill (S.C.) Herald*, 21 March 1960.

———. "Rock Hill Negroes Threaten Boycott," *Rock Hill (S.C.) Herald,* 1 March 1960.

Day, John Kyle. *The Southern Manifesto: Massive Resistance and the Fight to Preserve Segregation.* Jackson: University Press of Mississippi, 2014.

Debeljak, Julie. "Rights and Democracy: A Reconciliation of the Institutional Debate." In *Protecting Human Rights: Instruments and Institutions,* edited by Tom Campbell, Jeffrey Goldsworthy, and Adrienne Stone, 135–58. Oxford: Oxford University Press, 2003.

Debnam, W. E. *Weep No More, My Lady: A Southerner Answers Mrs. Roosevelt's Report on the "Poor and Unhappy" South.* Raleigh: Graphic, 1950.

"The Decision of the Supreme Court in the School Cases: A Declaration of Constitutional Principles." [The "Southern Manifesto."] *Congressional Record,* 84th Congress, Second Session 102 (March 12, 1956) 4459–60.

Declaration of the Occupation of New York City, 29 September 2011, https://archive.org/details/DeclarationOfTheOccupationOfNewYorkCity.

Deem, Melissa D. "Decorum: The Flight from the Rhetorical." In *Argumentation and Values: Proceedings of the Alta Conference on Argumentation,* edited by Sally Jackson, 226–29. Washington, D.C.: National Communication Association/American Forensic Association, 1995.

DeLaure, Marilyn. "Remembering the Sit-Ins: Performing Public Memory at Greensboro's International Civil Rights Center and Museum." *Liminalities: A Journal of Performance Studies* 7, no. 2 (2011): 1–28.

Del Gandio, Jason. "Extending the Eros Effect: Sentience, Reality, and Emanation." *New Political Science* 36, no. 2 (2014): 129–48.

———. "Performing Nonhuman Liberation: How the ALF and ELF Rupture the Political Imagination." In *Performance on Behalf of the Environment,* edited by Richard D. Besel and Jnan A. Blau, 27–49. Lanham, Md.: Lexington Books, 2013.

———. "Rethinking Immaterial Labor: Communication, Reality, and Neo-radicalism." *Radical Philosophy Review* 14 (2011): 121–38.

Delmont, Matthew F. *Why Busing Failed: Race, Media, and the National Resistance to School Desegregation.* Berkeley: University of California Press, 2016.

DeLuca, Kevin. *Image Politics: The New Rhetoric of Environmental Activism.* New York: Guilford, 1999.

———. "Unruly Arguments: The Body Rhetoric of Earth First!, ACT UP, and Queer Nation." *Argumentation and Advocacy* 36 (1999): 9–21.

DeLuca, Kevin, and Jennifer Peeples. "From Public Sphere to Public Screen: Democracy, Activism, and the 'Violence' of Seattle." *Critical Studies in Media Communication* 19 (2002): 125–51.

Delaney, Theodore Carter. "The Sit-in Demonstration in Historic Perspective." *North Carolina Historical Review* 57, no. 4 (2010): 431–38.

Demo, Anne, and Bradford Vivian, eds. *Rhetoric, Remembrance, and Visual Form: Sighting Memory.* New York: Routledge, 2012.

Derrida, Jacques. *Archive Fever: A Freudian Impression.* Translated by Eric Prenowitz. Chicago: University of Chicago Press, 1998.

"Determined Police Chief." *New York Times,* 23 July 1962.

de Velasco, Antonio, John Angus Campbell, and David Henry, eds. *Rethinking Rhetorical Theory, Criticism, and Pedagogy: The Living Art of Michael C. Leff.* East Lansing: Michigan State University Press, 2016.

Dickinson, Greg, Carole Blair, and Brian L. Ott, eds. *Places of Public Memory: The Rhetoric of Museums and Memorials.* Tuscaloosa: University of Alabama Press, 2010.

Dionisopoulos, George N., Victoria J. Gallagher, Steven R. Goldzwig, and David Zarefsky. "Martin Luther King, the American Dream, and Vietnam: A Collision of Rhetorical Trajectories." *Western Journal of Communication* 56 (1992): 91–107.

"A Disgusting Spectacle." *Tuscaloosa (Ala.) News*, 15 February 1940.

Dittmer, John. *Local People: The Struggle for Civil Rights in Mississippi*. Urbana: University of Illinois Press, 1994.

"Divine's Followers Give Aid to Strikers: With Evangelist's Sanction They 'Sit Down' in Restaurant." *New York Times*, 23 September 1939.

"Dogs, Kids, & Clubs." *Time*, 10 May 1963, 39.

Douglass, Frederick. *Great Speeches by Frederick Douglass*. Edited by James Daley. Mineola, N.Y.: Dover, 2013.

Dowden-White, Priscilla A. *Groping toward Democracy: African American Social Welfare Reform in St. Louis, 1910–1949*. Columbia: University of Missouri Press, 2011.

Doyle, Bertram Wilbur. *The Etiquette of Race Relations in the South: A Study in Social Control*. 1937. New York: Schocken Books, 1971.

Doyle, William. *An American Insurrection: James Meredith and the Battle of Oxford, Mississippi, 1962*. New York: Anchor, 2003.

Drane, Hank. "Genial Ancient City Businessman Caught in Middle of Race Issue." *Florida Times-Union*, 21 June 1964.

———. "Wild Incidents Precede St. Johns Jury Report Urging 30-Day Armistice." *Florida Times-Union*, 19 June 1964.

Dreier, Ted. "Remembering the Movement? A Question for the National Civil Rights Museum." *Truthout*, 8 July 2013, https://truthout.org/articles/remembering-the-move ment-a-question-for-the-national-civil-rights-museum/.

Driver, Justin. "Supremacies and the Southern Manifesto." *Texas Law Review* 92 (2014): 1053–135.

Du Bois, W. E. B. *The Souls of Black Folk*. Chicago: McClurg, 1903.

Dunbar, Anthony P. *Against the Grain: Southern Radicals and Prophets, 1929–1959*. Charlottesville: University Press of Virginia, 1981.

Duncan, Aaron M. "Reimagining the Self-Made Man: Myth, Risk, and the Pokerization of America." *Western Journal of Communication* 78, no. 1 (2013): 39–57.

DuRocher, Kris. "Violent Masculinity: Learning Ritual and Performance in Southern Lynchings." In *Southern Masculinity: Perspectives on Manhood in the South Since Reconstruction*, edited by Craig Thompson Friend, 46–64. Athens: University of Georgia, 2009.

Durr, Virginia Foster. *Outside the Magic Circle: The Autobiography of Virginia Foster Durr*. Edited by Hollinger F. Barnard. Tuscaloosa: University of Alabama Press, 1985.

Dworkin, Andrea. *Right-Wing Women*. New York: Perigee Books, 1983.

Eagleton, Terry. *The Ideology of the Aesthetic*. Oxford: Blackwell, 1998.

Eberhart, George M. "The Greenville Eight: The Sit-In that Integrated the Greenville (S.C.) Library." *American Libraries*, 1 June 2017, https://americanlibrariesmagazine .org/2017/06/01/greenville-eight-library-sit-in/.

Edgar, Walter B. *South Carolina: A History*. Columbia: University of South Carolina Press, 2011.

"An Editorial." *Louisville (Ken.) Defender*, 7 January 1960.

"Editorial: A Mockery of Democracy." *Nashville Globe and Independent*, 4 March 1960.

Egerton, John. *Speak Now against the Day: The Generation before the Civil Rights Movement in the South*. New York: Knopf, 1995.

Eick, Gretchen Cassel. *Dissent in Wichita: The Civil Rights Movement in the Midwest, 1954–1972*. Urbana: University of Illinois Press, 2001.

"Eleanor Roosevelt Reacts to Segregation," Oral History Interview with Modjeska Simkins, May 11, 1990. Interview A-0356. The University of North Carolina at Chapel Hill, Southern Oral History Program Collection (#4007).

"11 Pickets Arrested Sunday." *Cambridge (Md.) Daily Banner*, 22 April 1963.

Endres, Danielle, and Samantha Senda-Cook. "Location Matters: The Rhetoric of Place in Protest." *Quarterly Journal of Speech* 97, no. 3 (2011): 257–82.

Erickson, Keith V., and Stephanie Thomson. "First Lady International Diplomacy: Performing Gendered Roles on the World Stage." *Southern Communication Journal* 77, no. 3 (2012): 239–62.

Eskew, Glenn T. "The Alabama Christian Movement for Human Rights and the Birmingham Struggle for Civil Rights, 1956–1963." In *Birmingham Alabama, 1956–1963: The Black Struggle for Civil Rights*, edited by David J. Garrow, 4–114. New York: Carlson, 1989.

———. *But for Birmingham: The Local and National Movements in the Civil Rights Struggle*. Chapel Hill: University of North Carolina Press, 1997.

"Eviction Empties Motel Where Dr. King Died." *New York Times*, 3 March 1988, http://www.nytimes.com/1988/03/03/us/eviction-empties-motel-where-dr-king-died.html?emc=eta1.

Eyes on the Prize. DVD. Directed by Henry Hampton. New York and Washington, D.C.: Public Broadcasting Service, 1987.

Fairclough, Adam. *Better Day Coming: Blacks and Equality, 1890–2000*. New York: Viking, 2001.

———. Review of *The Sit-In Movement of 1960*, by Martin Oppenheimer. *Journal of Southern History* 57 (1991): 769.

Farber, David, and Beth Bailey. *The Columbia Guide to America in the 1960s*. New York: Columbia University Press, 2001.

Farmer, James. *Lay Bare the Heart: An Autobiography of the Civil Rights Movement*. Fort Worth: Texas Christian University Press, 1998.

Farrell, Thomas B. *Norms of Rhetorical Culture*. New Haven, Conn.: Yale University Press, 1993.

Fayer, Steve. "Ain't Scared of Your Jails." *Eyes on the Prize*, season 1, episode 3. Directed by Orlando Bagwell. Aired on PBS, 4 February 1987.

"Federal Intervention Necessary." *Louisville Defender*, 2 June 1955.

"Federation for Constitutional Government Issues Statement on Sit-In Demonstrations." *Nashville Banner*, 2 April 1960.

Fellowship of Reconciliation. "Lesson Plan on Non-violent Action." Box 18, folder 397, Pauli Murray Papers, Arthur and Elizabeth Schlesinger Library, Radcliffe Institute for Advanced Study, Harvard University.

Ferguson, Dougald. "Separate Beach Facilities on Coast Are Discussed." *New Orleans Times Picayune*, May 1, 1960.

Ferreri, Eric. "Civil Rights Protest Finally Gets Its Due." *Raleigh News & Observer*, 18 December 2007, http://nccueagles.yuku.com/topic/880/Royal-Ice-Cream-Parlor-Protestors-share-Durham-1957-Event#.UqdAKo1RZo5.

"Fighting Erupts during 'Protest.'" *Charlotte Observer*, 16 February 1960.

"The First Southern Conference for Human Welfare." Oral history interview with Virginia Foster Durr, 13–15 March 1975. Interview G-0023-2. University of North Carolina at Chapel Hill, Southern Oral History Program Collection (#4007).

"The First Southern Conference for Human Welfare." Oral history interview with Virginia Foster Durr, 16 October 1975. Interview G-0023-3. University of North Carolina at Chapel Hill, Southern Oral History Program Collection (#4007).

Fischer, David Hackett, and James McPherson, eds. *Freedom Riders.* Oxford: United Press, 2006.

Fischer, Roger A. "A Pioneer Protest: The New Orleans Street-Car Controversy of 1867." *Journal of Negro History* 53 (1968): 219–33.

Fitzgerald, Joseph R. "Days of Wine and Roses: The Life of Gloria Richardson." Doctoral dissertation, Temple University, 2005.

Fleming, Cynthia Griggs. *In the Shadow of Selma: The Continuing Struggle for Civil Rights in the Rural South.* Lanham, Md.: Rowman & Littlefield, 2004.

———. "White Lunch Counters and Black Consciousness: The Story of the Knoxville Sit-Ins." *Tennessee Historical Quarterly* 49 (1991): 40–52.

Foeman, Anita K. "Gloria Richardson: Breaking the Mold." *Journal of Black Studies* 26, no. 5 (1996): 604–15.

Foreman, Clark. "The Decade of Hope." *Phylon (1940–1956)* 12, no. 2 (1951): 137–50.

Formisano, Ronald P. *Boston Against Busing: Race, Class, and Ethnicity in the 1960s and 1970s.* Chapel Hill: University of North Carolina Press, 1991.

"44 are Released from Jail." *Cambridge (Md.) Daily Banner,* 8 April 1963.

Fosl, Catherine, and Tracy K'Meyer. *Freedom on the Border: An Oral History of the Civil Rights Movement in Kentucky.* Lexington: University Press of Kentucky, 2010.

Foster, Susan Leigh. "Choreographies of Protest." *Theatre Journal* 55 (2003): 395–412.

Foucault, Michel. *The Archaeology of Knowledge; and The Discourse on Language.* Translated by A. M. Sheridan Smith. London: Athlone, 1988.

———. *Society Must Be Defended: Lectures at the Collège de France, 1975–6.* Edited by Mauro Bertani and Alessandro Fontana. Translated by David Macey. New York: Picador, 2003.

Fox, Richard G. "Passage from India." *Humanities* 19, no. 1 (1998): 24–29.

Frankenberg, Ruth. *White Women, Race Matters: The Social Construction of Whiteness.* Minneapolis: University of Minnesota Press, 1993.

Franks, Dorothy, Ben Downs, and Sean O'Rourke. "Communicating Civic Responsibility & Reconciliation: A Keynote 'Conversation.'" Carolinas Communication Association, Greenville, S.C., 3 October 2014.

Frantz, Marge, and Cassandra Shaylor. "American Radical Traditions in Conference Organizing." *Social Justice* 27, no. 3 (2000): 176–79.

Fraser, Nancy. "Rethinking the Public Sphere: A Contribution to the Critique of Actually Existing Democracy." *Social Text* nos. 25–26 (1990): 56–80.

Frazier, E. Franklin. "The Negro and Non-Resistance." *Crisis* 27, no. 5 (1924): 213–14.

"Freedom—Now." *Time,* 17 May 1963, 23.

Friend, Craig Thompson. "From Southern Manhood to Southern Masculinities: An Introduction." In *Southern Masculinity: Perspectives on Manhood in the South Since Reconstruction,* edited by Craig Thompson Friend, ix–xxv. Athens: University of Georgia Press, 2009.

Gallagher, Victoria J. "Memory and Reconciliation in the Birmingham Civil Rights Institute." *Rhetoric and Public Affairs* 2 (1999): 303–20.

Gallagher, Victoria J., and Kenneth S. Zagacki. "Visibility and Rhetoric: Epiphanies and Transformations in the *Life* Photographs of the Selma Marches of 1965." *Rhetoric Society Quarterly* 37 (2007): 113–35.

———. "Visibility and Rhetoric: The Power of Visual Images in Norman Rockwell's Depictions of Civil Rights." *Quarterly Journal of Speech* 91 (2005): 175–200.

"Galleries: Royal Ice Cream Parlor Sit-in, 1957." And Justice for All: Durham County Courthouse Art Wall, 2013, http://andjusticeforall.dconc.gov/gallery_images/royal-ice -cream-parlor-sit-in-1957/.

Gamson, William. "Constructing Social Protest." In *Social Movements and Culture*, edited by Hank Johnston and Bert Klandermans, 85–106. Minneapolis: University of Minnesota Press, 1995.

Gardner, Christine J. "Created This Way: Liminality, Rhetorical Agency, and the Transformative Power of Constraint among Gay Christian College Students." *Communication and Critical/Cultural Studies* 14, no. 1 (2017): 31–47.

Garrow, David J. *Atlanta, Georgia, 1960–1961: Sit-ins and Student Activism*. Brooklyn, New York: Carlson Pub, 1989.

———. Preface to *The Sit-In Movement of 1960*, by Martin Oppenheimer, xi–xii. Brooklyn, NY: Carlson Pub, 1989.

———. *Bearing the Cross: Martin Luther King, Jr. and the Southern Christian Leadership Conference*. New York: Vintage, 1986.

———, ed. *St. Augustine, Florida, 1963–1964: Mass Protest and Racial Violence*. Vol. 10 of *Martin Luther King, Jr. and the Civil Rights Movement*. Brooklyn, N.Y.: Carlson, 1989.

Ghaemi, Nassir. *A First-Rate Madness: Uncovering the Links between Leadership and Mental Illness*. New York: Penguin, 2011.

Gilmore, Glenda Elizabeth. *Defying Dixie: The Radical Roots of Civil Rights, 1919–1950*. New York: Norton, 2008.

———. "From Jim Crow to Jane Crow, or How Anne Scott and Pauli Murray Found Each Other." In *Writing Women's History: A Tribute to Anne Firor Scott*, edited by Elizabeth Anne Payne, 142–71. Jackson: University Press of Mississippi, 2011.

Gladwell, Malcolm. "Small Change: Why the Revolution Will Not Be Tweeted." *New Yorker*, 4 October 2010, http://www.newyorker.com/reporting/2010/10/04/101004fa_fact _gladwell.

Glen, John. *Highlander: No Ordinary School: 1932–1962*. Lexington: University of Kentucky Press, 1988.

"Gloria Richardson: Lady General of Civil Rights." *Ebony* 19, no. 9 (July 1964): 23–31.

"Going to High Court—7 Fined in Trespass Case Here." *Durham (N.C.) Sun*, 18 July 1957.

Goldfeder, Jerry H., and Myrna Pérez. "After 'Shelby County' Ruling, Are Voting Rights Endangered?" Brennan Center for Justice at the New York University School of Law, 23 September 2013, http://www.brennancenter.org/analysis/after-shelby-county-ruling -are-voting-rights-endangered.

Goodman, Amy. "National Civil Rights Museum: The Motel Where Dr. King Was Shot Today a Museum that Preserves His Legacy." *Democracy Now!* 15 January 2007, http:// www.democracynow.org/2007/1/15/national_civil_rights_museum_the_motel.

Goodrich, Peter. "Rhetoric and Somatics: Training the Body to Do the Work of Law." *Law Text Culture* 5 (2000–01): article 9.

Gordon, Linda. *The Second Coming of the KKK: The Ku Klux Klan of the 1920s and the American Political Tradition*. New York: Liveright, 2017.

Gordon, Uri. *Anarchy Alive! Anti-authoritarian Politics from Practice to Theory*. London: Pluto, 2008.

———. "Dark Tidings: Anarchist Politics in the Age of Collapse." In *Contemporary Anarchist Studies: An Introductory Anthology of Anarchy in the Academy*, edited by Randall Amster et al., 249–58. New York: Routledge, 2009.

Gould, Jack. "TV: Study of Sit-Ins." *New York Times,* 21 December 1960.

Graeber, David. *Direct Action: An Ethnography.* Oakland, Cal.: AK, 2009.

Graham, Patterson Toby. *A Right to Read: Segregation and Civil Rights in Alabama's Public Libraries, 1900–1965.* Tuscaloosa: University of Alabama Press, 2002.

Gravely, William. "The Civil Right Not to Be Lynched: State Law, Government, and Citizenship Response to the Killing of Willie Earle (1947)." In *Toward the Meeting of the Waters,* edited by Winfred B. Moore Jr. and Orville Vernon Burton, 93–118. Columbia: University of South Carolina Press, 2008.

Graves, Carl R. "The Right to be Served: Oklahoma City's Lunch Counter Sit-Ins, 1958–1964." *Chronicles of Oklahoma* 59 (1981): 151–66.

Gray, Herman. "The Politics of Representation in Network Television." In *Channeling Blackness: Studies on Television and Race in America,* edited by Darnell M. Hunt, 155–74. New York: Oxford University Press, 2005.

———. *Watching Race: Television and the Struggle for Blackness.* Minneapolis: University of Minnesota Press, 1995.

Greenberg, Cheryl Lynn, ed. *A Circle of Trust: Remembering SNCC.* New Brunswick, N.J.: Rutgers University Press, 1998.

Greenberg, Michael. "On the Meaning of Occupation." In *The Occupy Handbook,* edited by Janet Byrne, 265–66. New York: Back Bay Books, 2012.

Greene, Christina. *Our Separate Ways: Women and the Black Freedom Movement in Durham, North Carolina.* Chapel Hill: University of North Carolina Press, 2005.

Greene, Ronald. "Communist Orator." *Philosophy and Rhetoric* 39 (2006): 85–95.

———. "Rhetoric and Capitalism: Rhetorical Agency as Communicative Labor." *Philosophy and Rhetoric* 37 (2004): 188–206.

"The Greensboro Chronology." International Civil Rights Center and Museum, http://www.sitinmovement.org/history/greensboro-chronology.asp.

"Greensboro Seeks to Take Over Civil Rights Museum." *USA Today,* 18 November 2014, http://www.usatoday.com/story/news/nation/2014/11/18/greensboro-international-civil-rights-museum/19250515/.

"The Greenville Civil Rights Movement." Panel Discussion at the Greenville County Library, Greenville, S.C., 22 August 2013.

Gregg, Richard. "NC Finally Recognizes Pre-Woolworth Sit-Ins in 1957." *Raleigh Telegram,* 30 November 2009, http://raleigh3.com/nc-finally-recognizes-prewoolworth-sitins-in-p2881-1.htm.

———. *The Power of Nonviolence.* 2nd rev. ed. Nyack, N.Y.: Fellowship, 1959.

Griffin, Charles J. G. "Movement as Memory: Significant Form in *Eyes on the Prize.*" *Communication Studies* 54, no. 2 (2003): 196–211.

Griffin, Leland M. "The Rhetoric of Historical Movements." *Quarterly Journal of Speech* 38 (1954): 184–88.

———. "A Dramatistic Theory of the Rhetoric of Movements." In *Critical Responses to Kenneth Burke,* in William H. Rueckert, 461–70. Minneapolis: University of Minnesota Press, 1969.

———. "When Dreams Collide: Rhetorical Trajectories in the Assassination of President Kennedy." *Quarterly Journal of Speech* 70 (1984): 111–31.

"Groans from Dying Practices." *Louisville Defender,* 17 January 1957.

Gronbeck, Bruce. "The Rhetorics of the Past: Argument and Collective Memory." In *Doing Rhetorical History: Concepts and Casesr,* edited by Kathleen J. Turner, 47–60. Tuscaloosa: University of Alabama Press, 1998.

Grossman, Ron. "The Birth of the Sit-In." *Chicago Tribune,* 23 February 2014, http://articles .chicagotribune.com/2014-02-23/news/ct-hyde-park-sit-in-0223-20140223_1_ezell-blair -lunch-counter-blacks.

"Gunfire Breaks Out as Races Clash in Greenville: Number of Arrests Are Made." *Greenville (S.C.) News,* 26 July 1960.

Gurian, Elaine Heumann. "Noodling Around with Exhibition Opportunities." In *Exhibiting Cultures: The Poetics and Politics of Museum Display,* edited by Ivan Karp and Steven Lavine, 176–90. Washington, D.C.: Smithsonian Institution Press, 1991.

Habermas, Jürgen. *The Structural Transformation of the Public Sphere: An Inquiry into a Category of Bourgeois Society.* Cambridge, Mass.: MIT Press, 1991.

Hailey, Foster. "Dogs and Hoses Repulse Negroes at Birmingham." *New York Times,* 4 May 1963.

———. "500 Are Arrested in Negro Protest at Birmingham." *New York Times,* 3 May 1963.

———. "4 Negroes Jailed in Birmingham as Integration Drive Slows." *New York Times,* 5 April 1963.

———. "Negroes Uniting in Birmingham." *New York Times,* 11 April 1963.

Haiman, Franklyn S. "The Rhetoric of the Streets: Some Legal and Ethical Considerations." *Quarterly Journal of Speech* 53, no. 2 (1967): 99–114.

Haines, Herbert H. *Black Radicals and the Civil Rights Mainstream, 1954–1970.* Knoxville: University of Tennessee Press, 1988.

Halberstam, David. *The Children.* New York: Random House, 1998.

———. "Fifth Avenue Tense as Rumors Fly." *Nashville Tennessean,* 1 March 1960.

———. "A Good City Gone Ugly." *Reporter,* 31 March 1960, 17–19.

———. "Negroes Served at Bus Terminal." *Nashville Tennessean,* 17 March 1960.

Halbwachs, Maurice. *On Collective Memory.* Chicago: University of Chicago Press, 1992.

Hall, Jacqueline Dowd. "The Long Civil Rights Movement and the Political Uses of the Past." *Journal of American History* 91, no. 4 (2005): 1233–63.

Hall, Stuart. "When Was the Post-Colonial? Thinking at the Limit." In *Post-colonial Question: Common Skies, Divided Horizons,* edited by Iian Chambers and Lidia Curti, 242–60. London: Routledge, 1996.

Halloran, S. Michael. "Text and Experience in a Historical Pageant: Toward a Rhetoric of Spectacle." *Rhetoric Society Quarterly* 31 (2001): 5–17.

Handler, Richard, and Eric Gabler. *The New History in an Old Museum: Creating the Past at Colonial Williamsburg.* Durham, N.C.: Duke University Press, 1997.

Hansen, Drew. *The Dream: Martin Luther King and the Speech that Inspired a Nation.* New York: Ecco, 2005.

Harcourt, Felix. *Ku Klux Kulture: America and the Klan in the 1920s.* Chicago: University of Chicago Press, 2017.

Hariman, Robert. "Decorum, Power, and the Courtly Style." *Quarterly Journal of Speech* 78 (1992): 149–72.

Hariman, Robert, and John L. Lucaites. *No Caption Needed: Iconic Photographs, Public Culture, and Liberal Democracy.* Chicago: University of Chicago Press, 2007.

———. "Problems and Prospects in the Study of Visual Culture." *Review of Communication* 8 (2008): 16–20.

Harley, Shannon. "Chronicle of a Death Foretold." In *Sisters in the Struggle: African-American Women in the Civil Rights & Black Power Movements,* edited by Bettye Collier-Thomas and V.P. Franklin, 174–96. New York: New York University Press, 2001.

Harold, Christine, and Kevin Michael DeLuca. "Behold the Corpse: Violent Images and the Case of Emmett Till." *Rhetoric and Public Affairs* 8 (2005): 263–86.

Harris, Cecily. "German Memory of the Holocaust: The Emergence of Counter-Memorials." *Penn History Review* 17 (2010): 1–26.

Harris, Clarence "Curly." "Curly Harris Talks about How He Took Signs Down and How He Could Have Worked with the Sit-In Participants." Interview. *Greensboro Sit-Ins: Launch of a Civil Rights Movement,* http://www.sitins.com/multimedia/curly1.mp3.

———. "Harris Decides to Integrate." Interview. *Greensboro Sit-Ins: Launch of a Civil Rights Movement,* http://www.sitins.com/multimedia/curly4.mp3.

———. "Harris Recounts What Happened on February 1, 1960." Interview. *Greensboro Sit-Ins: Launch of a Civil Rights Movement.* Online.

Hart, T. Robert Jr. "Amend or Defend: The End of Jim Crow in Greenville and Charleston." MA thesis, Clemson University, 1997.

Hartness, Erin. "Marker Commemorates Pioneering Durham Sit-In." WRAL.com, 23 June 2008. http://www.wral.com/news/state/story/3088736/.

Hauke, Kathleen. *Ted Poston: Pioneering American Journalist.* Athens: University of Georgia Press, 1999.

Hauser, Gerard A. *Vernacular Voices: The Rhetoric of Publics and Public Spheres.* Columbia: University of South Carolina Press, 1999.

Hawhee, Debra. *Moving Bodies: Kenneth Burke at the Edges of Language.* Columbia: University of South Carolina Press, 2009.

———. "Somatography." *Quarterly Journal of Speech* 93 (2007): 365–74.

Hay, James, Stuart Hall, and Lawrence Grossberg. "Interview with Stuart Hall." *Communication and Critical/Cultural Studies* 10, no. 1 (2013): 10–33.

"Heavy Vote Expected in Tuesday's Referendum." *Cambridge (Md.) Daily Banner,* 30 September 1963.

Height, Dorothy. *To Open Wide the Freedom Gates.* New York: Public Affairs, 2005.

Higgenbotham, Evelyn Brooks. *Righteous Discontent: The Women's Movement in the Black Baptist Church, 1880–1920.* Cambridge, Mass.: Harvard University Press, 1993.

Higginbotham, F. Michael. *Ghosts of Jim Crow: Ending Racism in Post-racial America.* New York: New York University Press, 2013.

"Highlander Delegates Propose Expanded Desegregation Drive." *Nashville Banner,* 4 April 1960.

Highlander Folk School Audio Archives (April 1–4, 1960). Audio Disks #39a–39d. Available at http://www.tn.gov/tsla/history/manuscripts.

Hill, Charles A., and Marguerite H. Helmers, eds. *Defining Visual Rhetorics.* Mahwah, N.J.: Lawrence Erlbaum, 2004.

Hill, Jennifer E. M. "Reframing the Victim: Rhetoric for Segregation in the Greenville News." *Young Scholars in Writing: Undergraduate Research in Writing and Rhetoric* 9 (2011): 45–57.

Hine, William C. "The 1867 Charleston Streetcar Sit-Ins." *The South Carolina Historical Magazine* 77 (1976): 110–14.

Hochschild, Adam. "Ku Klux Klambakes." *The New York Review of Books,* 7 December 2017, 16–18.

Hoelscher, Steven. "Making Place, Making Race: Performances of Whiteness in the Jim Crow South." *Annals of the Association of American Geographers* 93, no. 3 (2003): 657–86.

Hogan, Wesley C. *Many Minds, One Heart: SNCC's Dream for a New America.* Chapel Hill: University of North Carolina Press, 2007.

Holsaert, Faith S., Martha Prescod, Norman Noonan, Judy Richardson, Betty Garmin, Robinson, Jean Smith Young, and Dorothy Zellner, eds. *Hands on the Freedom Plow: Personal Accounts by Women in SNCC.* Champaign: University of Illinois Press, 2012.

Homan, Richard. "Negro Leaders Reject City Plan in Cambridge." *Washington Post,* 23 June 1963.

Hoover, Judith D., ed. *Corporate Advocacy: Rhetoric in the Information Age.* Westport, Conn.: Quorum, 1997.

"How Not to Attract." *Louisville Defender,* 19 May 1955.

"How to Lose Friends." *Cambridge (Md.) Daily Banner.* 10 April 1963.

Hubbard, Bryan, and Marouf Hassian. "Atomic Memories of the *Enola Gay*: Strategies of Remembrance at the National Air and Space Museum." *Rhetoric and Public Affairs* 1 (1998): 363–85.

Hudson, Janet G. *Entangled by White Supremacy: Reform in World War I Era South Carolina.* Lexington: University of Kentucky Press, 2008.

Huff, Archie Vernon Jr. *Greenville: The History of the City and County in the South Carolina Piedmont.* Columbia: University of South Carolina Press, 1995.

Huie, William Bradford. *Three Lives for Mississippi.* New York: WCC Books, 1965.

"Human Welfare Conference Brings Out Nationally Known Leaders." *Pittsburgh Courier,* 2 May 1942.

Hurst, Rodney L. *It Was Never about a Hot Dog and a Coke!: A Personal Account of the 1960 Sit-In Demonstrations in Jacksonville, Florida, and Ax-Handle Saturday.* Livermore, C.A.: WingSpan Press, 2008.

Huyssen, Andreas. *Present Pasts: Urban Palimpsests and the Politics of Memory.* Stanford, Cal.: Stanford University Press, 2003.

Ingalls, Robert P. "The Flogging of Joseph Gelders: A Policeman's View." *Labor History* 20, no. 4 (1979): 576–78.

Ingram, T. Robert, ed., *Essays on Segregation.* Houston: St. Thomas Press, 1960.

"It Can Happen Here." *Louisville Defender,* 10 March 1960.

"It's Time to Protest." *Tuscaloosa (Ala.) News,* 9 December 1938.

Jack, Jordynn, and Lucy Massagee. "Ladies and Lynching: Southern Women, Civil Rights, and the Rhetoric of Interracial Cooperation." *Rhetoric and Public Affairs* 14, no. 3 (2011): 493–510.

Jeyaraj, Joseph. "Liminality and Othering: The Issue of Rhetorical Authority in Technical Discourse." *Journal of Business and Technical Communication* 18, no. 1 (2004): 9–38.

Johnson, Charles S. "More Southerners Discover the South." *Crisis,* January 1939, 14–15.

Johnson, Davi. "Martin Luther King, Jr.'s 1963 Birmingham Campaign as Image Event." *Rhetoric and Public Affairs* 10, no. 1 (2007): 1–25.

Johnson, J. T. Interviewed by Andrew Young, Flagler College, St. Augustine, Florida, 2009. Video 1. Civil Rights Library of St. Augustine, http://flagler.contentdm.oclc.org/cdm/compoundobject/collection/p15415coll1/id/879/rec/17.

Johnson, Nan. *Gender and Rhetorical Space in American Life.* Carbondale: Southern Illinois University Press, 2002.

Johnstone, Christopher Lyle. "Greek Oratorical Settings and the Problem of the Pnyx: Rethinking the Athenian Political Process." In *Theory, Text, Context: Issues in Greek Rhetoric and Oratory,* edited by Christopher Lyle Johnstone, 97–127. Albany: SUNY Press, 1996.

Jolly, Kenneth S. *Black Liberation in the Midwest: The Struggle in St. Louis, Missouri, 1964–1970.* New York: Routledge, 2006.

Jones, Bob, Sr. *Is Segregation Scriptural?* Greenville, S.C.: Bob Jones University, 1960.

Jones, John Paul, III. "The Street Politics of Jackie Smith." In *The Blackwell Companion to the City,* edited by Gary Bridge and Sophie Watson, 476–87. Oxford: Blackwell, 2000.

Karp, Ivan, and Steven Lavine. *Exhibiting Cultures: The Poetics and Politics of Museum Display.* Washington, D.C.: Smithsonian Institution Press, 1991.

Kasher, Steven. *The Civil Rights Movement: A Photographic History, 1954–68.* New York: Abbeville, 1996.

Katriel, Tamara. "Our Future Is Where Our Past Is: Studying Heritage Museums as Ideological and Performative Arenas." *Communication Monographs* 60 (1993): 69–75.

———. "Sites of Memory: Discourses of the Past in Israeli Pioneering Settlement Museums." *Quarterly Journal of Speech* 80 (1994): 1–20.

Katsiaficas, George. *The Imagination of the New Left: A Global Analysis of 1968.* Boston: South End, 1987.

Kelley, Blair L. M. *Right to Ride: Streetcar Boycotts and African American Citizenship in the Era of* Plessy v. Ferguson. Chapel Hill: University of North Carolina Press, 2010.

Kempton, Murray. "Gloria, Gloria." *New Republic,* 11 November 1963, 15–17.

Kennedy, George A., trans. *Aristotle, On Rhetoric: A Theory of Civil Discourse.* New York: Oxford University Press, 1991.

Kermode, Frank. *The Sense of an Ending: Studies in the Theory of Fiction.* London: Oxford University Press, 1966.

Khanna, Samiha. "50 Years after Sit-in, a Reunion." *Raleigh News and Observer,* 16 September 2007.

Khazan, Jibreel (Ezell Blair, Jr.). "Oral History Interview with Jibreel Khazan and Franklin McCain by Eugene Pfaff." *Civil Rights Greensboro,* http://library.uncg.edu/dp/crg/oral HistItem.aspx?i=607.

———. "Something Must Be Done." Interview. *Greensboro Sit-Ins: Launch of a Civil Rights Movement,* http://www.sitins.com/multimedia/blair.mp3.

Kilpatrick, Carroll. "Bungled Opportunity: The Southern Conference for Human Welfare." *Washington Post,* 30 November 1938.

Kilpatrick, James Jackson. *The Southern Case for School Segregation.* N.p.: Crowell-Collier Press, 1962.

Kimbrough, Mary, and Margaret W. Dagen. *Victory without Violence: The First Ten Years of the St. Louis Committee of Racial Equality (CORE), 1947–1957.* Columbia: University of Missouri Press, 2000.

King, Martin Luther, Jr. *The Autobiography of Martin Luther King, Jr.* Stanford, Cal.: Stanford University, Martin Luther King, Jr. Research and Education Institute, http://mlkkpp01.stanford.edu/index.php/kingpapers/article/chapter_16_the_albany_move ment/ (accessed 14 January 2014).

———. "A Creative Protest." In *The Papers of Martin Luther King, Jr.,* vol. 5, edited by Clayborne Carson, Tenisha Armstrong, Susan Carson, Adrienne Clay, and Kieran Taylor, 367–70. Berkeley: University of California Press, 2005.

———. "I've Been to the Mountaintop." 1968. Martin Luther King, Jr. Research and Education Center, Stanford University. http://kingencyclopedia.stanford.edu/encyclopedia/documentsentry/ive_been_to_the_mountaintop/.

———. Speech at Fisk University, Nashville, 20 April 1960.

———. *Why We Can't Wait.* New York: Mentor, 1964.

King, Mary. *Freedom Song: A Personal Story of the 1960s Civil Rights Movement.* New York: Morrow, 1988.

"King—The Firewalker." *St. Augustine Record,* 24 June 1964 (reprinted editorial from *Tampa Tribune*).

Kinneavy, James L. "Kairos: A Neglected Concept in Classical Rhetoric." In *Rhetoric and*

Praxis: The Contribution of Classical Rhetoric to Practical Reasoning, edited by Jean Dietz Moss. Washington D.C.: Catholic University Press, 1986.

———. *"Kairos* in Aristotle's *Rhetoric." Written Communication* 17, no. 3 (2000): 432–44.

Kirshenblatt-Gimblett, Barbara. *Destination Culture: Tourism, Museums and Heritage.* Berkeley: University of California Press, 1998.

Kisseloff, Jeff. "Gloria Richardson Dandridge: The Militant." In *Generation on Fire: Voices of Protest from the 1960s: An Oral History*, 51–64. Lexington: University Press of Kentucky, 2007.

Klarman, Michael. *From Jim Crow to Civil Rights: The Supreme Court and the Struggle for Racial Equality.* New York: Oxford University Press, 2004.

Kluver, Randolph. "Rhetorical Trajectories of Tiananmen Square." *Diplomatic History* 34 (2010): 71–94.

K'Meyer, Tracy. *Civil Rights in the Gateway to the South: Louisville, Kentucky, 1945–1980.* Lexington: University Press of Kentucky, 2010.

Knott, Cheryl. *Not Free, Not for All: Public Libraries in the Age of Jim Crow: The Untold History of Public Library Integration.* Amherst: University of Massachusetts Press, 2015.

Kowal, Rebekah J. "Staging the Greensboro Sit-Ins." *TDR: The Drama Review* 48, no. 4 (2004): 135–54.

Krueger, Thomas A. *And Promises to Keep: The Southern Conference for Human Welfare, 1938–1948.* Nashville: Vanderbilt University Press, 1967.

Kruse, Kevin M. *White Flight: Atlanta and the Making of Modern Conservatism.* Princeton: Princeton University Press, 2005.

Kuettner, Al (UPI). "Motel Manager 'Shaken' After Protest Hits." *Atlanta Daily World*, 21 June 1964.

Landry, Stuart Omer. *The Cult of Equality: A Study of the Race Problem.* New Orleans: Pelican Publishing, 1945.

Lang, Clarence. "Black Power on the Ground: Continuity and Rupture in St. Louis." In *Neighborhood Rebels: Black Power at the Local Level*, edited by Peniel E. Joseph, 67–89. New York: Palgrave Macmillan, 2010.

———. *Grassroots at the Gateway: Class Politics and Black Freedom Struggle in St. Louis, 1936–75.* Ann Arbor: University of Michigan Press, 2009.

———. "Locating the Civil Rights Movement: An Essay on the Deep South, Midwest, and Border South in Black Freedom Studies." *Journal of Social History* 47, no. 2 (2013): 371–400.

Lau, Peter F. *Democracy Rising: South Carolina and the Fight for Black Equality Since 1865.* Lexington: University of Kentucky Press, 2006.

Laue, James H. *Direct Action and Desegregation, 1960–1962.* Brooklyn, N.Y.: Carlson, 1989.

Lawrence, Noah. "'Since It is My Right, I Would Like to Have It': Edna Griffin and the Katz Drug Store Desegregation Movement." *Annals of Iowa* 67 (2008): 298–320.

Lawson, James M. "A Conversation with James Lawson: Remembering the Nashville Movement." Nashville, 2006. https://video/npt_specials_conversation_james_lawson.

———. "From a Lunch-Counter Stool." In *Documentary History of the Modern Civil Rights Movement*, edited by Peter B. Levy, 71–74. Westport, Conn.: Greenwood, 1992.

———. Interview by William Barnes, October 21–22, 2002. Oral History Collection. Civil Rights Room, Nashville Public Library.

———. Interview by Robert Penn Warren. *Who Speaks for the Negro?* Special Collections, Jean and Alexander Heard Library, Vanderbilt University, 1964.

———. "Lunch Counter Sit-Ins in Nashville." Interview. 23 June 2009. https://lpb.pbs

learningmedia.org/resource/the-nashville-sit-ins/john-lewis-get-in-the-way/#.XapgnX 97mUk.

Lawson, Steven F. "Freedom Then, Freedom Now: The Historiography of the Civil Rights Movement." Review Essay. *American Historical Review* 96 (1991): 456–71.

Lawson, William H. "Citizenship as Salvation: The 1963 Mississippi Freedom Vote." *Advances in the History of Rhetoric* 11–12, no. 1 (2008): 159–229.

Lee, Barry Everett. "The Nashville Civil Rights Movement: A Study of the Phenomenon of Intentional Leadership Development and Its Consequences for Local Movements and the National Civil Rights Movement." Ph.D. diss., Georgia State University, 2010, http:// digitalarchive.gsu.edu/history_diss/16.

Lee, Ronald L. "The Rhetorical Construction of Time in Martin Luther King, Jr.'s 'Letter from Birmingham Jail.'" *Southern Communication Journal*, 56 (1991): 279–88.

Leff, Michael. "Dimensions of Temporality in Lincoln's Second Inaugural." *Communication Reports* 1 (1988): 26–31.

———. "The Habitation of Rhetoric." In *Rethinking Rhetorical Theory, Criticism, and Pedagogy: The Living Art of Michael C. Leff*, edited by Antonio de Velasco, John Angus Campbell, and David Henry, 143–62. East Lansing: Michigan State University Press, 2016.

———. "Rhetoric and Dialectic in Martin Luther King's 'Letter from Birmingham Jail.'" Keynote Address, International Society for the Study of Argumentation, Amsterdam, the Netherlands, June 26–28, 2002.

———. "Things Made by Words: Reflections on Textual Criticism." *Quarterly Journal of Speech* 78, no. 2 (1992): 223–31.

Leff, Michael, and Ebony Utley. "Instrumental and Constitutive Rhetoric in Martin Luther King, Jr.'s 'Letter from Birmingham Jail.'" *Rhetoric and Public Affairs* 7 (2004): 37–52.

Lehn, Melody. "In Defense of Crap Archives: Archival Possibilities for Researching First Ladies." *Carolinas Communication Annual* 31 (2015): 10–14.

Leonard, Thomas C. "Antislavery, Civil Rights, and Incendiary Material." In *Media and Revolution: Comparative Perspectives*, edited by Jeremy D. Popkin, 115–35. Lexington: University of Kentucky Press, 1995.

"Lesson Plan on Non-violent Action." Pauli Murray Papers, box 18, folder 397. Arthur and Elizabeth Schlesinger Library, Radcliffe Institute for Advanced Study, Harvard University.

Leuchtenburg, William E. *The White House Looks South: Franklin D. Roosevelt, Harry S. Truman, and Lyndon B. Johnson*. Baton Rouge: Louisiana State University Press, 2005.

Levy, Peter B. "The Black Freedom Struggle and White Resistance: A Case Study of the Civil Rights Movement in Cambridge, Maryland." In *The New Left Revisited*, edited by John McMillian and Paul Buhle, 67–91. Philadelphia: Temple University Press, 2003.

———. *Civil War on Race Street: The Civil Rights Movement in Cambridge Maryland*. Gainesville: University Press of Florida, 2003.

Lewis, Andrew B. *The Shadows of Youth: The Remarkable Journey of the Civil Rights Generation*. New York: Hill & Wang, 2009.

Lewis, Camille Kaminski. "A is for Archive: The Politics of Research in the Southern Archive." *Carolinas Communication Annual* 31 (2015): 15–18.

Lewis, George. *Massive Resistance: The White Response to the Civil Rights Movement*. London: Oxford University Press, 2006.

Lewis, John. "John Lewis: Acceptance Speech." John F. Kennedy Presidential Library and Museum, 21 May 2001, https://www.jfklibrary.org/events-and-awards/profile-in-courage -award/award-recipients/john-lewis-2001.

———. Interview by Judith Hoover, 11 December 2012. Transcript available from Judith Hoover.

———. *Walking with the Wind: A Memoir of the Movement.* With Michael D'Orso. New York: Simon & Schuster, 1998.

Linenthal, Edward T., and Tom Engelhardt. *History Wars: The Enola Gay and Other Battles for the American Past.* New York: Metropolitan Books, 1996.

Lingo, Al. Interview, Flagler College, St. Augustine, Florida, n.d. Videos 4 and 5, http://flagler .contentdm.oclc.org/cdm/compoundobject/collection/p15415coll1/id/ 509/rec/1.

Liston, Robert A. "Who Can We Surrender To?" *Saturday Evening Post,* 5 October 1963 78–80.

"Local Group Seeks Non-Segregated Facilities in Downtown Stores." *Nashville Globe and Independent,* 1 January 1960.

Loehwing, Melanie, and Jeff Motter. "Publics, Counterpublics, and the Promise of Democracy." *Philosophy and Rhetoric* 42 (2009): 220–41.

Loh, Jules. "St. Augustine Still Torn by Racial Strife." *Los Angeles Times,* 5 July 1964.

Loller, Michael. "National Civil Rights Museum in Memphis Will Have Presence during One-Year Hiatus." *Commercial Appeal,* 1 November 2012, http://www.commercialappeal .com/news/2012/nov/01/national-civil-rights-museum-in-memphis-will-one/?print=1.

"'Long, Hot Summer' Already under Way." *Baltimore Afro-American,* 27 June 1964.

Long, Michael G., ed. *First Class Citizenship: The Civil Rights Letters of Jackie Robinson.* New York: Time Books of Henry Holt, 2007.

Loughlin, Martin. "Rights, Democracy and the Nature of Legal Order." In *Skeptical Essays on Human Rights,* edited by Tom Campbell, Keith Ewing, and Adam Tomkins, 41–60. Oxford: Oxford University Press, 2001.

"Louisville Public Places Present Dismal Picture of Discrimination." *Louisville Defender,* 29 November 1956.

Lozano-Reich, Nina M., and Dana L. Cloud. "The Uncivil Tongue: Invitational Rhetoric and the Problem of Inequality." *Western Journal of Communication* 73, no. 2 (2009): 220– 26.

"The Lunch Counter: Overview." The Object of History, http://objectofhistory.org/objects/ intro/lunchcounter (accessed 19 September 2019).

"Lunchroom Counters Still Segregated Here." *Louisville Defender,* 19 January 1956.

Mallon, Winifred. "Sweeping Moves Urged to Aid South." *New York Times,* 23 November 1938.

Manis, Andrew M. *A Fire You Can't Put Out.* Tuscaloosa: University of Alabama Press, 1999.

"Marker Mania: Greensboro's Claim? Why, It's Mere Piffle." *Durham (N.C.) Morning Herald,* 13 January 1980.

Martinez, Elizabeth Betita. "Where Was the Color in Seattle? Looking for Reasons Why the Great Battle Was So White." *Colorlines,* 10 March 2000, http://colorlines.com/ archives/2000/03/where_was_the_color_in_seattlelooking_for_reasons_why_the_great _battle_was_so_white.html.

Mason, Gilbert R., and James Patterson Smith. *Beaches, Blood, and Ballots: A Black Doctor's Civil Rights Struggle.* Jackson: University of Mississippi Press, 2000.

May, Matthew S. *Soapbox Rebellion: The Hobo Orator Union and the Free Speech Fights of the Industrial Workers of the World, 1909–1916.* Tuscaloosa: University of Alabama Press, 2013.

"Mayor Charges that Mrs. Richardson Hopes to Defeat Amendment and Get Back in the News." *Cambridge (Md.) Daily Banner,* 28 September 1963.

"Mayor Names Biracial Group to Seek Peace." *Nashville Tennessean,* 4 March 1960.

McAdam, Doug. *Freedom Summer.* New York: Oxford University Press, 1988.

McAlpin, Harry. "Howard Students Picket Jim Crow Restaurant." *Chicago Defender,* 24 April 1943.

McCain, Franklin. "What Happened That First Day." Interview. *Greensboro Sit-Ins: Launch of a Civil Rights Movement,* http://www.sitins.com/multimedia/mccain12.mp3.

———. "Why We Did It." Interview. *Greensboro Sit-Ins: Launch of a Civil Rights Movement,* http://www.sitins.com/multimedia/mccain4.mp3.

McCarthy, Anna. *The Citizen Machine: Governing by Television in 1950s America.* New York: New York University Press, 2010.

McDermott, Nancie. "Civil Rights Sit-Ins: 'Sitting Down for a Cup of Coffee and Civil Rights.'" NCpedia, https://www.ncpedia.org/civil-rights-sit-ins/.

McElwee, Sean, and Jason McDaniel. "Economic Anxiety Didn't Make People Vote Trump, Racism Did." *Nation,* 8 May 2017, https://www.thenation.com/article/economic-anxiety-didnt-make-people-vote-trump-racism-did/.

McMillen, Neil R. "Black Enfranchisement in Mississippi: Federal Enforcement and Black Protest in the 1960s." *Journal of Southern History* 43 (1977): 351–72.

McNeil, Genna Rae. Interview with Pauli Murray, 1976. Interview number G-0044 in the Southern Oral History Program Collection, Lewis Round Wilson Special Collections Library. University of North Carolina at Chapel Hill.

McNeill, William. *Keeping Together in Time: Dance and Drill in Human History.* Cambridge, Mass.: Harvard University Press, 1995.

McWhorter, Diane. *Carry Me Home: Birmingham, Alabama: The Climactic Battle of the Civil Rights Movement.* New York: Simon & Schuster, 2001.

"The Meaning of Birmingham." *New York Times,* 10 May 1963.

Medina, Jose. *The Epistemology of Resistance: Gender and Racial Oppression, Epistemic Injustice, and Resistant Imaginations.* Oxford: Oxford University Press, 2012.

Meier, August. *Negro Thought in America, 1880–1915: Racial Ideologies in the Age of Booker T. Washington.* Ann Arbor: University of Michigan Press, 1963.

Meier, August, and Elliot Rudwick. "The Boycott Movement against Jim Crow Streetcars in the South, 1900–1906." *Journal of American History* 55, no. 4 (1969): 756–75.

———. *CORE: A Study of the Civil Rights Movement, 1942–1968.* Urbana: University of Illinois Press, 1975.

———. "Negro Boycotts of Segregated Streetcars in Virginia, 1904–1907." *Virginia Magazine of History and Biography* 81 (1973): 479–87.

Mendelson, Michael. *Many Sides: A Protagorean Approach to the Theory, Practice, and Pedagogy of Argument.* Dordrecht: Kluwer Academic Publishers, 2002.

Merelman, Richard. *Representing Black Culture: Racial Conflict and Cultural Politics in the United States.* New York: Routledge, 1995.

Michaeli, Evan. *The Defender: How the Legendary Black Newspaper Changed America.* Boston: Houghton, 2016.

Middleton, Michael, Aaron Hess, Danielle Endres, and Samantha Senda-Cook. *Participatory Critical Rhetoric: Theoretical and Methodological Foundations for Studying Rhetoric In Situ.* Lanham, Md.: Lexington Books, 2015.

"Militancy Is the Watchword." *Louisville Defender,* 22 November 1956.

Miller, Carolyn. "*Kairos* in the Rhetoric of Science." In *A Rhetoric of Doing: Essays on Written Discourse in Honor of James L. Kinneavy,* edited by Stephen P. Witte, Neil Nakadate, and Roger D. Cherry, 310–27. Carbondale: Southern Illinois University Press, 1992.

Miller, Douglas T., and Marion Nowak. *The Fifties: The Way We Really Were.* Garden City, N.Y.: Doubleday, 1977.

Miller, Keith D. "All Nations, One Blood, Three Hundred Years: Martin Luther King, Jr., Fannie Lou Hamer, and Civil Rights Rhetoric as Transatlantic Abolitionism." In *Rhetoric across Borders,* edited by Anne Teresa Demo, 92–108. Anderson, S.C.: Parlor, 2015.

——. *Martin Luther King's Biblical Epic: His Great, Final Speech.* Jackson: University of Mississippi Press, 2012.

——. *Voice of Deliverance: The Language of Martin Luther King, Jr., and Its Sources.* Athens: University of Georgia Press, 1992.

Miller, W. Jason. *Origins of the Dream: Hughes' Poetry and King's Dream.* Gainesville: University of Florida Press, 2015.

Milliken, Matthew E. "Civil Rights History Marked." *Durham (N.C.) Herald-Sun,* 23 June 2008, http://nccueagles.yuku.com/topic/880/Royal-Ice-Cream-Parlor-Protestors-share-Durham-1957-Event#.UqcinI1RZo5.

——. "Royal Ice Cream Sit-In Finally Makes Its Mark." *Durham (N.C.) Herald-Sun,* 23 June 2008.

Millner, Sandra Y. "Recasting Civil Rights Leadership: Gloria Richardson and the Cambridge Movement." *Journal of Black Studies* 26, no. 6 (1996): 668–87.

"Ministers Urge Lunch Freedom." *Nashville Tennessean,* 20 March 1960.

Mississippi Development Authority. "MDA Tourism Announces Mississippi Freedom Trail," http://www.visitmississippi.org/20110505-ms-freedom-trail.aspx.

——. "Mississippi Freedom Trail," http://www.visitmississippi.org/mississippi-freedom-trail.aspx.

"Mississippi Injustice." *Louisville Defender,* 15 September 1955.

Mississippi Truth Commission. "Civil Rights Movement in Mississippi," http://mississippitruth.org/pages/CRMtimeline.htm.

Mitchell, R. O. "Racial and Civil Disorders in St. Augustine: Report of the Legislative Investigation Committee, February 1965." 34. Appendix in *St. Augustine, Florida, 1963–1964: Mass Protest and Racial Violence,* vol. 10 of *Martin Luther King, Jr. and the Civil Rights Movement,* edited by David J. Garrow, 213. Brooklyn, N.Y.: Carlson, 1989.

Mitchell, W. J. T. *Picture Theory: Essays on Verbal and Visual Representation.* Chicago: University of Chicago Press, 1994.

Mixon, Harold. "The Rhetoric of States' Rights and White Supremacy." In *A New Diversity in Contemporary Southern Rhetoric,* edited by Calvin M. Logue and Howard Dorgan, 166–87. Baton Rouge: Louisiana State University Press, 1987.

Mohl, Raymond A. "Interracial Activism and the Civil Rights Movement in Postwar Miami." *Tequesta* 66 (2006): 28–48.

——. "'South of the South': Jews, Blacks, and the Civil Rights Movement in Miami, 1945–1960." *Journal of American Ethnic History* 18 (1999): 3–36.

Moody, Anne. *Coming of Age in Mississippi.* New York: Bantam Dell, 1968.

Moore, Charles, and Michael Durham. *Powerful Days: Civil Rights Photography of Charles Moore.* Tuscaloosa: University of Alabama Press, 2007.

Moore, Winfred B., Jr., and Orville Vernon Burton, eds. *Toward the Meeting of the Waters: Currents in the Civil Rights Movement of South Carolina During the Twentieth Century.* Columbia: University of South Carolina Press, 2008.

"More Arrests Made as Demonstrations Continue." *St. Augustine Record,* 18 June 1964.

Morgan, Iwan W. "The New Movement: The Student Sit-Ins in 1960." In *From Sit-Ins to SNCC: The Student Civil Rights Movement in the 1960s,* edited by Iwan W. Morgan and Philip Davies, 1–22. Gainesville: University Press of Florida, 2012.

Morgan, Iwan W., and Philip Davies, eds. *From Sit-Ins to SNCC: The Student Civil Rights Movement in the 1960s.* Gainesville: University Press of Florida, 2012.

Morris, Aldon. "Black Southern Student Sit-in Movement: An Analysis of Internal Organization." *American Sociological Review* 46 (1981): 744–67.

———. *The Origins of the Civil Rights Movement: Black Communities Organizing for Change.* New York: Free Press, 1984.

Morris, Charles E., III. "Contextual Twilight/Critical Liminality: J. M. Barrie's Courage at St. Andrews, 1922." *Quarterly Journal of Speech* 82, no. 3 (1996): 207–27.

Morris, Errol. "Will the Real Hooded Man Please Stand Up?" *New York Times,* 15 August 2007.

Morten, Baker E. "Man from St. Aug." *Baltimore Afro-American,* 4 July 1964.

Morton, Samuel. *Crania Americana, or, A Comparative View of the Skulls of Various Aboriginal Nations of North and South America: To Which is Prefixed an Essay on the Varieties of the Human Species.* Philadelphia: J. Dobson, 1839.

Mother Jones News Team. "Map: Occupy Wall Street, a Global Movement." *Mother Jones,* 4 October 2011, http://www.motherjones.com/politics/2011/10/occupy-wall-street-protest-map.

Mountford, Roxanne. "On Gender and Rhetorical Space." *Rhetoric Society Quarterly* 31 (2001): 41–71.

"Mrs. Bethune, Not 'Mary,' Gets into the Records." *Chicago Defender,* 3 December 1938.

"Mrs. Eleanor Roosevelt Greets Mrs. Mary Bethune." *Chicago Defender,* 3 December 1938.

"Muriatic Acid, Police Brutality Used against Non-violent Swim-In Demonstrators." *Associated Negro Press National News Service,* 24 June 1964.

Murphy, Troy A. "Civil Society, the Highlander Folk School, and the Cultivation of Rhetorical Invention." *Communication Review* 6 (2003): 1–22.

Murray, Pauli. "Ask India Freedom." *New York Amsterdam Star-News,* 15 August 1942.

———. "A Blueprint for First Class Citizenship." *Crisis* 51, no. 9 (1944): 358–59.

———. "Challenge to Us." *New York Times,* 13 September 1942.

———. "Freedom Here and There." *New York Herald Tribune,* 18 August 1942.

———. "Negroes Are Fed Up." *Common Sense* 12, no. 8 (1943): 274–76.

———. "Notes Taken by P.M. on Non-violence, March 1940." Pauli Murray Papers, box 86. Arthur and Elizabeth Schlesinger Library, Radcliffe Institute for Advanced Study, Harvard University.

———. *Song in a Weary Throat.* New York: Harper & Row, 1987.

———. "Why Negro Women Stay Single." *Negro Digest* 5, no. 4 (1947): 4–8.

Murray, Pauli, and Henry Babcock. "An Alternative Weapon." In *Moral Evil and Redemptive Suffering: A History of Theodicy in African-American Religious Thought,* edited by Anthony Pinn, 53–57. Gainesville: University Press of Florida, 2002.

Muste, A. J. "Sit Downs and Lie Downs." *Fellowship* 3, no. 3 (1937): 5–6.

Myerson, J. A. "How Do You Illustrate Corruption? Artist Rachel Schragis Explains." *Truthout,* 5 November 2011, http://www.truth-out.org/news/item/4600:how-do-you-illustrate-corruption-artist-rachel-schragis-explains.

"NAACP Backing Them, Sitters Told." *Nashville Tennessean,* 7 April 1960.

"NAACP Pickets Brown Theater." *Louisville Defender,* 31 December 1959.

Nakayama, Thomas K., and Robert L. Krizek. "Whiteness: A Strategic Rhetoric." *Quarterly Journal of Speech* 81, no. 3 (1995): 291–309.

Nash, Diane. Interview by Tavis Smiley. *The Tavis Smiley Show.* 10 May 2011. https://archive.org/details/WMPT_20110511_160000_Tavis_Smiley.

———. "She's the one to get." Interview. N.d. https://lpb.pbslearningmedia.org/resource/imlo4.soc.ush.civil.nash/diane-nash-and-the-sit-ins/#.XaplhX97mUk.

"Nashville Citizens Rally to Efforts of Militant Students." *Nashville Globe and Independent,* 4 March 1960.

Nashville: We Were Warriors (1960). Films for Humanities and Social Science. Civil Rights Room, Nashville Public Library.

Nashville Globe and Independent. 11 January 1907–December 1913, 5 January 1917–29 November 1935, 20 January 1939–July 1960. Library and Archives Holdings, Tennessee State Library.

"The Nashville Sit-Ins: Nonviolence Emergence." *Southern Exposure* 9, no. 1 (1981): 30–32.

Neal, Homer A. "Presenting History Museums in a Democratic Society." *University Record,* 7 April 1995, http://www.umich.edu/~urecord/9495/April17_95/perspect.htm

"Negro Children Held without Bail." *Christian Science Monitor,* 4 May 1963.

"Negro Is Beaten and Kicked at Lunch Counter in Mississippi's Capital." *New York Times,* 29 May 1963.

"Negro Press Creed." *Louisville Defender,* 18 March 1952.

"The Negro Press Is You." *Louisville Defender,* 18 March 1952.

"Negroes Conduct Orderly Segregation Protest Here: About 250 March on Airport." *Greenville (S.C.) News,* 2 January 1960.

"Negroes Fined in Dairy Bar Case." *Durham (N.C.) Sun,* 24 June 1957.

"Negroes Lose in Trespass Case Appeal." *Durham (N.C.) Morning Herald,* 11 January 1958.

"A New Attack on the Poll Tax." *Tuscaloosa (Ala.) News,* 12 September 1939.

Nelson, Jack. "Race-Mixing Center under Fire. Highlander Director Says School Not Communist, But in Same Field." *Atlanta Journal-Constitution,* 15 December 1957, http://vault.fbi/highlander.

Neuborne, Burt. "The Origin of Rights: Constitutionalism, the Stork and the Democratic Dilemma." In *The Role of Courts in Society,* edited by Shimon Shetreet, 187–207. Boston: Martinus Nijhoff Publishers, 1988.

"New Sit-Down Staged Here; Curfew Violator is Fined: Negroes Take Seats at 2 Variety Stores." *Greenville (S.C.) News,* 30 July 1960.

Newsom, Michael. "Marker Honors Struggle of Many." *Biloxi Sun Herald,* 18 May 2009.

Nichols, Bill. *Representing Reality: Issues and Concepts in Documentary.* Bloomington: Indiana University Press, 1992.

"9 pm Curfew Ordered to Ease Racial Unrest, No County Action at This Time: Persons 20 Years or Younger to Be Affected." *Greenville (S.C.) News,* 27 July 1960.

"No Trouble Here Unless . . . ." *Life,* 17 September 1956, 109–10.

Noakes, John, and Hank Johnston. "Frames of Protest: A Road Map to a Perspective." In *Frames of Protest: Social Movements and the Framing Perspective,* edited by Hank Johnston and John Noakes, 1–29. Lanham, Md.: Rowman & Littlefield, 2005.

Nora, Pierre. "Between Memory and History: Les Lieux de Memorie." Translated by Marc Roudebush, *Representations* 26 (1989): 7–24.

Norris, Marjorie M. "An Early Instance of Nonviolence: The Louisville Demonstrations of 1870–71." *Journal of Southern History* 32 (1966): 487–504.

North Carolina Department of Cultural Resources. "North Carolina Historical Marker Program: Royal Ice Cream Sit-In," http://www.ncmarkers.com/Markers.aspx?MarkerId=G-123 (accessed 10 December 2013).

"A Notable Anniversary." *Louisville Defender,* 12 May 1955.

Nunnelly, William A. *Bull Connor.* Tuscaloosa: University of Alabama Press, 1991.

O'Brien, M. J. *We Shall Not Be Moved: The Jackson Woolworth's Sit-In and the Movement It Inspired.* Jackson: University Press of Mississippi, 2013.

"Occupy Oakland: 400 Arrested after Violent Protest." NBC News, 30 January 2012, http://usnews.nbcnews.com/_news/2012/01/30/10268080-occupy-oakland-400-arrested-after-violent-protest?lite.

"'Occupy Wall Street' Protests Turn Violent When Demonstrators Clash with Police." Fox News, 6 October 2011, http://www.foxnews.com/us/2011/10/06/dozens-arrested-in-wall-street-protests-as-rallies-spread-across-hudson.

"The Odor in Birmingham." *Tuscaloosa (Ala.) News,* 24 November 1938.

"Ohio College to Aid Sitters." *Nashville Tennessean,* 11 March 1960.

Oldham, Marion O'Fallon. "Marion O'Fallon Recalls the CORE Lunch Counter Protests," http://www.umsl.edu/virtualstl/phase2/1950/events/ perspectives/documents/oldham.html (accessed 7 October 2012).

Olson, Lester C., Cara A. Finnegan, and Diane S. Hope, eds. *Visual Rhetoric: A Reader in Communication and American Culture.* Thousand Oaks, CA: Sage, 2008.

Olson, Lynne. *Freedom's Daughters: The Unsung Heroines of the Civil Rights Movement from 1830–1970.* New York: Scribner, 2001, 88.

O'Neill, Stephen. "Memory, History, and the Desegregation of Greenville, South Carolina." In *Toward the Meeting of the Waters,* edited by Winfred B. Moore Jr. and Orville Vernon Burton, 286–99. Columbia: University of South Carolina Press, 2008.

Oppenheimer, Martin. *The Sit-In Movement of 1960.* Brooklyn, NY: Carlson Pub, 1989.

"Ordinance Needed to End 'Accommodations' Bias." *Louisville Defender,* 4 December 1958.

O'Rourke, Sean Patrick. "Circulation and Noncirculation of Photographic Texts in the Civil Rights Movement: A Case Study of the Rhetoric of Control." *Rhetoric and Public Affairs* 15 (2012): 685–94.

———. "Greenville Airport Protest Started an Avalanche." *Greenville (S.C.) News,* 2 January 2010.

———. "Racism's Lessons Learned in Upstate: A 60-Year Retrospective." *Greenville (S.C.) News,* 14 June 2007.

"Origins of the Sit-In: A Sibling Remembers." Interview with Gloria Jean (Blair) Howard, Greensboro VOICES, 15 September 1982. The Object of History, http://objectofhistory.org/objects/brieftour/lunchcounter/ (accessed 16 February 2015).

Ortlepp, Anke. *Jim Crow Terminals: The Desegregation of American Airports.* Athens: University of Georgia Press, 2017.

Osborn, Michael. "In Defense of Broad Mythic Criticism—A Reply to Rowland." *Communication Studies* 41 (1990): 121–27.

———. "Rhetorical Distance in 'Letter from Birmingham Jail.'" *Rhetoric & Public Affairs* 7 (2004): 23–35.

"Our Anniversary." *Louisville Defender,* 2 April 1952.

"Outrage in Alabama." *New York Times,* 5 May 1963.

Packard, Jerrold M. *American Nightmare: The History of Jim Crow.* New York: St. Martin's Griffin, 2003.

"Parents Unanimously Approve Curfew But Teen-Agers Somewhat Reluctant." *Greenville (S.C.) News,* 17 July 1960.

Parry-Giles, Shawn J., and Diane M. Blair, "The Rise of the Rhetorical First Lady: Politics, Gender Ideology, and Women's Voice, 1789–2002." *Rhetoric and Public Affairs* 5, no. 4 (2002): 565–600.

Patton, John H. "A Transforming Response: Martin Luther King, Jr.'s 'Letter from Birmingham Jail.'" *Rhetoric and Public Affairs* 7 (2004): 53–66.

Patton, Stacey. "Why African Americans Aren't Embracing Occupy Wall Street." *Washington Post*, 25 November 2011, http://www.washingtonpost.com/opinions/why-blacks -arent-embracing-occupy-wall-street/2011/11/16/gIQAwc3FwN_story.html.

Payne, Charles. *I've Got the Light of Freedom.* Berkeley: University of California Press, 1995.

Phillips, Kendall R. "A Rhetoric of Controversy." *Western Journal of Communication* 63 (1999): 488–510.

———, ed. *Framing Public Memory.* Tuscaloosa: University of Alabama Press, 2004.

Perucci, Tony. "What the Fuck Is That? The Poetics of Ruptural Performance." *Liminalities: A Journal of Performance Studies* 5 (2009): 1–18.

Phillips, G. Mitchell, and Kendall R. Phillips, eds. *Global Memoryscapes: Contesting Remembrance in a Transnational Age.* Tuscaloosa: University of Alabama Press, 2011.

"Photos Tell Violent Story of St. Augustine." Special St. Augustine issue, *SCLC Newsletter,* June 1964, 6.

"Pilgrimage by Negroes Set Today." *Greenville (S.C.) News,* 1 January 1960.

Pitt, Matthew. "A Civil Rights Watershed in Biloxi, Mississippi." *Smithsonian Magazine,* 20 April 2010, http://www.smithsonianmag.com/history-archaeology/A-Civil-Rights -Watershed-in-Biloxi-Mississippi.html.

Plunkett-Powell, Karen. *Remembering Woolworth's: A Nostalgic History of the World's Most Famous Five-and-Dime.* New York: St. Martin's, 1999.

"Politics Enter Strike Picture as Candidate Reviews Laws on Cafes." *Carolina Times,* 13 February 1960.

"Poorly Timed Protest." *Time,* 19 April 1963, 30–31.

Poston, Ted, and Kathleen Hauke. *A First Draft of History.* Athens: University of Georgia Press, 2000.

Poulakis, John. "Toward a Sophistic Definition of Rhetoric." *Philosophy and Rhetoric,* 16 (1983): 35–48.

Powell, Rodney. Interview by Kathy Bennett, 29 March 2005. Civil Rights Oral History Project, Nashville Public Library, Nashville, Tennessee.

Prashad, Vijay. "Black Gandhi." *Social Scientist* 37, no. 1/2 (2009): 3–20.

"Protester Is Removed from King Motel Site." *New York Times,* 17 July 1990, http://www .nytimes.com/1990/07/17/us/protester-is-removed-from-king-motel-site.html?emc=eta1.

Proudfoot, Merrill. *Diary of a Sit-In.* Chapel Hill: University of North Carolina Press, 1962.

"Public Accommodations Bias Protest Begins." *Louisville Defender,* 22 January 1959.

Quigley, Joan. "How D.C. Ended Segregation a Year before *Brown v. Board of Education.*" *Washington Post,* 15 January 2016, https://www.washingtonpost.com/opinions/the -forgotten-fight-to-end-segregation-in-dc/2016/01/15/1b7cae2a-bafc-11e5–829c-26ffb874 a18d_story.html?utm_term=.8b8df3dce049 (accessed October 2, 2017).

"Race Segregation Blasted at Confab: But Races Forced to Sit Apart by Ruling." *Pittsburgh Courier,* 3 December 1938.

Racial and Civil Disorders in St. Augustin: Report of the Legislative Investigation Committee. 1965. Regional and Rare Materials. University of North Florida, Thomas G. Carpenter Library Special Collections and Archives. UNF Digital Commons, https://digitalcommons .unf.edu/northeast_fla_books/23/.

"Racial Peace in Birmingham?" *New York Times,* 17 April 1963.

Raiford, Leigh. "'Come Let Us Build a New World Together': SNCC and Photography of the Civil Rights Movement." *American Quarterly* 59 (2007): 1129–57.

Raines, Howell. *My Soul Is Rested: Movement Days in the Deep South Remembered.* New York: Putnam, 1977.

Ramsey, Paul. "Letter: Using Children in Alabama." *New York Times,* 10 May 1963.

Ransby, Barbara. *Ella Baker and the Black Freedom Movement: A Radical Democratic Vision.* Chapel Hill: University of North Carolina Press, 2003.

Ray, Angela G. "The Rhetorical Ritual of Citizenship: Women's Voting as Public Performance, 1868–1875." *Quarterly Journal of Speech* 93, no. 1 (2007): 1–26.

———. "The Transcript of a Continuing Conversation: David Zarefsky and Public Address." *Argumentation and Advocacy* 45 (2008): 64–79.

"Reader Used in State Held Unsatisfactory." *Tuscaloosa (Ala.) News,* 4 November 1962.

Reed, Linda. *Simple Decency and Common Sense: The Southern Conference Movement, 1938–1963.* Bloomington: Indiana University Press, 1991.

Regnault, John F. "Indictment of Christopher Jones in the Richmond City Hustings Court." *Remaking Virginia: Transformation Through Emancipation,* http://www.virginia memory.com/online-exhibitions/items/show/587.

Repass, Jerre. "Black Wall Street Durham, North Carolina." *About . . . Time,* 2006, 12–14.

Reporting Civil Rights: Part One: American Journalism, 1941–1963. New York: Library of America, 2003.

Reporting Civil Rights: Part Two: American Journalism, 1963–1973. New York: Library of America, 2003.

Richardson, Gloria. "Focus on Cambridge." *Freedomways* 4, no. 1 (1964): 28–34.

———, Interviewee. Joseph Mosnier and the U.S. Civil Rights History Project. Gloria Hayes Richardson Oral History Interview Conducted by Joseph Mosnier in New York, NY. 2011. https://www.loc.gov/item/2015669134/.

Riches, William T. Martin. *The Civil Rights Movement: Struggle and Resistance.* New York: St. Martin's, 1997.

Rickard, Carolyn. "Sit-In Site Will Get State Marker." *Durham (N.C.) Herald-Sun,* 18 December 2007.

"Rights Pact: A Truce Is Reached in Birmingham—But the Threat of Turbulence Remains." *New York Times,* 12 May 1963.

Rimpo, Maurice. "Tempo of Protests Steps Up." *Cambridge (Md.) Daily Banner,* 16 May 1963.

Ritchie, Gladys. "The Sit-In: A Rhetoric of Human Action." *Today's Speech* 18, no. 1 (1970): 22–25.

"Robert Kennedy Warns of 'Increasing Turmoil.'" *New York Times,* 4 May 1963.

Roberts, Gene, and Hank Klibanoff. *The Race Beat: The Press, the Civil Rights Struggle, and the Awakening of a Nation.* New York: Vintage, 2007.

Roberts, Elise. "Remembering the Biloxi wade-ins." Inside WLOX.com—Elise's Newsroom Blog, 11 May 2009, http://www.wlox.com/Global/story.asp?S=10337169.

Roberts, Kathleen Glenister. "Liminality, Authority, and Value: Reported Speech in Epideictic Rhetoric." *Communication Theory* 14, no. 3 (2004): 264–84.

Robinson-Simpson, Leola Clement. *Greenville County South Carolina.* Black America Series. Charleston, SC: Arcadia Publishing, 2007.

Robnett, Belinda. *How Long? How Long: African-American Women in the Struggle for Civil Rights.* New York: Oxford University Press, 1997.

"The Role of Gay Men and Lesbians in the Civil Rights Movement." *Teaching Tolerance,* https://www.tolerance.org/classroom-resources/tolerance-lessons/the-role-of-gay-men -and-lesbians-in-the-civil-rights-movement (accessed 19 September 2019).

"The Rollback of Civil Rights Era in America." Gates Public Service Law Program. 25 January 2008. https://www.law.washington.edu/multimedia/2008/rollback/transcript.pdf.

Roosevelt, Eleanor. Letter to Mrs. Henry M. Robert Jr., 26 February 1939. Franklin Delano Roosevelt Presidential Library, http://www.fdrlibraryvirtualtour.org/graphics/05-9/5-9-ER-7.pdf (accessed 1 September 2017).

———. "My Day," 24 November 1938. Eleanor Roosevelt Papers Project, http://www.gwu.edu/~erpapers/myday/displaydoc.cfm?_y=1938&_f=md055119 (accessed 1 September 2017).

———. *This I Remember.* New York: Harper & Brothers, 1949.

Rosenberg, Rosalind. "The Conjunction of Race and Gender." *Journal of Women's History* 14, no. 2 (2002): 68–73.

Rossi, Lisa. "Sons of Ice Cream Shop Owner Reflect on Sit-In." *Durham (N.C.) Herald-Sun,* 2 July 2008, http://nccueagles.yuku.com/topic/880/Royal-Ice-Cream-Parlor-Protestors-share-Durham-1957-Event#.Uqc2k01RZ05.

Rosteck, Thomas, and Michael Leff. "Piety, Propriety, and Perspective: An Interpretation and Application of Key Terms in Kenneth Burke's Permanence and Change." *Western Journal of Speech Communication* 53 (1989): 327–41.

Roswig, Bernard J. (UPI). "Grand Jury Rejects 'Good Faith' Bid." *Atlanta Daily World,* 20 June 1964.

Rowland, Robert C. "On a Limited Approach to Mythic Criticism—Rowland's Rejoinder." *Communication Studies* 41 (1990): 150–60.

———. "On Mythic Criticism." *Communication Studies* 41 (1990): 101–16.

Rowland, Robert C., and David A. Frank. "Mythic Rhetoric and Rectification in the Israeli-Palestinian Conflict." *Communication Studies* 62 (2011): 41–57.

Rozenzweig, Roy, and David Thelen. *The Presence of the Past: Popular Uses of History in American Life.* New York: Cambridge University Press, 1998.

"Rules . . . That Led to Jail." *Nashville Tennessean,* 28 February 1960.

Rushing, Janice Hocker. "On Saving Mythic Criticism—A Reply to Rowland." *Communication Studies* 41 (1990): 136–49.

Rustin, Bayard. "From Protest to Politics: The Future of the Civil Rights Movement." *Commentary,* February 1965, https://www.commentarymagazine.com/articles/from-protest-to-politics-the-future-of-the-civil-rights-movement/.

Rutenberg, Jim. "A Dream Undone: Inside the 50-year Campaign to Roll Back the Voting Rights Act." *New York Times Magazine,* 29 July 2015, https://www.nytimes.com/2015/07/29/magazine/voting-rights-act-dream-undone.html?mcubz=1.

Ruyter, Elena. "African Americans Sit-In against Segregation at Royal Ice Cream Parlor in Durham, N.C., 1957." Global Nonviolent Action Database, 2011, nvdatabase.swarthmore.edu/content/african-americans-sit-against-segregation-royal-ice-cream-parlor-durham-nc-1957.

Ryan, William Fitts. "Remarks in the House, Representative Ryan, of New York." In *Memorial Addresses in the House of Representatives: Together With Tributes on the Life and Ideals of Anna Eleanor Roosevelt: Eighty-Eighth Congress, First Session,* no. 152. Washington, D.C.: United States Government Printing Office, 1966.

Salinas, Chema. "Ambiguous Trickster Liminality: Two Anti-mythological Ideas." *Review of Communication* 13 (2013): 143–59.

Salisbury, Harrison E. "Fear and Hatred Grip Birmingham." *New York Times,* 12 April 1960.

"Saving a Lunch Counter." *America Magazine,* 15 February 2010.

Schiappa, Edward, ed. *Landmark Essays on Classical Greek Rhetoric.* Davis, Cal.: Hermagoras, 1994.

Schlosser, Jim. "Greensboro's Civil Rights Landmark Continues as National Newsmaker." Greensboro Sit-ins: Launch of a Civil Rights Movement, 1 February 1995, https://www .greensboro.com/sit-ins/headlines/greensboro-s-civil-rights-landmark-continues-as -national-newsmaker/article_375c2c4c-e323-11e6-8777-4b8507a7d2ae.html.

Schmidt, Christopher W. *The Sit-Ins: Protest & Legal Change in the Civil Rights Era.* Chicago: University of Chicago Press, 2018.

Schneider, Stephen. *You Can't Padlock an Idea: Rhetorical Education at the Highlander Folk School, 1932–1961.* Columbia: University of South Carolina Press, 2014.

Schwarze, Steve. "Juxtaposition in Environmental Health Rhetoric: Exposing Asbestos Contamination in Libby, Montana." *Rhetoric and Public Affairs* 6, no. 2 (2003): 313–36.

Sciullo, Nick J. "Social Justice in Turbulent Times: Critical Race Theory and Occupy Wall Street." *National Lawyers Guild Review* 69 (2012): 225–38.

Scott, Robert L., and Donald K. Smith. "The Rhetoric of Confrontation." *Quarterly Journal of Speech* 55 (1969): 1–8.

Seals, Donald Jr., "The Wiley-Bishop Student Movement: A Case Study in the 1960 Civil Rights Sit-Ins." *Southwestern Historical Quarterly* 106 (2003): 418–40.

Selected Digitized Correspondence of Eleanor Roosevelt, 1933–1945. Franklin D. Roosevelt Presidential Library and Museum, http://www.fdrlibrary.marist.edu/archives/collections/ franklin/?p=collections/ findingaid&id=504 (accessed 1 September 2017).

Sen, Rinku. "Race and Occupy Wall Street." *Nation,* 26 October 2011, http://www.thenation .com/article/164212/race-and-occupy-wall-street#.

"7 Negroes Pay Fines in Test-Case Action," *Durham Morning (N.C.) Herald,* 15 July 1958.

"17 Jailed Saturday." *Cambridge (Md.) Daily Banner,* 1 April 1963.

"79 Abused Arrested in Downtown Stores." *Nashville Globe and Independent,* 4 March 1960.

Sharp, Gene. *How Nonviolent Struggle Works.* Boston: Albert Einstein Institute, 2013.

———. *The Politics of Nonviolent Action. 3 vols.* Boston: Porter Sargent, 1973.

Sheffield, Michael. "Fighting for Civil Rights Tourism." *Memphis Business Journal,* 2 May 2012, http://www.bizjournals.com/memphis/print-edition/2012/03/02/fighting-for-civil -rights-tourism.html.

Shelton, Robert. "Source of Trouble." Letters to the Editor, *Tuscaloosa (Ala.) News,* 6 March 1960.

Sherter, Alain. "Days of Rage: 'Occupy Wall Street' Goes Global." *CBS MoneyWatch,* 14 October 2011, http://www.cbsnews.com/news/days-of-rage-occupy-wall-street-goes-global.

"Shocking and Surprising." *Tuscaloosa (Ala.) News,* 25 November 1938.

Shogan, Robert. "Labor Strikes Back." *American History,* December 2006, 36–43.

Shridharani, Krishnalal. *Selections from "War Without Violence."* New York: Fellowship of Reconciliation, 1939.

———. *War without Violence: A Study of Gandhi's Method and Its Accomplishments.* New York: Harcourt Brace, 1939.

Simons, Herbert. "Requirements, Problems, and Strategies: A Theory of Persuasion for Social Movements." *Quarterly Journal of Speech* 56 (1970): 1–11.

Sipiora, Phillip. "Introduction: The Ancient Concept of Kairos." In *Rhetoric and Kairos: Essays in History, Theory, and Praxis,* edited by Phillip Sipiora and James S. Baumlin, 1–22. Albany: SUNY Press, 2002.

"The Sit-Down Technique." *Fellowship* 3, no. 5 (1937): 6–7.

"Sit-Downs Prove Negroes Not Satisfied with Being of an Inferior Status." *Louisville Defender,* 31 March 1960.

"Sit-In." *NBC White Paper.* Aired 20 December 1960.

"Sit-In Halt Advisable–Lawyers." *Nashville Banner,* 4 March 1960.

"Sit-In Leader Advises Appeal to Moral Issues." *Louisville Defender,* 5 May 1960.

"Sit-In Leader Lawson at NAACP Meet Here." *Louisville Defender,* 28 April 1960.

"Sit-In Movement Sparks Social Change." CNN, 8 February 2017, https://www.cnn
.com/2017/02/08/us/gallery/tbt-civil-rights-sit-ins/index.html.

"Sit-Ins, a Weapon of Choice?" *Louisville Defender,* 11 August 1960.

"The Sit-Ins of 1960." Civil Rights Movement Veterans. http://www.crmvet.org/info/sitins
.pdf.

"Sit-Ins May Become Daily Occurrence Here." *Cambridge (Md.) Daily Banner,* 14 May 1963.

Sitton, Claude. "Birmingham Jails 1,000 More Negroes." *New York Times,* 7 May 1963.

———. "Birmingham Talks Reach an Accord on Ending Crisis." *New York Times,* 10 May
1963.

———. "Negro Sitdowns Disquiet South: Negro Sitdowns Stir Fear of Wider Unrest in
South." *New York Times,* 15 February 1960.

———. "Police Loose a Dog on Negroes' Group; Minister Is Bitten." *New York Times,* 29
March 1963.

Sloane, Thomas O. *On the Contrary: The Protocol of Traditional Rhetoric.* Washington, D.C.:
The Catholic University of America Press, 1999.

Smith, Daniel Blake. *February One: The Story of the Greensboro Four.* DVD. Directed by
Rebecca Cerese. 2003. San Francisco: California Newsreel, 2004.

Smith, J. Holmes. "Our New York Ashram." *Fellowship* 7, no. 1 (1941): 2.

Smith, Jacqueline. "Fulfill the Dream." http://www.fulfillthedream.net/pages/mlk.boycott1
.html.

Smith, Ralph R., and Russell R. Windes. "The Innovational Movement: A Rhetorical
Theory." *Quarterly Journal of Speech* 61 (1975): 140–53.

Smith-Rosenberg, Carroll. *Disorderly Conduct: Visions of Gender in Victorian America.*
New York: Knopf, 1985.

Snow, David, and Robert Benford. "Master Frames and Cycles of Protest." In *Frontiers
in Social Movement Theory,* edited by Aldon Morris and Carol McClurg, 133–55. New
Haven, Conn.: Yale University Press, 1992.

Snow, David E., Burke Rochford, Jr., Steven K. Worden, and Robert D. Benford. "Frame
Alignment Processes, Micromobilization, and Movement Participation." *American
Sociological Review* 51 (1986): 464–81.

Solomon, Martha. "Responding to Rowland's Myth, or In Defense of Pluralism—A Reply
to Rowland." *Communication Studies* 41 (1990): 117–20.

Sontag, Susan. *On Photography.* New York: Picador, 1977.

Southern Regional Council. "Special Report: Student Protest Movement, Winter, 1960."
Southern Regional Council Papers, 1944–68. Ann Arbor, Mich.: University Microfilms,
1984.

"Southern Whites Flay Jim Crow Laws in Open Meeting: Tired of Way South Treats Black
Race." *Chicago Defender,* 3 December 1938.

Spratt, Meg. "When Police Dogs Attacked: Iconic News Photographs and Construction of
History, Mythology, and Political Discourse." *American Journalism* 25 (2008): 85–105.

"St. Augustine Motel Is Scene of Wild Fracas." *Philadelphia Tribune,* 20 June 1964.

"St. Augustine Paper Charges Patrol Is Abridging Rights of White Citizens." *Florida Times-
Union,* 19 June 1964.

Stanley, Frank. "Being Frank about People, Places, and Problems." *Louisville Defender,* 18
August 1951.

———. "Being Frank about People, Places, and Problems." *Louisville Defender,* 2 April 1952.

———. "Being Frank about People, Places, and Problems." *Louisville Defender,* 6 January 1955.

———. "Being Frank about People, Places, and Problems." *Louisville Defender,* 15 September 1955.

———. "Being Frank about People, Places, and Problems." *Louisville Defender,* 9 February 1956.

———. "Being Frank about People, Places, and Problems." *Louisville Defender,* 15 March 1956.

———. "Being Frank about People, Places, and Problems." *Louisville Defender,* 29 November 1956.

———. "Being Frank about People, Places, and Problems." *Louisville Defender,* 6 December 1956.

———. "Being Frank about People, Places, and Problems." *Louisville Defender,* 20 August 1959.

———. "Being Frank about People, Places, and Problems." *Louisville Defender,* 21 April 1960.

———. "Being Frank about People, Places, and Problems." *Louisville Defender,* 22 September 1960.

———. "Being Frank about People, Places, and Problems." *Louisville Defender,* 9 March 1961.

Stanton, Mary. *Journey toward Justice: Juliette Hampton Morgan and the Montgomery Bus Boycott.* Athens: University of Georgia Press, 2006.

Starhawk. *Truth or Dare: Encounters with Power, Authority, and Mystery.* New York: Harper-Collins, 1987.

"State High Court Backs Local Setup, Says Private Firm May Accept or Reject by Whim." *Durham (N.C.) Sun,* 10 January 1958.

Stengren, Bernard. "Equality Is Goal of Race Congress: Group Pickets Group Here to Back Moves in South Over Lunch Counters." *New York Times,* 14 February 1960.

Stewart, Charles J. "A Functional Approach to the Rhetoric of Social Movement." *Central States Speech Journal* 31 (1980): 298–305.

Stewart, Warren. *Victory Together: For Martin Luther King, Jr.: The Story of Dr. Warren Stewart, Governor Evan Mecham, and the Historic Battle for a Martin Luther King, Jr. Holiday in Arizona.* Phoenix, Ariz.: A.W.O.L., 2015.

Stix, Judith Saul. Interview by Missouri Historical Society, 9 April 1996.

———. Interview by Krishna Murali, 6 December 2004.

Stokes, J. Hunter. "14 Young Negroes Are Arrested After Sit-In." *Greenville (S.C.) News,* 10 August 1960.

———. "7 Negroes Walk Into Library Here." *Greenville (S.C.) News,* 17 March 1960.

"Student 'Sit-Ins' Emerge as a Vital Force to Be Reckoned With." *Louisville Defender,* 3 January 1960.

"Student 'Sit-Ins' Is Top Controversy in United States." *Louisville Defender,* 24 March 1960.

"Students Form Non-violence Coordination Group at Raleigh Conference of Eight-State Leaders." *Louisville Defender,* 21 April 1960.

"Students Win Sit-in Victory in N.C. Court." *Louisville Defender,* 28 April 1960.

Stunte, Joel. "'Ice Cream Parlor' Negroes Found Guilty of Trespassing." *Durham (N.C.) Morning Herald,* 18 July 1957.

Sturken, Marita. *Tangled Memories: The Vietnam War, the AIDS Epidemic, and the Politics of Remembering.* Berkeley: University of California Press, 1997.

Sugrue, Thomas J. *Sweet Land of Liberty: The Forgotten Struggle for Civil Rights in the North.* New York: Random House, 2008.

Sullens, Frederick. "Dr. Mason and His Patients." *Jackson Daily News,* 3 May 1960.

Sullivan, Dale. "Kairos and the Rhetoric of Belief." *Quarterly Journal of Speech* 78 (1992): 317–32.

Sullivan, Patricia. *Days of Hope: Race and Democracy in the New Deal Era.* Chapel Hill: University of North Carolina Press, 1996.

———, ed. *Freedom Writer: Virginia Foster Durr, Letters from the Civil Rights Years.* Athens: University of Georgia Press, 2003.

———. "Virginia Foster Durr." In *The Eleanor Roosevelt Encyclopedia,* edited by Maurine H. Beasley, Holly C. Shulman, and Henry R. Beasley, 150–51. Westport, Conn.: Greenwood, 2001.

Sullivan, Patricia. "Lawyer Samuel Tucker and His Historic 1939 Sit-In at Segregated Alexandria Library." *Washington Post,* August 7, 2014, https://www.washingtonpost .com/local/lawyer-samuel-tucker-and-his-historic-1939-sit-in-at-segregated-alexandria -library/2014/08/05/c9c1d38e-1be8-11e4-ae54-0cfe1f974f8a_story.html?utm_term=.1e4 256ac1448.

Sumner, David E. "Nashville, Nonviolence, and the Newspapers: The Convergence of Social Goals with News Values." *Howard Journal of Communications* 6, no. 1–2 (1995): 102–13.

Sutton, David. "On Mythic Criticism: A Proposed Compromise." *Communication Reports* 10 (1997): 211–17.

Talley, James. "75 Students Arrested Here." *Nashville Tennessean,* 28 February 1960.

Taylor, Astra, and Keith Gessen, eds. *Occupy! Scenes from Occupied America.* Brooklyn, N.Y.: Verso, 2011.

"Television History: The First 75 Years." http://www.tvhistory.tv/facts-stats.htm.

Tell, Dave. *Remembering Emmett Till.* Chicago: University of Chicago Press, 2019.

"Tension Growing over Race Issue." *U.S. News and World Report,* 20 May 1963, 37–39.

"Tension Simmers in Biloxi." *Jackson (Miss.) State Times,* 25 April 1960.

Terrill, Robert E. "Rhetorical Criticism and Citizenship Education." In *Purpose, Practice, and Pedagogy in Rhetorical Criticism,* edited by Jim A. Kuypers, 163–76. Lanham, Md.: Lexington Books, 2014.

Terry, Wallace. "Birmingham Protest Had Slow, Reluctant Start." *Washington Post,* 12 May 1963.

Tesler, Michael. "Views about Race Mattered More in Electing Trump than in Electing Obama." *Washington Post,* 22 November 2016, https://www.washingtonpost.com/news/ monkey-cage/wp/2016/11/22/peoples-views-about-race-mattered-more-in-electing-trump -than-in-electing-obama/?utm_term=.4b79475f9e61.

"The Text of the Cambridge, Md., Accord." *New York Times,* 24 July 1963.

Tharoor, Ishaan. "Hands across the World." In *What Is Occupy?,* edited by *Time,* 25–33. New York: Time Home Entertainment, 2011.

Thomas, Jesse O. "Conflicts in Intra-racial Culture." *Chicago Defender,* 17 December 1938.

Thompson, AK. *Black Bloc, White Riot: Anti-Globalization and the Genealogy of Dissent.* Oakland, Cal.: AK, 2010.

Thompson, Heather Ann. *Blood in the Water: The Attica Prison Uprising of 1971 and Its Legacy.* New York: Pantheon, 2016.

Thompson, James W. "Whites, Negroes in Street Battle: Clash Follows Sit-Ins Here." *Green-ville (S.C.) News,* 22 July 1960.

"3 Jailed in Florida Had Area Connections." *Washington Post, Times Herald,* 20 June 1964.

"Thurgood Marshall Hails Progress." *Nashville Globe and Independent,* 8 January 1960.

Time, ed. *What Is Occupy? Inside the Global Movement.* New York: Time Home Entertainment, 2011.

Timms, Leslie. "3 Counter Sit-Ins Held in Greenville." *Greenville (S.C.) News,* 19 July 1960.

———. "8 Negroes Sit-In at Library Here: Arrested and Jailed Briefly," *Greenville (S.C.) News,* 17 July 1960.

Torigian, Michael. "The Occupation of the Factories: Paris 1936, Flint 1937." *Comparative Studies in Society and History* 41, no. 2 (1999): 324–47.

Torin, Jack. "Albany Foresaw Its Role as Racial 'Target City.'" *Los Angeles Times,* 6 August 1962.

Torres, Sasha. *Black, White, and in Color: Television and Black Civil Rights.* Princeton, N.J.: Princeton University Press, 2003.

Traister, Rebecca. *Good and Mad: The Revolutionary Power of Women's Anger.* New York: Simon & Schuster, 2018.

Tucker, Ray "Negroes' Sitdowns Stir New Discord." *Greenville (S.C.) News,* 22 March 1960.

Tumarkin, Nina. *The Living and the Dead: The Rise and Fall of the Cult of World War II in Russia.* New York: Basic Books, 1994.

Turner, Kathleen J., ed. *Doing Rhetorical History: Concepts and Cases.* Tuscaloosa: University of Alabama Press, 1998.

Turner, Victor. *Process, Performance and Pilgrimage: A Study in Comparative Symbology.* New Delhi: Concept, 1979.

———. "Process, System, and Symbol." *Daedalus* 106, no. 3 (1977): 61–80.

———. *The Ritual Process: Structure and Anti-Structure.* Ithaca: Cornell University Press, 1969.

———. "Variations on a Theme of Liminality." In *Secular Ritual,* edited by Sally F. Moore and Barbara G. Myerhoff, 36–52. Amsterdam: Van Gorcum, 1977.

"Two Sides to the Coin." *St. Augustine Record,* 18 June 1964.

Underground Railroad Freedom Singers. "Wade in the Water." *Freedom Is Coming: Songs of Freedom, Resistance, and the Underground Railroad.* Disc 1, track 4. Produced by New Orleans Jazz National Historical Park, National Park Service, 2011.

United Press International (UPI). "The Acid Test of Human Dignity." *Chicago Defender,* 20 June 1964.

———. "'Agitators' Ready for a 'Long, Hot Summer,'" *Chicago Defender,* 20 June 1964.

———. "All Biloxi Police Called to Duty in Race Crisis." *Jackson (Miss.) Clarion Ledger,* 26 April 1960.

———. "15 Rabbis Among New Fla. Arrests." *Atlanta Daily World,* 19 June 1964.

———. "Negro Doctor Breaks Color Line at Biloxi." *Jackson (Miss.) Clarion Ledger,* 18 April 1960.

———. "Negroes Fined in Biloxi Rioting." *Jackson (Miss.) Clarion Ledger,* 25 April 1960.

———. "Police Accused of Aiding Mob." *Memphis Commercial Appeal,* 10 August 1960.

———. "Rabbis Join Negroes in Fla. Freedom Battle; Acid Tossed in Pool." *Chicago Defender,* 20 June 1964.

———. "Racial Battle Enlivens Beach." *Memphis Commercial Appeal,* 24 April 1960.

———. "Racial Meeting Held at Capitol." *Memphis Commercial Appeal,* 29 April 1960.

U.S. Congress. Senate. Committee on the Judiciary. Testimony of Stokely Carmichael. 91st Cong., 2d sess., March 25, 1970. http://historymatters.gmu.edu/d/6461.

United States Department of Justice, Federal Bureau of Investigation. Racial Situation, St. Johns County, Florida (Jacksonville, Florida, June 19, 1964), 1–4. ProQuest History Vault.

"Vanderbilt University Group Urges Race Tolerance." *Nashville Tennessean,* 9 March 1960.

Vander Lei, Elizabeth, and Keith D. Miller. "Martin Luther King's 'I Have a Dream' in Context: Ceremonial Protest and the African American Jeremiad." *College English* 62 (1999): 83–99.

Vivian, Bradford. *Public Forgetting: The Rhetoric and Politics of Beginning Again.* University Park: Pennsylvania State University Press, 2010.

———. "'A Timeless Now': Memory and Repetition." In *Framing Public Memory,* edited by Kendall R. Phillips, 187–211. Tuscaloosa: University of Alabama Press, 2004.

Von Eschen, Penny. *Race against Empire: Black Americans and Anticolonialism, 1937–1957.* Ithaca, N.Y.: Cornell University Press, 1997.

"Wade in the Water." Songs for Teaching, http://www.songsforteaching.com/folk/wadein thewater.htm (accessed 18 September 2019).

Wagster Pettus, Emily. "Civil Rights Sit-In at Woolworth Changed Mississippi." *Associated Press,* 3 June 2013.

"Waiting for Miracles." *Time,* 3 August 1962.

Walker, Anders. "Legislating Virtue: How Segregationists Disguised Racial Discrimination as Moral Reform Following *Brown v. Board of Education.*" *Duke Law Journal* 47 (1998): 399–424.

Walker, Devona. "50 Years Ago, Children Helped Change Nation When They Sat Down." *Oklahoman,* 19 August 2008, http://newsok.com/article/3285497.

Walker, Jenny. "The 'Gun-Toting' Gloria Richardson: Black Violence in Cambridge, Maryland." In *Gender in the Civil Rights Movement,* edited by Peter J. Ling and Sharon Monteith, 169–85. New York: Garland Publishing, 1999.

Walker, Ruth. "Group of Young Negroes Enters Greenville Library: Building is Closed by Trustees," *Greenville (S.C.) News,* 2 March 1960.

———. "Integration Local Library Is Sought: Negroes File Federal Suit." *Greenville (S.C.) News,* 29 July 1960.

Warner, Michael. *Publics and Counterpublics.* Brooklyn, N.Y.: Zone Books, 2010.

Warren, Dan R. *If It Takes All Summer: Martin Luther King, the KKK, and States' Rights in St. Augustine, 1964.* Tuscaloosa: University of Alabama Press, 2008.

Watson, Bruce. *Freedom Summer: The Savage Season of 1964 That Made Mississippi Burn and Made America a Democracy.* New York: Viking Press, 2010.

Watson, Martha Solomon. "The Issue Is Justice: Martin Luther King, Jr.'s Response to the Birmingham Clergy." *Rhetoric and Public Affairs* 7 (2004): 1–22.

"Wave of Protest Gets Legion Action." *Louisville Defender,* 15 October 1959.

Webb, Clive, ed. *Massive Resistance: Southern Opposition to the Second Reconstruction.* Oxford: Oxford University Press, 2005.

West, Rebecca. "Opera in Greenville." *New Yorker,* 14 June 1947, https://www.newyorker .com/magazine/1947/06/14/opera-in-greenville.

West, William F. "Protestors from Royal Ice Cream Parlor Share How Event Shaped Durham." *Durham (N.C.) Herald-Sun,* 15 September 2007.

Whalen, Tracey. "Introduction: Rhetoric as Liminal Practice." *Rhetor* 1 (2004): 1–11.

"What a Record? Louisville Leads Nation in Sit-In Arrests." *Louisville Defender,* 27 April 1961.

"White and Negro Teen-Agers Clash: At Local Drive-In." *Greenville (S.C.) News,* 25 July 1960.

White, James Boyd. *When Words Lose Their Meaning: Constitutions and Reconstitutions of Language, Character, and Community.* Chicago: University of Chicago Press, 1984.

"Whites Hit at Conference in Birmingham: Condemn Meeting; Demand Resignations and Explanations." *Chicago Defender,* 3 December 1938.

Wiegand, Wayne A., and Shirley A. Wiegand. *The Desegregation of Public Libraries in the Jim Crow South: Civil Rights and Local Activism.* Baton Rouge: Louisiana State University Press, 2018.

Wilkinson, J. Harvie, III. "The Seattle and Louisville School Cases: There Is No Other Way." *Harvard Law Review* 121 (2007): 158–83.

Wilkerson, Isabell. *The Warmth of Other Sons: The Epic Story of America's Great Migration.* New York: Random House, 2010.

William Gravely Oral History Collection on the Lynching of Willie Earle. South Caroliniana Library of the University of South Carolina University Libraries. http://digital.tcl.sc.edu/cdm/landingpage/collection/gravely.

Williams, Juan. *Eyes on the Prize: America's Civil Rights Years, 1954–1965.* New York: Viking, 1987.

Wilson, Kurt H. "Interpreting the Discursive Field of the Montgomery Bus Boycott: Martin Luther King Jr.'s Holt Street Address." *Rhetoric and Public Affairs* 8, no. 2 (2005): 236–99.

Windham, Ben. "Southern Lights: Politics Isn't What It Used to Be." *Tuscaloosa (Ala.) News,* 20 October 2002.

Woodham, Rebecca. "Southern Conference for Human Welfare/Educational Fund." In *The New Encyclopedia of Southern Culture,* vol. 20, *Social Class,* edited by Larry J. Griffin and Peggy G. Hargis, 446–48. Chapel Hill: University of North Carolina Press, 2012.

Woodward, C. Vann. *The Strange Career of Jim Crow.* New York: Oxford University Press, 2001.

Workman, William D. Jr. *The Case for the South.* New York: Devin-Adair, 1960.

"Workshop Asks Further Sit-Ins." *Nashville Tennessean,* 4 April 1960.

Wright, Elizabethada A. "Rhetorical Spaces in Memorial Places: The Cemetery as a Rhetorical Memory Place/Space." *Rhetoric Society Quarterly* 35, no. 4 (2005): 51–93.

Wright, John A. *Discovering African American St. Louis: A Guide to Historic Sites.* 2nd ed. St. Louis: Missouri Historical Society Press, 2002.

Wynn, Linda T. "The Dawning of a New Day: The Nashville Sit-Ins, February 13–May 10, 1960." *Tennessee Historical Quarterly* 50, no. 1 (1991): 42–54.

Yahoo Contributor Network. "The Story of the Lorraine Motel in Memphis," http://voices.yahoo.com/the-story-lorraine-motel-memphis-14303.html (accessed 7 October 2013).

Yang, Guobin. "The Liminal Effects of Social Movements: Red Guards and the Transformation of Identity." *Sociological Forum* 15, no. 3 (2000): 379–406.

Yeingst, William. "Sitting for Justice." The National Museum of American History, http://amhistory.si.edu/docs/Yeingst_Bunch_Sitting_for_Justice_1996.pdf (accessed 15 July 2015).

Young, Andrew. *A Way Out of No Way.* Nashville: Nelson, 1994.

Young, James E. *The Texture of Memory: Holocaust Memorials and Meaning.* New Haven, Conn.: Yale University Press, 1993.

Young, Richard E., and Yameng Lu, eds. *Landmark Essays on Rhetorical Invention in Writing,* Davis, Cal.: Hermagoras, 1994.

Youngs, J. William T. *Eleanor Roosevelt: A Personal and Public Life,* edited by Oscar Handlin. New York: Longman, 2000.

Zald, Mayer N. "Culture, Ideology, and Strategic Framing." In *Comparative Perspectives on Social Movements: Political Opportunities, Mobilizing Structures, and Cultural Framings,* edited by Doug McAdam, John D. McCarthy, and Mayer N. Zald, 261–74. New York: Cambridge University Press, 1996.

Zarefsky, David. "Four Senses of Rhetorical History," in *Doing Rhetorical History*, edited by Kathleen J. Turner, 19–32. Tuscaloosa: University of Alabama Press, 1998.

———. "Interdisciplinary Perspectives on Rhetorical Criticism: Reflections on Rhetorical Criticism." *Rhetoric Review* 25, no, 4 (2006): 383–87.

Zarefsky, David, and Victoria J. Gallagher. "From Constitutional 'Conflict' to 'Constitutional Question': Transformations in Early American Public Discourse." *Quarterly Journal of Speech* 76 (1990): 247–61.

"A Zealot's Stand." *Time*, 11 October 1963.

Zimmerman, Samuel L. *Negroes in Greenville, 1970: An Exploratory Approach*. Greenville: South Carolina Tricentennial, 1970.

Zinn, Howard. *SNCC: The New Abolitionists*. Boston: Beacon, 1964.

Žižek, Slavoj. "Occupy Wall Street, or, the Violent Silence of a New Beginning." In *The Year of Dreaming Dangerously*, 77–89. London: Verso, 2012.

Contributors

WENDY ATKINS-SAYRE is chair and professor of rhetoric at the University of Memphis. She coauthored *Consuming Identity: The Role of Food in Redefining the South* and has a coedited volume coming out entitled *City Places, Country Spaces: Rhetorical Explorations of the Urban/Rural Divide*. She has a Ph.D. from the University of Georgia.

DIANA I. BOWEN is assistant professor of communication at Pepperdine University. She has published in *Communication Quarterly* and *Journal of Multimodal Rhetorics*, as well as having coedited the collection *Latina/o/x Communication Studies: Theories, Methods, and Practice*. Her research explores physical and psychological borderlands, a term coined by Gloria Anzaldúa to describe spaces of social, political, and cultural struggle. She is working on archival research with the Gloria Anzaldúa collection, and she is also interested in issues surrounding social movements, intercultural dialogue, public memory, and visual rhetoric. She has a Ph.D. from the University of Texas at Austin.

JASON DEL GANDIO is associate professor of instruction at Temple University. He has published one solo-authored book and three coedited collections. His expertise is the theory and practice of social justice. He has a Ph.D. from Southern Illinois University.

MARILYN DELAURE is associate professor of communication studies at the University of San Francisco. Her research investigates how people effect social change, focusing especially on embodied performance. She has published essays on dance, civil rights rhetoric, and environmental activism, and she is coeditor of *Culture Jamming: Activism and the Art of Cultural Resistance*. She is also a producer for the documentary film *Motherload* (2019). She has a Ph.D. from the University of Iowa.

VICTORIA J. GALLAGHER is professor of communication at North Carolina State University. She has published numerous articles and book essays featuring rhetorical criticism of civil rights related speeches, commemorative spaces, public parks, and public art and is the principal investigator of the Virtual Martin Luther

King project, a digital humanities project for the public. She has a Ph.D. from Northwestern University.

LINDSAY HARROFF is a doctoral candidate in communication studies at the University of Kansas. Drawing on perspectives from rhetorical studies, decolonial theory, and African studies, her research works to refigure matters of violence, identity, national community, justice, and democratic norms. Her dissertation, titled "Reimagining National Community through Truth and Reconciliation: A Rhetorical Analysis of Truth Commissions in South Africa, Kenya, and the United States," suggests how truth commissions in Kenya and South Africa offer alternative formulations of national community that decenter citizenship as the primary mode of public engagement and identity of belonging.

JUDITH D. HOOVER is professor emerita of communication at Western Kentucky University. She has published articles in *Electronic News, Journal of Intercultural Communication Research, Women and Language, Communication and Medicine, Omega: The Journal of Death and Dying, Storytelling, Self, and Society, American Behavioral Scientist, Presidential Studies Quarterly, Southern Communication Journal, Journal of Popular Film and Television,* and *Southern Quarterly,* as well as essays in *Who Says? Working-Class Rhetoric, Class Consciousness, and Community* and *Martin Luther King, Jr., and the Sermonic Power of Public Discourse.* Since retirement, she has published poetry and a novel, *Beyond Monongah: An Appalachian Story.* She has a Ph.D. from Indiana University.

WILLIAM H. LAWSON is assistant professor of communication at California State University East Bay. He has published in *Rhetoric and Public Affairs* and in *Advances in the History of Rhetoric.* He also has published *No Small Thing: The 1963 Mississippi Freedom Vote.* He has a Ph.D. from Florida State University.

MELODY LEHN is assistant professor of rhetoric and women's and gender studies and assistant director of the Center for Speaking & Listening at Sewanee: The University of the South. She has published articles and essays in *Rhetoric & Public Affairs,* the *Carolinas Communication Annual,* and several edited collections in political communication and rhetoric. She is also, with Antonio de Velasco, coeditor of *Rhetoric: Concord and Controversy* (2012). A previous version of the essay in this volume was presented at the 2016 Carolinas Communication Association Convention, where it won the Ray Camp Prize for Outstanding Faculty Research Paper. She has a Ph.D. from the University of Memphis.

CASEY MALONE MAUGH FUNDERBURK is associate professor of communication studies and serves as the vice provost for the Gulf Park campus at the University of Southern Mississippi. She publishes in areas of political communication and rhetoric. She has a Ph.D. from Pennsylvania State University.

ROSEANN M. MANDZIUK is university distinguished professor of communication studies at Texas State University. She has published numerous articles and book essays that analyze rhetorical dimensions of historical and contemporary discourse. She also is coauthor, with Suzanne Pullon Fitch, of the book *Sojourner Truth as Orator: Wit, Story, and Song* (1997). She has a Ph.D. from the University of Iowa.

KEITH D. MILLER is professor of English at Arizona State University. He is the author of *Voice of Deliverance: The Language of Martin Luther King, Jr., and Its Sources* and *Martin Luther King's Biblical Epic: His Great, Final Speech*. He recently assisted Rene Billups Baker with her memoir, *My Life with Charles Billups and Martin Luther King: Trauma and the Civil Rights Movement*. His essays about King, Malcolm X, Frederick Douglass, Fannie Lou Hamer, C. L. Franklin, and Jackie Robinson have appeared in flagship journals and in many scholarly collections. His current book project is tentatively titled "Who Wrote the Autobiography of Malcolm X?" He has a Ph.D. from Texas Christian University.

DAVID MIGUEL MOLINA is lecturer in communication at the University of Pittsburgh and a doctoral candidate in rhetoric and public culture at Northwestern University.

SEAN PATRICK O'ROURKE is coordinator of the Rhetoric Program, director of the Center for Speaking and Listening, and professor of Rhetoric and American Studies at Sewanee: The University of the South. He writes on rhetoric, rights, and protest, with a special interest in the period from 1948 to 1973. He holds J.D. and Ph.D. degrees from the University of Oregon.

LESLI K. PACE is associate professor and program coordinator of communication at University of Louisiana, Monroe. Her research focus is on the rhetoric of gender and social movements. She has published articles on feminist ontology, women's movements, and parenting discourses. She has a Ph.D. from Southern Illinois University.

JOSHUA D. PHILLIPS is assistant teaching professor of communication at Pennsylvania State University, Brandywine. His primary academic interest is studying how narratives shape culture. His current publications include the essays "The Culture of Poverty: On Individual Choices and Infantilizing Bureaucracies"; "The Case of Social Media Censorship in Germany: Public Good or Public Bad?"; and "Trial by Social Media: How Misleading Media and Ideological Protests led to Disastrous Results in *The State of Florida v. George Zimmerman*." His book, *Homeless: Narratives from the Streets*, uses narratives of the homeless in an effort to improve public policy. He has a Ph.D. from Southern Illinois University.

STEPHEN SCHNEIDER is associate professor of English at the University of Louisville. He has published essays in *Technical Communication Quarterly, College*

English, and *College Composition and Communication.* His first book, *You Can't Padlock an Idea: Rhetorical Education at the Highlander Folk School, 1932–1961* was published by the University of South Carolina Press in 2014. He has a Ph.D. from Pennsylvania State University.

JEFFREY C. SWIFT teaches writing and communication at Southern Virginia University. He researches communication technologies in public debate and manages community outreach strategy for political candidates and advocacy groups across the country. He has a Ph.D. from North Carolina State University.

REBECCA BRIDGES WATTS is curate (associate rector) at St. Thomas Episcopal Church in College Station, Texas. Previously, she was associate professor of communication and media studies at Stetson University. She is the author of *Contemporary Southern Identity: Community through Controversy* (2008). She has a Ph.D. from Texas A&M University as well as an M.Div. from the Seminary of the Southwest.

DAVID WORTHINGTON is associate professor of communication and theater at DePauw University. He has a Ph.D. from Indiana University.

KENNETH S. ZAGACKI is professor of communication at North Carolina State University. He has published numerous articles of rhetorical criticism in journals including the *Quarterly Journal of Speech, Rhetoric Society Quarterly,* and *Philosophy and Rhetoric.* He has a Ph.D. from the University of Texas at Austin.

Index